The
Geography
of
PUERTO RICO

Rafael Picó

ALDINE PUBLISHING COMPANY, Chicago

First Edition translation published 1974 by
Aldine Publishing Company
529 South Wabash Avenue
Chicago, Illinois 60605

ISBN 0–202–10056–1
Library of Congress Catalog Number 72-182916

Printed in the United States of America

Preface

The Geography of Puerto Rico deals with human activity and the different factors influencing life in the Island. It covers comprehensively the physical, economic and social geography of Puerto Rico using both the systematic and regional methods. The book incorporates the latest data available and the most recent developments and trends in our geography.

The Geography of Puerto Rico brings up to date the 1969 Spanish edition that in turn was based on two previous volumes: *Geografía Física* published in 1954 and *Geografía Económica* in 1964. It also supersedes the author's 1950 publication, *The Geographic Regions of Puerto Rico*, at the time an updated version of his 1938 PhD dissertation. These publications are mostly out of print after being used extensively in Puerto Rico, especially in its universities, as text and reference books on the geography of the island.

Puerto Rico is a small island but its geographic diversity is remarkable. Contrasts in topography provide lowlands, hills and mountains, further diversified by the variety of the rainfall regime. As a result, our soils and original vegetation typify numerous and much larger regions throughout the tropical and subtropical world. Crops adapted to this heterogenous environment also exhibit substantial changes: sugar cane, coffee, tobacco, fruits, starchy vegetables, native and imported grasses. Industrial, commercial and social activities add another level to this diverse background.

Interest in Puerto Rico's rapid progress from an underdeveloped and extremely poor island in 1940 to a land of promise, an example for developing nations in our diverse world, has prompted the publication of this book. Industrialists lured by "Operation Bootstrap," tourists and senior citizens seeking a warm climate and a different environment, scientists, students, public officials from many lands looking for new techniques of development, all demand basic information about Puerto Rico, its physical environment, its people and industries; in short, the whole

v

picture of modern Puerto Rico. It is the author's earnest hope that this volume serve as a source of information on Puerto Rico, both for our visitors as well as for citizens in the mainland who would like to understand better the Puerto Rican scene. One million Puerto Ricans now residing in continental U.S. also would like to know more about their homeland and its progress during the last decades.

The author wishes to express his sincere thanks to his colleague and friend for many years, Earl P. Hanson, for preparing an English draft for this book. His knowledge of the science as well as of Puerto Rico made him ideally suited for translating the original Spanish version.

Collaborator in the Spanish edition, Zayda Buitrago de Santiago, was very helpful in the preparation of the first part of this book. Others are duly recognized for their contributions to the *Nueva Geografía* in the Preface to the Spanish edition reproduced herewith.

Numerous Puerto Rican scientists helped with advice and revision of the first draft of the English manuscript. Among them, geologist Watson Monroe was outstandingly helpful. My colleague in Banco Popular de Puerto Rico, economist Augusto Amato, revised several chapters and provided the most recent data for sections of the book. For allowing me to use their maps, my thanks to geologist Reginald Briggs and geographer Margaret Howarth.

For providing valuable data, maps and photographs, the author is indebted to the Puerto Rico Industrial Development Company, the Water Resources Authority, the Highway Authority, the Ports Authority and the Government Development Bank for Puerto Rico.

My two lifelong collaborators, Leticia López and Zaida Rivera-Negrón, again provided careful editing and the painstaking task of putting together the different items incorporated in the final text. Thanks are also due for their excellent services to Mayra Díaz de la Bárcena, to my secretaries Nora Hernández and Lucy Muñoz and to my chauffeur Raúl Asencio. The work of updating maps and charts was done by draftsman Juan Pablo López of the Puerto Rico Planning Board, thanks to the authorization granted by Roger H. Wall, President of the Government Development Bank for Puerto Rico.

Finally, to my distinguished colleague, Professor Norton Ginsburg, of the University of Chicago, my sincere thanks for his help in advising on the book's acceptance and suggesting Aldine Publishing Company as its publishers. Recognition is hereby extended to Aldine executive Robert W. Wesner who became interested in my book and endorsed its publication, and to Mrs. Karla Heuer, Managing Editor of Aldine, who helped greatly throughout the printing process.

The Geography of Puerto Rico is undoubtedly the result of the efficient assistance and cooperation of several minds and many hands. To all of them the author owes a debt of gratitude for their splendid support.

Preface to the Spanish Edition

Nueva Geografía de Puerto Rico incorporates for the first time in a single volume the various aspects of our geography. In 1954 the author published his *Geografía Física de Puerto Rico* (*Physical Geography of Puerto Rico*) which was followed ten years later by his work on our *Geografía Económica* (*Economic Geography*). In a few years both books were out of print and, in answer to the requirements of the University Press which had published them, I decided to bring them up to date, eliminating duplications and incorporating the latest data and most recent points of view.

The strenuous demands of my work would have prevented the completion of this book, had it not been for the efficient and unselfish collaboration of Zayda Buitrago de Santiago and Héctor H. Berríos who already had contributed to the two previous books mentioned above. Leticia López of the Government Development Bank for Puerto Rico, and Zaida Rivera of Banco Popular de Puerto Rico, my loyal and dedicated assistants for many years, coordinated and edited the manuscript. To all of them I express my most profound and sincere gratitude.

Many other friends and associates helped with ideas and original research in the preparation of this book, either in its present form or through their assistance with the two previous texts on which the present volume is based: Professor Carlos Iñiguez, Dean Vernon R. Esteves, Professor Vicente Guzmán Soto, and Visiting Geography Professor, Dr. Antonio F. Chaves, all of the University of Puerto Rico.

I also wish to express my thanks to other professionals and technicians who contributed information, data, or photographs for insertion in the present revised version: Professor D. Clay McDowell, University of Puerto Rico; Frank H. Wadsworth, United States Forest Service; José F. Cadilla, Economic Development Administration of Puerto Rico; Félix Iñigo, Department of Agriculture of Puerto Rico; Watson Monroe, U.S.

Geological Survey; and officials of the Commonwealth Water Resources Authority and Soil Conservation Service.

I am greatly indebted to my excellent secretaries—Olga Casanova, Gladys Moyer, Lucy Muñoz and Norma Juarbe for their excellent work in preparing the final manuscript. For drafting maps and diagrams, I thank Juan López Méndez and Juan Solá of the Planning Board. In the matter of photographs I was helped greatly by Jacinto González Trías of the Metropolitan Photo Studio. I also owe much to Norberto Lugo Ramírez and Isabel Ortiz Espéndez of the University of Puerto Rico Press for their help, faith, patience, and encouragement that culminated in the publication of the *Nueva Geografía de Puerto Rico*.

RAFAEL PICÓ
San Juan, Puerto Rico

Contents

The
Geography
of
PUERTO RICO

Puerto Rico and The Antilles

Location, Shape, and Size

Puerto Rico is centrally located in the arc of submerged mountains which connects the two Americas and forms the archipelago of the Antilles (Fig. 1.1). The Greater Antilles—Puerto Rico, Hispaniola,[1] Jamaica, and Cuba—extend westward from Puerto Rico. The hundreds of small islands known as the Lesser Antilles curve toward the southeast and south as far as the coast of Venezuela.

Puerto Rico's total area, including the small, neighboring islands which are politically part of it, is about 3,435 square miles. The land area, excluding that of the lagoons, is 3,417.5 square miles. The main island is longest from east to west, with a maximum length of 111 miles between Punta (Point) Jigüero and Punta Puerca; its width from north to south averages 36 miles and is greatest in the west, reaching 39 miles between a point west of Isabela on the north and Punta Colón on the south coast, southwest of La Parguera.

The two largest adjacent islands, Vieques and Culebra, lie east of Puerto Rico proper. In the west, three islands are part of Puerto Rico: Mona, Monito, and Desecheo. Along all the coasts, but especially in the south and east, there are many smaller islands and cays, like fragments detached from the main body.

Puerto Rico and the Greater Antilles

Like Puerto Rico, the islands of Cuba and Hispaniola are surrounded by smaller islands and cays. Some of these are fairly large, like the Isle of Pines (Isla de Pinos) south of Cuba, which is almost one third as large as Puerto Rico; however, the term "Greater Antilles" refers only to the

---

1. Called Española in Spanish and also known by the names of its two countries: Dominican Republic (Santo Domingo) and Haiti.

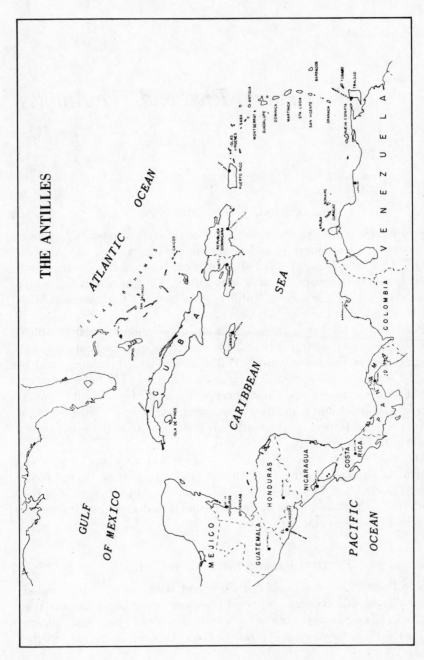

Figure 1.1. The Antilles. (Adapted from map published by the American Geographical Society.)

four largest (Table 1.1). Puerto Rico is the smallest, followed by Jamaica, which is about 20 per cent larger. Hispaniola is nine times and Cuba is thirteen times as large as Puerto Rico. Though differing greatly in shape, all four extend from east to west.

Jamaica, closest to Puerto Rico in size, is a little wider at the center and narrower at the ends. The main axis of Puerto Rico and of Jamaica are oriented from northwest to southeast and are slightly tilted. Both islands have mountainous interiors and coastal plains; in Puerto Rico these plains are widest in the north and in Jamaica in the south. Puerto Rico's mountainous spine extends through the island's entire length. Much of Jamaica's interior consists of a greatly dissected and eroded plain, and only in the northeast, in the Blue Mountains, are there true mountains which exceed in altitude Puerto Rico's Cordillera Central and the Sierra de Luquillo.

The two islands resemble one another greatly in climate. Kingston, on Jamaica's south coast with an average annual temperature of 79.3° F, is slightly warmer than San Juan, with 78° F; however, Guayama, located on Puerto Rico's south coast, has 79.9° F. On both islands, varying with altitude, the climate is cooler in the mountains. The amount and distribution of rainfall are also similar. Jamaica's north coast, like Puerto Rico's is rainy; on both islands the precipitation increases, and at the same rates, along the northern slopes of the mountains. Kingston's small precipitation (29 in.) compares with that in Puerto Rico's south; however, the more favorable orientation of the latter island's major axis permits a rainfall of 53 inches at Guayama. Only in Puerto Rico's Guánica zone, in the southwest, is the annual precipitation (about 30 inches) comparable to Kingston's.

Hispaniola is far less regular in shape than Puerto Rico and, though the two resemble one another in their predominantly mountainous interiors, the arrangement of Hispaniola's mountains, of the intermontane valleys, and the coastal plains, is more complex. Although, in general, the northern slopes of the mountains tend to be more humid than the southern, the distribution and quantities of Hispaniola's rainfall are also more complex.

Cuba, whose area is greater than that of all the other Greater Antilles combined, differs from the other islands in that at least three quarters of its territory is level or slightly undulating; its precipitation is, on the whole, markedly lighter, but the extremes of aridity found in Hispaniola, Jamaica, and Puerto Rico are rare. Because Cuba's western part extends considerably farther north than Puerto Rico, its winters are cooler. Havana's average annual temperature is 75° F.

Table 1.1 presents some basic data on the Greater Antilles. Followed by Haiti, Cuba has the largest number of inhabitants. The Dominican Republic, whose population has doubled over a thirty-year period, comes third, followed by Puerto Rico and, finally, Jamaica. Puerto Rico occu-

Table 1.1 The Greater Antilles: Area, population and commerce

Country	Area in square miles	1969 Population*		1968 GNP Per Capita U.S. $‡	1966 Commerce‡	
		total in thousands	per square miles		Exports total in million dollars	Imports total in million dollars
Cuba	44,218	8,250	187	310	714	1,015
Dominican Republic	18,703	4,174	223	290	180	191
Haiti	10,714	4,768	445	70	28	26
Jamaica	4,411	1,959	444	460	220	282
Puerto Rico	3,435	2,754	802	1,340	919	1,363
Total	81,481	21,905	269	–	2,061	2,877

Sources:

*For population: United Nations figures taken from *Diccionario Geográfico, 1971, Almanaque Mundial*, Editora Moderna, Inc., 1970.
‡*World Bank Atlas*, International Bank for Reconstruction and Development, September 1970.
‡*Information Please Almanac*, 1966.

pies first place in density of population with 800 inhabitants per square mile in 1969. Haiti, Jamaica, the Dominican Republic, and Cuba, follow in that order.

The Dominican Republic lies west of Mona Passage and it is difficult to imagine a greater contrast than is found on crossing that narrow strait. The Dominican Republic is much less densely populated and far richer in natural resources than is Puerto Rico. Until the nineteenth century, the Dominican Republic's population was considerably larger than Puerto Rico's, but during that period, as a result of struggles with Haiti and internal revolutions, the population decreased. However, statistics show that today the country's rate of population growth is greater than Puerto Rico's.

Climatic resemblances explain the similarity of agricultural products throughout the Greater Antilles. All the islands produce sugar, tobacco, coffee, subsistence crops and the same types of fruits; however, their relative importance varies from island to island. Cuba resembles Puerto Rico in that the agricultural economy of both depends heavily on sugar cane, followed at some distance by tobacco and coffee. In Haiti, coffee is the most important crop. In the Dominican Republic, coffee, cacao and bananas follow sugar cane, and crops for local consumption are important. In Jamaica, bananas follow sugar cane in importance.

Significant changes in the exports of those countries have taken place in recent years. Bauxite and alumina now comprise 45 per cent of Jamaica's exports. Cuba's commerce has shifted toward the countries of eastern Europe, primarily the Soviet Union. In Puerto Rico, whose evolution is toward an industrial economy, the value of exported manufactured goods now exceeds that of agricultural products.

While the United States has long participated to a considerable extent in the commerce of all the Greater Antilles, recent political changes in the area have altered that situation. The most notable change took place in Cuba, whose trade is now largely with the Soviet Union, China, and the countries of Eastern Europe. The United States continues to hold top place in Puerto Rico, which ranks fifth among all the countries of the world purchasing United States goods. The major part (78 per cent) of exports from the Dominican Republic is to the United States. Jamaica's exports to the United States (37 per cent) are on a par with those to the United Kingdom while imports from the United States (29 per cent) exceed those from the United Kingdom (25 per cent).

Puerto Rico and the Lesser Antilles

Due to the community of language, cultural interests, and social and economic contacts, Puerto Rico has maintained close relations with the Dominican Republic. Relations do not exist with Cuba due to the advent some years ago of the new political regime. Nor are close relations found with the Lesser Antilles, even though many of them are physically closer to Puerto Rico than is Cuba. Today, however, there is a trend toward the steady strengthening of ties and relations between Puerto Rico and the Lesser Antilles.

The area of the Lesser Antilles is about one and a half times that of Puerto Rico, but their total population is slightly smaller than Puerto Rico's (Table 1.2). The only truly large island is Trinidad, followed by

Table 1.2. The Lesser Antilles: Area and population

Country	Area in Square miles	Population	
		total (1969)	per square mile
British West Indies Subtotal	3,379	1,821,000	539
Barbados	166	254,000	1,530
Monserrat	33	15,000	462
Virgin Islands	67	9,000	134
Dominica	289	74,000	256
Grenada	133	105,000	789
St. Lucia	238	110,000	462
St. Vincent	150	95,000	637
St. Kitts, Nevis and Anguila	152	56,000	368
Antigua	171	63,000	370
Trinidad-Tobago	1,980	1,040,000	525
French Islands Subtotal	1,105	655,000	593
Guadeloupe	680	323,000	475
Martinique	425	332,000	783
Dutch Islands Subtotal	394	218,000	554
U.S. Virgin Islands Subtotal	133	50,000	376
Total	5,011	2,744,000	548

Source: United Nations figures taken from *Diccionario Geográfico, 1971, Almanaque Mundial*, Editora Moderna Inc., 1970.

Guadeloupe and Martinique. Those three islands constitute three fifths of the Lesser Antilles' total area. Trinidad has the largest population, followed by Martinique, Guadeloupe, and Barbados. Those four islands hold about two-thirds of the total population of the Lesser Antilles. The density per square mile varies between a mere 46 in St. John of the U. S. Virgin Islands, and 1530 in Barbados. As a whole, the density is far greater than in the Greater Antilles; virtually all of the Lesser Antilles are relatively more heavily populated than Cuba or the Dominican Republic. The population densities of Aruba, Grenada, and Martinique are closer to that of Puerto Rico.

Ethnographically the Lesser Antilles are a true Babel of races, languages, religions, and nationalities. In the British Antilles, the bulk of the population is Negro, and the prevailing language is a somewhat corrupted English. In Grenada, Santa Lucía, and Dominica, the predominant popular dialect is a derivative of French. Another exception is Trinidad, where the population is of African, Hindu, Spanish, Portuguese, and English descent; and while English predominates, many people use the language of their regions of origin.

In the French Antilles, by far the greatest number of people have African blood and speak a French dialect. As noted above, French influence is also felt in Santa Lucía, Grenada, and Dominica. On St. Thomas of the U.S. Virgin Islands there is a group of French descent, the Chachas, pure whites, who constitute a small part of the total, predominantly black, population.

The largest proportion of population of European origin is found in the Netherlands Antilles. In Saba, a small volcanic cone about as far from San Juan as Santo Domingo City, there is a population of Dutch origin and English language. The majority of those Antilleans of various generations are white, blond, and blue-eyed. The lack of local opportunities forces the men of Dutch descent to emigrate or to work as sailors; with time the population of African descent, now forming about half of the total, may come to predominate on the island.

Within the Antillean setting, Curacao and Aruba are extraordinary islands. They do not depend and never have depended economically on agriculture; their economy is geared to commerce, to the refining of Venezuelan petroleum, and to tourism. Their population is extremely varied, though African, Spanish and Dutch descendants predominate. The official language is Dutch, but all the tongues of the Caribbean are spoken, as well as one derived from all of these, called Papiamento.

In Puerto Rico, until fairly recently, one heard very little talk about the Lesser Antilles, which constituted a world far more remote than many countries of Europe, Asia, and Africa. The economic, political, and cultural life of those small islands developed in such a manner as to leave them as isolated cells, having contact with the rest of the world only through their ruling countries. Even within the British Antilles, each island had closer relations with England and Canada than with its neighbors. At times of difficult maritime transportation, as during World War II, many of those islands suffered great hardships.

The political changes which have occurred recently in the area, together with the accelerated economic development of Puerto Rico, have changed that situation and resulted in closer relationships between the peoples of the various islands.

Towards the goal of solving the serious social and economic problems referred to above, the Anglo-American Caribbean Commission was established in 1942; it was enlarged in 1946 by the addition of the French and Dutch dependencies and was thereafter called the Caribbean Commission. Puerto Rico was represented in that body, and several of its most important meetings were held in San Juan. The Caribbean Commission was an international advisory body which studied the economic and social problems of the Caribbean from a regional viewpoint; the problems, arising in part from geographic-social conditions common to the entire Caribbean area and affecting all of its inhabitants, were many and widespread; the solutions were hence of interest to all of the countries of the area. Although the Commission's role was exclusively that of orientation, the fact of its existence indicated recognition, by the participating countries, of the principle of regional cooperation as one of the bases for the improvement of the Antillean economy.

In September 1961, the Commission was replaced by the Caribbean Organization, whose aims were:

1. To direct general attention to the need for close regional cooperation toward the end of accelerating development.
2. To encourage the use of well-planned developmental practices in each territory.
3. To harmonize development on a regional level.
4. To win major cooperation of the region's inhabitants toward the implementation of the governments' development plans.

The fact that Puerto Rico was selected as the organization's headquarters indicates its role in regional and international cooperation.

The Organization initiated and developed many projects related to the stated aims but lacked powers to implement them toward the end of contributing effectively to the area's economic progress. Together with political motivations, that fact contributed to the organization's eventual dissolution in 1964. The work of the Commission, however, resulted in the creation in 1969 of a Caribbean Development Bank, financed by the countries of the British area plus the United Kingdom and Canada, for the purpose of stimulating investment in the area, particularly in the smaller islands. I suggested this proposal in 1963 during a seminar sponsored by the Commission.

Through a law passed June 15, 1965, Puerto Rico's Legislature created the Corporation for the Caribbean Economic Development (CODECA, Corporación de Desarrollo Económico del Caribe); through that organization Puerto Rico has returned to participation and shares its experiences with those of the other Caribbean islands toward social, economic, and cultural improvement, aimed at accelerated progress.

Puerto Rico in the Caribbean

A country's geographic location is undoubtedly one of the most important factors in its overall development. The land's location in a specific part of the world subjects it to the region's climatic conditions and so delimits its agricultural possibilities, its agricultural resources, and its general conditions of life. Moreover, the country is subjected to an unavoidable series of relationships, determined by its location and neighbors as well as by its relative significance in the world scene.

The agricultural economy of the Caribbean area, through its location in the tropical zone, complements that of the temperate-zone countries. The possibilities of selling the Caribbean's agricultural surpluses to countries like the United States, Canada, England, and France are far greater than are those of selling them to neighboring countries whose agricultural production is similar. To provide itself with certain foods as well as machinery, the Caribbean necessarily turns to countries which produce them in excess of their own needs, generally those in the temperate zones. These complementary economies permit commercial exchange. Countries strive to obtain what they want to satisfy their own needs in return for what they can produce in excess of local demands. As a part of the Caribbean region, Puerto Rico is no exception; and, as noted above, 85 per cent of its commerce is with a complementary area, the United States mainland.

Beside that general orientation of markets, Puerto Rico's special position in the Caribbean has played an important role in its life as a people. Almost always, that role has been in the vanguard. When the Spaniards arrived, Puerto Rico was inhabited by the Arawak Indians, a peaceful aboriginal people who occupied the Greater Antilles and differred greatly from the war-hardened Caribs of the Lesser Antilles. However, before the arrival of the Spaniards, Puerto Rico's east had begun to be invaded by those fierce warriors. The island was the frontier between two worlds, the peaceful world of the Arawaks and the warlike, expansionist world of the encroaching Caribs.

History tells us that both of those races came from the northern part of South America, the Orinoco regions; first came the Arawak wave, followed later by that of the Caribs, who eliminated the Arawaks from all the Lesser Antilles and were beginning to establish themselves in Puerto Rico's east when the Spaniards arrived.

Because of Puerto Rico's location, the fact that it was the largest island first reached by the Arawaks in their westward movement and the first they occupied which offered optimum possibilities for the growth of their culture, the island's Arawak Indian developed a culture superior to that on the other islands. When the white man arrived on Puerto Rico, he found the Carib and Arawak in mortal combat, the former striving to invade the other Antilles and the latter resisting this invasion.

Shortly after the Spanish Empire began to be established in America, we again find Puerto Rico in a vanguard position, with corresponding responsibilities. Despite being nearer to Spain and the Canary Islands than are the other Greater Antilles, Puerto Rico was not among the lands discovered by Columbus in the course of his first voyage. Later, because the island did not contain the abundance of gold sought by the conquistadores, it was almost ignored. The majority of the conquistadores, though first landing on the Greater Antilles, soon moved toward the mainland where the riches of Mexico and Perú began to be exploited. However, the transportation of those riches to Spain demanded bases for the protection of the fleets; and Puerto Rico, dominating some of the most important sailing routes, again became strategically important. The occupation of the Lesser Antilles by the European powers which tried to preempt Spain's hegemony in America, soon brought Puerto Rico to the forefront again, this time in Spain's American empire. Little by little, the Spaniards made Puerto Rico, or rather the Port of San Juan, their first line of defense, endowed with formidable fortifications (Fig. 1.2). San Juan not only served as a base of protection and refuge for Spanish ships but could also play a similar role for other powers into whose hands it might fall. Thence stemmed the determination to defend the island and recover it, as in 1598 when it fell into British hands for a few months.

That strategic importance began to diminish with the disappearance of piracy, the introduction of new commercial practices during the eighteenth century, and the loss of Spanish colonies on the continent in the beginning of the nineteenth. Nevertheless, Puerto Rico was beginning to exploit its own possibilities while its position on many navigation routes

Figure 1.2. Section of Morro Castle in San Juan. Its construction made the port of San Juan the first line of defense against the enemies of Spain. (Courtesy Government of Puerto Rico. Photo by Rotkin.)

and near the great markets of Europe and American facilitated the development of its agricultural wealth.

Later, the opening of the Panama Canal made Puerto Rico more than ever the Caribbean's strategic key. It dominates several important routes between Europe and the Canal, through Anegada Passage or Mona Passage. In addition, through its central location Puerto Rico is an ideal stronghold for naval or air forces needed for controlling sea lanes in the rest of the Antillean area arc. Modern progress in aerial navigation, with radio extending the operations of aircraft, further heightens Puerto Rico's value. Even before the United States entered World War II Puerto Rico's strategic importance was fully realized and the island's military and naval bases were fortified for the defense of a large part of the Caribbean. Here, too, were established the general military and naval headquarters for the forces which covered the entire Antilles.

In discussing the Caribbean Sea, which he called the American Mediterranean, Spykman[2] says there are three strongholds for the defense of the east coast of the United States. One is Newfoundland, another is Bermuda and the anchoring point of that outer line is Puerto Rico. These military bastions, with their air fields, can serve as a barrier to an enemy approaching from the east.

In a wartime economy, Puerto Rico is also in a key position. Petroleum from Venezuela and Trinidad, bauxite from the Guianas, Jamaica, and the Dominican Republic, are essential for a major effort like that of World War II. On their way to the United States, the largest parts of such materials must be taken through a considerable part of the Caribbean Sea. No base is better located than Puerto Rico for the transcendentally important role of keeping the Caribbean areas free of enemy ships, submarines and aircraft, so that such strategic cargoes could safely reach their ports of destination.

Many of those basic strategic concepts changed with the advent of guided missiles. Nevertheless, if Puerto Rico's importance has diminished in the strictly military sense, the value of the island's strategic location has in recent times increased considerably vis-à-vis commercial relations with the east coast of the United States, the development of the Antilles, and international relations between the Hispanic-American and Anglo-American countries.

Puerto Rico's location is important in times of peace as well as war. In these days of commercial aviation's great development, the island serves as a connecting point for many transoceanic flights. It is located directly north of South America's north coast, especially Venezuela's and is more directly on the route to South America's east than are the rest of the

2. Nicholas J. Spykman, *America's Strategy in World Politics* (New York: Harcourt, Brace, Jovanovitch, Inc., 1942), pp. 431–32.

Figure 1.3. Aerial View of the International Airport of Isla Verde. It is
the most active in the Caribbean. (Courtesy of the Ports Authority of
Puerto Rico.)

Greater Antilles. Today, the international airport of Isla Verde, which
has replaced that of Isla Grande as San Juan's principal airport, is the
busiest in the Caribbean (Fig. 1.3). Puerto Rico's role in the future of
commercial aviation is made obvious by a mere glance at the map of the
Caribbean and the realization that the cost of flights is steadily going
down while their volume rises. Though commercial planes, steadily increasing their radii of action, tend to decrease the numbers of their stops,
Puerto Rico, conveniently located at the half-way point and with good
airports and modern installations, continues to be an essential stopping
place. Its favorable position is highlighted still more by the fact that it is
ideally located for the airlines connecting Central and South America
with Europe.

2

The Geographic Environment and
Its Influence on the Life
of Puerto Rico

In comparison with the world's rich regions, Puerto Rico's physical base is limited in natural resources. Nevertheless, a careful analysis and evaluation of those resources are fundamental for reaching an understanding of the island's real possibilities.

The Geographic Environment

LOCATION

As discussed in the previous chapter, geographic location has been of great importance to the history and development of Puerto Rico.

Today Puerto Rico is still a cultural frontier between the predominantly Anglo-Saxon world to the north and the Latin American lands to the south. Furthermore, the influence of these cultures is, on balance, beneficial to the island, although the Puerto Ricans are doing their best to preserve their distinct personality.

AREA

Puerto Rico's total area, including that of its adjacent small islands, is about 3,435 square miles; deduction of the lagoons leaves some 3,417.5 square miles of land. The factor of available space profoundly affects the island's economy, whose total output is limited by the small area as well as by the paucity of natural resources. Those who maintain that area is unimportant and that several small countries have reached high points of economic development, mention Switzerland, Belgium, and Holland, the smallest of which is more than three times as large as Puerto Rico (Table 2.1). In the Caribbean region, while the island is larger than any of the Lesser Antilles, it is the smallest of the Greater Antilles. The Dominican Republic is almost six times as large as Puerto Rico while Cuba, with 44,000 square miles, is nearly thirteen times as large. With more

13

Table 2.1. Total population, area and density for various countries

Country	Population in Thousands (1968)	Area in Square Miles	Density per Square Mile
Puerto Rico	2,754	3,435	802
Switzerland	6,230	15,944	397
Belgium	9,646	11,779	819
Netherlands	12,783	13,025	981
Dominican Republic	4,174	19,129	223
Cuba	8,250	44,217	187

Source: Population figures according to the United Nations, taken from *Diccionario Geográfico, 1971, Almanaque Mundial,* Editora Moderna Inc., 1970.

than 2 million inhabitants, Puerto Rico's relation between space and population is alarming.

The island's crowded condition has strongly influenced the industrialization program which started to be developed during the 1940's. Its aim was to accelerate employment in manufacturing through increased production for local consumption and export. Migration to the mainland United States also eased the pressure of population on resources. Puerto Rico's success in raising levels of living would seem to refute the concept of geographic determinism. Before the development program the island's per capita average annual income was $121; today it is more than $1,400, the highest in Latin America and comparable to that of many of the world's developed countries.

TOPOGRAPHY

Puerto Rico is topographically rugged; its surface consists largely of hills and mountains. It is estimated that not more than a third of the island can be classified as level or undulating. Almost one-fourth of Puerto Rico consists of steep slopes of 45 degrees and more. Nearly half of the total area lies at more than 500 feet above sea level. Approximately 40 per cent of the island consists of mountains, 35 per cent of hills, and 25 per cent of plains.

While that situation imposes serious limitations on agriculture, there are compensations: the uplands can be used for hydroelectric development and the countryside's spectacular scenic beauty offers powerful attractions for local and external tourism.

The topography, always a limiting factor from the point of view of agricultural expansion, now also tends to handicap industrial development. In order to stimulate investments, most of the municipalities in the western, rugged mountainous areas offer tax exemption for seventeen instead of ten years. Nevertheless, the establishment of new industries in those regions proceed at a much slower pace than on the coastal plains, the humid, hilly region of the north, or the semiarid ones in the south. While it is true that the topographic limitations can be overcome through such improvements in transportation facilities as the elimination of tortuous roads and narrow bridges, it is equally true that the cost of such work is far higher than in the more level regions.

IRRIGATION AND HYDROELECTRIC ENERGY

Two indications of Puerto Rico's successful effort to overcome its geographic limitations are the irrigation service and the generation of hydroelectric energy. While the island's best soils are in the south (Ponce, Coamo, Santa Isabel, Paso Seco, and San Antón), the precipitation, as low as about 30 inches per year on the southern coastal plain, is at all of those points insufficient for agriculture. At Isabela, in the northwest, other limiting factors are the high rate of evaporation and the drainage of water into the porous soil.

The transfer of sovereignty over Puerto Rico from Spain to the United States (1898) resulted in the expansion of markets for the island's sugar. One result of that expansion was the construction of the first reservoirs in the south at Patillas, Carite, Coamo, and Guayabal. These were built primarily for irrigation; hydroelectric energy was regarded as a by-product. Later, however, growing demands stimulated the development of new sources of hydroelectric energy and resulted in the construction of a large number of reservoirs, primarily in the mountainous regions where abundant rainfall and steep streambeds assured steadier and more permanent yields. In 1936–37, 81 per cent of all the electricity produced in Puerto Rico came from such sources (Fig. 2.1).

Figure 2.1. The Dos Bocas Dam. Construction of the dam greatly beautified the countryside by the vast area of its reservoir. The electric generating plant is seen near the dam. (Courtesy, Government of Puerto Rico.)

However, the transformation of a predominantly agricultural economy
into one more industrialized and diversified demanded a rate of expansion in the production of electric energy much greater than that which
could be achieved through the development of hydraulic sources. Thermoelectric generating plants now came to be built at such a rate that, in
1965, hydroelectric stations produced only 14.5 per cent of the electricity
generated, 85.5 per cent coming from thermal sources.

Spurred by the government's objectives of island-wide industrialization, electrification of the rural areas, and lower costs of electric services,
the Water Resources Authority, with cooperation from the U.S. Atomic
Energy Commission, has continued its expansion with great success,
reaching a technological climax in the BONUS project, operated by nuclear energy. The effectiveness of that plant has led to plans for the construction of a 600,000 KW nuclear installation in Aguirre starting in 1971.
With that plant, expected to be in operation by 1976, the Authority will
produce sufficient electric energy to meet the demands of constant expansion and so guarantee the growth of the economy's main sectors.

MINERALS

Despite the fact that Puerto Rico began its historic life with mining,
the island is relatively poor in commercially exploitable minerals. The
mining industry languished as a result. According to the 1950 census, only
1,500 workers, including those who labored in the rock quarries, were engaged in mining, comprising a mere 0.2 per cent of the total labor force.
In 1960 the figure was 1,396, indicating a reduction in the number of
those who could properly be called miners.

In the face of existing low prices for metals, though without having
made thorough investigations, the Puerto Ricans have long insisted that
their island lacked commercially exploitable metallic mineral resources.
However, explorations brought to a head in 1965 by the Ponce Mining
Corporation and the Bear Creek Mining Company revealed the existence
of large deposits of low-grade copper ores whose commercial exploitation is today possible. With the exploitation of these deposits, a mining
economy would replace the traditional agrarian economy in the Lares-
Utuado-Adjuntas region. The construction of flotation plants for the concentration of copper ores would transform the region's geographic
landscape.

The latest word on a potential mining industry came from R. P. Briggs,
director of a program conducted jointly by the U.S. Geological Survey
and the Commonwealth's Economic Development Administration. He
recommended a thorough investigation of ocean bottoms surrounding
Puerto Rico, beginning if sufficient funds are available with the bottom
of Mona Passage.

Only very few metals, limited to gold, manganese, iron, and a little
high-grade copper, have in the past been exploited commercially in vari-

ous parts of the island. However, the companies which mined gold and manganese have stopped their operations.

The most promising of the iron ores occurring here and there are the limonites in the Cerro de las Mesas and in the vicinity of Guanajibo. In Guanajibo there are 46,800,000 tons of laterites which contain nickel, cobalt, and iron. Their exploitation is held up, however, pending the development of new methods of extracting the metals. The other iron deposits like the hematites and magnetites of Juncos and Humacao, can not be exploited commercially. According to Briggs, the ores of urbanized Cerro de las Mesas are worth less than the high cost of the land.

Puerto Rico's most important mining industry has been, and is, the exploitation of coarse building materials such as limestone and quarry stone, together with the production of sand and other construction materials. However, the acceleration of the latter industry, now amounting to more than $1 billion annually, has alarmingly reduced the availability of sand, especially in the San Juan metropolitan area. The mounting need for sand has resulted in the excessive exploitation of several beaches, to the detriment of the shores' scenic beauty.

Clays are abundant on the island but have not, for various reasons, been used by a flourishing ceramics industry. However, the siliceous sands used in the manufacture of glass have enabled the bottle factory in Guaynabo to increase its production from 2,000 gross daily in 1951 to 3,500 in 1966.

FISHING

While employing a mere 3,000 workers, fishing is another extractive industry. It seems paradoxical that a land surrounded entirely by water provides poor fishing. However, the paucity of Puerto Rico's oceanic resources is easily understood by those who recognize the factors needed for an appreciable fishing industry, such as the presence of ocean currents with various temperatures, great rivers flowing into the sea, and banks with maximum depths of 100 fathoms. The fact that Puerto Rico's annual catch does not exceed some 11 million pounds explains the yearly importation into the island of some 30 million pounds of dried fish, the equivalent of 125 to 150 million pounds of the fresh product.

Recent plans for the improvement of the fishermen's lives and production include: training for navigation on the high seas, the provision of better boats with modern equipment for locating schools of fish, and the improvement of villages where fishermen's cooperatives can obtain advice toward raising their social-economic levels.

While the natural limitations on fishing cannot be removed, a thorough study of the location of neighboring banks, going hand in hand with improved knowledge of fish culture, should result in greater fishing yields.

In the matter of fresh-water fishing, the potentialities of 1950 are to-day's realities. Black-bass, catfish, "tilapias," bluegills, sunfish, and other varieties have been bred in Maricao and distributed in the island's rivers as well as in the man-made lakes. Fish abound in the La Plata, Añasco, Arecibo, Manatí, Loíza, and Mameyes rivers and in the lakes of Guajataca, Guineo, Guayabal, Garzas, Carite, Patillas, Comerío, Dos Bocas, and Matrullas. Within its program for the development of fresh-water fishing, the Commonwealth's Department of Agriculture has created artificial farm ponds in various places which lacked natural sites for breeding fish.

The development of sport fishing began about 1947. In 1949, the Office of Tourism began to investigate nearby ocean currents and the presence of fish species of interest to sportsmen. It was found that Puerto Rican waters abound in species of marine fauna for which such sport centers as Miami, Acapulco, and others, have long been famous. The Office of Tourism began to organize international fishing tournaments which proved so successful that they are today annual affairs, patronized by the various yacht clubs (Fig. 2.2). Competitions for blue marlin and sailfish are especially famous. Several world records set by men and women have earned for Puerto Rico the title "Capital of the Blue Marlin."

Figure 2.2. Aerial View of the Cangrejos Yacht Club. The growing number of boats with their equipment indicates the growth of sport fishing, which with its international competitions can stimulate the maritime pursuits of the Puerto Ricans. (Courtesy of the Economic Development Administration.)

CLIMATE

The climate is another environmental factor which must be studied with care. Puerto Rico's location in the tropical zone, plus the lack of extreme temperatures, permits year-round production. The mild winters also play an important role in the development of the tourist industry which brought in $15 million in 1950, $96 million in 1964, $139 million two years later, and $223 million in 1970. While total rainfall is abundant, with an annual average of more than 70 inches, large level areas are arid in the south and subhumid in the northwest. Human ingenuity has partially overcome that climatic limitation by rechanneling waters from the humid north to the south, to convert the semi-desert there into an oasis of production. (Fig. 2.3).

Topography, soils, and climate form the physical environment for agriculture which, employing about 74,000 Puerto Ricans in 1970, remains one of the island's important industries. Through the intensive utilization of natural resources, supplemented by large investments of capital, the sugar industry is trying to reach levels of production which, in quantities and efficiency, would equal those of the world's principal sugar zones. Other branches of agriculture are in bad shape. In coffee, tobacco, and minor fruits, the yield per acre is far below those in other lands where the production of such crops is a major occupation. In coffee, however, the trend, stimulated by government help, is toward yields substantially higher than the traditional two hundred weight per acre.[1] Such increased production will call for smaller areas of cultivated lands for the same yields of coffee and will permit the remaining lands to be used for the cultivation of minor fruits, oranges, bananas, plantains, and cattle.

The juxtaposition of a constantly growing population with limited agricultural resources inevitably demands employment in other economic activities. The trend toward sources of income other than agriculture, already noticeable in 1950, resulted in a total income of $3,821 million in 1970, of which agriculture produced only $184 million. Obviously, agriculture's increases in total production are far lower than are those attained in manufacturing, commerce, transportation, and other nonagricultural activities.

The annual production of beef cattle and chickens is expected to reach some $120 million by 1975 while the total consumption of animal products will come to about $220 million. Such conditions call for a new era in agriculture based on "the modernization of all traditional aspects, including maximum mechanization, continuous and intensive experimenta-

---

1. The figures correspond to the Puerto Rican terms of "quintales" per "cuerda." However, a "quintal" (46 kg.) corresponds so closely to 100 pounds and a "cuerda" (0.9712 acres) to an acre, that the terms are used interchangeably in round-number discussions of this kind.

Figure 2.3. Eastern Part of the Lajas Plains. The foreground shows cultivated fields ascending to the bases of the hills. In the background are the Bay of Guánica and the Former Guánica Lagoon drained as part of the Lajas Valley project. The conversion of that semi-desert (30 inches of rain per year) into an important agricultural area is a triumph of Puerto Rico's efforts to overcome the environmental limitations. (Courtesy of the Puerto Rico Water Resources Authority.)

tion, the introduction of new plant varieties, and the development of new methods of cultivation in sugar cane, coffee, and tobacco."[2]

VEGETATION

The resources for direct exploitation are far more limited than are those for agriculture. The natural vegetation which once covered the island, consisting almost entirely of forests, has diminished to the point where today less than one-fourth of the island is covered by trees while a century ago at least three-quarters of the area was forested. The remaining forested mountain areas are less valuable for their lumber than for the protection they afford for the entire island, impeding soil erosion and the undue flooding of rivers. Of the 500,000 acres (22 per cent of the island's total) which should, according to forestry experts, be covered by trees, only 114,000 produce timber trees while more than half of the area is completely devoid of trees of any kind.

In recent years, however, the island seems to have turned the corner from its most critical period of forest denudation. Federal and Commonwealth agencies have carried forward a vigorous program of reforestation, while there is a growing trend toward using the steeper slopes for pasture or trees. The growing awareness on the part of the citizens of the value of trees holds promise for the immediate as well as distant future. The introduction of a number of new species of trees, including Honduran pine and "mahore," promises not only better conservation of the soils but also the expansion of forested areas for recreation and the conservation of trees.

SOILS

Puerto Rico's soils are profoundly affected by the topography. Surveys have shown that a large part of the soils lack depth and plant nutrients. Less than one-third of the island's soils, located almost solely in the plains, are classified as having good or average qualities. Studies made by the island's experimental station and the Federal Government show that no more than 400,000 acres, some 28 per cent of the island's total area can be classified as ranking in productivity between the better grade, 1 and 5. The remaining soils have far inferior productive capacities, falling between grades 6 and 10.

Erosion has begun to show its damaging effects, especially in the mountainous interior. The Soil Conservation Service estimates that a conservation of Puerto Rico's soils demands the cultivation of no more than 850,000 acres and that the major parts of those require complex and intensive conservation practices to be truly productive. The experts main-

2. Rafael Picó *Puerto Rico. Planificación y acción* [*Planning and action*] (San Juan: Government Development Bank for Puerto Rico, 1962), p. 186.

tain that the remaining area, some 60 per cent of the total, should be used
only for pasture or forests. However, studies made by the Puerto Rican
Department of Agriculture revealed that in 1951 nearly 900,000 acres
were cultivated while an additional 100,000 acres, normally in pasture,
were used for the same purpose. The figures indicate that Puerto Rico
surpassed its limit and has long cultivated lands which according to the
specialists should not be so used.

Countries which practice scientific agriculture have overcome limitations. Denmark's low-quality, sandy soils, administered by expert agronomists who apply the interaction of fertilizers, irrigation, the introduction
of new plant species, and the control of diseases, yield more than other
regions with good natural fertility. It is expected that in Puerto Rico's
new agricultural era, the soils will produce economic yields comparable
with those resulting from industrial development.

Projections for the Future

As stated above, a country's geographic environment consists primarily
of its natural resources which, in Puerto Rico, and especially in relation
to the island's high population density, are extremely limited. Puerto Rico
presents a discouraging contrast to other parts of the world blessed with
abundant natural resources.

I recall a visit to the prairies of the Midwestern United States where I
saw some of the finest black soils in the world; in several places these
soils were removed and destroyed for the purpose of reaching a four-foot
seam of coal in the subsoil. Nature had there been prodigal in not only
providing one of the world's finest soils but in also adding mineral resources a few feet below the surface. Not enjoying similar advantages,
Puerto Rico must plan carefully the utilization of its scant natural resources.

In view of the limited acreage of good lands recommended for cultivation, there is need for confining cultivation to the best lands, devoting the
remainder to pastures for the growing cattle industry. Obviously, the
scant agricultural lands which comprise almost the only natural resource
of the island must be put to optimum use. Erosion control is a sine qua
non toward that end. According to the experts, only about 28 per cent of
the island's lands show a minimum of erosion or none at all; on the rest
of the island the destructive action of erosion, while more acute in some
places than in others, is truly a serious problem.

The urgent task is to promote good usage of natural resources, drain
swampy lands and irrigate arid regions, as has been done in the Lajas
Valley which today enjoys irrigation services. A proposed similar program in the Coamo–Bauta area promises economic success some time in
the future. Other projects must be undertaken. The Land Authority has

already improved by drainage some 5,600 acres in the so-called Caño de Tiburones, near Arecibo. But Puerto Rico still has large remaining areas of undrained, or inadequately drained, lands.

The restoration and conservation of soils, going hand in hand with reforestation, provides ample opportunities for enlarging Puerto Rico's productive areas. Programs for such restoration and conservation must be intensified, not only to preserve the land's productivity but also to conserve the water resources and so increase the generation of hydroelectric energy.

As a result of a thorough study of the conservation of natural resources by the Commonwealth's House of Representatives, the Legislature in 1970 created a public body, the Environmental Quality Board, with the purpose of establishing standards for environmental protection to be followed by all industries and other economic activities that might cause pollution and contamination.

Industrialization and the Geographic Environment

Despite all labors to augment the island's cultivated regions and expand the extractive industries to the maximum, the scarcity of natural resources demands that developmental efforts be channeled toward other economic activities. The Commonwealth Government, largely through its Industrial Development Company, is developing a vast program of industrial expansion. Under the auspices of the Industrial Development Company, about 1,700 new industries have to date been established in Puerto Rico (Fig. 2.4).

Figure 2.4. Petroleum Refinery of Phillips Puerto Rico Core, Inc., in Guayama.

Analysis of the nature of those industries shows that most of them use imported raw materials and that very few process materials obtained on the island. Among those which use local resources are the cigar factories, plants which make paper from bagasse (the end product of grinding sugar cane), canneries for fruits, juices, and vegetables, industries processing the by-products of sugar cane cultivation, and those which process coffee.

It is obviously necessary to redouble efforts to use increasing quantities of local raw materials for that great industrial program. All sugar, for instance, should be refined on the island; the fact that it is not is caused by an absurd restriction imposed on the principal industry by mainland economic forces. Copper production and refining is another possibility for a local resource-based new industry.

However, the principal incentive for the establishment of new industries is not, and will not become, the utilization of the island's natural resources, but the abundance of available manual labor, transportation facilities, tariff protection which gives Puerto Rico a "common market" with the United States, and other economic and financial advantages which Puerto Rico's new generation has created.

3

The Relief

Importance of the Study

Knowledge of the relief of a country is essential for the study of its geography. The relief gives us the configuration of the land in terms of differences in altitude, the slopes within a given area, and the resulting regional distribution of various land forms. The study of the relief gives us the general aspects of various parts of a country and hence the setting for other geographic elements. Often those elements are intimately related to the relief, and the shapes in which they manifest themselves are directly related to the shapes of the relief. So, for example, the climate, the vegetation, and the soils differ from place to place, depending on whether the land is level or mountainous. Even the geographic elements stemming from man's labor, such as cultivated fields, cities, and roads, differ according to the relief of the land in which they are found.

Aspects to be Studied

The study of relief begins with the topography, the description of the various places in which distinct forms of relief are encountered. Hence we see which parts of the island are mountainous and which are level. Next we come to the physiography, or the description of the nature of those forms of relief. As the topography reveals where the various forms of relief are encountered, physiography explains the reasons for them and their occurrence in the various regions. The topography gives a statistical picture of the relief as it is today, and physiography gives a dynamic picture in which the relief is seen as resulting from a series of processes and transformations which began in the past and continue today and into the future. It will therefore be interesting to turn to the past and give space to the study of Puerto Rico's geologic origins, including two subjects related to the relief, the rocks and the earthquakes.

Topography

GENERAL NATURE OF TOPOGRAPHY

Puerto Rico's topography[1] is dominated by mountains (Fig. 3.1). From any vantage point in San Juan, one sees the imposing wall of mountains in the south covering that whole part of the horizon, in contrast to the small coastal plain which extends northward from the foothills to the Atlantic Ocean. The same thing can be seen from Ponce to the south coast. In the east and west, the narrow, deep valleys originating in the mountains and spreading out fanwise to end at the sea also tend to bring out the magnificence of the mountain masses from where they stem and by whose spurs they are flanked.

A study of Puerto Rico's mountainous areas[2] reveals that 55 per cent of the island's land is located at altitudes below 500 feet above sea level; 21 per cent lies between 500 and 1,000 feet, and 24 per cent above 1,000 feet. In terms of gradient, almost one fourth of the surface slopes steeply, some at 45 degrees or more from the horizontal. In terms of altitude, almost half of the total area is more than 500 feet above sea level.

As to relief forms, it is estimated that about 40 per cent of the island is covered by mountains and some 35 per cent by hills, while 25 per cent is level. In other words, less than half of the lands lower than 500 feet in altitude can be considered level. The rest are covered by hills which also compose parts of the lands above 500 feet, and the remaining parts are mountainous.

Those mountains form the true nucleus or spine of the island, extending almost without a break from one end to the other. The relief map (Fig. 3.2) shows the distribution of the mountainous and hilly regions in relation to the plains. The axis of the mountainous spine begins near the west coast, in the Mayagüez area where the Uroyán Mountains and the Cerro de las Mesas are found, and spans the island toward the east, forming the Cordillera Central (Central Range), the Sierra (Range) of Cayey, and the Sierra de Luquillo.

Along the coast is a zone of interrupted coastal plains, covered by river alluvium, beach sands, or aeolian dunes. On some of those plains, especially in the southeast, the deposits are shaped like alluvial fans.

1. The best sources for the study of topography are the excellent maps published by the U.S. Geological Survey and Puerto Rico's Department of the Interior (today the Department of Public Works), which cover the island in 64 sheets at a scale of 1:20,000. Interpretation of those maps is facilitated by a study of the hundreds of aerial photographs which are used in their compiling. There is also a topographic map of the entire island, recently published in one sheet, reduced from the 64 sheets and using two scales, namely: 1:120,000 and 1:240,000. The so-called Aeronautical Chart of Puerto Rico, produced by the U.S. Coast and Geodetic Survey to the scale of 1:250,000 for use in aerial navigation, is also useful for the study of topography.

2. A. Upson, *El area montañosa definida* [Description of the mountain area] First Conference on the Problem of Mountains, June, 1946. *Revista de Agricultura de Puerto Rico* [Journal of Puerto Rican agriculture], July–December 1946.

Figure 3.1. Aerial View of Strong Relief along the Island's Backbone and the Wide Valley of the La Plata River. The town of Comerío is in its midst. (Courtesy, Government of Puerto Rico. Photo by Rotkin.)

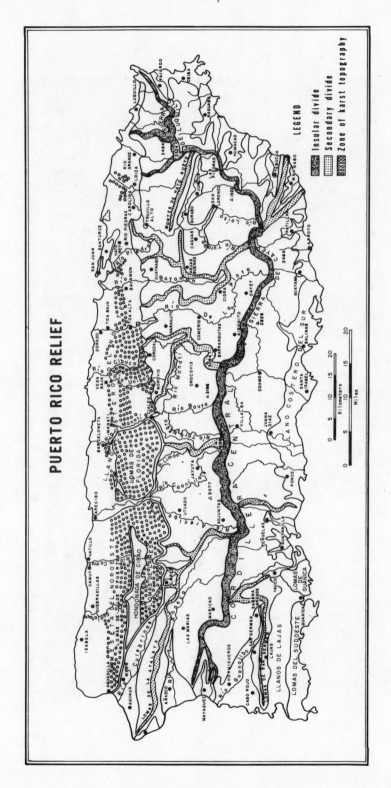

Figure 3.2.

Figure 3.3. Sinkhole and Cavern of *Tres Pueblos* (Three Towns). It is so called because of its location at the junction of Camuy, Hatillo, and Lares. It is part of the extensive system of caves of the Camuy River. The speleologists who have studied it believe it to be among the world's most spectacular. (Courtesy of Watson Monroe.)

In Puerto Rico's northwest, between the mountainous spine and the coastal plain, is found a true "lunar" landscape, characterized by hundreds of funnel–shaped holes without outlets, called "sinkholes" (locally "sumideros") hundreds of cone–shaped limestone hummocks called "haystacks" ("mogotes" or "pepinos") and numerous caves (Fig. 3.3). The drainage of that entire region of haystacks and sinkholes is subterranean, through the caves which cross the haystacks and feed on the waters caught in the sinkholes. The special topography of hummocks, sinkholes, and caves resulted from the ease by which certain pure limestones are dissolved by rainwater which destroys them chemically, riddling them with holes which are in time converted into caves containing subterranean rivers. The region in which those phenomena are found is said to have a "karst" topography, after the region in Yugoslavia of similar origin. The caves are thought to represent the first step in the process of erosion, following the appearance of sinkholes whose bottoms drain into the caves. The sinkholes, gathering rainwater, feed the subterranean rivers which flow through the caves, enlarging them little by little, until, finally, the roofs cave in and the remaining walls form hummocks or "haystacks" (Fig. 3.4).

Figure 3.4. Haystack Hill (Mogote) South of Montebello near the Town of
Florida. (Courtesy of Watson Monroe.)

The forces and processes active in Puerto Rico's geologic evolution permit us to divide the island (according to Monroe)[3] into three large physiographic regions: (1) the interior mountainous zone, (2) the karst region in the north, and (3), the coastal plains. However, from the
geographic point of view, which considers the various degrees of homo-
geneity in the ways of life, produced independently as well as resulting
from natural forces, we continue to divide the island into thirteen geographic regions discussed in Chapter 18.

THE INTERIOR MOUNTAINOUS ZONE

The Cordillera Central extends through the island's entire interior,
from Mayagüez to Aibonito. The higher parts of that range, with altitudes of more than 3,000 feet, are generally found to the southwest of
Adjuntas and to the north of Villalba. Between Adjuntas and Mayagüez,
in the Cerro de las Mesas, altitudes diminish to 700 or 1,000 feet. East of
Villalba the decline is less, to about 2,800 feet southeast of Aibonito,

3. Watson Monroe, (U.S. Geological Survey) *Dominio litológico en la formación
de algunas formas de relieve en Puerto Rico* [Lithologic control in the development
of some land forms in Puerto Rico], *Unión Geográfica Internacional,* Conferencia
Regional Latinoamericana, Proceedings, 2:286–91.

where the highway from Cayey to Salinas crosses the divide which separates the Cordillera Central from the Sierra de Cayey.

The divides and rivers provide clues for understanding the topography of the mountainous regions. A divide is a line which connects the high points where rainwaters divide or flow in opposite directions to form rivers. Puerto Rico's most important divide is the "Insular" (Fig. 3.2), which separates the rivers flowing toward the north from those which flow southward. It coincides approximately with the crest of the mountainous spine. Some of the island's highest peaks, like the Cerro de Punta (4,389 feet) and the Cerro de Doña Juana (3,539 feet), are found on this divide, and the rest are quite near it (Fig. 3.5). It may be seen that the divide does not run along the island's center. It is about twice as far from the north coast as the south. South of Barranquitas, Aibonito, and Cayey, the divide turns toward the southeast and then runs only 9 miles from the south coast and 27 from the north, or three times as far.

The Sierra de Cayey may be said to be merely a part of the Central Range, where the divide is closest to the south coast. The highway between Cayey and Salinas can serve as an arbitrary line which separates the two mountain groups. All along the Sierra de Cayey, toward the east, the altitude diminishes until, between Las Piedras and Humacao, where

Figure 3.5. Cerro de Punta (Point Hill). This is Puerto Rico's highest point, 4,389 feet. Its morphology justifies the term. (Courtesy of Dr. Carlos Iniguez.)

the Sierra de Cayey ends, it is only some 400 feet. A branch of the Sierra de Cayey runs southeast to form the Sierras Guardarraya and Pandura. The divide turns northward and ascends rapidly, again reaching high altitudes in the peaks of the Sierra de Luquillo, some of which exceed 3,400 feet. Among these are el Toro (the Bull, 3,524 feet) and el Yunque (the Anvil, 3,494 feet) (Fig. 3.6).

The southward descent from the crest of the Cordillera Central and the Sierra de Cayey is very steep. Most of the rivers are short and torrential, generally flowing only when it rains, which is not often. After their rapid descent, the mountains become hills which form a band between the Cordillera proper and the plain; they are called the foothills, or piedmont hills, because they are located at the feet of the mountains. Here and there, as in the case of the limestone hills between Yauco and Ponce, they unite with the system of coastal hills discussed above. Northwest of Yauco, the foothills form the divide between the valleys of Yauco and Guanajibo and connect the hills of San Germán with the Cordillera Central.

The descent toward the north from the Cordillera Central and the Sierra de Cayey is much gentler. Precipitation is heavier in this part of the mountains, and the rivers have been able to do a more complete job of erosion. There are many more rivers than in the south, and they have consolidated into a few systems, forming large basins whose divides are shown on the map (Fig. 3.2). The most important are that of the Añasco, west of Adjuntas; of the Arecibo and its large tributary, the Caonillas; and those of the Manatí and the La Plata. The divide between the basins of the Añasco and Arecibo runs northward but twists toward the northwest to end near Rincón, forming the Lomas (Hills) de la Atalaya.

The Arecibo River and its tributaries have actively eroded the mountainous region, forming a large basin in the triangle between Utuado, Adjuntas, and Jayuya. Near Jayuya, however, the resistance of the rocks to erosion has been greater, and the entire upper valley of the Caonillas is filled with spurs which separate it from the valley of the upper Arecibo and the Limón River. The spurs west of the Jayuya culminate in the Cerro Prieto with an altitude of 3,077 feet. South of the same insular divide is the Cerro de Punta, Puerto Rico's highest mountain, 4,389 feet above sea level. Toward the east, in the spur which runs northward toward the hills of Florida, are the "Tres Picachos" (Three Peaks), with altitudes of more than 3,615 feet.

In the east is the important basin of the Río de la Plata (Silver River), narrow but long, the longest in Puerto Rico (Fig. 3.7). With its tributaries, the river has excavated valleys which are generally deep and steep, but the valley of the La Plata widens near Cayey and creates an undulating plain of considerable extent, the Interior Plain of Cayey.

Figure 3.6. El Yunque. Seen from Luquillo Beach.

Figure 3.7. The Wide Valley of the La Plata River near Cayey. The Puerto Rico Reconstruction Administration (PRRA) located a resettlement project here. Today, in addition to tobacco and sugar cane, its production of chickens and eggs are among the island's largest. (Courtesy of Watson Monroe.)

THE CAGUAS VALLEY

East of the La Plata basin is the island's largest river basin, that of the Loíza, Puerto Rico's widest stream, with its tributaries, the Turabo and Gurabo. The combined erosion of those three rivers in their mid-course carved a large interior plain, the Caguas Plain, almost entirely surrounded by mountains (Fig. 3.8). To the west are the Aguas Buenas and Cidra mountains, south the Cayey Range, and in the northeast that of Luquillo. A spur of the Sierra de Luquillo, the mountains of Hato Nuevo and Aguas Buenas, bound the plain in the north, but between them are two passages, the valley of the Loíza River and the highway from Caguas to Río Piedras.

THE KARST REGION IN THE NORTH

In Puerto Rico's northwest there is a relatively low region called La Meseta del Noroeste (The Northwest Plateau). In it is a coastal belt, mostly level or lightly undulating, with altitudes of 100 feet near the coast and 700 feet inland, traversed by ridges of low limestone hills which are seen from Highway #2 between Arecibo and Aguadilla (Fig.

Figure 3.8. Aerial View of the City of Caguas, in the Heart of the Loíza River Valley. (Courtesy of the Government of Puerto Rico. Photo by Rotkin.)

3.9). That coastal belt is called the Llano de Quebradillas (Quebradillas Plain).

The topography becomes quite irregular toward the interior. The terrain is covered by hundreds of "haystack hills" and "sinkholes," extending from Aguadilla and the valley of the Culebrinas River to the valley of the Loíza. The belt is cut by deep north-south canyons of the Guajataca, Camuy, Arecibo, and Manatí Rivers, as well as by the Hondonada de Cibao (Cibao Lowland), consisting in part of the valleys of various streams which flow into the Culebrinas, Guajataca, and Camuy Rivers, and in part of low hills. The lowland is partially divided into two belts, those of the north and south, by a zone of haystacks and depressions. The northern belt is the Lomas de los Puertos, parts of which are locally called the Sierra de Jaicoa (near Aguadilla), the Sierra de Aymamón (west of the Guajataca River), and the Montes de Guarionex (between the Guajataca and the Camuy Rivers). The southern belt is called the Lomas de Lares (Lares Hills).

The Los Puertos Hills, as well as those of Lares, are bounded in the south by steep escarpments. That of the Lares Hills, called the Cuesta de Lares (Lares Cuesta or Escarpment), is seen clearly toward the north from the towns of Lares and San Sebastián. The road from San Sebastián to Lares runs partly along the escarpment's foot but soon, about 3 kilometers east of San Sebastián, it climbs it and runs the rest of the way

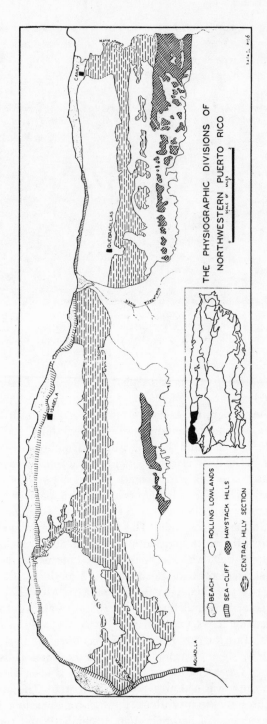

Figure 3.9.

along its top. The Cuesta de Lares continues toward the northwest until it joins the Cuesta de Los Puertos, but it becomes less marked when passing the Cibao lowlands, appearing more like a steep slope in the bottom of the Culebrinas River Valley. North of Moca both cuestas run together and parallel, that of the Los Puertos forming the higher ridge, its crest crowned with "haystacks" or "mogotes," while that of Lares is the lower and softer slope which descends into the valley. Near Aguadilla the escarpment has an altitude of some 300 feet; its maximum of 1,600 feet occurs some ten kilometers east of Lares, in the barrio of Caguana.

The Northwest Plateau also terminates in escarpments in the west, the north, and the east. Those scarped borders, on the four sides, are precisely the features which give individuality to the region. Those in the west and north drop in stair-step terraces near the coast, especially marked in Aguadilla, Isabela, and Quebradillas. They are lower near Camuy, and virtually disappear between Hatillo and Arecibo. On the plateau's eastern border, near Arecibo, there are no pronounced escarpments but only a line of hills which ends abruptly in the alluvial plain of the Arecibo River but reappears toward the south, by the Arecibo-Utuado highway, to arrive at the "mogote" chains of los Puertos and Lares.

East of the Northwest Plateau, between the Arecibo and Manatí Rivers, is a related region, the Florida hills. Those hills are virtually a continuation of the chains of haystacks and sinkholes of Los Puertos and Lares, being separated from them by the valley of the Arecibo River. On their southern border they also have an escarpment, a continuation of the Cuesta de Lares, with an altitude of about 1,000 feet near the Arecibo River, where the Dos Bocas (Two Mouths) reservoir is located, and about 700 feet in Ciales on the Manatí River. Along the valleys of the Arecibo and Manatí Rivers, the Florida hills are also bordered by escarpments, but in the north the "mogotes" comprising them end at the northern plains which at this point have an altitude of some 300 feet.

Between the karst region and the coastal plain east of the Arecibo River's alluvial plain, the topography is dominated by "haystacks," interspersed by regions of rolling relief. Between the La Plata and Piedras Rivers, the surface is rolling to hilly, with few "haystacks." East of the Piedras River, the "haystacks" virtually disappear; only a few are found near San José Lake and the Loíza River. The dominant relief is rolling, like that found in Río Piedras, or with low hills, like that at the beginning of the road from Río Piedras to Caguas.

THE COASTAL PLAINS

The Northern Coastal Plain. The Northern Coastal Plain (Fig. 3.10) extends from the lower Arecibo River to Cape San Juan which forms the island's extreme northeast corner. Near the coast is a truly level region, interrupted only by rocky outcrops and sandy dunes in the littoral.

Figure 3.10. Mouth of the Río Grande de Loíza.

Among the former are that of El Vigía (the Lookout) at Arecibo and the one on which San Juan is located. Many parts are so level and low that the drainage is deficient, a matter which is aggravated by the sand dunes which impede drainage directly to the coast. In those places the coastal plain contains swamps, marshes, and some lakes like the Caño Tiburones (Shark Channel), between Arecibo and Barceloneta, and Lake Tortuguero and the Piñones Lagoon.

Toward the interior of the coastal plain the topography becomes more irregular; the only level regions of any importance are found in the alluvial plains of the rivers which cross the region, such as the Arecibo, the Manatí, the Cibuco, the Loíza, and the La Plata.

Between the Arecibo and Manatí Rivers the topography is gently rolling, or with low hills, including, however, a chain of haystacks which extends westward from Barceloneta, like a belt of the hills of Florida.

The Eastern Coastal Valleys. Near the east coast, the mountains come close to the sea and the rivers have cut narrow, triangular valleys through them, which in places combine to form larger ones (Fig. 3.11). The more important of these valleys are those of Fajardo, Naguabo, Antón Ruiz, Humacao, Yabucoa, and Maunabo.

The South Coastal Plain. The south coastal plain, extending uninterrupted from Patillas to Ponce, is formed by the consolidation of the bottoms of the valleys which extend southward from the Cordillera Central and the Sierra de Cayey. Lacking haystacks and sinkholes, it is much more narrow and regular than is that of the north coast. Drainage is good and occasional swamps are found only at the coast. The rising slope toward the interior is gentle; the plain ends at the foothills of the mountain spine. Between Guayama and Salinas, the plain consists of a series of large alluvial fans.

Coastal Valleys of the Southwest. West of Ponce are some limestone hills which, extending to the coast, form part of the mountains' piedmont as well as the western border of the Ponce-Patillas coastal plain. Level regions are found only where the Tallaboa, Guayanilla, and Yauco Rivers have cut through the hills and formed valleys of considerable size, extending toward the mountains.

The Lajas Plains. In the southwest a large plain extends westward to Boquerón from Yauco and Guánica in the east. In the north it is bordered by the range of hills called las Lomas de San Germán, in the south by that called las Lomas del Suroeste (Southwest). The plain, called el Valle (the Valley) de Lajas (Fig. 2.3), was until fairly recently covered by the sea and has a middle elevation of only some 40 feet. Its low altitude and gentle slopes result in markedly poor drainage. At its eastern end were the Anegada Swamp and Lake Guánica, and on the west is Lake Cartagena. Another swamp and lagoon are found south of Boquerón. Construction of the Lajas Valley irrigation system necessitated drainage

Figure 3.11. Western End of the Yabucoa Valley. In the background, note the steep descent of the Sierra de Cayey. (Courtesy of the Government of Puerto Rico. Photo by Rotkin.)

of the Anegada Swamp and Lake Guánica, but Lake Cartagena remains as an irrigation lake and an excellent bird refuge.

The Southwest Hills. South of the Lajas plains is a chain of rather low hills which in the days when the plain was covered by the sea formed a long island between Guánica and Puerto Rico's southwest corner. The highest point of those hills is about 1,000 feet above sea level, in the Sierra Bermeja.

The Coastal Valleys of the West. Puerto Pico's west coast resembles the east coast in that the mountains encroach close to the sea and the rivers have carved triangular valleys through them, their vertices inland and the bases on the coast. However, in the west some rivers are more powerful than those in the east and have formed valleys which are considerably larger and longer. Three large valleys, those of the Culebrinas, Añasco, and Guanajibo Rivers are found on the west coast; between them are two small valleys, Córcega at Rincón, and the Yagüez River, at Mayagüez.

Physiography

THE PHYSIOGRAPHIC PROCESSES

Puerto Rico's present relief resulted from a series of processes which have operated through the eons and may be classified as the "constructive" and "destructive" processes.

Sedimentation is among the former and occurs when clay, sand, and other materials, transported by rivers and rains, settle on the ocean floor. Those sediments harden in time to form "sedimentary" rocks such as shales. The sea itself helps to form sedimentary rocks. Calcareous shells, deposited on the bottom, form limestones, and the corals form limestone islands called coral islands. The sea is a great factory in which future lands are made, always by the process of sedimentation by which they are amassed while still submerged.

The so-called *tectonic* processes also belong to those called "constructive." Resulting from little understood natural forces within the earth, they cause various regions to rise and so lift the sediments from the ocean bottom to the surface. The rise may be gradual, like a gentle vertical uplift, or due to powerful lateral pressures which crush the sediments, bend them, and at times break them to form *"faults."* The pressures may be sufficiently great to harden sedimentary rocks and even to convert them into other kinds of rocks, called *metamorphic rocks.*

Finally, without seeming to be so, volcanic eruptions are among the constructive processes. These are known as *vulcanism* when melted rock from the earth's interior emerges to the surface through vents along a surface fracture to form a volcano and cools rapidly into a glass. At times, however, the melted rock does not emerge but accumulates in great masses beneath the surface, cooling so slowly that large crystals are formed. That process is *plutonism*. Those processes contribute to the formation of rocks and mountains. The tectonic processes jointly with those of vulcanism and plutonism, are called *orogenic* because they form mountains.

But the forces of nature are not merely constructive. There are also forces of erosion, or attrition, which wear down what has been built up and attempt to reduce everything to the level of the sea. Their aim is to form one perfect plain. They never reach that objective, but they often lower the surface so much that it almost resembles a plain, which is known as a "peneplane" (also written peneplain). Erosion is unable to form a perfect plain because as the rivers lose gradient they stop flowing and so lose the power to erode. In the middle of every peneplane may be seen remaining marked elevations, caused by the fact that the hardest rocks resisted erosion and stayed as remainders of the mountains which had once been there in the past. Those surviving heights are called *monadnocks*.

Often, when a peneplane has been formed or is close to being formed, the tectonic processes start to work again and raise the eroded area. The rivers again cut their valleys in this plain. Small plain areas then remain above the valleys, or the tops of new mountains stay at the same level, indicating that both formations had previously been parts of a peneplane. Those remains form a so-called elevated peneplane, of which there are two in Puerto Rico.

STUDIES BY LOBECK AND MEYERHOFF

The first complete and detailed study of the island's physiography was made by Armin K. Lobeck as a part of the *Scientific Survey of Porto Rico and the Virgin Islands,* which began publication in 1919 under the auspices of the New York Academy of Sciences.

With its nineteen volumes, the *Survey* is a notable contribution to the study of Puerto Rico's geology, physiography, paleontology, zoology, botany and archeology. Volumes I, II, and III contain the geologic and physiographic materials resulting from the labors of a series of specialists; D. R. Semmes studied the San Juan region; E. T. Hodge that of Coamo-Guayama; G. J. Mitchell worked in the Ponce district, and Bela Hubbard in that of Lares. Charles R. Fettke worked around Humacao, and Howard A. Meyerhoff studied the districts of Fajardo, Culebra, and the Virgin Islands. Those works were published in New York between 1919 and 1931.

The study of the physiography, by Lobeck, was included in a single volume which appeared in 1922. Lobeck there recognized three distinct levels of erosion, representing three successive stages in the island's attrition. During each stage the entire island had remained stable and tranquil, resulting in time in its lowering by the processes of erosion which formed plains, beginning at the coasts and extending inland along the rivers.

The lowest of the three levels of erosion, represented by the coastal plains and the adjoining alluvial plains, such as the valley of the Guanajibo River, the Caguas Plain, and the low valley of the Arecibo River, represents the most recent stage, so recent that those plains were only beginning to be formed.

The second stage was represented by a low but elevated peneplane, easily recognized from a distance by the divides in the piedmonts in the mountainous regions of Ciales and Luquillo and also in the low hills of equal altitude extending between Gurabo and Humacao. Lobeck called this level the "Lower Peneplane." It stemmed from an erosion stage earlier than that which had formed the coastal plain. That stage was also longer and gave time for the formation of a plain far larger than the present coastal plain. Before it could level the entire island, however, Puerto Rico was again uplifted by tectonic movements which left the plain high and as though fossilized, not only unable to expand, but even reduced greatly by the later erosion which began to form the present coastal plain representing the first level.

The third stage may be recognized in the remains of another elevated peneplane, marked by the divides toward the middle and high parts of the mountains, and especially in certain high plains like that of Aibonito (Fig. 3.12). It represents the first of the three stages of erosion. In the course of that stage the entire island was being eroded into one peneplane which was eventually raised by the tectonic movements which raised the erosion cycle to its present altitude and produced the lower peneplane, and was finally uplifted again together with the latter, to give way to the present cycle producing today's coastal plain.

Finally, crowning the upper penelane, are the island's highest peaks, regarded by Lobeck as monadnocks, or the remains of ancient mountains which had been destroyed through the formation of the Upper Peneplane (Fig. 3.13). According to Lobeck, those monadnocks extend from south of Maricao to south of Barranquitas, and through all of the Sierra de Luquillo.

Further, Lobeck recognized the existence of a series of zones resembling plateaus, including those known locally as the Meseta del Noroeste (the Northwest Plateau), las Lomas de Florida, (the Low Hills of Florida) and las Colinas Calizas (the Limestone Hills) between Guánica and Ponce. He also recognized, and showed on the map accompanying his work, the regions of "haystacks" which were discussed under topography, and analyzed their origins as caused by subterranean drainage in the limestone.

In 1931 and 1932, Professor Meyerhoff again visited the island, broadened his studies of its geology and physiography, and wrote a book sum-

Figure 3.12. Section of the Cordillera Central. The ancient surfaces were reduced by the leveling agents to the condition of peneplanes. The photograph
shows the San Cristobal Canyon in the foreground and Aibonito and the St.
John peneplane to the rear. (Photo by Watson Monroe.)

Figure 3.13. Monadnocks in the Sierra de Cayey, between Cayey and Salinas. (Courtesy of the Government of Puerto Rico.)

marizing the observations of his colleagues as well as, in general, every-thing then known about Puerto Rico's geology. In that work, *The Geology of Puerto Rico*, published in 1933 by the University of Puerto Rico, he presented his map of Puerto Rico's geology which, until very recently, was the last word on the subject.

In addition to today's geology, Meyerhoff presented in his book his own theories on the island's geologic origins, as well as broadening and im-proving Lobeck's studies of physiography. He accepted Lobeck's monadnock zones but limited the Upper Peneplane largely to the high point of the divides between Adjuntas and Lares, and to 1,600 feet in the Sierra Luquillo region. He named that peneplane "St. John" because it corresponds to the highest erosion level observable on the island of that name in the Virgin Islands.

Below the St. John peneplane, separated from it by escarpments some 800 feet high, are the remains of the "Caguana" peneplane, corresponding to Lobeck's "Lower" peneplane. Meyerhoff gave it that name because the typical location where it is found is in the Caguana barrio of Utuado, about halfway along the road between Lares and Utuado. Much more re-mains of the Caguana peneplane than of the St. John peneplane. When it was formed, the St. John peneplane covered all of the island, but when the island was raised and the Caguana peneplane was formed, the edges of the St. John were trimmed off and its remains now exist only in the island's interior. The 800-foot escarpments which separate the two were produced by the upward movements which ended the St. John erosion cycle and began that of the Caguana. While the lands were rising, erosion had no time in which to attack them much more but when, after rising some 800 feet, the island again became stable, the processes of erosion began to attack this plain now at a great altitude. In the begin-ning, great ravines were formed near the coasts which, as a result of the uplift, must have been much farther from the mountains than today, and gradually worked their way inland. As that happened, the coastal valleys widened, producing plains or triangular valleys, more or less like those which are today seen in Maunabo, Yabucoa, and Humacao. After much time, the ravines which had begun at the coasts had worked their way into the island's heart, destroying the St. John Peneplane in their advance and leaving behind large valleys which continued widening more and more, establishing a large plain near the coasts, which possibly sur-rounded the entire island.

In such manner, while the Caguana peneplane was being formed and enlarged near the coasts, the St. John peneplane, at 800 feet altitude, was being destroyed. From a large and continuous plain, it was reduced to a series of small highland plains near the island's center, separated by the ravines which had penetrated to the very zone of monadnocks. Some of those ravines still exist, almost in their primitive forms, as may be seen from those which remain between Aibonito and Barranquitas, to which town they gave its name. (*Translator's note:* the Spanish word for ravines is "barrancas".) The Caguana peneplane continued to grow and became very wide along the north coast, though considerably smaller on the others. Some tongues of low ground extended from this peneplane toward that of St. John in the interior, following the bottoms of the ravines and valleys; they gave rise to the small interior valleys which abound in the mountains, as for instance in Adjuntas, Jayuya, and Caguas.

When Puerto Rico was again uplifted, the Caguana peneplane could not extend itself farther and began, in turn, to be destroyed by new ravines which began to form along the coasts, and there, after many thousands of years, produced today's coastal plain.

The uplift which ended the Caguana peneplane erosion cycle differed from its predecessor, in which the island had been raised as one block, all at once. The later uplift consisted of an unequal arching, inclined toward the east, in which some parts were raised more than others. The greatest elevation, to some 2,200 feet, took place in the Lares region. Toward the east the uplift was milder, reaching only 500 to 700 feet near the Luquillo Range, and even less at Fajardo. East of Fajardo there was actual submersion; in the Virgin Islands the Caguana peneplane lies under the sea.

One important way in which Meyerhoff modified Lobeck's physiographic ideas was giving a much greater area to the Caguana peneplane and reducing considerably the area of St. John. Meyerhoff had more materials and more time available for his study and credit due to Lobeck should not be diminished. His work served as a basis for later investigations.

The physiographic map (Fig. 3.14) shows the island's zones in which signs are seen of the three levels of erosion as well as the intermediate transition zones. The map was prepared according to the studies and conclusions of Lobeck and Meyerhoff, plus the analysis and interpretation of the 64 sheets of Puerto Rico's topographic map.

While the plain created by the third erosion cycle is still in its early stages, forming largely a series of bands along the coasts, it penetrates considerably inland in the island's eastern part. Here, too, the Loíza River and its tributaries encountered softer rocks among the harder, wore away the softer more rapidly, and produced the interior plain in Caguas. The harder rocks remained to form the Cayey Range and the mountains of Cidra, Aguas Buenas, Hato Nuevo, and Asomante, which border the plain on three sides. The higher parts of those mountains form sections of the St. John peneplane, while parts of the foothills and many low hills are at the level of that of Caguana. The low, flat-topped hills around Las Piedras, which form the divide between Juncos and Humacao, also form parts of the Caguana peneplane.

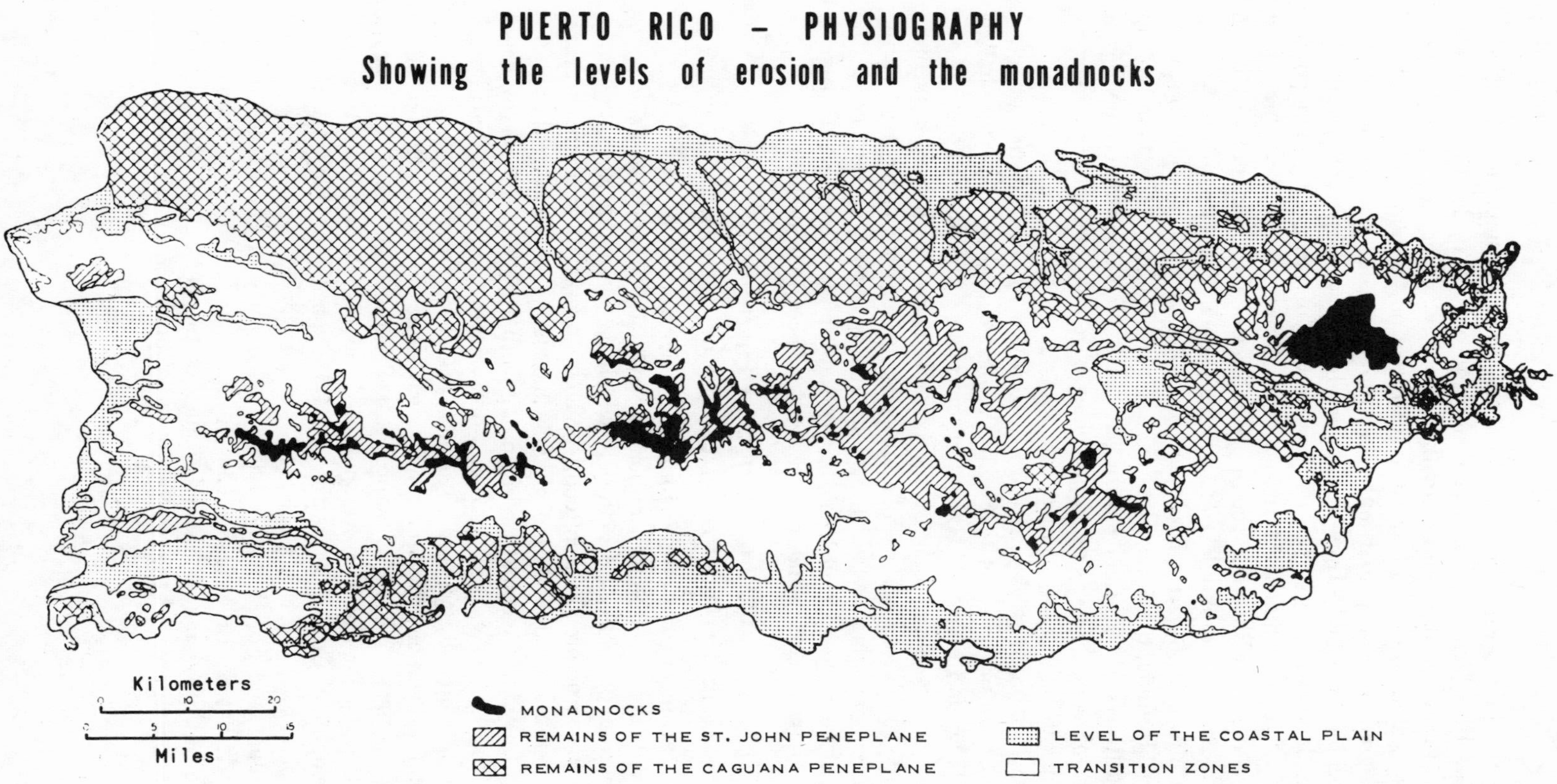
PUERTO RICO – PHYSIOGRAPHY
Showing the levels of erosion and the monadnocks
Kilometers
0 10 20
0 5 10 15
Miles
MONADNOCKS
REMAINS OF THE ST. JOHN PENEPLANE
REMAINS OF THE CAGUANA PENEPLANE
LEVEL OF THE COASTAL PLAIN
TRANSITION ZONES

Figure 3.14. (Based on topographic map of the USGS)

The incline toward the east and north which accompanied the island's folding by which the Caguana peneplane erosion cycle was terminated also caused certain changes in the erosive work of the island's rivers. Those which flowed northward or westward on the northern slope found their gradients steepened and so acquired greater powers of attrition, deepening their beds. However, those which flowed eastward found their slopes lessened, lost a part of their powers of attrition, and deposited some of their sediments, forming large alluvial plains. The three most typical cases are shown in the upper courses of the La Plata and Gurabo Rivers and in the middle course of the Loíza. On losing slope, the La Plata River deposited a large part of its sediment in a widening of its valley, forming the internal alluvial plain of Cayey; the Gurabo and Loíza Rivers did the same east of Caguas. Later, those three rivers began again to deepen their beds, approaching base level, and are forming new canyons in the regions of their courses.

Such, in broad strokes, is the nature of Puerto Rico's forms of relief. Comparison of the relief map with the physiographic brings out similarities between the two. The zones of low plain correspond to those of the lowest erosion level, that of the coastal plain; the plains of medium altitude and the zones of hills and plateaus represent the level of the Caguana peneplane, while the mountainous regions correspond to the level of the St. John peneplane, to the transition belt between the two, or to the monadnocks which extend above the St. John peneplane.

Geologic Origin of Puerto Rico

SOURCES OF INFORMATION ON THE GEOLOGY OF PUERTO RICO

The arrangements of the forms of relief and their minor details is understood best through acquaintance with the underlying geology, or the classes of rocks and materials which compose the island, together with the structure or architecture which governs their occurrence and distribution. The foundation of such knowledge is found in the studies made by various geologists, beginning with the scientific survey sponsored by the New York Academy of Sciences, and its masterful summary presented by Meyerhoff in his *Geology of Puerto Rico*.

After Meyerhoff, important work was done on the north and south coasts in 1944–45, by A. D. Zapp, H. R. Bergquist, and C. R. Thomas, of the U.S. Geological Survey, sponsored by the Puerto Rico Industrial Development Co. in its search for oil deposits. In 1948 Charles L. McGuinness of the U.S. Geological Survey, working for the Puerto Rico Aqueduct and Sewer Authority, made a survey of the island's underground waters. In 1949–51, Clifford A. Kaye of the U.S. Geological Survey (USGS) made detailed studies of the geology of the San Juan metropolitan area, of the coastal physiography, and of Mona Island.

Since 1952, the USGS, cooperating with the Puerto Rico Economic Development Administration, has carried on a detailed study of Puerto Rico's geology, directed until 1966 by Watson H. Monroe, and carried on thereafter by R. P. Briggs. The geology of 37 of Puerto Rico's 64 topographic sheets has been studied under that program, and by 1971 geologic maps with their proper annotations have been published by the USGS. The geologic map of Puerto Rico (Fig. 3.15) is a generalization of the map published by Briggs in 1964.

In 1954, a Section of Mineralogy and Geology, consisting of three geologists under the direction of Mort D. Turner, who was succeeded later by José Cadilla and Eduardo Aguilar was organized within the Economic Development Administration. The group makes studies of minerals and rocks which are, or may be, economically important to Puerto Rico, especially clay, iron, limestone, dolomite, marble, and sand.

Concurrently with those studies, others were made by various United States universities, especially Princeton, Rice, and Texas Christian. The studies sponsored by the Department of Geology of Princeton University, directed by the late Harry H. Hess, resulted in knowledge of the geology of Puerto Rico's southwest corner (P. H. Mattson), as well as of fossils (E. A. Passagno).

A geological section in the Department of Public Works, directed by Pedro A. Gelabert Marqués, produces geologic information on the distribution of building materials and the geology of the beaches.

A group of engineers and geologists of the USGS, working in collaboration with the Water Resources Authority, the Aqueduct and Sewer Authority, and the Industrial Development Company, has since 1957 studied the waters of the rivers and the underground water, their quantities, quality, and the natures of their sediments. That group also studies the history of floods in Puerto Rico.

CLASSES OF ROCKS

Understanding Puerto Rico's geologic origins demands knowledge of the classes of rocks found on the island, their distribution and their ages.

The rocks which compose the crust of the earth are divided into three large groups: igneous, sedimentary, and metamorphic. The igneous rocks were formed from *magma*, the rock found in the earth's interior. When that magma emerges on the surface it is called "lava," or "volcanic ash," which on cooling becomes "volcanic rocks." Those which don't emerge on the surface, but cool off slowly within the crust, are the "plutonic rocks." Those which result from deposition and sedimentation are the "sedimentary" rocks. The metamorphic rocks, which are rare in Puerto Rico, are formed through the transformation of igneous as well as sedimentary rocks. For instance, marble is the result of the meta-

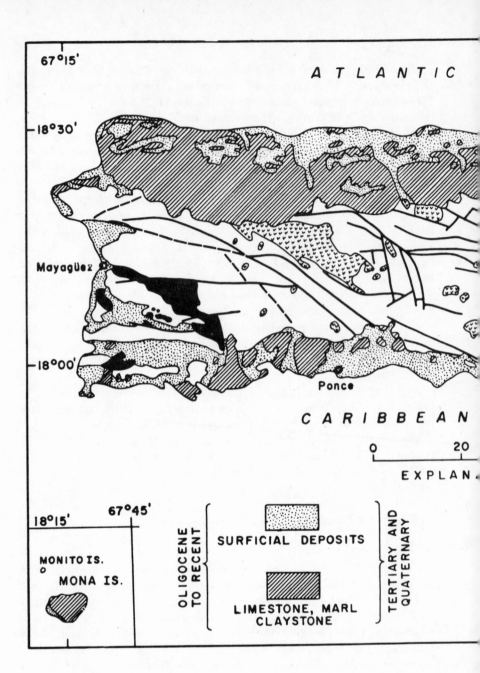

ATLANTIC

67°15'

18°30'

Mayagüez

18°00'

Ponce

CARIBBEAN

0   20

EXPLAN

18°15'   67°45'

MONITO IS.
MONA IS.

OLIGOCENE TO RECENT

SURFICIAL DEPOSITS

LIMESTONE, MARL
CLAYSTONE

TERTIARY AND QUATERNARY

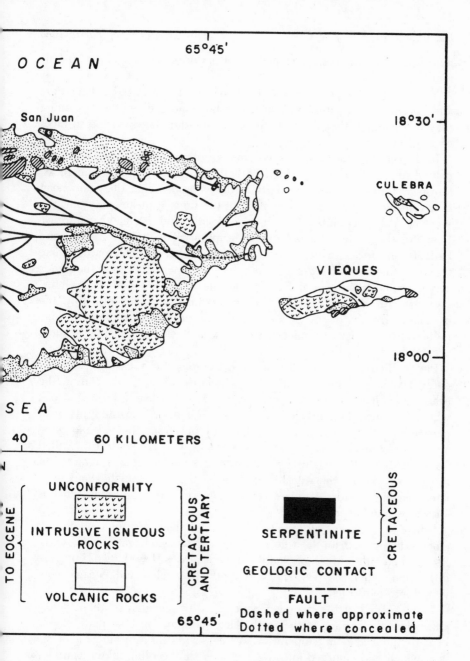

OCEAN

San Juan

65°45'

18°30'

CULEBRA

VIEQUES

18°00'

SEA

40   60 KILOMETERS

UNCONFORMITY

INTRUSIVE IGNEOUS ROCKS

VOLCANIC ROCKS

TO EOCENE

CRETACEOUS AND TERTIARY

SERPENTINITE

CRETACEOUS

GEOLOGIC CONTACT

FAULT
Dashed where approximate
Dotted where concealed

65°45'

Figure 3.15. Generalized Geologic Map of Puerto Rico. (Reprinted from Reginald P. Briggs, "Mineral Resources of Puerto Rico," *Revista del Colegio de Ingenieros de P. R.* 19, no. 2 [April–June, 1969].)

51

morphism of limestone, and serpentine of peridotite (a crystalline igneous rock).

Volcanic rocks abound in Puerto Rico. Vulcanism lasted a long time and enormous quantities of lava and ashes emerged; in the beginning they hardened on the ocean's bottom, but in later stages on the surfaces of volcanic islands.

In the quiet periods between volcanic eruptions, sedimentary rocks appeared and became interbedded with the igneous. The volcanic rocks, however, formed the largest parts of the deposits. That does not mean that volcanic activity took place most of the time; it means only that the volcanic rocks accumulated much more rapidly, and in greater quantities, than did the sedimentary. A single eruption, like that of the volcano Paricutín in Mexico, which lasted a few months, is enough to accumulate the same thickness of rocks as results from sedimentation over thousands of years. The thousands of feet of volcanic rocks in Puerto Rico, interspersed with a few hundred feet of sedimentary, are probably the cumulative results of several centuries of eruption, interrupted by some millions of years of quiet, during which the sedimentary rocks accumulated.

Puerto Rico's volcanic rocks consist of "pyroclastic" rocks and "consolidated lava," or simply "lava." The pyroclastic rocks resulted from the ashes which had issued from volcanos which on hardening formed a rock which is generally hard despite having originally consisted of small particles. In many cases, the masses erupting from the volcano were larger, and these on hardening formed rocks of a cruder texture called "volcanic tuff." When still larger particles emerged—true fragments of rocks destroyed by the volcanic explosions—they accumulated and were later cemented with calcareous or siliceous materials, forming what is known as "agglomerates."

When the volcanic eruptions were less violent, the pieces did not emerge flying; instead, lava flowed from crevices and craters and solidified at their sides. Much of Puerto Rico's lava is pillow-shaped, implying deposition under the sea. The lava gradually cooled and became converted into hard rock.

Near the end of the period of vulcanism, the magma solidified while still below the surface of the earth. That solidification took place slowly because the change in temperature was not as violent as in the case of the lava which had emerged into the air. Such slow cooling allows time for the formation of minerals and crystals in the magma; the lava contains few crystals because the cooling is so sudden that the greater part of the magma solidifies to a kind of glass. In the plutonic rocks, on the other hand, the crystals are plainly visible. Examples of plutonic rocks are granite, granodiorite, quartzdiorite, diorite, and gabbro.

Those rocks were formed beneath the surface and appeared on the surface after long periods of erosion had removed the covering rocks; today plutonic rocks appear on the surface in many places.

In the tropics, granites offer little resistance to erosion perhaps because they are composed of large grains and crystals, clearly defined, which makes it easier for the heat and humidity to disintegrate them. The proof is encountered in the interior valleys, like that of Caguas, which were excavated from such soft, weathered granites, as well as in the region between the Caguas Valley and Humacao, and in that between Utuado and Jayuya. The largest region of plutonic rocks is in the southeast, in the entire area between Juncos and Yabucoa. The earth's surface is there virtually covered by great crags or boulders which are the eroded remains of blocks of plutonic rocks.

The island's igneous rocks are used primarily for road building, for which the lavas, being the most resistant, are preferred.

The sedimentary rocks originated from particles deposited beneath the water where they were consolidated. There are also a few cases where the sedimentary rocks were formed by the wind which carried sand which, in turn, became cemented by something.

Limestones are Puerto Rico's most abundant sedimentary rocks. These are composed of calcium carbonate, deposited in sea water through precipitation, or more often extracted from the water by animals or plants. In the island's interior a very useful limestone rock is found. As a result of contact with very hot volcanic rock, under great pressure, that stone has often hardened so much that it is almost marble. It is the best stone for road building and is known as *caliza azul* (blue limestone).

Some of the limestone deposits show the work of subterranean waters which produced caves, sinkholes, and the hills known as *mogotes*. Elsewhere the limestone bands have produced mountain ranges, like the Cerro de las Cuevas, north of Juana Díaz.

Another of the sedimentary rocks, shale, is quite abundant in the mountainous regions. It was formed by the induration of clays, and in some cases volcanic ashes, brought to the sea from their original sites of deposition (Fig. 3.16).

There are also sedimentary rocks known as conglomerates. Not only does their name resemble that of agglomerates of volcanic origin, but the two rocks also resemble one another. They differ in that the agglomerates of volcanic origin are composed of fragments whose sides are made up of angles and edges, while the conglomerates are composed of pebbles whose surfaces have been rounded by river waters. In both kinds of rocks the fragments, or pebbles, are embedded in a matrix, or cement, which holds them together as rocks. The conglomerates are very resistant rocks and are found in large quantities in the Cordillera Central.

Figure 3.16. Folded Cretaceous Shales in the Luquillo Range.

The sandstones are composed of fragments of shells, grains of quartz or other minerals, and volcanic rocks. The grains are cemented by some material, generally calcium carbonate, silica, or oxide of iron.

The metamorphic rocks generally originated at great depths where they were subjected to high pressures and temperatures, which are the agents through which the rocks were metamorphosed or transformed into other kinds of rocks. One example is slate, a metamorphic rock derived from the laminated rock known as shale. When the latter's layers are compressed further, they harden and refine greatly to form slate.

Because of Puerto Rico's relative youth, metamorphic rocks are rare on the island. Among them are marble, derived from limestone; serpentine, derived from the intrusive rock called peridotite; and hornfels, derived from lava.

THE GEOLOGIC AGES

In dealing with geologic evolution it is necessary to refer to spans of time which are much longer than those used in dealing with human affairs. Geology's time limits are those of the earth's entire history, from the beginning of its independent life as a planet until the present time. That history spans perhaps 4,500 to 6,000 million years. However, on seeing the rocks and fossils of Puerto Rico, the geologist realizes that the island began to be formed about 150 million years ago; since that is a very short time, Puerto Rico, geologically, is young.

In dealing with such long ages, the current historic pattern of years before and after Christ is not practical. The geologist measures time by certain epochs, identified by types of rocks, and especially by fossils of animals or plants which are known to have lived in one or the other of the epochs and which, on dying, left their prints on the rocks which in those days were dust, mud, or sand, which covered the remains. Those remains may be shells, bones, teeth, or simply an animal's footprint or the impression of a leaf.

The geologist groups the world's ages into great eras and periods. In table 3.1, the right hand column indicates the number of years each period is entitled to in the world's geological history. The table shows, especially, the periods and epochs which were important in Puerto Rico's geologic history.

Table 3.1. Divisions of geologic time

Era	Period	Epoch	Approximate Age Preceding the Present, in Millions of Years
	Quaternary	Pleistocene Holocene	1
		Pliocene	11
		Miocene	25
Cenozoic	Tertiary	Oligocene	40
		Eocene	60
		Paleocene	70
	Cretaceous	Upper	90
		Lower	135
Mesozoic	Jurassic		180
	Triassic		225
Paleozoic	Six Periods		600
Cryptozoic			3,000 plus

The estimates of years are taken from the Holmes Time Scale. (Holmes, A. 1960. A Revised Geological Time Scale: Edinburgh Geological Society. Trans. v. 17, pt. 3, p. 204.)

The table should be read from the bottom upward because, when a geologist examines a cut in the rocks, the most ancient is usually at the bottom.

The first two eras, the Cryptozoic and the Paleozoic, do not interest us since rocks that old have not been found in Puerto Rico. The island began to be formed in the Mesozoic Era and the oldest rocks known in Puerto Rico stem from the Cretaceous Period. Those rocks are found in the interior mountains. The youngest rocks are from the Cenozoic Era, and those of its Tertiary Period include the limestones which today occupy the greater parts of the coastal regions.

The still younger rocks of the Quaternary Period are composed of unconsolidated materials, like the sandstones of the San Juan Formation, the river alluvium, the coastal plains, and the beach sands.

THE ISLAND'S EVOLUTION

The table of Puerto Rico's geological evolution appearing on pages 58–63 of this chapter (Table 3.2) presents, in summarized form, the main steps in the island's formation. It should be read from left to right, following the numbers. The events of any one epoch appear in the same horizontal column. Events of a similar nature, like those related to drainage, erosion, deposition, or paleogeography, appear in the same vertical column. Orogenic phenomena and changes in the relative levels of sea and land are inserted horizontally in the columns.

No direct evidence remains of Puerto Rico's earliest times; the island has no rocks which antedate the Cretaceous Period. From what is known of the rest of the Antilles and what happened to them later, it is supposed that in those days the islands didn't exist, and the space now occupied by them was covered by deep seas, or the Atlantic Ocean, quite far from the nearest land (1^4 in Table 3.2).

At some time not precisely known, late in the Jurassic Period or early in the Cretaceous, powerful movements within the earth caused the opening of crevices in the earth's crust. This occurrence may have coincided with the sinking of the Gulf of Mexico and the growth of California's Sierra Nevada. Streams of lava emerged from those fissures and melted rocks poured from the crevices for millions of years (2). At times the rocks solidified, but pressures within the earth were so great on the magma that there were violent explosions and the magma appeared in the ocean's waters like a glowing cloud of powder and fragments of lava known as volcanic ash.

Those events continued through a large part of the Lower Cretaceous Epoch and the rocks formed from the lava flows, together with the volcanic ash, constitute the Pre-Robles rocks of eastern Puerto Rico (2a). That formation has a thickness of more than 6,000 feet of volcanic rock, deposited below the sea.

After a long time, tens of millions of years, the mountains of volcanic materials emerged and appeared as volcanic islands (3) which were soon subjected to erosion (4). At that time, sea animals formed reefs near the island, creating the Río Matón Limestone which is now found near Cayey and Aibonito, as well as other limestones near Barranquitas, Comerío, and Cidra. At the same time, volcanos cast lava and ashes into the sea and air, which gave rise to the volcanic formations in Puerto Rico's eastern and central parts. Known as the Robles and Río Orocovis Formations, these are located between Coamo and Ciales and between Salinas and San Juan. Submarine volcanic eruptions of lava and ashes

4. This and other numbers in parentheses refer to the summary table at the end of this chapter, and indicate the different stages in Puerto Rico's geologic evolution.

now also began in the west, giving rise to the lava and volcanic tuff of the Río Loco Formation (5) (Fig. 3.18a).

The temporary volcanic island grew in area (6) and became permanent (7). Rainfall began the process as of weathering and erosion (8), and the new rivers came to be filled with mud, sand and gravel derived from the weathered fragments of the volcanic rocks. On arrival at the sea, the rivers deposited their loads near their mouths in thick layers of gravel. The sea's currents and waves moved the finer particles farther out and deposited them as clay and sand. At some sites, where the sea was cleaner, the marine fauna, especially the large shellfish called rudistids, extracted calcium carbonate from the water and built limestone reefs. All those sediments constitute the Cariblanco Formation of Puerto Rico's southeast. In the north, the eruption of lava of the Río Orocovis Formation continued. Farther west vulcanism continued to deposit lava and volcanic tuff while clay and much limestone were deposited by the sea. Those materials came to constitute the Mayagüez Group which consists of many lenticular formations (9). At the end of the Cretaceous Period there was a long volcanic island, extending from the Virgin Islands to Santo Domingo, through Puerto Rico (10). At times that island reached a high altitude above sea level, at others it was lower (11). Vulcanism continued, but not as strongly as before. There was deposition of mud, sands of volcanic origin, and limestone along the island's north and south edges, which today constitute the Coamo Formation. The sea waters farther west were cleaner and deposited limestone, today's San Germán Limestone, with a thickness of 2,000 feet (12).

Those matters may be read on the geological map (Fig. 3.15). Among the rocks of the Cretaceous Period (see the key below the map) we encounter extrusive or volcanic rocks, mainly lavas and largely andesites. These are found southeast and southwest of the Luquillo Range (southwest of Ceiba and northeast of Juncos); in the Cayey Range (north of Patillas); in the hills of Aguas Buenas (northwest of that town); in the Cordillera Central (west of Adjuntas); and in the hills of Atalaya (south of Aguada).

The Upper Cretaceous formations also include pyroclastic rocks which are accumulations of fragments produced by volcanic explosions, and shales as well as tuff, partly calcareous, which had been deposited on the ocean bottom as sediments around the volcanoes. The shales had grown through the accumulation of clay and mud brought by the rivers, the tuffs through the accumulation of volcanic ash. They are both calcareous through the accumulation of marine organisms which lived during the intervals of volcanic inactivity. There are also some thin beds of marble and crystallized limestone which had been metamorphosed and recrystallized through the action of heat and pressure in the earth's interior.

Table 3.2. Synopsis of the geologic evolution of Puerto Rico

Based on studies by Meyerhoff, Thomas, Berquist, Zapp, and McGuinness; revised by Watson Monroe

Period	Epoch	Paleogeography	Erosion	Deposition	Drainage
Time before Cretaceous		1. At the site of Puerto Rico, there was deep ocean far from the nearest land.			
	Lower Cretaceous	2. Lava erupted through fissures in the ocean floor in the eastern part of today's Puerto Rico. After millions of years of explosive eruptions of lava and ashes, mountains of volcanic deposits reached the surface of the ocean to form transitory islands.		2a. Deposition of the Pre-Robles rocks; more than six thousand feet of volcanic rocks, lava, and tuff, deposited almost entirely under the sea.	
		3. After a long time, tens of millions of years, the volcanic islands grew and became permanent islands.	4. Erosion of the volcanic islands.	5. Deposition of the Robles Formation, consisting in general of shaly volcanic tuff but including a limestone bed Rio Matón Limestone (member of Robles) which was a reef of rudistids (ancient shellfish) near a volcanic island, and two thick beds of lava (Lapa Lava Member and Las Tetas Lava Member) each more than 1,000 feet thick. The thickness of the Robles Formation is more than 3,000 feet. In the west, the Rio Loco formation, consisting of lava and volcanic tuff, began to be deposited on the ocean bottom.	
		6. Vulcanism continued.			
	Upper Cretaceous	7. A chain of volcanic islands arose in the area corresponding to the present municipalities of Orocovis and Barranquitas.	8. Rapid erosion of 7.	9. Deposition of the thick mass of lava between Barranquitas and Corozal. Deposition of the Cariblanco Formation south of Aibonito. This formation consists of a conglomerate of rounded lava fragments near Aibonito, and of shale farther	

CRETACEOUS

south. It is more than 2,500 feet thick. In the west, deposition of the Mayaguez group, consisting of limestone formations, volcanic tuff, shale, and lava, whose thickness varies from 2,400 to 10,000 feet.

10. Growth of a large volcanic island extending from the Virgin Islands to the Dominican Republic and including Puerto Rico.

11. Erosion of 10, at times rapidly, at others more slowly.

12. Deposition of mud, sands of volcanic origin, and limestone, at the island's sides. Today represented by the outcrops of shale, sandstone, and limestone of the Coamo Formation in Puerto Rico's southern part (more than 4,500 feet thick) and by the San German limestone in the southwest (with a thickness of 2,000 feet).

13. Compression from the southwest and northeast created a series of folds and faults with a general orientation from west-northwest to east-southeast, as far as St. Croix, without continuing into the Lesser Antilles. In the west they probably extended to the Dominican Republic, in the course of that folding a part of the earth mantle (the part beneath the crust), rose in great folds in Puerto Rico's western part and became converted into serpentine. East of Cabo Rojo are masses of amphibolic gneiss, perhaps a metamorphosed part of the basaltic crust previously under the sea. The folding of the volcanic rocks and the sedimentary rocks deposited earlier pushed several layers to great depths. Those rocks were melted again at the "root" of the folded area.

CRETACEOUS

Table 3.2 (continued)

Period	Epoch	Paleogeography	Erosion	Deposition	Drainage
TERTIARY	Paleocene	14. The melted rock began to cool in great masses—the batholiths of San Lorenzo and Utuado, and in many minor bodies in Sierra Luquillo, Morovís, Cuyón, and other places. The volcanic rocks subsided because of their density while the lighter plutonic rocks rose. Those movements, vertical as well as horizontal, occurred through great faults along thousands of fractures in the Puerto Rican mountains. At that time there were great horizontal movements everywhere in the Caribbean area. Among other possibilities the southern part of Cuba may have moved eastward to become southern Hispaniola and northeastern Puerto Rico many miles eastward to face the central part. 15. Those great tectonic movements produced a narrow chain of mountains which continued to rise, especially where there were large masses of intrusive rocks.	16. Intensive erosion of the rising mountains until the intrusive rocks of Jayuya were uncovered.	17. Deposition of several hundred feet of sandstone, conglomerate, shale, and limestone in the seas north and south of the range. These included fragments of volcanic and intrusive rocks. They include the Cuevas limestone on the south coast and the Jicara Formation in the west.	18. The drainage is complex because of the complex structure of the new mountain range.
	Eocene		19. The Lower Peneplane, today beneath the coastal plain. There were high hills in the peneplane, especially in the neighborhood of Utuado and Ciales.		20. With many exceptions, the drainage of this period flowed largely toward the north and south.
	Oligocene		21. A depression was formed on the north coast, penetrating southward as far as Lares and the area		

west of Ciales. Another depression in the south from Juana Diaz to Yauco. These resulted in an arching of the island along an east-west straight axis.

22. A very large island that extended from the Virgin Islands to Hispaniola. Two depressions in the north and south gave the island the form of an hourglass. High islands projected from the sea north of today's Utuado and east of Corozal.

23. Immediately after 21, accelerated erosion stripped the island of its surface soils.

24. First there was deposition of the soils stripped in 23, to form the deposits of gravel, sand, and clay, known in the north as the San Sebastian Formation and in the south as the Juana Diaz Formation. As the seawaters in the north soon became clear owing to lack of sediments, the Lares Limestone was deposited amid surroundings of coral, algae, and other marine life. In the south, the deposition of the Juana Diaz Formation continued.

25. Drainage continued in general toward the north and south.

26. New depressions in the north and moderate bending along the island's axis.

27. The islands near Utuado are submerged.

28. Slight increase of erosion.

29. In the north, deposition of the marl of the Cibao Formation, except in the area north of Utuado where there were no large rivers to bring deposits. In that region limestone was deposited near the coast, going hand in hand with the growth of coral reefs. Far from shore, in the north, the ocean currents carried clay and sand, and today, north of the limestone, there are deposits similar to those in other parts of the Cibao Formation; these are found only in deep wells drilled for petroleum. In the south, the deposition of the Juana Diaz Formation continued.

30. Generally, the island's drainage ran from the axis toward the coasts. Gravel lenses in the Cibao Formation indicate the river channels of those times near the coast.

31. Erosion continued more slowly, without additional uplift of the island's axis.

32. Along a large part of the north coast, the lack of sediments allowed deposition of limestone, the

TERTIARY

Table 3.2 (continued)

Period	Epoch	Paleogeography	Erosion	Deposition	Drainage
				Aguada Limestone. Ancient rivers, having the same courses as during Cibao time, transported some quantities of sand toward the sea, which is why the Aguada limestone is more sandy near the mouths of those rivers than elsewhere. On the south coast the deposition of the Ponce Limestone began.	
TERTIARY	Miocene	33. The large island continued to extend from the Virgin Islands to Hispaniola.	34. Erosion in the island's center, after a long period of stability without uplift, reduced the mountains to a peneplane, known as the St. John peneplane.	35. The paucity of sediments, resulting from small erosion in the peneplane, caused the deposition of the purest limestone found in all the formations: in the north the Aymamón limestone and in the south the upper part of the Ponce limestone.	36. The rivers flowed slowly toward the coasts, with many meanders but carrying little sediment.
			37. Orogenic movements occur in the Antilles; formation of the Bartlett Trough; folding in Haiti, Hispaniola, Sierra Maestra in Cuba; Blue Mountains of Jamaica; in Puerto Rico bending suddenly increased along the axis while the Tertiary beds are slightly inclined and emerge from the sea. With continuation of the bending, the north coast submerged. Chemical erosion of the limestone began, resulting in sinkholes and haystacks ("mogotes").		
			38. Renewal of erosion.	39. Deposition of the Camuy Formation, containing much sand, clay, and iron-bearing limestone.	40. The rivers resumed erosion, producing entrenched meanders.
		41. Uplift of the entire island. Faults occurred on the four sides, cutting the island to its present shape. Two isolated faultblocks re-			

main between Hispaniola and Puerto Rico as the present Islands of Mona and Desecheo.

41a. Birth of the rivers that flow east and west.

Pliocene

42. Formation of the Caguana Peneplane. Chemical erosion continues on the northern coastal plain. Uplift of the entire island with bending along an axis near the Cordillera Central. Several faults in the Tertiary formations.

43. Erosion of the Caguana and St. John Peneplanes. Chemical erosion continues on the northern coastal plain.

44. In the north, entrenchment of many rivers and deposition of floodplains (Gurabo, La Plata), now preserved as terraces. In the south, loss of grade and distribution of gravels and sands in the valleys while vertical erosion is intensfied near the mouths.

Pleistocene

45. The sea recedes as a result of continental glaciations. The melting of the ice results in new submersions. Those occurrences are repeated several times.

46. Bays and low valleys were cut when the ocean receded. Marine terraces, today 200, 150, 115, and 75 feet high, were cut when the ocean rose. Deep valleys, like those of the Rio Grande of Arecibo and the Manati River, filled with alluvium. Submersion of the Lajas Valley.

47. The San Juan Formation of aeolian dunes formed of sand blown from the beaches; sand bars separate the sea from lagoons. The lagoons begin to be filled with alluvium as the sea rises.

48. Changes in drainage as some rivers capture others; rapid growth of westward flowing rivers (such as Añasco and Culebrinas) as well as of those flowing eastward (such as Humacao and Guayanés).

Recent

49. The island attains almost its present shape.

50. Erosion. Upland rivers are more deeply entrenched. Seacliffs emerge over the waters. Barrier reefs formed near the coast.

51. Most of the lagoons are filled; deposition of alluvial fans along the south coast. Filling of estuaries (Arecibo, Manati, Guayanés, etc.).

52. Entrenchment of almost all the rivers in the mountains.

QUATERNARY

Originally, very few of those rocks appeared near the surface. Most of them formed beds or strata hundreds, and even thousands, of feet below sea level. Even deeper were the bodies of magma which fed the volcanoes and which at times also emerged as projections or tongues, without necessarily reaching the surface, to cool and form the porphyries and peridotites.

The fact that not all those rocks are found today in Puerto Rico points toward two things. Possibly none of them is where it had been originally during the Upper Cretaceous Epoch, having later been mixed up and displaced by violent tectonic movements, before emerging from the sea. Also, erosion by the rivers which formed on the new surface may have been so intensive as to have removed all such materials and uncovered their very entrails. Such degrading happened near the end of the Upper Cretaceous Epoch and at the beginning of the so-called Antillean Revolution. The rocks deposited throughout the Cretaceous Period were compressed and folded, and a series of folds was formed in an arch that extended from Cuba to the vicinity of the Island of St. Croix; as a result there was probably a time when there was an unbroken chain of mountains from one end to the other of the Greater Antilles (13) (Fig. 3.18b). Under their great compression, the roots of the folds sank to great depths, were again melted as a result of heat and pressure, and again became magma. As the pressure lessened, the magma tended to rise somewhat, and at the same time crystallization began. Depending on the original composition of the magma and the degree of crystallization of the various minerals, Puerto Rico's intrusive rocks were so formed; these are largely granodiorites and quartz-diorites, but they include diorite, gabbro, and granite. Those rocks solidified at great depths but most of them, especially the granodiorites, are less dense than the lavas basalt and andesite. The large bodies of intrusive rocks, plutons and batholiths, therefore began to rise through the denser folded rocks (14). After a long time they had risen so high that streams began to cut valleys through them (Fig. 3.17). These rocks are the diorites, quartz-diorites, and granites which are found in many places in Puerto Rico, but especially in the region between Utuado and Jayuya, and in the entire area of Caguas, Gurabo, Juncos, San Lorenzo, Las Piedras, Humacao, Yabucoa, and Maunabo.

The crystals which make up these rocks are large. As a result, in the tropics, that kind of granitic rock is quite susceptible to erosion. In temperate climates, granite is a very hard rock (hence the expression "hard as granite") but in tropical climates, under the combined action of temperature and humidity, the crystals loosen and separate, forming a friable sand. In the tropics those crystalline rocks rarely form mountain peaks; more often they form valleys and bottom lands. The latter occurred recently in the two regions mentioned above. In the Utuado-

Figure 3.17. Intrusive Rock. Plutonic rocks, such as granodiorite and quartz-diorite, suffer conchoidal fractures as a result of meteorization. At the end of the process they adopt a round form, as shown in this photograph from the Caguas Valley. (Courtesy of Dr. Carlos Iñiguez.)

Jayuya region the Caonillas River has excavated a deep valley along the entire deposit of weathered granite, from Dos Bocas to Los Picachos, turning aside on reaching the harder rocks (andesite porphyry) which bound the rivers. In the Caguas-Humacao region, the Loíza River and its tributaries excavated the large Caguas Plain, as the rivers of the east coast dug the valleys of Humacao, Yabucoa, and Maunabo. The headwaters of both river systems have so lowered the divide which runs from the Sierra de Cayey to that of Luquillo that, in place of mountains, they left only the Las Piedras elevated plain, which is part of the Caguana peneplane. With the passage of time, it is not surprising that the east coast rivers succeeded in destroying that elevated plain, leaving only one large plain from Caguas to Humacao.

In Puerto Rico's west, folding raised a part of the earth's mantle, the part beneath the crust, which is composed of peridotite. Through the action of time and humidity, this became converted into a metamorphic rock, serpentinite, and is so indicated on the map. Serpentinite appears in the axis of many anticlines in Puerto Rico's southwest. With the formation of fold-mountains along the island's length (15), erosion was accelerated (16) and with it the deposition of sediments on both sides. The Cuevas Limestone north of Ponce contains fragments of granodiorite derived from the Utuado batholith (17). Before the deposition of that limestone, the intrusive rock had risen to so high an altitude that erosion could drag down pieces and the rivers transport them to the sea, where they fell into the limestone deposit. Volcanic ashes were deposited at the same time, today forming a green tuff which is very common near Juana Díaz and Río Piedras (17).

After the deposition of those Paleocene and Eocene sediments, the entire island rose and a long, high mountain range was formed from the Virgin Islands to Santo Domingo (22). That was followed by a period of intense erosion (23).

The first stages of destruction of the folds by erosion occurred in the remote time which followed the Antillean Revolution; its intensity causes many geomorphologists to doubt that those mountains could ever have attained an altitude of four miles, since the folds have no sooner emerged from the sea than the rivers, the rains, and the heat began to attack them and wear them down. Those rivers were all of the "consequent" type in that they followed courses determined by the original slope of the land. As the surface was folded, the rivers could follow only two kinds of courses: one was along the synclines or natural channels between folds, the other was on the surface of the blocks which had dropped at the sides of the faults. As a general rule, however, the rivers flowed by the shortest routes toward the sea.

The general drainage picture, seen on a map of that time, would be one of very long east-west rivers with many short north-south tributaries and, at the coasts, very short rivers flowing northward on the north coast and southward on the south.

Since those coastal rivers had very steep gradients, their erosive work was powerful; gorges were soon formed which opened passages across the folds, reaching the synclinal rivers. When that happened, the synclinal rivers were "captured" in the sense that their waters, instead of continuing to flow along the length of the synclinal channel, turned to pour into the sea through the opening formed by the river which had captured them. Many of the independent rivers which had flowed along the synclines began to disappear in that manner and to become tributaries of the north-south streams, so increasing the latter's flow and importance.

That process was much more important on the north coast than the south since then, as now, the north coast was the rainier of the two, the rivers flowed more steadily, and their erosive power was greater. Hence, little by little, the north coast rivers continued to consolidate into a few large systems. That phenomenon can be seen on every map of the island. Many streams rise on both the north and south slopes of the Cordillera Central; in the south, however, only a few unite to form some of the nearly dry rivers which reach the coast, while in the north many streams continue, little by little, to unite to form ever growing rivers, to the point where only about ten rivers which had risen high in the mountains reach the coast. That process, begun near the end of the Cretaceous Period, reached its full development at the beginning of the Tertiary, during the epochs called Paleocene and Eocene (18).

Logic and imagination lead one to suppose that intense erosive activity took place throughout that time, though direct evidence in the form of peneplanes is lacking. One also supposes that the materials carried down by those rivers were deposited beyond the coasts to form large layers of terrestrial sediment to which deposits of marine origin were added from time to time. There is no direct evidence of those sediments since the coasts of those days were farther out than are today's and one would have to seek them (the sediments) on the bottoms of the oceans surrounding Puerto Rico. But sediments of the Eocene and the early and middle Oligocene epochs are found in some of the other Antilles.

Finally, that entire period of erosion culminated in the creation of a peneplane which Meyerhoff calls the Lower Peneplane (19) but which should not be confused with Lobeck's Lower Peneplane, Meyerhoff's "Caguana," which was formed much later. That peneplane is not well-known because it is today covered by younger rocks, but it probably extended along the north coast from Aguadilla to Luquillo. Its surface was not quite level; some hills and mild undulations survived. Nor did it extend very far into the island's interior; it probably didn't reach beyond the Northwest Plateau, the hills of Florida, and the inner limits of today's coastal plain.

In the interior, in the region where Cretaceous rocks are found today, the drainage had already been established more or less like today's pattern. All the rivers which had followed synclines had been captured by the north-south rivers (20). As a result of the greater erosive powers of the rivers flowing north, their headwaters wore down the mountains more rapidly than did those of the streams flowing south. This situation resulted in the southward displacement of the insular divide to more or less its present location.

The drainage situation did not change much during the Upper Oligocene, but two things of importance to the island's shape occurred during that epoch. For reasons scarcely known, parts of the north and south coasts began to sink and the sea penetrated to the interior (21) (Fig. 3.18c). Those depressions grew with time, but while they sank they were also refilled by sediments. Gravel, sands, mud, and clay, brought by the rivers, were deposited in the north and finally mixed with marine sediments, producing impure limestone. This sequence is the San Sebastián Formation with a thickness of about 300 feet (24). The nature of those sediments indicates the conditions under which they were deposited. Sediments of terrestrial origin, brought by the rivers, predominate (25); occasionally, however, in the shallow bays, the marine organisms and their shells multiplied, giving a limestone character to at

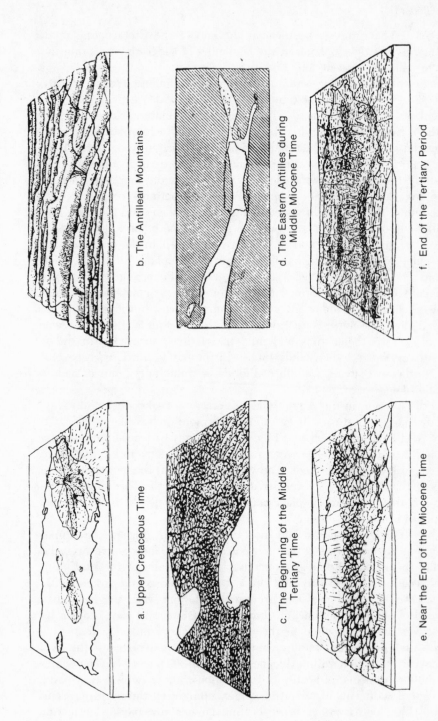

b. The Antillean Mountains

d. The Eastern Antilles during Middle Miocene Time

f. End of the Tertiary Period

a. Upper Cretaceous Time

c. The Beginning of the Middle Tertiary Time

e. Near the End of the Miocene Time

Figure 3.18. Geologic Evolution of Puerto Rico. (From Howard A. Meyerhoff, *The Geology of Puerto Rico.*)

68

least parts of the terrestrial deposits. As the subsidence continued, the gulf grew larger and its edges moved farther and farther inland (26), meaning that the terrestrial deposits also moved inland along its edges. However, far from the coast, at sites not reached by at least the finer clays brought by the rivers, deposits consisting entirely of large quantities of marine life, including coral, began to be added to the San Sebastián formation. That was the Lares Formation (24) of pure limestone, which eventually grew to a thickness of 1,200 to 1,300 feet. Eventually the subsidence of the region stopped and the gulf came to be filled increasingly by deposits of Lares Limestone, until the rivers could again reach them, bringing large quantities of fine terrestrial sediments such as sands and clays. Nevertheless, except for the corals which cannot live in dirty water, the marine organisms persisted and the sands and clays came to be mixed with beds of marl, giving rise to the Cibao Formation with a thickness of about 1,000 feet. Occasionally the deposits in the gulf arrived at the point where marine sediments were scarce and terrestrial sediments, such as gravel, sand, and clay predominated, resulting in today's Guajataca and Miranda sands which are found in the Cibao Formation and were created when the erosion of the island's interior was accelerated (28). The subsidence was renewed shortly thereafter and the sediments again assumed the predominantly marine character of the Cibao Formation, leaving the sands as enclosed deposits between two beds of Cibao. All of those sediments of the Oligocene epoch comprise what is now called the Río Guatemala Group because they are best represented along that river's valley in Puerto Rico's northwest.

Between the Lares area and the Florida hills were various mountains of volcanic origin which had become islands in the sea in the Lares epoch. In part because of those mountains there were no large rivers in that part of the island, and hence there were few clastic sediments in the sea. As a result, the Cibao Formation is pure limestone in that region, with marl and sand at the sides (29).

Along the south coast the deposition was much simpler, consisting only of the Juana Díaz Formation, which is composed of terrestrial deposits such as mud, sands, and conglomerates, alternating with limestones of marine origin. On the geologic map, the muds are described as shales. Originally they were deposited as muds, but were soon consolidated by the weight of later deposits, hardened, laminated, and converted into the laminated rock so abundant in Puerto Rico, called shale.

The large island extended from the Virgin Islands to Santo Domingo as before (33) (Fig. 3.18d). During the Lower Miocene epoch, erosion continued, but more slowly, the rivers carrying few sediments (30-31). In the north the Aguada Limestone was deposited, its lower part consisting of limestone and marl, and the upper part of limestone (32). That formation is a transition between the underlying Cibao and the overlying

Aymamón. Resting on the Aguada limestone is found the Aymamón Limestone, the purest found in Puerto Rico. There are so few clastic sediments in this limestone (35) that it is evident that the rivers of that time carried little sediment to the sea (36). It is therefore also thought that erosion had by that time reduced the mountains to the peneplane known as the St. John peneplane (34).

The entire island was converted into a vast plain cut by shallow valleys, except near the divides where the highest peaks of the Sierra de Luquillo remained as monadnocks, as did those of the Sierra de Cayey and the Central Cordillera. In the west, the branches of the sea which covered the plains of Lajas and the lower valley of the Guanajibo, more or less isolated the southwestern hills and those of Lajas from the rest of the island and its erosive processes. Nevertheless, the tops of those hills are more or less at the same altitude, which probably resulted from the erosion to which they were subjected while the rest of the island was reduced to the level of St. John.

Thick sediments of Ponce Limestone, full of deep sea fossils, were deposited in the south. Like that of Aymamón, this contains coral reefs of pure limestone.

After that deposition, the island was bent along an east-west axis; the limestone emerged but, as the bending continued, the northern part of the Aymamón Limestone was again submerged. The rivers again carried sediments resulting from the erosion of the peneplane, and these were deposited in the sea off the north coast in layers of iron-bearing limestone, sand, and reddish marl of the Camuy Formation (39). There was more slight bending, immediately followed by uplift of the entire island, with renewal of erosion (38).

The orogeny which lifted those regions above sea level, giving rise to the Tertiary deposits along the north and south coasts, occurred in various manners in all the Greater Antilles (37). In Puerto Rico it was characterized by mild north-south thrusts which produced some low folds in the southern limestones and slightly bent the entire island in such a way that the Tertiary beds, which had been entirely horizontal, emerged from sea level for the first time and in the north became inclined toward the coast by some four to six degrees. That is known to have occurred after the Lower Miocene epoch, since the higher and hence more recent strata in the Camuy Formation do not go beyond that time. However, since it is not known when those which remained above them were destroyed by erosion, there is no precise indication as to when the deposition stopped.

At the time of the elevation of recently deposited calcareous strata, Puerto Rico probably had the aspect of a chain of low hills with an average altitude of 700 feet, flanked in the north and south by narrow coastal plains which were merely ocean bottoms, recently uplifted. In general, the shape resembled today's Puerto Rico (41). The higher mountains were in the east, in the Luquillo Range which projected some 2,300 feet above sea level. Near the center, in the vicinity of Jayuya, the highest peaks probably reached about 1,700 feet.

Since, before the beginning of the uplift, those mountains were much lower and hills predominated in Puerto Rico, it is clear that the increase in altitude brought about a renewal of the rivers' erosive forces (40).

However, on the west coast, the orogeny which bent and uplifted the entire island apparently caused a depression, probably through movements along the faults which formed Mona Passage. According to McGuinness, that seems indicated, among other things, by the discovery of foraminifera (fossils characteristic of the age) in various wells drilled in Mayagüez, Añasco, and the Guanajibo and Lajas Valleys. Since, Puerto Rico until then was probably joined to Santo Domingo, it can be assumed that the depression formed the beginning of today's west coast, though it is not known whether it had the same shape it has now.

The immediate consequences of those events, in the matter of drainage, soon became manifest (41a). On the formation of the west coast through depression, the east-west valleys of that region became much steeper and their rivers (the Añasco, Yagüez, and Guanajibo) acquired enormous erosive powers. They rapidly extended their headwaters toward the interior mountains, along such lines of weakness as soft rocks and the valleys of other rivers which they proceeded to capture. The Añasco proved to be the most active in that process, decapitating the Guajataca and Camuy Rivers and pushing its headwaters almost to Adjuntas; it was followed by the Guanajibo which, in the region of Sabana Grande, probably captured various streams which had previously drained the Lajas Valley. The Yagüez was the least active; it could not even reach the vicinity of Maricao, and its basin is today much smaller than are those of the other two.

On the other hand, north of Añasco the land was uplifted into what are today the mountains of Atalaya; the tertiary limestones of the north coastal plain are on the other side of those mountains. In the base of those limestones was the San Sebastián Formation of very soft rocks. Typical of a submerged coast, that formation did not stop its deposition; as the north coast was submerged, its gravels, sands, and mud were deposited farther and farther south, ascending the northern slopes of the Atalaya Mountains and always serving as the base for the limestone formation which followed. When deposition stopped on the coastal plain, that extension of the San Sebastián Formation was found on the surface far south of the present outcrops, probably south of today's Río Culebrinas. The Culebrinas River was perhaps only a stream among the hills southeast of San Sebastián, but when that region was uplifted, the unconsolidated rocks of the San Sebastián Formation were easily eroded and the zone served as a natural channel for the waters from San Sebastián to Aguada. That was the beginning of the present Culebrinas River. Very soon the river excavated a deep channel from east to west in the San Sebastián Formation. Since this formation crops out in only a relatively narrow belt and slopes toward the north beneath the limestone formations, these were undermined. As the San Sebastián was eroded lacking the base of support, large limestone fragments fell into the valley bottom to be hauled to the sea by the river. In this way the Culebrinas, little by little, deepened its valley north of the hills which formed the present Atalaya Mountains, while the Añasco did the same in the south. In that manner, too, the channel of the Culebrinas continued to shift northward until it reached its present position, always following the line of weakness represented by the San Sebastián Formation which rested on the old north slope of the Atalaya Mountains. Today that ancient surface is deeply eroded, but forms the relatively smooth southern border of the valley of the Culebrinas, in contrast to the northern side, which is high and steep and forms part of the rugged cuesta of the Lares Formation which extends from Lares to Aguadilla.

In the southwest, while the coastal part was submerged during the Upper Oligocene and Lower Miocene, while receiving the limestones of the Ponce Formation, the area which is today the Lajas Plains remained above water, exposed to erosion. There the foldings of the Antillean Revolution had created a series of east-west belts with dissimilar resistance. The soft belts were easily eroded by the rivers, so forming the primitive valleys of the Guanajibo and the Lajas. The hard belts remained standing as chains of hills among which, today, are the hills of San Germán and those of the southwest. Soon, like the lower parts of the valleys of the Añasco, Yagüez, and Guanajibo Rivers, the primitive valley of Lajas was submerged, and for the first time the sea reached from Boquerón to Guánica. The so-called Lajas Valley remained submerged throughout that time.

The rivers which eroded the northern coastal plain probably had little trouble in wearing down the newer strata of the upper limestone layers, but soon older and more consolidated strata were exposed. Here the surface erosion was more difficult, but chemical erosion, dissolving the limestone, began to appear; probably the higher southern part of the northern coastal plain began to be riddled with caves and sinks.

Near the end of the Miocene the entire island was uplifted some 800 feet without bending or tilting. During the period of calm which followed that elevation, erosion again reduced considerable parts of the island to sea level, to form the Caguana peneplane (42). The areas affected by that cycle of erosion are shown on the physiographic map. Erosion continued on the northern coastal plain, largely chemical, until the topography assumed the aspects it has today (43) (Fig. 3.18f). The

Lares cuesta, begun by various east-west rivers along the contact between Tertiary limestones and the Cretaceous rocks of the interior, became more pronounced. The west coast had also been uplifted; parts of it, which had previously been inundated, emerged from the sea, and deposition stopped. It is possible that for a time Puerto Rico again became united with Santo Domingo in the west and the Virgin Islands in the east and that the emerged lands extended far beyond the present coasts to the very edge of the submarine platform on which the island rests.

In the southwest, the uplift led to the uncovering of the Lajas plains and the rivers promptly began to reexcavate the recently deposited marine sediments. Among the island's rivers only minor readjustments took place.

Near the end of the Pliocene, fresh orogenic movements bent the island along the same axis on which it had been bent during the Middle or Upper Miocene, which ended the Tertiary deposition on the north and south coasts. At the same time, the entire island was tilted toward the northeast, and fractures, or faults, occurred along the four sides. The outer blocks of those fractures fell into the ocean, and the insular platform was thus trimmed down to its present proportions. Toward the west, north, and south, its edges remain fairly near the coasts, but in the east they extend far enough to include Vieques, Culebra, and the Northern Virgin Islands. In the west, the islands of Mona and Desecheo remained as isolated blocks, and in the east St. Croix remained separated. At the extreme western end of the bending, the west coast subsided again and the sea once more penetrated into the low valleys of the Añasco, Yagüez, and Guanajibo Rivers, as well as the Lajas plains.

So began the Pleistocene Epoch, only a million years removed from the present. The uplifting which had begun near the end of the Pliocene continued slowly throughout that time; as a result the Caguana peneplane, which in the beginning must have been nearly horizontal, is today inclined toward the sea, from south to north, with a grade of about 100 feet per mile. As a result of the depression toward the west, the highest part of the peneplane is not on the west coast but in the vicinity of Lares (2,200 ft.), whence it descends to 500 feet on the north coast and 100 to 200 feet on the west coast.

Erosion, which had reached a minimum in the region of the peneplane, recovered intensity with that uplifting, and the peneplane began to be dissected (44). The effects on the drainage were varied, according to the manner in which the tilting toward the northeast affected each river. The rivers which drained the north slopes gained in gradient and entrenched themselves, excavating their channels vertically to form trenches. But on some rivers which flowed wholly or in part from east to west, the tilting toward the northeast lessened the gradients and, as they lost power to tear down, they deposited large parts of the sediments on the alluvial plain, as happened in the case of the Gurabo, in the interior plain of Caguas, the La Plata River, and in the interior plain of Cayey. The rivers of the southern slopes also lost gradient and inundated their valley with sediments while, toward their mouths, the uplift increased their slopes, causing them to entrench their channels vertically. Today the Gurabo and La Plata, like the south slope rivers, have managed with their vertical excavations to readjust their gradients to the zones they traverse and to their volumes of flow and have begun again to cut horizontally in the alluvium they have deposited, excavating terraces on both sides of their channels.

All subsequent events are dated within the last million years and have had only minor effects on the island's relief, giving it, so to speak, the finishing touches. In all that time there were two main agents of change: the slow, but continuing, rise of the island which still goes on and the changes in the ocean's level caused by continental glaciations.

During the Pleistocene epoch, the earth is known to have gone through four periods of glaciation, each lasting several tens of thousands of years. During each such period, the winters became colder and the summers cooler; on several continents enormous quantities of snow accumulated year after year, and every summer less of this melted than fell in winter. Since the snow fell from the clouds which had obtained their moisture from the oceans and since the snow, not melting, could not return to the sea, the oceans little by little but inevitably lost some of their waters. It is estimated that, at the height of a glacial period, the ocean level was reduced by some two hundred to six hundred feet, depending on the amount of snow held back. The reduction in the ocean level affected Puerto Rico because, when the sea level was from two to six hundred feet below normal, it was as though the island has risen by that much and the erosive powers of the rivers had been greatly increased; with the passing of the glacial period the snows melted, the ocean rose to its former level, and the island seemed to have been submerged by that depth.

In the course of some of those oscillations (45), marine terraces, which are today elevated because of the island's continued uplift, were probably cut as the ocean rose. This cut occurred in the coastal region of the Northwest Plateau, at altitudes of 150 to 200 feet (46). At the same time the San Juan Formation, consisting of aeolian dunes, appeared on the north coast. A number of lakes, some of which still exist, appeared behind it. The San Juan Formation has almost been destroyed by erosion, but in the north its remains exist as a chain of dunes parallel to the coast and in the east as sandbars near the coast.

The oceans rose during the Sangamon interglacial period immediately before the Wisconsin glaciation. The terraces which today lie at an altitude of some 75 feet in the northwest were probably cut then.

On the other hand, the Lajas Valley, which had also experienced a series of submersions and emergings, was submerged for the last time.

The lakes behind the San Juan Formation were enlarged by that rise and at that time began their definite filling which still continues. Similarly, the sea inundated the lower parts of some river valleys, forming estuaries which began to be filled by the rivers' sediments. On the south coast those sediments were at times so scant that the inundated parts have remained as bays (Guánica, Guayanilla, Aguirre). On the north coast one relatively large invasion by the sea (San Juan Bay) was only partly refilled. The process of inundation and refilling went through two stages. Near the end of the Pleistocene Epoch, apparently because of the final return of the waters, the entire platform of Puerto Rico and the Virgin Islands came to be submerged to a depth of 40 to 45 feet.

At the beginning of the recent (Holocene) epoch (about 15,000 years ago), the island's submersion had reached a maximum and the process of refilling was continued (51). Soon the ocean withdrew, dropping mean sea level about 15 feet. That could have been caused, simply, by the latest oscillation in the glaciation cycle, though the process of uplifting may also have played a part. Meanwhile erosion continued, giving rise to the present rather small entrenchment which is noted in the courses of nearly all the rivers. Continued uplift had placed beyond the reach of the waves the cliffs most recently cut by the sea, leaving small beaches between them and the present coasts and in the sea shallows covered by reefs (49). The island had attained almost its present shape.

Finally, and in the present epoch, the process of erosion continues, with the entrenchment of almost all the rivers in the mountains.

SUMMARY

Summarized, the history of Puerto Rico's geologic evolution falls into the following stages:

One: Volcanic stage and Cretaceous Sedimentation. Near the end of the Jurassic Epoch, or the beginning of the Cretaceous, fissures opened on the bottom of the Atlantic Ocean through which enormous quantities of lava, powder, ashes, and gases poured. Those deposits grew as submarine mountains and finally formed volcanic islands. Erosion of the islands provided clastic sediments and reefs were formed in their vicinity.

Two: The Antillean Revolution. An arch of folded mountains and fault blocks, direct antecedents of today's Greater Antilles, grew near the end of the Cretaceous period. Plutonic intrusions were injected into the heart of those mountains, giving rise to granitoid rocks which are most prevalent in the valley of the Caonillas River and in the zone from San Lorenzo to Yabucoa.

Three: The Stage of Limestone Deposition. During the first third of the Tertiary period, Puerto Rico's mountains were eroded so powerfully that, in the Lower Oligocene epoch, they were reduced to a peneplane, the Lower peneplane. The north and south borders of the island were submerged between the Upper Oligocene and the Lower Miocene epochs and received thousands of feet of limestone sediments. In the north those sediments extend from Aguada to Loíza but are thickest between Lares and Camuy. In the south the calcareous sediments extend from Cabo Rojo to Santa Isabel. During the last stages of that deposition, erosion culminated in the formation of the St. John peneplane whose remaining monadnocks are today the highest peaks of the Cordillera Central, the Sierra de Cayey, and the Sierra de Luquillo.

Four: Stage of Uplift, Erosion, and Formation of the Other Peneplane. After the Lower Miocene epoch, orogenic forces uplifted Puerto Rico some 800 feet; a new period of erosion followed which destroyed the edges of the St. John peneplane and gave rise to the formation of the Caguana peneplane.

Five: Stage of Faulting, Elevation, and Glaciations. Near the end of the Pliocene epoch, the island was again uplifted, this time with the occurrence of faults on its edges, resulting in almost its present-day shape. That final uplift occurred only a million years before the onset of the present epoch and continues very mildly to this day. In the course of those million years the borders of the Caguana peneplane were destroyed by erosion to form the present coastal plains and valleys. The destruction of that peneplane extended to the soft granitoid rocks of the interior, forming the interior Caguas Plain. Although the uplift movement continued, variations in sea level, produced by continental glaciations, resulted in periods of submersion during which large quantities of alluvium were deposited in the coastal plains and valleys, together with a sand dune along the north coast, today known as the San Juan Formation.

Earthquakes in Puerto Rico

The faulting which took place near the end of the Pliocene epoch not only helped to trim down the island's borders and separate it from neighboring islands, giving it more or less its present shape, but even today affects Puerto Rico profoundly through the seismic movements caused by faulting (Fig. 3.19).

It has been proved that the tremors which shake the island are related to the faults. The blocks depressed along the faults, in other words, the parts which now lie at great depths on the ocean's bottom, continue their tendency to drop down. That downward movement does not take the form of a continuing, mild displacement, but rather, because of the resistance offered by both faces of the fractured rock, the new displacement occurs after pressure, accumulating day after day, and is sufficiently powerful to overcome the resistance. The new displacement is therefore sudden and violent, producing in the earth's crust the strong vibrations which are called earthquakes.

Figure 3.19. Displacement along a Fault in
the Volcanic Rocks of the Luquillo Range.

The displacement is generally small, of only a few centimeters, and the
vibrations are not very strong. But that displacement, though rapid, does
not dissipate all the tension which accumulates for years until the crust
can no longer resist, and a large displacement occurs, at times a yard or
more. The vibrations so set up are so strong that they cause what is
known as an earthquake.

The two most active and dangerous faults, which cause most of the
tremors and earthquakes experienced in Puerto Rico, are at the extreme
northwest and southeast points of the insular platform, at Mona Passage
in front of Aguadilla and at the Anegada Trough. The epicenters are
located there where the seismic waves originate. These waves travel over
the entire crust, are registered on all the world's seismographs and do the
greatest damage in the regions nearest to the epicenters.

The fact that those two extremes of Puerto Rico, the northwest and
southeast, are the most dangerous spots is proved, according to Meyer-

hoff, by the 25 important tremors which occurred in Puerto Rico during nearly a century, from 1832 to 1918. Of those 25, 9 originated in the northwest and 13 in the southeast. The other three were divided among the far more stable faults in the island's north and south. The most recent violent earthquakes were those of 1918. Before that, the greatest were the earthquakes of 1867, which were probably more violent than those of 1918. Miller[5] says that 1867 was a true year of calamities for Puerto Rico.

On October 29, the hurricane San Narciso caused great property damage; agriculture and commerce suffered large losses. A terrible earthquake occurred November 18, which was probably the worst in Puerto Rico's history. The tremors lasted several days. Many San Juan residents abandoned the city because of the damage suffered by the buildings. The churches of Coamo, Gurabo, and Juncos were rendered unusable. Crevices opened in the fields and virtually all the smokestacks of the plantations were destroyed. Many structures built of masonry were damaged.

History as well as science tells us that the origin of those earthquakes was in the Anegada Trough, and some of the towns mentioned, Gurabo and Juncos, indicate that the shock waves came from the east. That is also corroborated by the history of St. Croix in the Virgin Islands. In that year the United States first began to think of buying those islands from Denmark. A U.S. Commission was sent to investigate them and the ship which had brought it was anchored in Christiansted bay. The earthquake was accompanied by an enormous tidal wave which carried the American ship several yards into the town. The commissioners suffered no harm, but when they mentioned in their report that the islands had been devastated by a storm the preceding month and that an earthquake had occurred shortly thereafter, interest in buying the Virgin Islands diminished. The acquisition of islands which were plagued by hurricanes and earthquakes at the same time was said to be bad business. In 1917, because of the possibility that the Virgin Islands might fall into the hands of Germany, the United States decided to buy them for $25 million.

Earthquakes and hurricanes are unrelated and what happened in St. Croix and Puerto Rico in 1867 was mere coincidence. Hurricanes are meteorological phenomena while earthquakes result from the pressures and the structures, of the rocks beneath the surface.

As stated above, the most recent of Puerto Rico's destructive earthquakes was that of 1918. The strong tremors began October 11, but they were followed by a series of aftershocks which inspired terror. Those strong shocks, occurring October 24 and November 12, were experienced at intervals through an entire month. The fact that in Fajardo the quakes

5. Paul G. Miller, *Historia de Puerto Rico* (New York: Rand McNally, 1922), p. 278

had a violence of 5, and in Aguadilla and Mayagüez of 9,[6] proved that those earthquakes originated in the northwest, a fact also proved by the damage done in Mayagüez and Aguadilla.

The accompanying Isunami or Seismic tidal wave was especially strong at Aguadilla. Such a wave is caused by the sinking of a block in the bottom of the sea and large quantities of water rushing in to fill the hole. The water rushes in enormous quantities toward the ocean bottom where, since more has come than is needed, it rebounds toward the coast like a ball, flooding the coasts with great violence. However, the sea soon returns to its normal level. The destruction was greatest at Aguadilla and Mayagüez because those towns are backed on the land side by a rim of mountains and hills.

Those earthquakes caused 116 deaths and 241 wounded; losses in property destroyed throughout the island amounted to $3,472,000.

6. The shocks are graded, according to intensity, from 1 to 10.

4

The Internal Hydrography and Its Utilization

The Internal Hydrography

The general regimen of precipitation, whose geographic distribution varies greatly despite the island's small size, is closely related to the topography. The range of mountains running from west to northeast is in a sense a barrier to the prevailing east-northeast winds; loaded with moisture, these are forced to rise to atmospheric regions where they are chilled. The resulting condensation causes relatively heavy rainfall north of the divide. The precipitation on the narrow belt of south coastal plains is low because on crossing the mountains the air masses lose much of their humidity. On the other hand, the descent on the southern slopes causes the contraction and adiabatic warming of those air masses, so raising their capacity for moisture; evaporation is thereby accelerated, contributing to the region's aridity.

In other specific parts of the island the characteristics of the precipitation are, like those of the north and south coasts, more or less related to their topographies and their locations in regard to the prevailing east-northeast winds.

RIVER SYSTEMS

There are four principal slopes that conduct the precipitation toward the sea. These are the northern or Atlantic slope; the southern or Caribbean slope; the eastern slope to Vieques Passage; and the western to Mona Passage.

Together with such factors as topography and geology, the geographic distribution of rainfall lends certain characteristics to those slopes with their approximately 1,300 streams. Of the latter, despite the ample rainfall in most parts of the island, only 17 form true river systems (Table 4.1), a fact for which the small sizes of many catchment basins are responsible.

80

The north slope stands out by the relative abundance of its precipitation and the persistence and greater volume of its rivers. Most of the rivers rise in the Central Cordillera, crossing the humid foothills to reach the coastal plain (Fig. 4.1). Many parts of the plain are so low that drainage is deficient, giving rise to the formation of swamps and marshes, among them Tiburones, Tortuguero, and the Piñones lagoons. Elsewhere the rivers submerge in regions of karst topography, characterized by sinkholes and caves, formed through the ease with which certain pure limestones were dissolved and chemically destroyed through the ages by the rainwaters. More than half of the basins of three of those rivers—the

Table 4.1. Puerto Rico's largest river basins

	Drainage Area (Square Miles)	Length of the Basin (Miles)	Fall from the Highest Point (Feet)	Average Slope (Feet per Miles)
Rivers flowing toward the north				
Río Guajataca	71	17	1,740	102
Río Camuy	62	16	2,300	144
Río Grande de Arecibo	289	24	4,390	183
Río Grande de Manatí	224	25	4,150	166
Río Cibuco	100	18	2,200	122
Río de la Plata	239	30	3,090	103
Río de Bayamón	105	21	2,000	99
Río Grande de Loíza	308	26	3,520	
	1,398 total	22 average	2,920 average	132 average
Rivers flowing eastward				
Río Guayanés	50	12	2,130	178
Rivers flowing toward the south				
Río Nigua (Salinas)	53	13	2,830	218
Río Coamo	78	17	2,890	170
Río Jacaguas	94	16	3,540	221
Río Tallaboa	35	10	3,410	341
Río Yauco	47	15	3,540	236
	307 total	14 average	3,242 average	237
Rivers flowing westward				
Río Guanajibo	129	19	2,950	155
Río Grande de Añasco	185	29	3,950	136
Río Culebrinas	114	21	1,680	80
	428 total	23	2,960	124
Summary of 17 Rivers	2,183 total	18	2,788	168

Source: *Puerto Rico Water Resources, A Progress Report,* Water Resources Bulletin No. 4, prepared by the United States Geological Survey in cooperation with The Commonwealth of Puerto Rico, 1964.

Guajataca, Camuy, and Cibuco—are located in the karst region of the coastal plain. The upper courses and large parts of the middle courses of the other rivers flow through the basic complex of the island's interior.

The eastern slope has a peculiar topography. The mountains come close to the sea and the rivers have cut triangular valleys into them. Some of these valleys combine to form larger ones.

Figure 4.1. The Arecibo (formerly Abacoa) River. Its waters flow slowly in the transition zone between the humid hills and the northern coastal plain. (Courtesy of Dr. Carlos Iñiguez.)

The most important are the Fajardo, Naguabo, Humacao, Yabucoa, and Maunabo. In the mountainous interior, the courses of those rivers are well defined by the topography and they remain within their basins; when they cross the coastal plains, however, the basins become shallow, causing the rivers to overflow in times of heavy rains.

The southern slope is more complex. Because of the proximity of the Central Cordillera to the coast, the rivers are much shorter than are those of the north. As stated above, the precipitation along the south coast is low, causing many of the rivers to dry up during the dry winters. The high evaporation of the region limits the flow of the rivers, many of which have formed large alluvial fans. The plains of the southwest which form the Lajas Valley are low in altitude and with short slopes, causing poor drainage. The lakes of Guanica and Cartagena once formed small basins, the former of which virtually disappeared on the construction of the Lajas Valley public irrigation system.

The western slope is characterized by a rainy season with relatively heavy precipitation during the months from May to November. The river basins are relatively large, with considerable flows. The shortest of the rivers flowing west is longer than any of those on the southern slope. The most important is the Río Grande de Añasco; its volume is the second largest, and its drainage basin the fifth largest in the island (Table 4.1). Like those in the north, the west-flowing rivers flow the year round, though the prevailing regimen of precipitation causes considerable diminution in volumes during the dry season from December to April.

The characteristics of the river systems, combined with the topography and the regimen of precipitation, have hampered the integrated utilization of the waters for domestic, agricultural, and industrial purposes. The need for overcoming those hindrances has aroused the creative energies of the Puerto Ricans, resulting in the construction of a series of works for irrigation and generation of electric energy.

Utilization

IRRIGATION

The South Coast. The south coastal plain extends without interruption from Patillas to Ponce bordering the southern foothills. With an average annual precipitation of less than 60 inches, it is the VI zone of precipitation outlined by Margaret Howarth.[1] During the first four centuries following Puerto Rico's discovery, the zone was used principally for pasture and cattle ranches because the meager rain and long dry season made agriculture uncertain outside of certain valleys where primitive irrigation systems were established since the middle of the nineteenth century.

Early in the twentieth century the production of sugar increased enormously in Puerto Rico, stimulated by United States capital and a sure and accessible market in the mainland. From 103,152 tons in 1900–1901 production soared to 277,093 tons by 1907–08. The best lands on the north, east, and west coasts were planted for sugar cane and producers were seeking additional areas for the crop. The south coastal plains were therefore examined carefully and the idea came up of overcoming aridity through irrigation. The main problem was that of finding enough water. Wells would yield only enough for the irrigation of limited areas, and pumping from them would be costly for lack of cheap electricity. The solution would be water from the mountains where rainfall was plentiful, especially north of the insular divide, but the project would be too costly to be undertaken by anybody but the government.

In 1908, therefore, the Insular Legislature passed a law creating the "Puerto Rican Irrigation Service." Technical studies began the same year

1. Margaret Howarth studied the climate of Puerto Rico during 1934 for her master's thesis at Clark University.

and construction of the first reservoirs was completed during the years 1910–14. It was a propitious time; after reaching a total of 398,000 tons in 1911–12, the island's production of sugar had fallen off to 345,000 tons in 1914–15.[2]

The original system included four reservoirs: one on the Patillas River, called the Patillas Reservoir; another, the Coamo Reservoir, on the river of that name; a third, the Guayabal Reservoir on the Jacaguas River (Fig. 4.2); and finally the Carite Reservoir on the headwaters of the La Plata River. The waters of those reservoirs were brought, by gravity and through canals, to the coastal plain, for distribution to the various cane fields.

Since the Patillas, Coamo, and Guayabal reservoirs were south of the insular divide, it was a simple matter to bring their waters to the coast. But the Carite reservoir lay north of the divide. To bring its waters to the south side, the engineers built a diversion tunnel about 2,700 feet long, crossing the Sierra de Cayey. In addition, for the purpose of increasing the sources of water for the Guayabal Reservoir, the "Toro Negro" tunnel was bored through the Cordillera Central in 1913 to divert, towards the south, waters of the Toro Negro River and the Doña Juana Brook. While

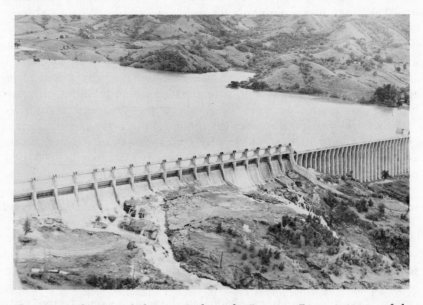

Figure 4.2. The Guayabal Dam. Built on the Jacaguas River, it is part of the original Puerto Rican Irrigation Service created in 1908. Its waters supply the South Coast Irrigation District. (Courtesy of the Puerto Rico Water Resources Authority.)

2. After the addition of the south coast to the cane-producing areas, the production rose to 483,000 tons in 1915–16 and 503,000 in 1917–18.

the waters brought to the south side via that tunnel were sufficient in the beginning, their quantities had to be increased after some years by enlarging the Toro Negro project through the construction of the Guineo and Matrullas Reservoirs and diversion from seven brooks north of the divide.

The law governing public irrigation on the south coast stipulated the annual provision of four acre-feet[3] of water per irrigated acre, the equivalent of bringing to the lowlands some four inches of water per month. The irrigator had to pay an annual fee of $15 per acre. However, the benefits accruing to the system from the utilization of the drops for the production of electricity were applied for the lowering of those fees or preventing them from soaring. In 1952, the fee paid for irrigation was $14.99 per acre, while the lands of the district's enlargement of 1937 paid an additional $6.00.

Since some parts of the land were sandy and hence needed more than four acre-feet of water, the irrigators, now having cheap electricity from the hydroelectric system which came into being as a by-product of irrigation, began to install pumps to make up for the deficiency while also extending the irrigated area. Today some 33,000 acres in the area are irrigated by gravity flow from the reservoirs, occasionally supplemented by pumping, while 18,000 acres are irrigated entirely by pumping (Fig. 4.3).

In time, private irrigation by pumping was extended to the areas west of Ponce, in the valleys of the Tallaboa, Guayanilla, and Yauco Rivers, as well as in the Lajas Valley. In the zone between Ponce and the Jacaguas River, not reached by the government's irrigation system, private entities installed a system using pumps, taking the water from the subsoil as well as the rivers and freshwater lakes, like Guánica and Cartagena in the Lajas Valley. That raised the total land irrigated on the south coast to about 75,000 acres.

Since the cultivation of cane requires much water, the need for irrigation is pressing along the entire south coast. As mentioned earlier, a good cane harvest requires at least 75 inches per year, evenly distributed. Where the precipitation is only 30 inches, as at Guánica, at least 45 inches must be added. Moreover, because of the high evaporation, it is believed that 75 inches is a low figure and that 96 to 126 inches of water are actually needed. Obtaining that additional water is expensive, but warranted by the results. An acre of pasture on the south coast was worth $100 in 1950; the cultivation of sugar cane increased the value from five to ten times. The region has the best soils in Puerto Rico, and irrigation permits the water to be applied at the time when it will do the most good. In 1947–48 the south coast, while using only some 16 per cent of the island's

3. One acre-foot is equivalent to 12″ of water covering an acre or approximately 325,000 gallons.

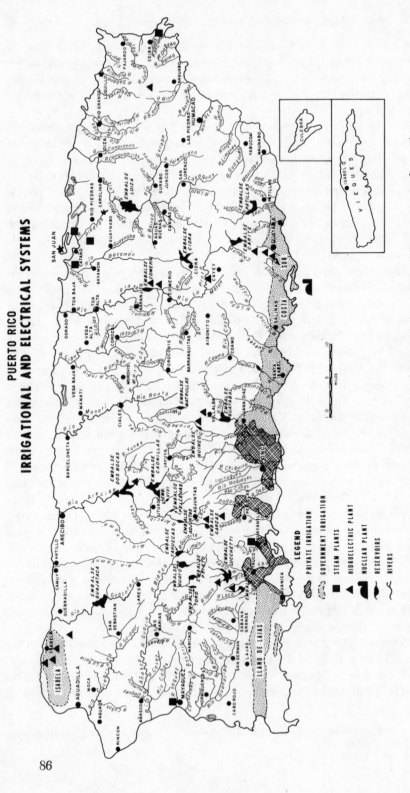

Figure 4.3. (Adapted from map prepared by the Puerto Rico Water Resources Authority.)

total land in sugar cane, produced about 19.17 per cent of the total crop. In 1963, six sugar mills in the region ground more than 25 per cent of the island's total production (978,303 tons).

The Northwest. Encouraged by the success of irrigation on the south coast, the government decided to help other areas in that manner. The region between Aguadilla and Isabela, at the western end of Margaret Howarth's rainfall region No. I, seemed promising because of its gentle relief and the possibility of bringing water by gravity from the Guajataca River. The project was initiated by the Department of the Interior, now the Department of Public Works, and was completed in 1928 at a cost of $4 million. It was expected that a total of 15,000 acres would be irrigated, but apparently neither the nature of the soil nor the region's geography were sufficiently taken into account in the planning stage.

The reservoir was built in the Cibao lowlands, at the point where the Guajataca River becomes narrower and crosses through a deep canyon, the arch of Aymamon limestone haystack hills and sinkholes about five miles south-southeast of Quebradillas. The canal draining the reservoir runs a little more than two miles along the canyon, by the river's west bank; soon, however, it turns toward the northwest through the zone of haystack hills and continues so for three miles through several small tunnels which had to be built to permit the canal to cross the walls separating the sinkholes whose bottoms it uses in its course.

Finally, once in the irrigation district, the canal system distributed its water to porous lands with a high percentage of sand. As a result much water was lost through seepage; irrigation came therefore to be concentrated on areas which could make use of it more economically. Never were even half of the projected 15,000 acres irrigated. The maximum was 6,000 but at times the irrigated areas came to fewer than 2,000 acres. Even for 6,000 acres, the investment in irrigation was extremely high. It amounted to $500 per acre, which was more than the land was worth. While the farmers had been expected to pay a total of some $100,000 annually for irrigation they never paid more than $30,000 to $40,000. Finally, the government had to subsidize the Isabela Irrigation Service and tax the entire island for the purpose of wiping out its deficits.

In 1955 the system was transferred from the Isabela Irrigation Service to the Water Resources Authority and its hydroelectric phase was integrated into the Authority's network.

Other parts of Puerto Rico, beyond the southern and northwestern regions came to be irrigated, though not as intensively. Some lands in the rest of the northwest's subhumid region received irrigation, as did some toward the east, as far as the Central (sugar mill) Constancia, close to the 75 inches average annual rainfall line.

The Lajas Valley Project. Two projects emerged from numerous studies, namely the Southwest Project also known as the Lajas Valley Project and as another possibility the so-called Coamo-Bauta Project.

The first, begun in 1948, was planned to irrigate, through gravity flow, some 26,000 acres in the Lajas plains. Through tunnels, it would bring water from various rivers north of the insular divide to the Loco River, west of Yauco, and thence distribute it to the plains via canals (Fig. 4.4). Later it was decided that some 6,000 acres could not be used, narrowing the area to be irrigated down to 20,000 acres.

Figure 4.4. Concrete Irrigation Canal near Yauco, partly Underground. (Courtesy of the Government of Puerto Rico.)

Five reservoirs were built for the project (Fig. 4.5). The first, on the Yahuecas River, stores water brought westward through a tunnel to another reservoir on the Guayo River. From here, another tunnel brings the waters westward to the Río Prieto, crossing under the latter at a depth of 100 feet and ending at the Chiquito River. Water from a reservoir on the Río Prieto pours into the tunnel through a vertical conduit; the latter reservoir also receives the waters of the Toro River which have been diverted by means of a dam and appropriate conduits. From the Chiquito River, the waters flow south, crossing the insular divide though a tunnel almost 6¼ miles long to a large reservoir (the Lucchetti) on the Yauco River which flows to the south coast (Fig. 4.6). Before entering the Lucchetti Reservoir, the waters turn the turbines of a hydroelectric station. Below Lake Yauco, another tunnel brings the waters to another hydroelectric station, whence they flow into a smaller lake formed by a dam on the Loco River. From the latter they are brought by canals to irrigate the

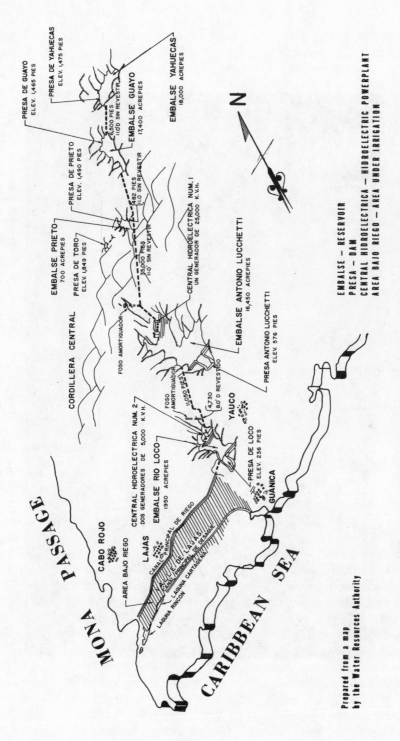

Figure 4.5. Hydroelectric Power and Irrigation in the Lajas Valley Project.

MONA PASSAGE

CARIBBEAN SEA

CABO ROJO

AREA BAJO RIEGO

LAJAS

CORDILLERA CENTRAL

PRESA DE GUAYO
ELEV. 1,465 PIES

PRESA DE YAHUECAS
ELEV. 1,475 PIES

EMBALSE GUAYO
17,400 ACREPIES

EMBALSE YAHUECAS
18,000 ACREPIES

N

EMBALSE PRIETO
700 ACREPIES

PRESA DE TORO
ELEV. 1,849 PIES

PRESA DE PRIETO
ELEV. 1,490 PIES

6,500 PIES
110 SIN REVESTIR

482 PIES
110 SIN REVESTIR

35,000 PIES
110 SIN REVESTIR

CENTRAL HIDROELECTRICA NUM. I
UN GENERADOR DE 25,000 K.V.H.

EMBALSE ANTONIO LUCCHETTI
16,450 ACREPIES

PRESA ANTONIO LUCCHETTI
ELEV. 576 PIES

FOSO AMORTIGUADOR

FOSO AMORTIGUADOR
1,050 PIES

4,730
80'D REVESTIDO

YAUCO

CENTRAL HIDROELECTRICA NUM. 2
DOS GENERADORES DE 5,000 K.V.H.

EMBALSE RIO LOCO
1950 ACREPIES

CANAL PRINCIPAL DE RIEGO

CANAL PRINCIPAL DE DESAGÜE

LAGUNA CARTAGENA

LAGUNA RINCON

PRESA DE LOCO
ELEV. 236 PIES

GUANICA

EMBALSE – RESERVOIR
PRESA – DAM
CENTRAL HIDROELECTRICA – HIDROELECTRIC POWERPLANT
AREA BAJO RIEGO – AREA UNDER IRRIGATION

Prepared from a map
by the Water Resources Authority

Figure 4.6. The Lucchetti Reservoir. Built on the Yauco River, it also receives waters from other reservoirs north of the divide after they have crossed the Cordillera through a tunnel of almost six miles. (Courtesy of the Puerto Rico Water Resources Authority.)

plains of Lajas. Altogether, there are almost 12.5 miles of tunnels. The power plants have an installed capacity of 28,000 kva. and produce an average of 50 million kWh annually. The totel cost of the combined hydroelectric and irrigation project has been estimated at $35,996,047 (Table 4.2).

Table 4.2. Cost of Lajas Valley irrigation system

	Commonwealth Funds	Funds of the Water Resources Authority	Total
Sources of Water	$10,890,210	$ 8,352,676	$19,242,886
Hydroelectric System	0	6,180,016	6,180,016
Subtotal	$10,890,210	$14,532,692	$25,422,902
Irrigation and Drainage System	10,573,172	0	10,573,172
Total Cost	$21,463,382	$14,532,692	$35,996,074

Source: Puerto Rico Water Resources Authority.

The Lajas Valley Irrigation Project started in 1949 and began to function partially in 1955. At the end of the fiscal year 1962–63, 16,250 acres were irrigated and by June 1966, the figure had risen to 18,140.

The region's economy has improved greatly as a result of irrigation. The value of Lajas Valley products rose from $2 million in 1956 to about $7.3 million in 1963 and nearly $10 million in 1966.

The Provisional Irrigation District of the Lajas Valley was officially established in February 1965. During the provisional or trial period, extended to 1971, the Commonwealth Department of Agriculture, collaborating with other government agencies, will determine which areas should be permanently included in the district.

Possibilities for Expansion. The construction of the Coamo-Bauta project is still contemplated for the future. The water will be brought through a tunnel from a reservoir on the Bauta River, north of the divide, to be added to that in a small reservoir in the upper basin of the Toa Vaca River[4] whence it will be brought through a tunnel and canals to another on the Coamo River. The project is planned to include another hydroelectric plant producing 14,900,000 kWh annually and eventually to irrigate some 4,800 acres near Coamo (Fig. 4.7). The high cost of the project ($10 million according to the estimates of 1954) has forced its temporary postponement. More recent estimates place the total cost of the Coamo-Bauta project at between $14 million and $16 million.

4. This reservoir is located about 5.5 miles upstream from the Guayabal Reservoir and should not be confused with the reservoir on the lower Toa Vaca River near Guayabal, now under construction.

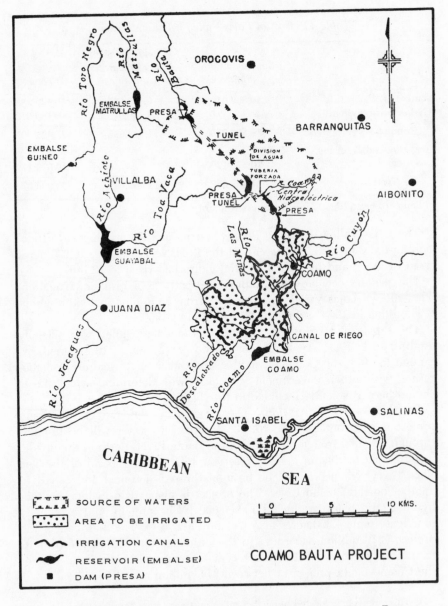

Figure 4.7. (Adapted from the report of the Puerto Rico Water Resources Authority on the Coamo-Bauta project.)

92

DEVELOPMENT OF ELECTRIC ENERGY

The Private Companies. Private companies were the first to produce and distribute electricity in Puerto Rico. The most important was the Puerto Rico Railway Light and Power Company, also known as the San Juan Light Company. That company served the entire north coast from Barceloneta to Luquillo, the east coast from Fajardo to Yabucoa, and interior regions as far as Ciales, Orocovis, Barranquitas, Aibonito, Comerío, Naranjito, Guaynabo, and Trujillo Alto, as well as from Caguas to Yabucoa. The district included approximately half of Puerto Rico's population and was also the easiest and most lucrative to serve, the relatively short transmission lines being able to reach more customers.

The San Juan Light Company built a thermal generating plant in Santurce, by the Condado Lagoon, using oil to fire the boilers which generated steam for turbogenerators. All thermal generating plants must use some kind of fuel, coal, gas, or petroleum, to heat their boilers or a nuclear reactor in place of boilers; their operating cost is therefore higher than that of hydroelectric plants which use falling water. The San Juan Light Company, to lower the cost of production, therefore also operated hydroelectric plants.

There were two such installations; one on the Río La Plata, north of Comerío, and the other on the Río Blanco, south of the Sierra de Luquillo. The Comerío dam is the oldest in Puerto Rico and its reservoir came rapidly to be filled with silt. That is the main problem of reservoirs for hydroelectric development. The power plant needs a steady and uniform flow of water, for the provision of which a reservoir is built; but if that comes to be filled with silt brought by the river, the reserve capacity for use in the dry season gives out. Dredging a reservoir is so expensive that it is often better to abandon it and build a new one. The capacity of the Comerío reservoir has been so reduced by such means that it is practically useless for the storage of water. The two stations of that project therefore use essentially the run-off of the river.

The franchise for the Río Blanco plant was granted in 1928 after much public discussion. The "Bureau for the Utilization of Water Resources" had been in existence since 1925 as a part of the Department of the Interior[5] and maintained that, in the public interest and according to the law which created it, all water resources should be developed by government agencies. The franchise was granted despite great public opposition, with the stipulation that the plant should be turned over to the government upon payment of its fair value after 15 years. Accordingly, in 1939, legal steps began toward the transfer of the Río Blanco station. The litigation was soon solved through the expropriation, as a war measure,

5. Today the Department of Public Works.

of the entire system by the Federal Government. The Puerto Rico Railway Light and Power Company with all its properties was bought later in 1944, by the Puerto Rico Water Resources Authority (created in 1941) at a cost of $11,218,000.

The second private company of importance was the Mayagüez Light, Power, and Ice Company which with a thermal generating plant in Mayagüez served the island's entire southwest district, including Mayagüez, Hormigueros, Cabo Rojo, San Germán, Lajas, and Sabana Grande. The company was finally bought by the Water Resources Authority in 1944, for $1,700,000.

The third large private company was the Ponce Electric Company which served the municipio of Ponce with a thermal plant. That was the first company to be acquired by the Insular Government. Its purchase in 1937, for $1,400,000, was the government's first step in its efforts to produce and distribute *all* of the island's electricity.

A certain number of small installations were found in the towns not served by any of the three large companies, some of them, like those of Yauco, Cayey, Utuado, and Adjuntas, using hydroelectric generating plants. Various sugar mills also produced electricity for their own use and sold the surplus to the public. After the creation of the Water Resources Authority and the development of the hydroelectric systems, some of the small companies bought power from the authority for resale to the public at much higher rates, so serving solely as distributors rather than producers of electric energy. The service was bad. Virtually all of those small companies have by now disappeared together with the large ones, absorbed by the Water Resources Authority.

The Guánica, Aguirre, Rufina, Mercedita, and Coloso sugar mills still generate electric energy during the harvest season, part of which is bought by the Water Resources Authority.

Origin and Scope of the Water Resources Authority (WRA). The production of hydroelectric energy as a government enterprise grew out of the irrigation service on the south coast.

There was a large drop in the Carite project, south of the divide, from the reservoir at 1,800 feet altitude to almost 1,000 feet. It was decided to use that drop for the generation of electricity to run irrigation pumps. Hydroelectric station Carite No. 1 was built in 1915, with a generating capacity of 700 kva. Later that capacity was enlarged to 4,200 kva (3,360 kW), while another generating plant, Carite No. 2, with a capacity of 800 kva (640 kW)[6] was built a little farther down. About 85 per cent of

6. The capacity of turbogenerators does not diminish appreciably with time. However, the capacity of 800 kilo-volt-amperes (kva) with a 0.8 energy factor is conventionally converted to 640 kilowatts (kW) which is the term commonly used for describing generating capacity. It is different in the case of Toro Negro because there the capacity was later raised.

the electricity produced in those two plants was used for running irrigation pumps; the remaining 15 per cent was distributed to the towns in the region.

In 1925, aware of the need for making cheap electricity available to the entire population, the government passed a law creating the "Bureau for the Utilization of Water Resources" as a branch of the Department of the Interior. The law stated that all of Puerto Rico's natural sources of energy would be developed by the government; for the purpose of financing new projects, a tax of one-tenth of 1 per cent, for five years (1925–30) was levied on all real and personal property in Puerto Rico.

The first of these new projects, hydroelectric plant No. 1 of Toro Negro, in Villalba, was begun in 1929 with an initial capacity of 5,400 Kva (4,320 kW). Two more reservoirs were later built in the Toro Negro region: one called el Guineo, on the same Toro Negro River, northwest of Villalba; the other the Matrullas, on the Matrullas River, northeast of that town. Those artificial lakes, north of the cordillera, served to regulate the flow of their respective rivers; through tunnels and canals they also supplied more water to the Toro Negro plant and to Lake Guayabal, so also aiding irrigation. Water from several brooks and small streams was also diverted to increase the generating capacity of the Toro Negro No. 1 plant.

Near the end of 1935, the (Federal) Puerto Rico Reconstruction Administration (PRRA) was established, with an important program, among others, of rural electrification which came to contribute heavily to the expansion of the "Utilization of Water Resources" system. Early in 1936 the PRRA undertook the construction of various projects which had been planned by the insular water resources organization, and which were turned over to that body on their completion in 1937. The capacity of station Toro Negro No. 1 was enlarged to 10,800 kva (8,640 kW), through the installation of a new hydroelectric group. Another plant, Toro Negro No. 2, with a capacity of 2,400 kva (1,920 kW), was built northeast of the Guineo and just north of the divide. A third plant, with a capacity of 800 kva (640 kW), was built in Carite, north of Guayama, at an altitude of 400 feet, making use of the considerable drop which had remained below Plant No. 2. The projects of the Puerto Rico Reconstruction Administration are estimated to have enlarged the system's capacity by 80 per cent. On the other hand, the demand also increased rapidly.

In 1931, the Carite plants produced annually 10 million kilowatt-hours, and the Toro Negro 9.5 million. The total electric energy produced that year was 27,600,000 kWh, 70 per cent of which came from hydroelectric plants. In 1936–37, the total production had risen to 109,650,000 kWh, four times that of 1931. Seventy-three per cent of that energy was supplied by the "Utilization of Water Resources." About 81 per cent was produced by hydroelectric means, in publicly and privately owned plants.

In 1937, the Puerto Rico Reconstruction Administration also started the Garzas and Dos Bocas projects.

The Garzas project included the construction of an earth dam 202 feet high on the Vacas River, a tributary of the Arecibo; the waters of its reservoir were brought to the south of the divide through a tunnel 11,700 ft. long. The project was similar to those of Carite and Toro Negro. Generating plant No. 1 was built at the bottom of a drop of 1,200 feet; No. 2 located another 800 feet down. Their combined capacity was 15,300 kva (12,240 kW). Work on the project was stopped December 1938 because during the course of construction the PRRA had run into financial difficulties. In 1939 the project was transferred to the Puerto Rican government which resumed the work with funds from the Federal Public Works Administration. Garzas plant began to produce limited quantities of electricity in November 1941 and has produced at full capacity since its completion in 1942–43.

The Dos Bocas project, with an original capacity of 15,000 kva, was completed in 1942, adding 7,500 kva (6,000 kW)[7] to the island's generating capacity.

Within its program for rural electrification, the Puerto Rico Reconstruction Administration also built lines for transmission and distribution in rural areas. Altogether, until 1941 when the program of rural electrification was suspended, the PRRA had spent $9,209,000 on hydroelectric plants and $200,000 on transmission lines.

As shown above, both the PRRA and the BUWR ("Bureau for the Utilization of Water Resources") contributed to the island's electrification. However, except in the Ponce region, the lines of the BUWR had been built largely in the rural districts, beyond the territories of the San Juan Light Company, the Mayagüez Light Company, and the Isabela Irrigation Service. The last-named supplied electric energy to the northwest plain, the lower valley of the Culebrinas as far as Moca, and the region of the Atalaya hills as far as Añasco.

In 1938–39 the total production of the four systems came to almost 146,000,000 kWh, of which some 67 per cent originated in hydroelectric plants. That figure seems to indicate a reduction from the 81 per cent produced in 1936–37. Actually, the production of hydroelectric energy had increased from 90 million kWh in 1936–37 to 98 million in 1938–39, but the increase in both demand and consumption had been far larger. In the ensuing years that imbalance increased considerably: in 1940–41, when the production of hydroelectric plants was 120.3 million kWh, the island's total came to 231,016,000 kWh, meaning that 48 per cent of the total originated in thermal generating plants.

On May 2, 1941, the Island's Legislature created the Water Resources Authority ("Autoridad de las Fuentes Fluviales," known as AFF in Span-

---

7. The Dos Bocas plant contains three turbogenerators of 7,500 kva each, or a total capacity of 22,500 kva, the equivalent of 18,000 kW.

ish and WRA in English), which was granted powers to acquire, operate, and develop plants and installations for the production and distribution of electricity for use by the public, with a view to establishing an integrated, island-wide system.

The "Bureau for the Utilization of Water Resources" disappeared, absorbed by the WRA which also took over the South Coast Irrigation Service and the production of energy in the Carite plants Nos. 1 and 2, while the operation of the irrigation services came under a separate division of the WRA.

The following year, using its wartime powers and with the objective of economizing on fuels, the federal Public Works Administration seized the San Juan Light Company and that of Mayagüez, placing both under the WRA, which finally bought them in 1944.

The incorporation of those two systems into the WRA in 1942, plus the completion that same year of the Garzas and Dos Bocas projects, resulted by 1943 in the reduction of the island's consumption of fuel oil from an estimated 19 to 8 million gallons. The WRA, in other words, saved 11 million gallons of petroleum products in a war year when such fuels were extremely scarce.

The WRA also continued the practice of acquiring the small companies which distributed electricity locally.

Construction of the Caonillas project began in wartime and was completed in 1948 at a total cost of $10,500,000. Plant No. 1 of Caonillas had a capacity of 17,600 kW. The following year work began on the project's enlargement at a cost of $4,107,000 contributing an additional 4,000 kW to the total generated by hydroelectric means.

In 1949 the Water Resources Authority began a multiple-purpose project known as the Project of Puerto Rico's Southwest, at a cost estimated at $32 million. In addition to providing water for irrigating 26,000 acres in the Lajas Valley for domestic and industrial uses, that project protects the region's lives and properties against floods. It also provides water for moving turbogenerators in the Yauco plants Nos. 1 and 2, with capacities of 20,000 and 8,000 kW, respectively.

The enormous growth of consumption after World War II also demanded expansion of thermoelectric plants. This need was made more urgent since the anticipated industrial development being promoted by the government would create new demands in the years to come. The need to be prepared for extraordinary droughts which might reduce the output of the hydroelectric plants added to the urgency of building steam power plants. Moreover, the construction of hydroelectric plants had been delayed by wartime and post-war difficulties.

To meet the immediate problem created by the need for rapid expansion, the WRA acquired from the Federal War Surplus Administration a floating steam power plant called the "Seapower," with a capacity of 30,000 kva which was installed in the San Juan bay and began operating in August 1946. Earlier, in 1945, the Authority had leased the thermal plant of the U.S. Naval Base at Ensenada Honda, Ceiba (Roosevelt Roads), interconnecting it into its system of transmission lines and so obtaining an additional 10,000 kva.

The thermal plants of Santurce and Mayagüez were enlarged. An additional unit of 7,500 kva was installed in the Santurce plant, and one of 5,000 kva in that of Mayagüez.

The floating power plant, "Seapower," was used until 1950 when it was sold in public auction to the Brazilian Traction, Light, and Power Company. That year saw the completion of a new steam plant, located at the site of Puerto Nuevo (New Port), called "San Juan Steam Power Station." The plant's net original capacity was 60,000 kW (now 598,000 kW) and its cost is estimated at about $48 million, including the installation of storage tanks for fuel, a substation of 110 kva, a pier 1,700 feet long which was sold to the Puerto Rico Ports Authority, and such additional facilities as warehouses, repair shops, and garages.

The intensive droughts between 1947 and 1950 greatly diminished the productive capacities of the hydroelectric plants, while the demand for electric energy kept growing, so forcing the thermal plants to supply an ever growing share of the total.

In 1951–52, out of a total of 674,003,840 kWh produced by the WRA,[8] 413,434,000 kWh, or 60.3 per cent, were generated in the four thermal plants and 260,569,840 kWh, or 38.1 per cent, by 13 hydroelectric plants.

Of the capacity in 1970, only 107,920 kW were installed in hydroelectric plants, while 1,393,000 kW were in thermoelectric plants, despite the fact that the hydro plants of Yauco No. 1 with 8,000 kW and Yauco No. 2, with 20,000 kW, both part of the Lajas Valley project, were added to the system in 1961. Total steam generating capacity grows constantly, and the latest figure for WRA total name plate rating for June 1970 was 1,500,000 kW (Table 4.3).

The energy produced by the Authority was distributed as follows: 27.7 per cent to private residences; 22.1 per cent to commerce; 34.8 per cent to industries; 1.5 per cent to public illumination; 5.2 per cent to the South Coast Irrigation Service; 1.0 per cent to new projects or constructions of the WRA; 5.6 per cent to other public authorities; and 1.8 per cent to various public services. In 1950 the Authority served more than 190,000 customers in all parts of the island. In 1965 it serves a total of 552,111.

The Old Hydroelectric System of the Isabela Irrigation Service. In 1950, at Isabela, four hydroelectric plants were producing energy, in addition to irrigation service. The oldest, dating back to the start of the service, is located southeast of Isabela and has an installed capacity of 1,760 kva. In 1940–41, its production was about 5,306,000 kWh. As the

8. Compared with 27,600,000 kWh produced in all plants in 1931.

Table 4.3. *Puerto Rico Water Resources Authority installed generating capacity 1970*

Plants	Capacity in kW	Location
Thermoelectric		
San Juan	598,000	San Juan
Mayagüez	50,000	Mayagüez
South Coast	263,000	Peñuelas
Palo Seco	411,000	Toa Baja
Other	71,000	
Total	1,393,000	
Hydroelectric		
Toro Negro, No. 1	8,640	Villalba
Toro Negro, No. 2	1,920	Villalba
Carite, No. 1	3,360	Guayama
Carite, No. 2	640	Guayama
Carite, No. 3	640	Guayama
Garzas, No. 1	7,200	Peñuelas
Garzas, No. 2	5,040	Peñuelas
Caonillas, No. 1	17,600	Utuado
Caonillas, No. 2	4,000	Utuado
Dos Bocas	18,000	Arecibo
Comerío No. 1	1,600	Comerío
Comerío No. 2	3,200	Comerío
Río Blanco	5,000	Naguabo
Yauco, No. 1	20,000	Yauco
Yauco, No. 2	8,000	Adjuntas
Isabela, No. 1	1,280	Quebradillas
Isabela, No. 2	800	Quebradillas
Isabela, No. 3	1,000	Quebradillas
Total hydroelectric	107,920	
Grand total	1,500,920	

Source: Puerto Rico Water Resources Authority.

capacity was insufficient to meet the demand at certain times, an additional 1,069,510 kWh were bought from the WRA in that year. Plant No. 2, begun by the PRRA and boosting the system's capacity by 900 kva, was completed in 1941 southwest of Isabela. Later, Plant No. 3, west of Isabela and with a capacity of 1,250 kva, was built with insular government funds. In 1950 the system's total installed capacity, in four plants, had risen to 5,535 kva, distributed as follows: No. 1—1,760 kva; No. 2— 900; No. 3—1,250; and No. 4—1,625 kva.

The Isabela system served the northwest from Hatillo to Añasco, including the air base at Punta Borinquen, known as Ramey Field. There, as on the south coast, the production of electric energy began as a by-product of irrigation. Recently, in December 1965, the Water Resources Authority stopped the production of electricity by the Isabela hydro-electric plants because of the relatively high cost of such production, while the hydraulic installations continue to supply water for irrigation to the lands included in the Isabela Irrigation District. However, more water from the Guajataca reservoir, the only one in the zone, is used for domestic purposes than for irrigation. The WRA supplies water to Ramey Air Base, as well as to the Aqueduct Authority for distribution to the people of Aguada, Aguadilla, Isabela, Moca, and Quebradillas. During the fiscal year 1965–66, the consumption of water through these aqueducts was 7,900 acre-feet and that for irrigation was 1,600 acre-feet.

Thermal and Hydroelectric Plants. The relative superiority of thermal or hydro plants has often been debated in relation to the development of the WRA's generating system. Each has its advantages, and actually they complement one another. The original investment in steam plants is relatively low, and such plants can be built near the centers of consumption, especially in the case of urban populations. For hydroelectric plants it is necessary to build reservoirs high in the mountains and to install conduits and tunnels for bringing the water to the generating plants. As a result, the initial cost is much higher and it is necessary to build long transmission lines. The loss of power from these is considerable.

On the other hand, the high initial cost of hydroelectric plants is offset by low operating costs. When the reservoir also supplies irrigation water to a nearby district, or water for industrial and domestic uses, its several functions absorb part of the project's cost, the total cost being divided between the users of electricity, the irrigators, and other consumers. Moreover, the Puerto Rican government has received federal aid which has supported large parts of the initial costs.

After a hydroelectric station has been built, the only costs connected with it are those of operation and maintenance. In some cases, like that of Toro Negro No. 2 which is operated automatically from Villalba, human operators are not needed. Because of the small personnel required, the operating costs of hydro plants are lower than those of thermal plants. During the emergency war years and immediately after, the hydroelectric plants gave Puerto Rico sufficient electricity to meet the island's needs. But thermal plants continued to be built for service in periods of drought. Since then the needs created by industrial development and population growth gave decisive advantages to thermal over hydroelectric plants. To meet the growing demand, the installations had to be increased at a rate of some 80,000 kW per year. Hence the Water Resources Authority which, in the beginning, had generated exclusively in hydroelectric plants, must today rely on steam plants for the generation of some 95 per cent of its total production.

Suitable sites for further hydroelectric projects are today virtually unavailable. Not one has the capacity required by modern conditions; they lack river basins of sufficient size, rainfall, or sites for large reservoirs. The situation siffers drastically from that of 1936–37, when 81 per cent of the production depended on hydraulic forces.

The Control of Production and Distribution: Private Enterprises and the Government. This subject is current and important. In the United States, too, there are large government-owned generating plants, like those of the Tennessee Valley Authority (TVA). The history of Puerto Rico's case is even more interesting since, today, virtually the entire production is controlled by a government agency, the Water Resources Authority which also controls practically the entire distribution.

The question can be debated pro and con according to one's personal concepts of such government action and the limits to which it should be allowed to go. Nevertheless, it cannot be doubted that governmental control has many advantages.

A large enterprise can distribute electricity at lower cost, with the added advantage that the profits can be used for such beneficial purposes as the three listed below:

1. Maintenance and constant expansion of the system to meet the ever growing demands for electricity, and bring it to the point where it can help new industries which need much low-cost power.

2. Distribution of electricity in the rural areas. Since electric energy is unquestionably a civilizing agent, distribution is very important. Much of the rural population which in 1950 comprised about 60 per cent of the total lacked electricity. Here was a magnificent opportunity to bring to the rural areas the benefits which the service bestows on the urban. While it is undoubtedly more expensive to distribute electricity in rural than in urban areas, it proved possible to subsidize rural electrification. Since 1946–47 the Commonwealth government has annually appropriated $500,000 which, together with $100,000 of WRA funds, has made feasible an island-wide program of rural electrification. In 1952 the WRA borrowed $6,000,000 from the Federal Rural Electrification Administration (REA) for the purpose of accelerating the program. Between 1952–53 and 1961–62, 83,262 families came to be served at an investment of $21.7 million. Today, electricity is obtainable on almost 100 per cent of the island. In 1970 service went to 690,725 customers, about half of whom live in the rural areas.

3. Reduction of electricity rates. That was begun by the Utilization of Water Resources in Ponce, where the rates were lowered to three quarters of what they had been before the agency acquired the district. Theoretically that entailed an annual loss of $150,000; however, since the lowered rates increased the consumption one and a half times, there was an actual gain of $30,000, or 12 per cent, over previous receipts. Other adjustments have since been made, according to the costs of production, but the objective of making electricity available to everybody has been reached.

Future: The Expansion of the Hydroelectric System and its Importance. On February 28, 1942, Engineer Antonio Lucchetti, the first executive director of the Water Resources Authority, answering a letter of inquiry directed to him by the author as to the potentialities for hydroelectric development in Puerto Rico, wrote that a total annual production of 400 million kilowatt-hours was a feasible objective. That was almost equal to the production of total electric energy in 1950 and double of that year's production of hydroelectric energy.

In contrast, the Brookings Institution in its 1930 report on Puerto Rico and its problems said that the maximum hydroelectric energy which the island could generate was 200 million kWh. annually. That was the quantity which could be produced in 1950 by the plants then in existence, but there remained other feasible projects for expanding the productive potentiality considerably more. The report of the Brookings Institution was too conservative. Other estimates of the island's total productive capacity of electric energy have gone as high as 600 million kWh annually.

In 1950–51, preferences for hydroelectric development were based on certain above-named advantages such as certainty of service in wartime, lower cost of maintenance and operation, and the use of reservoirs for irrigation and other domestic and industrial purposes. However, the fact that the supply of hydroelectric energy diminished temporarily during periods of drought and permanently with the silting of reservoirs, plus the impossibility of maintaining a rate of production growth at the level of accelerated needs caused by the growth of industrialization, has caused those preferences to run in favor of thermoelectric generation.

Under the former point of view, a series of improvements were planned, to augment the production of existing plants. The Caonillas plant was enlarged with the addition of 4,000 kW generating capacity. The Guayabal dam was raised and plans were drafted for building a new reservoir and generating plant in the Río Blanco. The Yunque zone seemed promising. Its high precipitation and various young, closed valleys, traversed by steep rivers with considerable flow, seemed ideal for the construction of reservoirs. The Southwest Project, with two generating plants, became a reality. Studies were made of the basin of the La Plata River, especially south of Comerío. Five promising sites were studied in the Manatí River basin, and thought was given to the possibility of building five additional reservoirs on the Arecibo River. Another project was considered on the Añasco River, near las Marías.

Under the later swing toward thermoelectric plants, the new plant at Puerto Nuevo, with an original capacity of 40,000 kW was begun in 1947 and completed in 1950. The system was further enlarged through the construction of the Thermoelectric Plant of the South, the gas turbine station of Mayagüez, and the Palo Seco station (Fig. 4.8). The steam plant of the south went into operation in December 1963. Since then, new units have been added to bring its capacity to 263,000 kW.

Figure 4.8. Thermoelectric Plant of Palo Seco. Many steam plants were built to meet the needs of constant industrial expansion. The Palo Seco plant we see here has a present capacity of 411,000 kW. (Courtesy of the Puerto Rico Water Resources Authority.)

Figure 4.9. Experimental Thermonuclear Power Plant BONUS, in Rincón.

The San Juan or Puerto Nuevo plant after the addition of new units has a capacity of 598,000 kW, the largest in the island as of 1971.

The culmination of that admirable development program was the construction of the nuclear power plant, BONUS which, at 11:30 A.M., on August 15, 1964, began for the first time in Latin America to generate electric energy by nuclear means (Fig. 4.9). Although it is still an experimental project under the auspices of the Atomic Energy Commission of the United States in cooperation with the Water Resources Authority, its production of electricity totalled 2,519,200 kWh. during 1964–65.

The success of the project led to the planning of a new thermonuclear plant of 600,000 kW. Construction at Aguirre of the $135 million plant will begin in 1971.

The prolonged debate over hydroelectric versus thermoelectric energy seems to be resolving in favor of nuclear energy as a new fuel and new procedure. For a country like Puerto Rico, lacking coal, gas, and petroleum, and with limited hydraulic resources, the nuclear era promises to open a source of energy with enormous possibilities.

5

Minerals

Mining Developments during Colonization

Puerto Rico began its historic life as a mining island. Gold was the main product of its soils from 1509 to 1536. The first small group of settlers explored the land avidly for the precious metal and expertly worked the gold-bearing sands of the rivers. Historians disagree on the total quantity extracted during that period and vary in their estimates of the length of the mining era which some extend to the middle of the sixteenth century. Calculations as to value fluctuate between $42 million according to Horacio Ray and a mere $3 million. The differences stem from fluctuations in the value of gold and from the fact that estimates were based on the share which was turned over to the Spanish Crown since there were no estimates on the totals mined. The true production was somewhere between those two figures.

The accumulation of many centuries was extracted during those first twenty-seven years of the sixteenth century. The work of the Spanish miners was so effective that the former deposits are today almost entirely depleted. Puerto Rico, and the Antilles in general, disappointed the first wave of adventurous colonists, determined to enrich themselves at any cost. Most of them sailed away to the continent, where the rich gold and silver mines in Mexico, Perú, and Bolivia, many of them already worked by the Indians, continued to yield on a large scale.

Other important facts which contributed to the loss of interest in mining in Puerto Rico seem to be the tropical climate and the dense vegetation which impeded exploration; in the three countries mentioned above, with much dryer and cooler climates, the relative scarcity of vegetation facilitated such exploration. Hence the great current of migration veered toward the continent, leaving on the island only a few settlers, devoted to agriculture and commerce.

The truth is that Puerto Rico has been poor, not only in gold but in economically exploitable minerals in general. The mining industry has therefore seen very little development. According to the Census of 1950, mining employed only 1,161 men, or fewer than 0.2 per cent of Puerto Rico's total labor force, including the workers in gravel pits.[1]

At the beginning of the century, the figure was more or less the same, showing that by 1950 there had been no substantial change in opportunities for mine workers. What did change was the number of workers in certain activities which have by now lost their importance. For instance, in 1900 many more workers were extracting clay to make bricks used then for building much more than they are today.

The Census of 1960 shows 524 workers in mining at that time, a marked decline from the number ten years earlier.

Investigations

Puerto Rico's development has been impeded by a pronounced lack of interest in mining, which seems to stem in part from the causes behind the abandonment of goldmining in the sixteenth century. While it is true that much of the former dense natural vegetation has been cleared to permit farming, much of the latter, as in the case of coffee, covers the land permanently and impedes exploration. The lack of "free" land for prospecting and staking without interference, has been suggested as another bar to the development of mining; the abundance of free land was important in furthering mining in Mexico and in the western United States. Other contributing factors were the virtual cessation of mining since the sixteenth century, the absence of a mining tradition and adequate knowledge of the resources available, the lack of skilled miners and of audacity and enterprise for such exploitation on the part of capital.

The Committee on Mineral Resources, organized in 1932, and the Bureau of Mines of the Department of the Interior,[2] organized in 1935, furthered the investigation of mineral resources and the diffusion of information about them. Act 243 was passed in 1946, abolishing the Bureau of Mines and transferring its functions to the Puerto Rico Industrial Development Company. The Economic Development Administration was created in 1950, taking over industrial investigations under the direction of Rafael Fernández García. The Mining Commission, attached to the Governor's Office with the task of encouraging and regulating mining in Puerto Rico, was established in 1954. In that same year, the section of mineralogy and geology was established within the Economic Development Administration.

1. In the census classifications, work in gravel pits is considered mining.
2. Today the Department of Public Works.

The search for oil encouraged by the Industrial Development Company was among the first mineral investigations. Those of more recent times were the searches for copper by private entities, which culminated in the discovery of promising deposits in the region of Lares-Utuado-Adjuntas.

Mineral deposits fall into three categories: metallic, nonmetallic, and hydrocarbon.

Metallic Minerals

The number of metals exploited commercially in Puerto Rico is very small; only gold and manganese were in that category (Fig. 5.1). However, the exploitation of both stopped quite long ago. Today the copper deposits in the Utuado-Adjuntas region are recognized as other metallic minerals with commercial value.

GOLD

Gold was one of Puerto Rico's most exploited metals. An estimated 6,000 ounces, with a value of $100,000, was extracted between 1900 and 1932. There are two types of deposits: (1) the placers, or accumulations of gold-bearing sands in streams, and (2) veins of gold-bearing quartz. In the early days of colonization the most important placers were in the Corozal, Luquillo, and San Germán regions, of which the first two, yielding four-fifths of the total were the richest. The placers have been the most exploited deposits but are today virtually exhausted.

Working the veins, the original sources of gold, seems now to offer greater possibilities. Veins which may prove profitable are found in six of the island's regions. The old Bureau of Mines reported that those regions are at Corozal, San Germán, Guayama, Barranquitas, Luquillo, and Utuado. The geologist R. P. Briggs of the United States Geological Survey reported that the exploitation of gold as a by-product of copper offers possibilities today.

MANGANESE

In the course of the present century, manganese has been Puerto Rico's most important export mineral. The industry was established in 1915, in the Tijeras and Guayabal barrios of Juana Díaz, in a mine belonging to the Atlantic Ore Company, a subsidiary of the General Dry Batteries Co. of Cleveland, Ohio. The manganese was used in the manufacture of dry batteries and was so pure that it was ideally suited for that purpose.

In this zone, from the Guayabal Dam toward the southeast, early tertiary limestone is faulted in an intense and complex manner, in a belt one mile wide and two and a half long, forming a pronounced range northeast of Juana Díaz. The pressure of the orogenic forces which gave

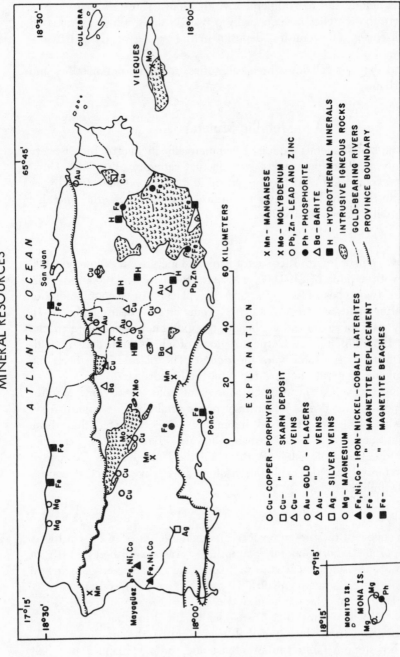

Figure 5.1. Map Showing Occurrences of Metals, Phosphorite, Barite and Hydrothermal Minerals in Puerto Rico. (Reprinted from Reginald P. Briggs, "Mineral Resources of Puerto Rico," *Revista del Colegio de Ingenieros de P. R.* 19, no. 2 [April–June, 1969].)

108

rise to the faulting created a series of fractures in the limestone, to which rainwaters had easy access. Meyerhoff writes as follows about the appearance of manganese in those fractures:

> The island's one operating mine is located about three miles northeast of Juana Díaz. Here one of the bands now known to be early tertiary limestone comes to the surface, and a complex series of folds has spread it over the crest of the prominent ridge east of the Guayabal reservoir. The calcium carbonate composing it is soluble, and the many fractures which developed when the formation was folded have furnished meteoric waters an easy means of entry into the rocks. Solution has occurred extensively, and large caves have been opened in the recesses of the mountain. But the percolating waters have not confined their activities to the destructive work of solution. Along some of the fractures and in many older cavities, they not merely removed the calcium carbonate but left highly concentrated deposits of manganese oxide in its place. Black prisms of manganite contrast with the calcareous matrix of the fracture zones, and sooty masses of pyrolusite and psilomelane fill the irregular chambers which the waters dissolved. Each pocket of manganese ore is more or less isolated, and thick pillars of pure limestone must be penetrated to get from one pocket to the next; but the deposit is of such excellent quality that it pays to remove the barren limestone to reach the ore.[3]

The mine produced an annual average of 2,500 tons, with an export value of about $100,000. The method of extraction seems to have been quite primitive and, as the work progressed, it became increasingly difficult to obtain the ore. That fact, plus an increase in wages from 12 to 25 cents per hour made mandatory in 1938 under the Federal Reasonable Working Standards Law, plus the company's greater interest in its El Cristo mines north of Santiago, Cuba, were the main reasons for the closing of the mine. The manganese of the Cuban mines is inferior in quality, but the deposits are larger and the wages lower, making their exploitation more profitable than at Juana Díaz. In January 1939 the Puerto Rican operation was suspended and the technical personnel was moved to the El Cristo mines.

The deposits at Adjuntas, Aguada, Lares, Lajas, and Juana Díaz were once considered exploitable; recent studies, however, showed them to be not worth the risk of too small production.

IRON

The metal of which the largest deposits are found on the island is iron. In the Cerro de las Mesas, southeast of Mayagüez, there is a deposit of limonite which originated from the decomposition of the serpentine

3. H. A. Meyerhoff, *Geology of Puerto Rico* (Monographs of the University of Puerto Rico, Series B, No. 1) (Rio Piedras: The University of Puerto Rico, 1933), pp. 133–34.

which forms the range, stretching six miles toward the southeast. Under the influence of heat and humidity, the upper layers of serpentine were transformed from a greenish rock containing a mere 8 per cent of iron into a reddish earthy mantle which is quite poor as cultivable soil but rich as an iron-bearing mineral, containing from 55 to 60 per cent of iron-oxide (limonite), about 20 per cent of alumina, and some 15 per cent of water. The large amount of water is a disadvantage in that it raises the cost of transporting the ores. The presence of alumina is also a disadvantage, hampering the metallurgical processes for obtaining the iron, and so raising costs. Those matters impede the economic development of the ores. A possible compensation for those drawbacks is found in the proximity of the deposit to Mayagüez and the resulting possibility of setting up a system of transporting the ores cheaply by gravity down the mountain slopes.

In an interview I had in 1962 with the former Director of Industrial Research, Mr. Carlos Vincenty, he expressed himself as follows:

> We have completed a study of Puerto Rico's west coast which reveals the presence of more than 90 million tons of ore containing eight tenths of one per cent of nickel, but including 15 million tons with 1.25 per cent nickel and 0.1 per cent cobalt. The nickel content is considered sufficient to permit exploitation, and the quantity of ores with that content is large enough to justify detailed studies aimed at commercial working.

Nevertheless, the fact that the nickel is found partly in serpentine and partly in laterite means that known methods of extraction may not be applicable to Puerto Rico's limonites. The geologist of the U. S. Geological Survey, R. P. Briggs, believes that the buildings on the Cerro de las Mesas are more valuable than the scant minerals underneath. He reports that in Guanajibo (Mayagüez) there are 46,800,000 tons of laterite with an average content of 0.88 per cent nickel, 0.88 per cent cobalt, and 20.54 per cent iron. But its exploitation, too, requires the development of a new method of extracting the metals.

Iron ores other than limonite are found on the island. While their deposits are much smaller than are those at Mayagüez, their quality is higher. Magnetite, a blackish, magnetic ore, is found in the barrio Tibes, four miles north of Ponce, by the Portugués River, as well as in the so-called Alto de la Bandera on the Jayuya-Ponce road south of Adjuntas, and in the Monte Morales near Utuado. Magnetite is also a prominent constituent of some of the beach sands in Puerto Rico. Investigations have shown those deposits to be commercially unexploitable, unless a Puerto Rican iron industry is based in some other larger body of ore; in that case magnetite from these sources could be exploited.

Magnetite is also found in the region between Juncos and Humacao, where they are mixed with hematite, a red iron ore. The largest deposit is in a hill a mile east of Juncos. The former Spanish-American Ore Company explored the deposit but abandoned it as commercially unexploitable. It contains an estimated 250,000 tons of rich ores. From 1951 to 1953 the West Indies Mining Company worked the deposit, taking out a daily 800 tons of rich ore containing 63 per cent iron. During the calendar year 1951, the island exported 42,255 tons of iron ore from the Juncos mine. Today the operation is abandoned and the remaining reserves are thought to amount to less than half of the past production.

COPPER

Until 1965, the high-grade copper deposits in Naguabo, Ciales, Morovis, San Germán, Corozal, and Comerío were regarded as unexploitable because of limited reserves, although those of Naguabo had been worked between 1866 and 1868. It has been virtually inexplicable, however, that Puerto Rico, composed 65 per cent of igneous rocks and with two large batholyths at San Lorenzo and Utuado-Jayuya, should not offer copper ores, like the other Antilles. The geologists were therefore not surprised by the discovery of significant deposits in Lares, Utuado, and Adjuntas. The composition of those deposits promises new wealth in copper. The exploratory work has been done by the Ponce Mining Corporation, a subsidiary of the American Metal Climax, Inc., and by the Bear Creek Mining Company, a subsidiary of the Kennecott Copper Company, in the borders of the Utuado, Adjuntas, and Lares municipalities, where borings penetrated to a depth of some 1,500 feet (Fig. 5.2). While there are discrepancies as to the copper content the average came to some 0.8 per cent, or 16 pounds of copper per 2,000 pounds of extracted materials. The total content of the deposits is estimated as at least 250 million tons of copper ores. Further investigations may result in changes in the estimated commercial yield, but present knowledge assures a copper mining industry for Puerto Rico if market prices remain stable.

After ten years of exploration and the expenditure of $9 million, the mining companies in 1969 formally submitted to the Commonwealth Government their second proposal to start a copper mining industry in the Rio Viví-Río Pellejas area on the border of the municipalities of Utuado and Adjuntas. A total investment of $200 million is contemplated. After concentrating the low-grade ore from an average content of 0.8 per cent to 26 per cent, the partly processed mineral would then be piped to the smelter proposed to be established near Guayanilla on the southern coast together with a sulphuric acid plant. Copper anodes of 99.3 per cent copper would be produced in the smelter ready for final refining to completely pure copper. No terminal refinery operations are proposed for Puerto Rico until local demand for the metal increases. However, the companies are willing to supply refined copper to local manufacturing plants at U.S. mainland prices.

Figure 5.2. Core Drill Used in the Search for Copper in Lares. Cylindrical samples (cores) obtained from depths as far as 1,500 feet permit determination of the copper content. (Courtesy of the Economic Development Administration.)

Total volume of copper to be annually produced for at least 30 years is estimated at 50,000 tons worth about $50 million at the present market price of $0.50 per pound. The companies further estimate an annual gross profit of $20.3 million to be split equally three ways among the two companies and the Commonwealth Government. About 1,600 workers will be employed during the three year construction period and 800 permanently thereafter. It is estimated that these operations will create indirectly from 6 to 8,000 additional jobs.

It is expected that a transition from a depressed agricultural economy into one of modern mining will bring substantial changes to the whole west-central mountains of Puerto Rico. Strong opposition to these operations has been voiced by some conservationists and also especially by many nationalists. However, it is expected that the proposed mining plans will be approved by the Commonwealth Government after assuring itself that the antipollution devices and the economic plan are in the best interests of Puerto Rico.

TITANIUM

Titanium is found in solid solution with magnetite as well as in association with basic intrusive rocks, near Humacao, in beach sands at Barceloneta, Mercedita, Humacao, Vieques, and elsewhere. Its exploitation, however, is questionable, due to difficulties encountered in its metallurgic separation and to the relatively small size of the ore bodies.

Nonmetallic Minerals

BARITE

This mineral is found in Juncos as well as in Lares, Coamo, and Ciales. However, the deposits are so small that successful commercial extraction cannot be expected.

QUARRY STONE

In view of the great demand for crushed stone for use as concrete aggregate in the present period of active construction, stone quarrying employs the largest number of workers engaged in mining. Fortunately, the island has large amounts of quarry rock suited for various uses in construction work.

The *Cretaceous Limestones* (Blue Limestones), very hard and resistant, are greatly in demand for the construction of roads and buildings (Fig. 5.3). At times the owners of quarries call igneous rocks blue limestone. Among the known reserves of this material are the quarries of barrio Matón at Cayey, Aguas Buenas, Aibonito, and others.

Figure 5.3. Quarry for Blue Limestone along the Cayey-Aibonito Road. (Courtesy of the University of Puerto Rico. Photo by Samuel A. Santiago.)

The *granites* and *diorites* in the island's interior are also useful for such purposes but it is generally necessary to obtain fresh rock from some depths since those near the surface have been weathered and decomposed by the actions of heat and humidity. Some important granite quarries are located in the interior where limestone is scarce. The rock was widely used for the construction of naval installations on the island of Vieques. Granitic rocks are also sources of monumental stones for ornamentation but in Puerto Rico there is as yet no demand for them.

Andesite rocks, whether pure andesite or andesitic tuffs, have been widely used in Puerto Rico for the preparation of concrete. The rock is generally hard and resistant and does not react to highly alkaline cements. The aggregate used in the construction of Dos Bocas dam was about 30 per cent andesite.

LIME

Lime is made from limestone by a simple method, employing special kilns (Fig. 5.4). It is best produced in small units to meet local demands, requiring small investments of capital and labor. The kilns are set up near deposits of pure Tertiary limestone which abound along the north and south coasts; at times deposits of limestone accumulated during the Quaternary period are also used. Cretaceous limestone is not as good because of its hardness and many impurities.

Lime is used principally in the sugar industry and in construction. Formerly, one of the most important deposits was that of Hicaco Island, northeast of Fajardo, whose limestone was extraordinarily pure. Today, the only important plant belongs to the Ferré Enterprises, in Ponce.

MARBLE

Marble is another stone with possibilities. One of the most important deposits is north of Juana Díaz, in a belt about 2.5 by 0.6 miles; others are in Coamo, Rosario, Las Marías, Caguas, and Cidra-Aguas Buenas. Because of its size, the Juana Díaz deposit promises the most lasting exploitation (Fig. 5.5). Its color ranges from pure white to a beautiful light beige. Today it is used for gravestones, for floors and stairs, and in chips for the preparation of *terrazo*, which is a mixture of marble fragments and white cement.

Such, almost exclusively, was the utilization of the island's marble until recently. In 1965, highly experienced Italian experts, with cooperation from the Government Development Bank and the Economic Development Administration, formed a corporation for studying the economic possibilities of the working of marble. In 1967 the work of that corporation resulted in the establishment, in the San Juan Metropolitan Area, of a modern factory for meeting the growing demands of Puerto Rico's construction industry (Figs. 5.6, 5.7).

Figure 5.4. Tertiary Limestone. Base for the production of lime in special kilns. (Courtesy of the Agricultural Extension Service.)

Figure 5.5. Plant for Processing Marble in Juana Díaz. Chips for making terrazo are obtained here. (Courtesy of Dr. Carlos Iñiguez.)

Figure 5.6. Modern Machinery Imported from Italy for Processing Marble.

CLAYS

For a long time, pottery and ceramics were small, native industries. In some towns, kilns and people who model clay for making various receptacles may still be found.

Many clay deposits, potentially useful for a ceramic industry, are found in Puerto Rico. Red and yellow clays, resulting from the decomposition of Cretaceous clay-shales, abound in the island, especially in

Figure 5.7. Processed Marbles. Samples show the diversity of colors, designs, and structures of Puerto Rican marbles.

alluvial plains and residual soils. Some deposits of kaolin (white clay) are located in Hato Tejas (Bayamón), Isla Verde (Carolina), Caguas, Cayey, Cerro La Tiza (between Aguas Buenas and Comerío), San Germán, and elsewhere.

The red and yellow clays were widely used during the years of Spanish rule, for the manufacture of bricks, flagstones, and roofing tiles. Today, reinforced concrete and concrete blocks are preferred for permanent buildings.

The factory of the Puerto Rico Clay Products Company, capitalized at $1,900,000 and located in Carolina, began to operate in 1947. It manufactured terracotta blocks, roofing tiles, bricks, and sanitary ware such as washbowls, sinks, and toilets. It used clays from an adjoining deposit as well as another at the St. Just Development, southeast of Río Piedras.

During the first eleven months of 1948–49, production was $535,388.28. In 1950, 17,081 tons of earthenware products were produced, valued at $286,000. The trend was to concentrate on the production of bricks and tiles. The island's mounting industrialization and economic improvement promised a good future for the ceramics industry. Nevertheless, the Carolina plant was eventually closed because of technical difficulties and other problems.

A ceramics factory still in existence, Caribe China, which specializes in the manufacture of chinaware for hotels and institutions, was established in Vega Baja, but uses kaolin imported from Cornwall, England. Puerto Rican clays are used largely in the cement and construction industries.

SILICEOUS SANDS

The siliceous sands which abound between Carolina and Camuy are used for the manufacture of glass. The only factory which today makes glass is in the municipality of Guaynabo. It produces bottles exclusively and its principal markets are the industries producing liquor and other beverages. The market for bottles is therefore subject to the ups and downs of those industries.

In 1939–40 some $800,000 worth of bottles were imported into Puerto Rico. During World War II, the island's rum industry grew enormously but was confronted by a serious shortage of bottles. In 1944, the import of bottles reached $4 million. In 1942, the Industrial Development Company built a glass factory in Guaynabo, at an investment of almost $4 million. It began to produce in January 1945. In 1951, the factory was sold to private interests. The decline in the production of rum in 1947–48 and the change from bottles to cans in the case of other products such as beer reduced the demand for bottles. Nevertheless, a strong demand from the rest of the Caribbean has stimulated the industry. With rising production in other branches of the beverage industry, such as beer and soft drinks, and the possible switch back to glass for ecological reasons, the future promises a growth in the demand for bottles which will place the factory in a good economic position. Moreover, the factory is a guarantee that any future expansion of the liquor industry will not be hampered by a shortage of containers, as happened in the past. At the end of 1951 its average daily output was 2,000 gross, or about 100 million bottles per year. In 1966 it produced 3,500 gross daily, or 1,200,000 gross annually, equivalent to 55,000 tons.

SALT

Lacking deposits of rock salt, Puerto Rico extracts its salt from sea water, a process which amounts to manufacturing rather than mining.

The operation is simple. Shallow tanks with large surface areas are built in low places near the coast and are filled with sea water through sluices (Fig. 5.8). After days in the tank, the water is evaporated by the sun, leaving salt crystals on the bottom to be recovered and packed. Generally, for industrial use nothing more is needed. For table use the salt must be refined and ground; however, those operations are simple.

Figure 5.8. General View of Salt Drying Tanks in the Cabo Rojo Salt Works. (Courtesy of the Government of Puerto Rico. Photo by Delano.)

The requirements for a salt factory are low land near the coast to permit the water to flow into the tanks and a dry climate with many days of sunshine for rapid evaporation of the water. At times, one strong rainstorm can ruin the work of weeks. The ideal region for salt factories is therefore the dry south coast, and especially the southwest. Most of the salt consumed in Puerto Rico comes from plants in Cabo Rojo and west of Ponce. East of Ponce the rainfall increases to about 50 inches per year, while at the salt works of the southwest precipitation is about 29 inches or less. Such regions, with scanty rain, yield the largest quantities of salt.

The annual production of Puerto Rico's salt factories, about 30,000 tons, is used for industrial and domestic purposes. In 1952 a modern factory for the manufacture of salt from sea water, destined to produce for the local market, was built in Tallaboa, near Ponce (Fig. 5.9). Today the factory supplements its own production with salt imported in bulk from the Bahama Islands. In the extreme southwestern tip, in Cabo Rojo, another modern salt plant produces salt for local consumption.

Figure 5.9. A modern factory for the manufacture of salt established in Tallaboa, near Ponce, where salt, imported from the Bahama Islands in bulk, is refined.

CEMENT FACTORIES

Raw materials for the manufacture of cement are limestone, clay, siliceous sands, and gypsum. The last is the only imported material; all the others are plentiful on the island. The cement factories in Ponce, Guaynabo, and Dorado with a capacity of 12 million barrels per year are located near good deposits of the required basic materials.

The Guaynabo factory near the town of Cataño across the bay from San Juan was started by the Puerto Rico Reconstruction Administration (PRRA) in 1938, shortly before the war, and its development and expansion were financed by the federal and insular governments. The factory began to produce cement in 1939. Though some pessimists predicted an early, disastrous failure for it, the factory became highly successful and amortized the invested capital through the earnings of a few years. The Ponce factory was built shortly afterwards by private enterprise. During the war years, when it was all but impossible to import cement from the outside, both factories worked at full capacity, so preventing the stoppage of construction in Puerto Rico. In 1950, the government's factory was sold to the Ferré Enterprises which also own the Ponce factory.

Today, Puerto Rico's construction industry absorbs most of the local production plus limited imports from Colombia. In 1940–41, total production was 385,000 barrels, but about 850,000 additional barrels were imported. During and after World War II, the imports of cement virtually ceased, while the local production rose correspondingly. In 1950, more than 3,000 barrels were produced daily, which left a considerable number for export after local demands had been met. Current production of the

Puerto Rico Cement (Ferré Enterprises) factories exceeds 9 million barrels, while the newly built San Juan Cement Factory can produce 2.5 million.

HYDROCARBONS

Puerto Rico's oldest rocks stem from the Cretaceous period. Nowhere on the island are there rocks from the Carboniferous period which was much older and during which by far the largest part of the earth's coal deposits were formed. Nevertheless, in the Tertiary period during which the clays originated, including the clay-shales of the San Sebastian formation, a dense vegetation sprang up in the swamps along the northeast depression; on being buried, together with the swamp muds, these plants came through the centuries to be deposited into layers, first of peat and later of lignite. The lignites, which yield a very poor coal, appear today as carbonaceous lenses within the shales of the San Sebastián formation. The new route of Highway III around Lares cuts through several of those lenses which are very thin, with no commercial value although they were used in the past in local blacksmith shops.

As to the existence of petroleum in Puerto Rico it is of interest to quote U.S.G.S. geologist Watson Monroe's remarks to the author in March 1971.

> You may want to mention the two authentic natural occurrences of petroleum in Puerto Rico. Lynn Glower found drops of petroleum in limestone concretions in a shale of the Cretaceous Cariblanca Formation near Coamo, as reported in the American Association of Petroleum Geologists Bulletin. An oil seep is present beneath the waters of Lago No. 2 northeast of Ponce. Mort Turner collected the soil containing the oil and Fomento's laboratory extracted the oil. Both occurrences are in Cretaceous rocks, but neither is considered commercial. Nevertheless they are encouraging.

Petroleum may be found also in rocks of the Tertiary period. These abound along the island's north and south coasts, and it has been thought possible that they contain oil. A careful study of the Tertiary formation, sponsored by the Development Company, revealed certain possibilities. The sedimentary rocks of the island's two Tertiary basins were deposited in a marine environment. Most of the world's oil-bearing sediments have a similar history, though many are not of Tertiary age. Despite the fact that no positive evidence of oil has been found, the constant rise in prices of oil derivatives, as well as Puerto Rico's industrial expansion, make it imperative that the possibility of oil production on a commercial scale not be overlooked.

Seismographic studies have revealed four interesting structural regions. Only four test wells have been drilled into those structures: three on the south coastal plain in the Santa Isabel-Ponce region and one at Barceloneta on the north coastal plain. None of these found oil or gas.

Despite the negative results of drilling carried on to date, it remains a fact that there are propitious structures of the kind which have yielded oil in various regions of the earth; the prudent attitude should therefore be that "we haven't found it yet," without categorically denying that it exists.

MINERAL WATERS

At times, the presence of certain minerals dissolved in the underground waters makes the latter valuable for the curative powers ascribed to them. Among Puerto Rico's mineral waters, the most famous are those of Coamo which are thermal and, years ago, gave rise to the construction of a spa which is soon to be rebuilt. There are also mineral waters in the Baths of Quintana, north of Ponce, in San Lorenzo and in Arroyo.

The Future of Mining in Puerto Rico

INDUSTRIALIZATION OF THE MINERALS

In *The Geology of Puerto Rico*, Meyerhoff pointed out that the island's principal natural resources are largely materials of low economic value and called attention to the possibilities of developing a few of them, such as clay, siliceous sands, and limestone. Those minerals are now being exploited as raw materials for some of the island's principal industries.

Meyerhoff also remarked on the problems and difficulties involved in the exploitation of metals. The lack of large deposits and of precise information on the existing smaller ones have to date been the main obstacle to development. Among the more promising, he mentioned, with caution, the manganese of Juana Díaz, the gold of Corozal, and the iron of Las Mesas and of the Juncos-Humacao area.

Nevertheless, as has been noted, recent years have opened good prospects for the exploitation of copper ores in the Lares-Utuado-Adjuntas region. The overall effects of such exploitation on the country's economic life must resemble those observed in the new plants which sprang up as a result of oil refining and petrochemical industries in Peñuelas, Guayama, and Yabucoa.

The 1954 Act which created the Mining Commission stated:

> The Commission shall by all reasonable means endeavor to have all commercial minerals extracted in Puerto Rico given the highest degree of refining possible in Puerto Rico, and this requisite shall be a condition for any lease and a factor to be considered in determining the amount of the royalty. Transportation of unrefined or partially refined or processed mineral shall be permitted only after it is established by unquestionable proof before the Commission that it is not commercially sound to carry out more complete refining operations in Puerto Rico.

This is a very valid objective that merits observance in order to further Puerto Rico's development.

The two principal companies which will exploit the copper deposits believe that total production might mount to 200 tons of refined copper per day. That would require an investment (for access roads, shops, warehouses, dams, canals) of about $100 million. The labor force could vary from 800 to 1,000 and its wages would be much higher than those of the present agricultural workers in the region. Some of the laborers will be trained in cooperation with the Division of Vocational Training of the Department of Education, and within the "Scientific Community" project about to be established in Mayagüez where it is planned to create a School of Mining. As evidence of new industrial development, in the definitive contract with the companies, the Director of Development states that a modern plant will be built for the manufacture of sulphuric acid.

The establishment of a sulphuric acid plant will largely solve the problem of air pollution while also producing a raw material used in the manufacture of insecticides, detergents, explosives, fertilizers, and other possible industries.

Significantly, the contract with the copper companies stipulates that only one-third of the metal produced may be used for the manufacture of cables and wire. The remainder is to be used for making a variety of articles for export to the United States and foreign countries.

Mention should here be made of the report submitted by the Senate Commission on Industry and Commerce, in the regular session of July 1965. Working jointly with the Special House Commission and the Senate's Commission on Public Works and Lands, the Commission, in view of the prospects for mining developments, insisted that "the presence and vigilance of the public power should never be absent from such matters." The report mentioned "a possibility of direct participation in the activity by the Economic Development Administration" but, aware of the impact on private enterprises which the administration's attitudes could have in the task of economic development, stressed the matter in the following terms: "A country in the full process of development, such as Puerto Rico certainly is, must maintain a climate favorable for the foreign investors who risk their capital." In the Commission's judgement, that thought does not preclude the possibility of private enterprises with social orientation, insisting that "social responsibility and reasonable profits" are perfectly compatible.

The Commission recommended that exploitation concessions should continue to be granted, always providing that the processing be done locally as far as possible and that lands bought be adequately paid for. It also insisted on the necessity for a vocational mining school and a scholarship fund for the training of professionals specializing in mining. Finally, it endorsed the projects recommended by the Mining Commission for "studying the kaolin deposit in Utuado, Adjuntas, Maricao, San Lorenzo, Las Piedras, and Cabo Rojo; evaluating the quantity and quality of marble deposits available for industrial development; contracting for the services of geologists and chemists for the study of peat and its developmental possibilities; and authorizing the funds required for the extraction of iron from the laterite soils in the Mayagüez-Maricao-Cabo Rojo region."

6

Marine Resources:
The Fishing Industry

Studies of Fishing

Puerto Rico is not a land of fishermen. The condition is commonly ascribed to the scarcity of commercially valuable fish in the waters which surround the island. The Puerto Rican people, however, are large consumers of fish, principally dried fish. In 1950–51, 41 million pounds of fish and fish products were imported while the local production of fresh fish, according to a study made by the Division of Fisheries and Wild Life of the Department of Agriculture, was about 3 million pounds. That situation has led to many investigations of the fishing industry, aimed at increasing its production as well as its contributions to the local market.

Progress has been made in the fishing industry, but the goal is far from being reached. The most recent estimates of the total local fish catch is still annually 3 million pounds worth $1 million. Imports of salted and pickled cod and haddock (the bulk of the fish imports for local consumption) decreased to 24 million pounds worth around $6 million in 1967–68. It is estimated that all seafood products imported for local consumption in 1969 were worth $18 million.[1]

Parallel to this picture of slow growth or actual retrogression in fresh and imported fish consumption another significant fact stands out. Puerto Rico has become the most important tuna-canning center in the Western hemisphere. In 1967–68 canneries in Puerto Rico brought in their own vessels or imported from foreign sources for processing there 152.6 million pounds of tuna valued at $25.8 million.

The study of local fish from a scientific point of view began during the past century with the works, published between 1873 and 1875, of the

---

1. Félix Iñigo, Ralf Juhl, and José A. Suárez-Caabro, "El fomento de la industria pesquera en Puerto Rico y sus perspectivas," *Contribuciones agropecuarias y pesqueras,* Department of Agriculture, San Juan, vol. 11, no. 3 (May 1970).

German naturalist Jean Gundlach and the work in 1883 by the Puerto Rican Dr. Agustín Stahl. In 1898, the Fish and Wild Life Commission of the United States sent a mission to Puerto Rico and the results of their extensive investigations were published in 1900. In 1914, I. T. Nichols made important studies which came to be included in Volume X of the series *Scientific Survey of Puerto Rico and the Virgin Islands*, published by the New York Academy of Sciences.

The most complete investigation of the island's fisheries was made by N. D. Jarvis, technologist of the Federal Bureau of Fisheries, in 1931. A little later, in 1933, S. F. Hildebrand, under the auspices of the Puerto Rican Department of Agriculture and Commerce, studied the Puerto Rican fishing grounds. In 1934, a "Division of Fisheries and Wild Life" was established in the Department of Agriculture to work on the development of marine and freshwater fishing.

In 1951, Félix Iñigo published a study of Puerto Rican fishing entitled *Informe preliminar sobre un estudio de la pesca comercial en Puerto Rico* (Preliminary Report on a Study of Commercial Fishing in Puerto Rico), which was presented at the Conference on Fishing in the Caribbean, held in Trinidad in March 1952. In June 1951, the University of Miami published an excellent "Bibliography on the Fishes and Fisheries of Puerto Rico," by Professor Pedro J. Soler, as Appendix 1, pp. 143–49, of the *Proceedings of the Gulf and Caribbean Fisheries Institute*, November 1950. In 1956, D. S. Erdman, ichthyologist in the Division of Fisheries and Wild Life, published a list of Puerto Rican fish in his work *Informes recientes sobre peces de Puerto Rico* (Recent Reports on Puerto Rican Fish).

During the Second World War, due to increasing difficulty in the importation of fish and the rise in price of dried fish, intensive investigations were made of the commercial phase of fishing. In 1941, the Federal Government contributed with the construction of a laboratory for fishing investigations, located on the grounds of the College of Agriculture in Mayagüez. The laboratory, provided with the most modern equipment, was the fourth of its kind in the hemisphere. In the fiscal year 1941–42, the Laboratory for Fishing Investigations, in cooperation with the Division of Fisheries and Wild Life, started a working program which continued until 1944–45. This program included studies of various methods of preserving fish, such as freezing, salting, drying, and canning, as well as ways of utilizing the industry's various by-products. The program included oceanographic studies of the waters surrounding the island to determine the species of edible fish found there, the times of year when they are most abundant, the location of new fishing banks, the types of boats and equipment best suited to local conditions, and studies on the nature of the ocean bottoms.

After 1944–45, under an agreement between the United States Fish and Wildlife Service and the University of Puerto Rico, the laboratory was transferred to the University of Puerto Rico to serve as a marine biological station, an operation which it still carries out. At present it is known as the Institute of Marine Biology.

In 1945 in an effort to help the fishing industry, the Department of Agriculture and Commerce obtained an appropriation of $250,000 from the Emergency Council and the Insular Legislature that was used for the purchase of refrigeration equipment, to build warehouses, and to acquire fishing gear. Twelve warehouses were established in the principal fishing centers for the purpose of making such materials and equipment available to fishermen.

The Land Authority cooperated by granting lots to fishermen in various fishing zones and establishing fishermen's communities.

Since 1945, the Fisheries Division of the Puerto Rican Agricultural Company developed a two-phase fishing program. One phase of this program was the purchase of a fishing boat, "La Reina del Caribe" (The Queen of the Caribbean) for exploring fishing possibilities in Puerto Rican waters and adjacent zones off the north coast of South America. Biological studies were undertaken to determine the potentialities of fishing grounds north of Venezuela, the Dominican Republic, Haiti, Cuba, and the Bahamas. The high cost of the project and lack of funds forced the Agricultural Company to drop this activity in 1951.

The other part of the program started by the Agricultural Company was direct aid to fishermen, largely by helping them in the sale of their products in the local market. In Fajardo the Company had a purchase station and a supply store. In 1948–49 the Company bought some 215,480 pounds of fish and lobsters from fishermen. The supply store sold the fishermen about $4,401 worth of fishing equipment.

Long before the Agricultural Company folded up in 1955, its fishing program had been terminated and for some years there was no activity in that field. The development of fishing, once again attached to the Department of Agriculture, came gradually to be resumed. In 1966 the following four programs were in operation.

1. Centers for the distribution of materials and fishing gear. These facilities aimed to help the fishermen to acquire, at moderate prices, not only conventional equipment but also that which had been newly developed by fishing technology. That program is conducted by the Administration of Agricultural Services.

2. A credit program for fishermen. In 1959, a joint program by the Department of Agriculture and the Government Development Bank was initiated. Under that program, loans were granted to some 800 fishermen for the acquisition of equipment, such as outboard motors, fishing gear,

and boats. This equipment has improved safety and efficiency and extended the fishermen's radii of operations. The fact that about 65 per cent of the island's fishing boats are now motorized has been one of the basic factors contributing to the marked increase of the catch (Fig. 6.1). In October 1966, that type of credit was taken over by the Agricultural Credit Corporation.

Another source of credit has emerged through the program sponsored by the Federal Economic Opportunities Act.

3. Construction of minimal facilities for fishing ports. This program aims to overcome obstacles encountered by fishermen at their shore bases. This includes: (*a*) construction of piers; (*b*) acquisition of land for launching skids; (*c*) storage sheds for fish; (*d*) beach cabins where the fishermen can keep their motors and gear (Fig. 6.2).

4. Training for fishermen. This is considered the most essential of all the programs for without the proper training of the human element all efforts to fully develop a fishing industry would be virtually futile. The training includes: general principles of mechanics and the operation of gasoline and diesel engines; coastwise navigation, using the compass and navigation charts; demonstrations of the use of modern, improved fishing gear; safety measures on board; sanitary measures and the conservation of fish on board; carpentry, construction, repair and maintenance of fishing gear, and biologic, economic, and social aspects of the fishing industry. The training program is conducted by the Department of Education in collaboration with the Department of Agriculture.

Despite the success of these programs, it has been considered necessary to broaden them through additional projects such as the following.

1. Design of a boat that would meet the conditions best suited for Puerto Rican fishing. The design would include more covered space, a cabin for the fishermen's protection, refrigeration equipment for the conservation of the catch in ice, more tonnage, and echo-sounding equipment with which to locate the banks and avoid the loss of time caused by unfamiliarity with ocean depths.

2. Establishment of a Fishing Industry Laboratory under the program of Federal Law 88–309, known as the "Commercial Fisheries Research and Development Act of 1964." The laboratory would concentrate its investigations on the following: (*a*) potentialities of natural fish resources; (*b*) technology of fishing techniques and methods; (*c*) the technology and marketing of fish products.[2]

3. A project for the development of Caribbean fishing, with headquarters in Barbados. The project is sponsored jointly by the United Nations and the region's ten countries, including Puerto Rico. The project

2. Report on the pilot project for the improvement of the fishing industry and on the living conditions of fishermen, prepared by former Secretary of Commerce Jenaro Baquero and submitted to the Governor of Puerto Rico, December 1965.

Figure 6.1. Fishing Boats. The use of outboard motors improves the fishermen's safety and efficiency and expands their radii of operations. The motors were acquired through a credit program for fishermen carried out jointly by the Department of Agriculture and the Government Development Bank. (Courtesy of the Department of Agriculture of Puerto Rico.)

Figure 6.2. Storage Sheds. Fishermen keep their motors and fishing gear in these sheds near the beaches. (Courtesy of the Department of Agriculture of Puerto Rico.)

will evaluate the region's fishing resources and train officials and teachers to spread knowledge of fish native to each of the respective countries. Conducted by specialists, this program is expected to bring out the special potentialities of tuna and other migratory fish whose catch seems capable of major expansion.

4. Project of fishing villages.[3] In view of the relative backwardness of the fishing industry and the low incomes derived by the Puerto Rican families engaged in it, the Governor of Puerto Rico in 1965 started a pilot project of fishing villages to determine the desirability of establishing similar communities throughout the island. Studies in various parts of the island led to the recommendation of the areas Playuela de Aguadilla and Humacao beach as regions with favorable conditions. Later Barrio Bajos de Patillas was added. The selection of the latter was based on a series of conditions among which the following deserve mention: (a) proximity to relatively rich fishing banks east of Puerto Rico; (b) location near markets; (c) availability of electricity, water, transportation and communications; (d) a generally favorable attitude among members of the community as well as in the municipal authorities of the towns involved; (e) finally some 90 acres, belonging to the Department of Agriculture, and 115 privately owned but undeveloped acres located at the edge of the roadstead (Fig. 6.3).

3. Ibid.

The project of Humacao Beach had the advantage of facing the island's largest "platform," known to extend across the Virgin Islands to Anegada Passage. The majority of fishermen work as such the year round, but some take advantage of the winter season, when the region's ocean current moves away from the coast, to work in agriculture or on public works projects. The discontinuation of sugar shipments from Humacao has forced many dock workers to go into fishing.

Figure 6.3. Cooperative Fishing Boats. Within its projects designed to contribute to the general well-being of fishermen, the government of Puerto Rico acquired these four fishing boats to be operated by the Fishermen's Cooperative of the Bajos de Patillas. (Courtesy of the Department of Agriculture of Puerto Rico.)

The project of Aguadilla Beach had as one of its most important stimuli the opportunity of larger catches and higher incomes as a result of considerable increases in the tuna catches. Here, too, a favorable attitude toward measures for progress is found in the community and its fishermen. There are 26 fishermen and almost all own their boats and fishing gear. The Playuela (Small Beach) was considered the most advisable for the establishment of the pilot project on fishing villages.

On the Playuela in Aguadilla, as well as in the Bajos in Patillas, the sites finally selected for the project, the Department of Agriculture built small cabins for fishermen and storage places for fish, as the first improvements for the fishermen's general well-being.

5. The Institute of Marine Biology is engaged in biologic and oceanographic work, principally in Mona Passage, to increase knowledge both on species and organic productivity. For that purpose it acquired a vessel equipped for studies of salinity, temperatures, and animal and

vegetable plankton. Pending receipt of the results of those investigations, it is difficult to make reliable estimates of Puerto Rico's living marine resources.

6. In July 1967, a project to collect and analyze the statistics of the fishing industry was established in the Department of Agriculture as part of the Fisheries Research and Development Program (PL 88–309) also sponsored by the U. S. Department of Interior. A survey is regularly carried out among Puerto Rico's fishermen, using a sales ticket system. It is estimated to be about 75 per cent accurate.

Production and Employment

Puerto Rico's annual fishing catch was between 3 and 4 million pounds in 1950, or about one and one-half to two pounds per inhabitant, and to date these figures have not changed much. The fact that the annual per capita consumption of fish, in all forms, was some 20 pounds makes it clear that the local production constituted an insignificant part of market needs.

The consumption of 20 pounds of fish per person is relatively high, but it could be higher. In the United States, where meat plays a much more important role in the diet, the per capita consumption of fish is only about 15 pounds, while in Japan, where meat is scarce, it rises to 65 pounds. Both meat and fish are sources of proteins, important in the diet, and people tend to compensate for deficiencies in the one, as do the Japanese, by increasing consumption of the other. The Puerto Ricans should occupy a position halfway between those of the United States and Japan, for though the island, like Japan, is poor in beef cattle, Puerto Ricans have access to nearby sources of beef like the Dominican Republic and the United States and are therefore not forced to consume as much seafood. Nevertheless, meat is generally more expensive than fish and the condition in which it arrives at the market—refrigerated, frozen, or treated in some other manner—drives the cost still higher; the people therefore tend to eat more fish as long as its price remains as low as that of dried fish. Actually, the Virgin Islands, where the per capita annual consumption of fish is 30–35 pounds, occupy the middle position. Since their population is much smaller than Puerto Rico's, and the coast lines are therefore relatively longer than those of the latter, the local fishing industry has come to contribute more to the market; it is calculated that about half of those 30–35 pounds is fresh fish.

The total number of fishermen in Puerto Rico has been variously calculated, but there is agreement on the fact that they comprise a small part of the total population (Fig. 6.4). According to the 1940 Census, out of a total of 601,920 Puerto Rican workers, only 1,090, or a few more than one per thousand, were employed full-time in the fishing industry or silviculture—which is the manner in which the census lumps the occupation.

The 1930 Census listed 1,403 fishermen, using nine motorboats, 240 sail-boats, and 462 rowboats. In 1931, N. D. Jarvis estimated the total number of fishermen at about 1,400, of whom some 600 worked full-time at the trade. During World War II, L. C. Bonnet of the Fisheries Division of the Department of Agriculture and Commerce, estimated the total number of fishermen at about 3,000, reduced in wartime to some 1,500 because of the difficulties encountered in obtaining materials for making and repair-

Figure 6.4. A Day's Catch. The fisherman is happy over the results of one day's efforts. On the bottom of the boat are fine lobsters in addition to fish. (Courtesy of the Department of Agriculture of Puerto Rico.)

ing the required equipment. The Department of Agriculture, which maintains a register of fishermen and their equipment, and requires every fisherman to be licensed, gives the number as of 1970 as 2,200 and the fishing boats as 900. About 62 per cent of them were part-time, only 38 per cent full-time.

According to a study published by the University of Puerto Rico in 1945, the average fisherman sold only 571 pounds of fish monthly, yielding a net income of $47, of which $24 went to the boat's owner, and $23 to the crew, averaging 1.7 men.[4] The earnings, thus, were insignificant.

More recent studies show an annual average catch of 1,500 lbs. per fisherman, a very low figure.

The Geography of Fishing

The reasons given for the small importance of the local fishing industry both in production as well as in employment and income are varied, yet they all boil down undoubtedly to the lack of good fishing banks near Puerto Rico.

Marine life is known to reach its full development at shallow depths of less than 100 fathoms.[5] Fish are scarce at great depths because the sun, source of all animal and vegetable life, cannot penetrate that far. In shallower waters, under the influence of sunlight, an infinite number of microscopic organisms develop, small animals, larvae of larger animals, and diminutive plants. All these float in the water and are called plankton. The small fish eat the plankton and the larger fish gather around the smaller which are their food. The existence of plankton is thus indispensable for an abundance of fish.

Certain other factors, beside that of relatively shallow waters, favor the existence of plankton. Among them are believed to be the mingling of submarine currents with different temperatures, as well as the enormous quantities of organic matters poured into the sea at the mouths of large rivers. The great banks of Newfoundland, Labrador, Europe's North Sea, parts of the coast of the Gulf of Mexico, the west coast of North America and the east coast of Asia, are regions of that type. Puerto Rico's coastal waters, however, are deep and lack great rivers and mixed currents.

The scarcity of fishing banks resulted from certain geologic phenomena at the time of the island's formation. As explained in Chapter 3, the transition from the Tertiary to the Quaternary period was characterized by the appearance of large faults which sheared off Puerto Rico's edges. The outer blocks of those faults plunged to great depths and became part of the ocean bottom. The "Brownson Trough" was formed in the ocean along Puerto Rico's north coast, extending eastward to Anegada Passage and westward to the island of Santo Domingo. In its center, a little north of Mona Passage, is the deepest part of the Atlantic Ocean, the "Nares Deep," or Puerto Rican trench, with a depth of almost 30,000 feet.

Along the south coast there is another great depression, the Tanner Basin, reaching to almost 16,500 feet. Minor depressions in the east and

4. M. Vélez, S. Díaz Pacheco, and P. B. Vázquez Calcerrada, *La pesca y distribución de pescado en Puerto Rico* [Fishing and the distribution of fish in Puerto Rico] (Río Piedras: University of Puerto Rico, Agricultural Experiment Station, June 1945).
5. One fathom equals approximately 5.7 feet (see Appendix T).

west gave rise respectively to the Passages of Anegada and Mona. However, in the middle of all those faults which sheared off, a block remained standing like a submarine platform, or pedestal, jutting out of the sea in the west to form the island of Puerto Rico, and in the east to form those of Vieques, Culebra, and the Virgin Islands (with the exception of St. Croix).

That submarine platform is Puerto Rico's best fishing zone and, as indicated by the map (Fig. 6.5), it is quite small. Along the north coast, the limit of 100 fathoms is about two miles from shore. The same is true along the west coast from Aguadilla to Añasco, but at the latter point the platform widens and between Mayagüez and Boquerón it attains a width of some 17 miles. Along the south coast the platform is a little wider than in the north, especially at La Parguera and between Ponce and Guayama. The platform's greatest extent is in the east coast where, between Fajardo and the island of Anegada of the Lesser Antilles, the depth never exceeds 40 fathoms. In the last-named region, the submarine platform has an area of some 1,500 square miles. That permits Puerto Rico's fishermen to work eastward as far as the edge of the Lesser Antilles; the sea is not too deep, there are fishing banks, and a number of roadsteads and bays are available for shelter in bad weather.

The outlines of the coasts are also important. In Puerto Rico, as a result of faulting and elevation, the coasts tend to be regular and offer few bays and places of shelter. Only a small part of the population is in direct contact with the sea. In other countries, irregular and broken coasts permit the inhabitants to become well acquainted with the sea and look on it as a source of subsistence. Examples of that are ancient Greece and today's North Sea countries. Even in the smaller islands of the Lesser Antilles there is a greater tendency to depend on the sea than in Puerto Rico.

That phenomenon can be observed within Puerto Rico itself. The northwest coast, with its rocky cliffs, isolates people from the sea and does not encourage a fishing industry (Fig. 6.6). The east and south coasts, however, present more favorable conditions. The worst of all coasts for fishing is that of the north, with its straight shore, its absence of fishing banks, and its lack of protection against the Atlantic Ocean, often a very rough body of water.

Fishing Zones

Four fishing zones are recognized in Puerto Rico: the north, south, east, and west coasts.

The North Coast while it is the longest, does not offer very good fishing because of its regularity and the narrowness of the submarine platform extending from it. It extends from Point Agujereada in the northwest to

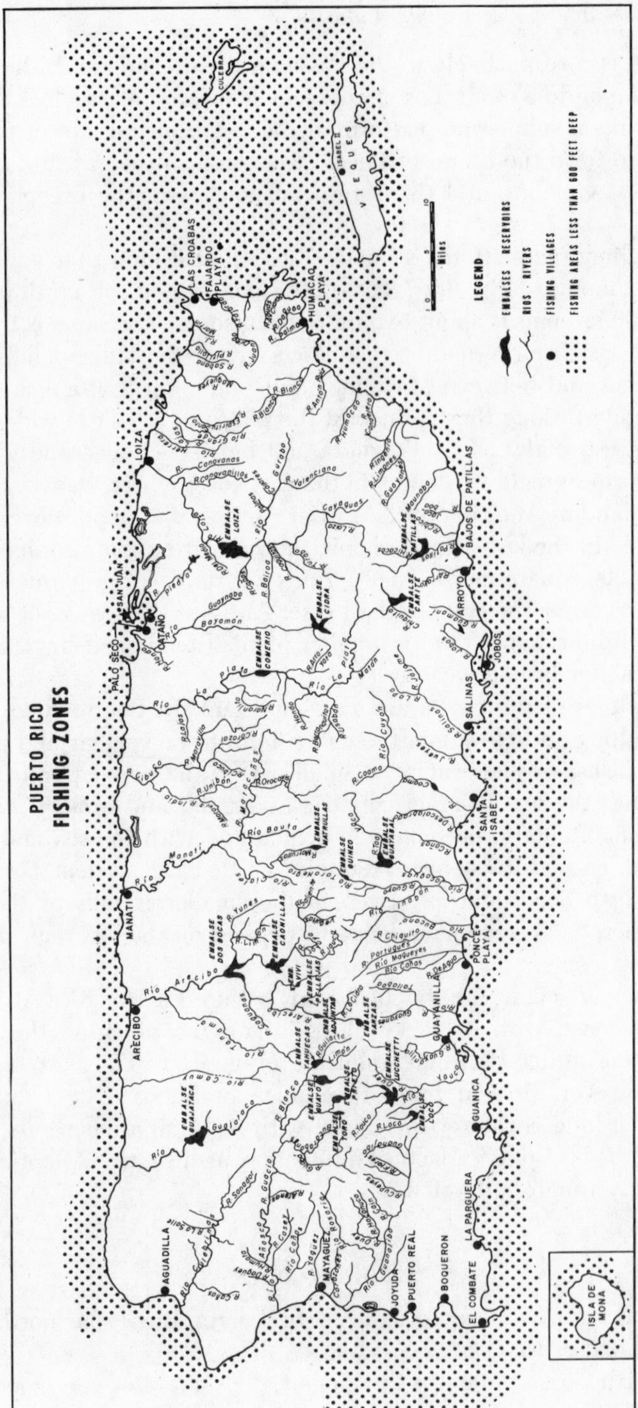
PUERTO RICO
FISHING ZONES
LEGEND
EMBALSES · RESERVOIRS
RIOS · RIVERS
FISHING VILLAGES
FISHING AREAS LESS THAN 600 FEET DEEP
Miles
AGUADILLA
ARECIBO
MANATI
PALO SECO
CATAÑO
SAN JUAN
LOIZA
LAS CROABAS
FAJARDO PLAYA
HUMACAO PLAYA
BAJOS DE PATILLAS
ARROYO
JOBOS
SALINAS
SANTA ISABEL
PONCE PLAYA
GUAYANILLA
GUANICA
LA PARGUERA
EL COMBATE
BOQUERON
PUERTO REAL
JOYUDA
MAYAGUEZ
VIEQUES
CULEBRA
ISABEL II
ISLA DE MONA

Figure 6.5.

Figure 6.6. View of a Section of the Northwest Coast of Puerto Rico, near the Mouth of the Guajataca River. (Courtesy of the University of Puerto Rico. Photo by Samuel A. Santiago.)

Cape San Juan in the northeast. The fishing sites are located near the mouths of the Arecibo, Manatí, and Bayamón Rivers, in San Juan Bay, at Boca de Cangrejos, and at the mouth of the Loíza River. The most important fishing ports are Arecibo, Cataño, San Juan, and Loíza.

In 1950,[6] out of a total Puerto Rican catch of 3,080,000 pounds, about 360,773 pounds, or some 9 per cent, came from the north coast. Nevertheless, in 1946–47, out of a total of 1,906 registered fishermen, 660, or more than 34 per cent, were on the north coast. The reason that so many fishermen were there seems to be that a large number of customers for fresh fish are in that zone. The San Juan Metropolitan Area and the increasing population on the north coast assure a good market and encourage more people to engage in fishing, even if only on a part-time basis. Of the 660 fishermen on the north coast, 165 were in Arecibo, 171 in the San Juan Metropolitan Area, and 155 in Loíza. West of Arecibo there were only 24 fishermen. The remaining fishermen were scattered between Arecibo and the metropolitan area.

The South Coast is the longest. It extends from Cabo Rojo (Red Cape) in the southwest to Punta Yeguas in the southeast. Its shoreline is somewhat irregular, with three important bays, and faces the Caribbean Sea which is much more tranquil than the Atlantic Ocean. The insular platform is also wider than in the north. The sites where the greatest number of fish are found are La Parguera, Guánica, Guayanilla, Playa de Ponce (Ponce Beach), Santa Isabel, Salinas, Arroyo, and Patillas.

In 1950, the South Coast supplied 1,252,525 pounds of fish, or about 30 per cent of the total. On the other hand, in 1946–47, only 479 fishermen were registered there—a little less than 25 per cent of the total. Those men depend on the fishing industry much more than do the fishermen in the North. In the southwest zone (Guayanilla, Guánica, Parguera, Lajas) there were 210 fishermen. The central zone (Ponce, Juana Díaz, Santa Isabel, Peñuelas) had 130, most of them in Ponce where there were 98. The southeast zone (Arroyo, Guayama, Aguirre, Coamo) had 139, more than half of whom (72) were in Arroyo.

The West Coast fishing zone extends from Punta Agujereada in the north to Cabo Rojo in the southwest, and includes Mona Island. The relative abundance of shallows and the irregular coastline are favorable for fish which are especially plentiful at Mona Island, Boquerón, Puerto Real, and Joyuda. The important fishing ports are Aguadilla, Mayagüez, Joyuda, Puerto Real, Boquerón, and El Combate. In 1950 the west coast produced 1,595,200 pounds of fish, or about 37 per cent of the island's total. That figure is considerably higher than that of the south coast. In

6. More recent data by fishing zones are not considered entirely reliable until the fishing statistical project is fully developed.

1946–47, 214 fishermen were registered on the west coast—a little less than 12 per cent of the island's total. It is possible that many of the fishermen on the north and south coasts worked as such only part of the time, devoting the remainder to agriculture or other activities while the west coast had more permanent fishermen, another indication of the region's richness in fishing possibilities.

The East Coast fishing region extends from Cabo San Juan in the northeast to Punta Yegua in the southeast. Despite the coastline's marked irregularities, it is the shortest of the four; however, it includes the islands of Vieques and Culebra and so, when the coastlines of those two bodies are added, it becomes the longest except for the north coast. The sites most favorable for fishing are at Humacao, Naguabo, Ensenada Honda, Vieques, and Culebra. The most important fishing villages are on the beaches of the above-mentioned four cities, at Isabel Segunda (Vieques), and Culebra. Parts of the fishing grounds off the island of Vieques and Ensenada Honda have suffered from the military installations which have made fishing difficult or impossible as they have become "restricted areas." In 1950, production was about 1,036,502 pounds, or about 27 per cent of the island's total, giving the east coast fisheries third place. In 1946–47 there were 553 fishermen, a few less than 29 per cent of the total. The ratio between fishermen and their catch is almost exactly the same as for Puerto Rico as a whole.

Potentialities of the Fishing Industry

The insufficiency of Puerto Rico's internal resources in relation to population bodes well for a flourishing fishing industry. Many of the countries where fishing has become highly developed are poor in internal resources; among them are Norway, Newfoundland, and Iceland, as well as countries and regions whose populations exceed economic possibilities and exert great pressure on them, such as Japan, Java, Spain, Portugal, Scotland, and Brittany. Fish play important roles in all those countries, not only in the people's diets but also as important sources of income through their export in dried, salted, and canned forms throughout the world.

Even though the Puerto Ricans might not aspire to export fish but only to meet local demands, their fishing industry is susceptible to considerable expansion. To produce the 30 to 40 million pounds of dried fish which were imported annually would require the catching and preparation of 175 million pounds of fresh fish. The island's fishing industry would have to expand its present production over 50 times in order to meet the demand for dried fish.

While the local fishing banks cannot support so massive an expansion, it is nevertheless possible to increase greatly the local production and to benefit the fishermen economically by improving the methods of fishing, preserving, and marketing the catch. In 1930, Jarvis estimated that production could be tripled.

In the program described earlier in the chapter, it is contemplated to train and improve the island's fishermen and to develop their industry to the point where they may eventually go beyond local waters, as far as the rich banks off the continental coasts of the Caribbean Sea and the Gulf of Mexico, the Galapagos Islands, and even to the waters off Newfoundland and Labrador which produce most of the dried fish now consumed in Puerto Rico. Fishing far from home is neither very difficult nor dangerous. Most of the fishing nations send their ships to all the world's seas. The Japanese fish as far away as the coasts of the United States, while the Norwegians and the Portuguese swarm in large numbers to the Newfoundland fishing banks.

A part of that objective has been reached. Boats belonging to the tuna fish canneries located in Puerto Rico fish off West Africa and Perú's equatorial coast, whence they bring their catches through the Panama Canal to Puerto Rico.

As a result of government's efforts, four tuna fish canneries have been established in Puerto Rico, three in Mayagüez and the fourth in Ponce; these help the economy considerably by employing more than 1,500 workers. The island's geographic location is ideal for such plants, permitting the fishing boats of the Pacific and the African west coast to unload their catches of tuna in Puerto Rico instead of continuing to the west coast of the United States where the canning plants for fish are located. The fish are processed and canned in Puerto Rico for shipment to the large markets in the eastern United States, with considerable savings, not only through the shorter distances involved, but also because of the lower cost of ocean transportation as compared to overland haulage.

Another possibility for expanding the fishing industry, though of lesser importance, lies in freshwater fishing which has always been important in the larger countries with great rivers and lakes. In some countries, like China, where the pressure of population is so great that fishing at sea as well as in rivers and lakes is not enough, farms include ponds where the country people fish in order to enrich their diets with the needed proteins. Puerto Rico has no large rivers or lakes, but there are many small rivers and some artificial lakes which are used for the propagation of edible freshwater fish.

A basic part of the freshwater fishing program of the Division of Fisheries and Wild Life of the Department of Agriculture is the establishment of fish ponds in those parts of the island where there are no natural sites for propagation. Since a one-acre pond can produce from 200 to 400 pounds of fish annually, that program has been fairly well accepted by the farmers. Today some 400 fish ponds are in operation in Puerto Rico.

Since 1939, the Division of Fisheries and Wild Life has also operated the fish hatchery of Maricao, which produces large numbers of fresh-water fish such as large mouth, black bass, sunfish ("chupas"), cat-fish ("barbudos"), tilapias and others. The hatchery is used for the accli-matization and multiplication of fish which are later distributed to the island's rivers and reservoirs.

Fish have so far been distributed in the reservoirs ("embalses") of Guajataca, Dos Bocas, Garzas, Guineo, Guayabal, Caonillas, Cidra, Matrullas, Patillas, Carite, and Loíza. Bass have also been planted experi-mentally in the Adjuntas, Lares, and Maricao Rivers, and the species has been found to adapt readily to conditions in Puerto Rico's swift-water streams. The project has therefore not been limited to seeding fish in lakes, but has been extended to rivers and ponds as well as irrigation waters.

Today freshwater fish abound in the La Plata, Añasco, Arecibo, Manatí, Loíza, and Mameyes Rivers, as well as in the above-mentioned lakes (Fig. 6.7).

The Division of Fisheries and Wild Life of the Department of Agri-culture experiments with species which might adapt themselves to fresh water, toward the end of improving production as well as quality.

The development of sport, as opposed to commercial, fishing is ex-tremely promising in Puerto Rico. In 1949 the Office of Tourism began to

Figure 6.7. Freshwater Fishing in the Mameyes River near the Town of Palmer. (Courtesy of the University of Puerto Rico. Photo by Samuel A. Santiago.)

investigate the ocean currents of nearby waters, as well as the various kinds of fish which interest sportsmen. Puerto Rican waters were found to be full of the varieties of marine fauna which have made such sports centers as Miami, Acapulco, and others, famous. The Office of Tourism began to organize international tournaments which proved so successful that today two such tournaments for game fish are held every year, organized by yacht clubs. The competition for blue marlin and sailfish is especially rigorous. Several records for men and women have been established and have won for Puerto Rico the title "Capital of the Blue Marlin."

7

The Climate

Weather is the condition of the atmosphere at any one time and place. It is determined through consideration of a number of elements of which the most important are: temperature, precipitation, humidity, winds, and air pressure. These are subject to a series of controls such as latitude, bodies of water, winds, frontal zones, easterly waves, cyclones, hurricanes, troughs (*vaguadas*), and topography or relief. Each of these is carefully observed and the sum of the observations gives us the weather.

Climate is the generalized state of the atmosphere in a given area. It is like a composite picture summarizing the distinct conditions of the atmosphere which have occurred day after day, year after year, over a long period of time. The longer the period, the more representative of the climate are the generalizations which can be made.

The Work of the Weather Bureau

In Puerto Rico the work of the U.S. Weather Bureau goes back to 1898. Earlier, only isolated studies and observations of particular aspects had been made, but a general and continuing picture for the entire island was lacking. The observations dealt mainly with temperatures in their relation to people's comfort and welfare, precipitation in its relation to agriculture, and hurricanes because of their destruction. Since the establishment of the Weather Bureau in San Juan in November 1898, careful and constant observations of the weather have been made and gathered in many parts of the island. As a result of that work we are now able to arrive at a series of generalizations about weather conditions which give us Puerto Rico's climate. One of the most distinguished investigators of the Weather Bureau was Dr. Oliver L. Fassig who spent years in studying the island's climatology and published various articles on the subject. He died before publishing his work on Puerto Rico's climate, but his research was continued by Robert Stone.

The Weather Bureau[1] is in the United States Department of Commerce but, because of the relations between weather and crops, the Federal and Commonwealth Departments of Agriculture are also interested in its work. *The Agricultural Almanac of 1944*[2] published a study by Richard W. Gray on the annual and geographic distribution of rainfall in Puerto Rico. Miles F. Harris, Weather Bureau meteorologist, wrote a study of temperatures in Puerto Rico which was published in the *Agricultural Almanac of 1947*. Other studies of Puerto Rico's climate have been published in the 1941 Annual of the U. S. Department of Agriculture, in *Soil Survey of Puerto Rico* by R. C. Roberts (1942), and in the work on *Types of Agricultural Exploitation in Puerto Rico*, by McCord, Serrallés, and Picó, published in Spanish by the Agricultural Experiment Station of the University of Puerto Rico. In 1935, the Federal Agricultural Experiment Station in Mayagüez, with help from the Puerto Rico Emergency Relief Administration (PRERA), also prepared a study, in the form of graphs, of the island's rainfall. In 1934 Miss Margaret Howarth made Puerto Rico's climate the subject of the thesis for her Master's degree at Clark University.

In recent years many Weather Bureau reports have been published on the island's meteorology and climatology. Outstanding among them is the part about Puerto Rico in the tract *Climates of the States—Puerto Rico and the Virgin Islands*, written by David Smedley in 1961 and translated into Spanish by the Puerto Rico Department of Education in 1965. In March 1966, Dr. José A. Colón present director of the U.S. Weather Bureau prepared a paper "On the Mechanisms for the Production of Rainfall in Puerto Rico" for a seminar on "Water Resources in Puerto Rico."

The most popular part of the work of the Weather Bureau is that related to forecasts, especially during the hurricane season. Among studies of Puerto Rico's hurricanes are those by I. R. Tannehill of the Washington office of the Weather Bureau extending to 1944 and by Professor Rafael W. Ramírez de Arellano of the University of Puerto Rico. The latter deals largely with historic aspects. In 1950, Dr. Luis A. Salivia published his *Historia de los Temporales de Puerto Rico (1508–1949)* (History of Puerto Rico's Storms), a thorough study, arranged chronologically, of all the hurricanes which have swept over the island. The book has an appendix containing a study of the hurricanes which had apparently been headed for the island but changed their courses without affecting it. The book also offers a tabulation of hurricanes by centuries and months.

Among general works which refer to Puerto Rico that by Dunn and Miller, *Atlantic Hurricanes*, published in 1960 and revised in 1964, is outstanding.

---

1. On July 1, 1965, the Weather Bureau was reorganized and combined with the U.S. Coast and Geodetic Survey to form a new subdivision of the Department of Commerce, called the "Environmental Science Service Administration."
2. Annual publication of Puerto Rico's Department of Agriculture and Commerce.

The Institute of Tropical Meteorology

The Institute of Tropical Meteorology of the University of Puerto Rico played an important role in the development of basic theories on modern tropical meteorology. It was established in 1943 in collaboration with the University of Chicago as a center for research and teaching. Among other basic concepts, the institute contributed those of the easterly wave, frontal zones, and the intertropical zone of convergence. It also published important work on the formation and nature of hurricanes.

The University of Chicago withdrew from the work in 1946 and recalled its personnel. The institute then ceased functioning as a research center but continued as a Department of Meteorology in the School of Natural Sciences of the University of Puerto Rico. Today it has its own meteorological observatory and an excellent library and keeps up-to-date a collection of maps and meteorological data on the Caribbean. In gathering observations, it maintains close contacts with the Weather Bureau and other meteorological organizations on the island.

Climatic Controls

The most important factors which influence the island's climate are the following.

1. Latitude. Puerto Rico lies between 17° 52′ and 18° 30′ north of the equator, in the tropical zone. That location gives rise to a series of climatic conditions. In the first place it locates the island within the zone of maximum insolation, between the Tropics of Cancer and Capricorn, where the sun rays at noon are nearly vertical, powerfully heating the earth. Because the earth's axis is inclined 23° 27′ to the plane of its orbit around the sun, always pointing in the same direction (toward the North Star), the noonday sun rays, in the course of a year, fall vertically on a series of points in the entire zone between 23° 27′ north and south of the equator.

Once a year in Puerto Rico, during the second half of December, the noonday sun reaches its farthest distance from the zenith, some 40° to 41° south of that imaginary point in the heaven. The sun rays strike the earth at an angle of 50° to 51° to the horizontal and are unable to warm it as effectively as previously, so marking the onset of the tropical winter. The weather is cool for about three months after December, but the sun then moves again toward the noonday zenith and the weather grows warmer until the end of May, when the zenith is reached and the noon rays are vertical to the earth. That phenomenon marks the beginning of the tropical summer, lasting five months, with many hot days, when the noonday sun stays close to the zenith a relatively long time. Early in June it continues its northward course, changing from the sky's southern half to the northern and moving slightly from the zenith until June 21, the day of the summer solstice, when it is about 5° from Puerto Rico's zenith. Then it returns toward the south, again passing the zenith in Puerto Rico about the middle of July, after which it continues descending until the winter solstice, December 23, when it returns to its original maximum distance from the vertical.

During three months, from early May to early August, Puerto Rico's noonday sun is always almost directly over head, never departing from the zenith by more than five degrees. Before and after that period there are two periods of two months each when the sun departs between 5 and 20 degrees from its vertical noon position. In the first of these, in March and April, when summer is approaching, the sun draws steadily nearer to the zenith; in the second, in August and September, it moves farther away. During seven months of the year, from March to September, the island receives an enormous quantity of solar heat; from October to February, the quantity is smaller, but still appreciable.

2. Insularity. Because Puerto Rico is a relatively small island, the ocean exerts a large influence over its climate. The maritime influence is a moderating one since it is well known that the sea warms up and cools off more slowly than the land, and therefore tends to warm the island in winter and cool it in summer. Puerto Rican temperatures therefore never reach the great extremes of heat and cold which are encountered in the interior of continents as well as, to smaller degrees, on larger islands. The same circumstances of location also results in the fact that maximum and minimum temperatures do not coincide with the dates of maximum and minimum insolation, but there is a lag of one or two months; when the earth should logically begin to cool at the beginning of August, or start to grow warmer in February, the surrounding ocean, warmer than the earth in winter, and cooler in summer, affects the island's temperature during those months.

3. Location with respect to the great masses of earth and water. Puerto Rico is located east of the middle part of the great continent of the Americas and west of the North Atlantic Ocean. That position, together with the island's latitude, places it within the influence of the Great Northern Equatorial Current (Fig. 7.1). The current originates along the African coast, near the Cape Verde Islands, traverses the Atlantic from east to west, and divides into several branches on reaching the Lesser Antilles: one flows toward Florida, passing north of Puerto Rico, Cuba, and the Bahamas; the other flows toward the Gulf of Mexico, south of Puerto Rico, Hispaniola, Jamaica, and Cuba. The latter is reinforced by a branch of the South Atlantic Equatorial Current, proceeding from the Gulf of Guinea.

The fact that the North Equatorial Current is warm and the air above it humid tends to intensify those characteristics in Puerto Rico's climate

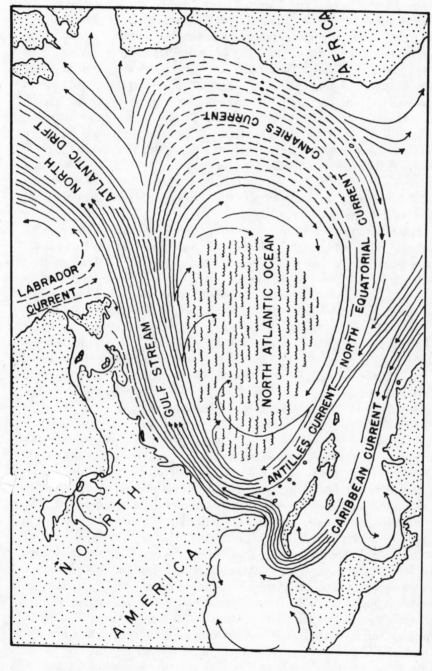

Figure 7.1. Ocean Currents of the North Atlantic. The North Equatorial Current affects Puerto Rico. (Adapted from map published by the American Geographical Society.)

147

which, for that reason and like that of the Antilles in general, is a little warmer than it should be. The fact that evaporation is heavy from the surface of those warm waters results in much cloudiness in the entire Antillean area, and so also in greater opportunities for precipitation.

4. The Trade Winds. The Trades are easterly winds which normally blow between 5° and 30° on either side of the equator and toward that line, NE in the north and SE in the south. When they reach the surface an easterly direction prevails. In the course of the year, following the apparent movements of the sun toward the poles, those two windbelts move, with some lag, in such a manner that in summer the trade winds of the northern hemisphere may extend to 35° N, while their southern edge is about 11° N. In winter the northern edge may reach only to 26° N, while the southern edge of the northern trade winds may extend as far as the equator or even beyond.

Within its latitudes, Puerto Rico is clearly always within the zone of the trade winds which blow from the east (NE-SE) throughout almost the entire year. They are generally characterized as "drying" in that they tend to absorb moisture from the places they pass; however, when forced to rise they cool off and hence drop part of their moisture to produce rain. When the rise is forced by mountain barriers what is called "orographic," or "mountain," rain is produced.

5. The Easterly Waves. Modern developments in the field of tropical meteorology have brought to light an interesting phenomenon: the easterly waves ("las ondas alisias"). They are known to occur in both of the trade wind belts, on both sides of the equator, but have been studied more thoroughly in the North Atlantic and Caribbean regions.

These are simply deformations in the form of horizontal waves which are observed in the isobars (lines of equal pressures), near the earth's surface, moving from east to west (like undulations along a shaken cord) with a constant velocity of 10 to 15 miles per hour. Normally, the isobars curve softly, but when an easterly wave occurs the curvature becomes more pronounced and moves with the trade wind toward the west. The deformation grows more marked with altitude.

The effect of the deformation is to create barometric depressions of low intensity. When the wave is approaching, the wind is from the northeast; when it has passed, the wind veers rapidly to the southeast. Ahead of the wave, west of the axis, the air descends toward the earth and the weather is good, with clear skies and relatively cool temperatures. Behind the wave, east of the axis, the air ascends and there is convection (heat transfer); the skies are cloudy and the weather is stormy, with rain.

Easterly waves play an important part in the island's climate. They move westward across the Caribbean Sea with a frequency of one every 4–5 days, causing frequent rains which at times last two or three days without interruption. The rain comes from the moisture accumulated in the atmosphere through the normal process of convection. The wave abets convection on certain days and hinders it on others, giving rise to successions of rainy and dry days.

6. Fronts. The polar air masses and other circulation systems of middle latitudes are displaced southward toward the tropics contributing greatly to the variety of the climate. The process resembles that of the easterly waves, but with reversed movements and characteristics. These masses are accompanied by large areas of clouds and rains, usually of much less intensity, but longer duration, than those caused by easterly waves. The occurrence of winter days cooler than usual, and at times relatively cold, results from the north winds ("nortes") which follow the fronts. The nearer to the continent, the more accentuated is the phenomenon. It is quite pronounced in Cuba's west where the temperature at times falls below 50° F. Along Puerto Rico's coasts, the drop is normally not below 60° F.

7. Hurricanes. Hurricanes are centers of very low pressure, characteristic of tropical regions east of the great continental lands, marked by devastating winds blowing in circular fashion. Fortunately, few hurricanes pass over Puerto Rico, but every year some pass near enough to affect the island's climate. Aside from their destructiveness, the main effect of hurricanes is heavy rain. The high precipitation of August, September, and October is caused partly by hurricanes.

8. Topography. The island's relief has a double effect on its climate. Air temperatures decrease with increases in altitudes, causing the mountainous regions to be considerably cooler than those along the coasts. As obstacles to the trade winds, the mountains also force them to rise and drop some of their moisture as orographic rains. After the winds have crossed the mountains, they begin to descend and become warmer, again becoming "drying" winds which bring aridity to the regions they traverse. A further role of the mountains is to serve certain areas as a screen and protection against winds, causing those regions to develop other rain-producing processes which would otherwise not occur there. As a result of those matters Puerto Rico, despite its small size, displays a number of distinct and contrasting climatic regions.

Elements of Climate

TEMPERATURE (REFER TO TABLE 7.1)

Puerto Rico has two temperature zones, differentiated by altitude; the "tierra caliente" (hot, tropical) on the plains and low hills and the "tierra templada" (moderate, subtropical) in the upper parts of the mountains (Fig. 7.2). The two zones may be regarded as being separated by the

Table 7.1. Monthly and annual averages of temperature
(in degrees Fahrenheit)

Station	Altitude (feet)	Jan.	Feb.	Mar.	Apr.	May	June	July	Aug.	Sept.	Oct.	Nov.	Dec.	Year
Aguirre	10	75.9	75.6	76.0	77.4	79.4	80.4	81.0	81.4	81.2	80.6	79.2	77.2	78.8
Aibonito	2,000	67.9	67.8	68.6	69.9	71.9	73.4	74.4	74.3	74.1	73.2	71.6	69.4	71.4
Arecibo	50	74.1	74.0	74.8	76.2	78.5	79.5	80.0	80.6	80.5	80.0	78.0	75.4	77.6
Caguas	250	72.4	73.5	73.4	75.5	78.0	79.0	79.2	79.5	79.4	78.5	76.6	73.8	76.5
Canóvanas	30	74.3	74.6	75.4	77.2	79.5	80.5	80.4	81.0	80.7	79.8	78.0	75.8	78.1
Cayey	1,300	69.1	69.1	70.2	71.6	74.0	75.0	75.6	76.0	75.8	75.0	73.2	70.8	73.0
Cidra	1,400	69.3	69.2	70.1	72.2	74.0	74.8	75.5	75.6	75.7	74.9	73.5	71.0	73.0
Corozal	400	72.5	72.4	73.2	74.9	77.2	78.2	78.3	78.5	78.4	78.0	76.2	73.8	76.0
Fajardo	30	76.5	76.1	76.8	78.2	80.2	81.2	81.8	82.1	81.6	80.8	79.2	77.6	79.3
Guayama	50	77.4	77.2	78.0	79.0	80.4	81.1	81.8	82.2	81.8	81.2	80.0	78.6	79.9
Humacao	90	73.8	74.0	75.1	76.8	78.4	79.5	80.0	80.2	79.8	79.0	77.3	74.8	77.4
Isabela	275	74.7	74.4	75.4	76.6	78.4	79.2	80.0	80.1	80.0	79.4	78.0	76.0	77.6
Jayuya	1,700	71.4	71.6	72.0	72.9	74.7	76.5	77.3	77.7	77.1	76.2	74.8	72.6	74.6
Lares	1,200	72.0	71.6	72.6	73.8	75.3	76.5	77.1	77.4	77.1	76.6	75.4	73.2	74.9
Manatí	60	73.2	73.4	74.2	75.9	78.0	79.4	79.7	80.0	79.5	78.8	76.9	74.6	77.0
Maricao	1,500	70.1	69.7	69.9	71.1	72.1	73.3	74.0	74.7	73.4	72.7	72.1	70.9	72.0
Mayagüez	80	74.5	74.4	74.8	76.0	77.8	78.8	78.9	79.2	79.4	79.1	77.6	76.1	77.2
Ponce	40	75.4	75.2	76.0	77.4	79.4	80.6	81.1	81.5	81.2	80.5	79.0	77.0	78.7
Río Piedras	75	73.2	73.0	74.1	75.2	77.8	78.8	79.0	79.4	79.5	78.8	77.0	74.5	76.7
San Germán	350	74.2	74.4	75.0	76.3	78.4	79.6	80.0	80.2	79.9	79.5	78.0	75.8	77.6
San Juan	50	74.9	74.9	75.5	76.7	78.7	79.7	80.0	80.5	80.5	80.0	78.3	76.4	78.0
Puerto Rico	—	73.2	73.2	73.9	75.3	77.2	78.3	78.8	79.1	78.9	78.2	76.7	74.5	76.4

Source: M. F. Harris, "La Temperatura de Puerto Rico," Agricultural Almanac of Puerto Rico, 1947, San Juan, P.R.: Department of Agriculture and Commerce General Administration of Supplies, Office of Services, Printing Division, 347 pages.

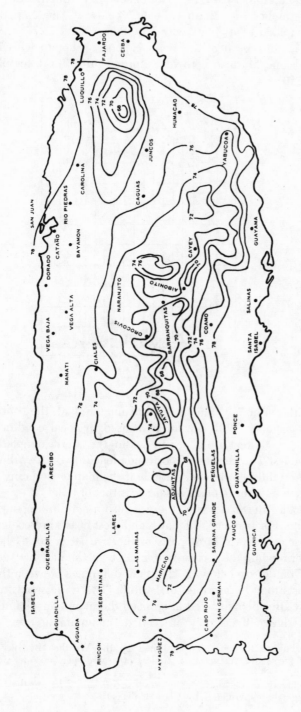

Figure 7.2. Mean Annual Temperatures in Fahrenheit Degrees. (Source: U. S. Weather Bureau in San Juan.)

mean annual isotherm of 74° Fahrenheit (23° Centigrade)[3] above the
74° isotherm lies the "tierra caliente," below it (in temperatures), the
"tierra templada." San Juan, with 78°, Ponce, with 78.7°, and Mayagüez
with 77.2°, are typical of the tierra caliente. Aibonito with 71.4°, Cidra
with 73.3°, and Maricao with 72°, represent the "tierra templada" (Figs.
7.3 and 7.16).[4]

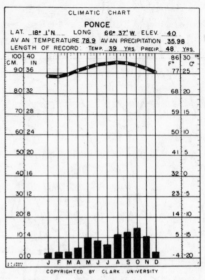

Figure 7.3.

The isotherm of 74° coincides approximately with the contour of 1,000
feet (300 meters). With deviations caused by local conditions, the terrains above 1,000 feet are generally within the "tierra templada," the subtropical zones. The degree of correspondence of the two lines could of
course be established more accurately if the map of isotherms were based
on as large a number of observations as is that of relief.

Within the "tierra caliente" there is also a certain amount of regional
distribution. For instance, the north and west coasts are cooler than those
of the east and south. Most parts of the two latter coasts lie above the
78° isotherm while the former two, except for the part between San Juan
and Río Grande, are below it. The small difference between the north and
south coasts may be ascribed to latitude. The trade winds arrive at the
west coast after being cooled in crossing the mountainous interior; due to
their refreshing effects they are called "mountain breezes," which will

3. According to the custom established by the Weather Bureau and accepted
throughout the island, temperatures, unless otherwise specified, are always given in
degrees Fahrenheit.

4. The climatic charts shown as figures 7.3, 7.6, and 7.13 use the format of their
English originals, copyrighted by Clark University.

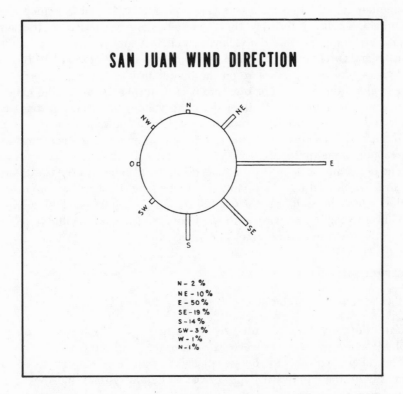

Figure 7.4. Data from the U.S. Weather Bureau in San Juan, Puerto Rico.

ments called "land breezes," which are much gentler than those from the sea.

The trade winds and sea breezes tend to cool the climate, tempering extremes to make the summer heat bearable, especially in the shade. While the trade winds blow steadily throughout the year from virtually the same direction, the breezes, quite variable in intensity, change direction daily. There are many tranquil intervals and two periods of calm: in the first hours of the morning and at dusk. The breeze, moreover, is a low–altitude wind and its principal effect is on the temperature, ventilating and cooling the atmosphere near the coasts. However, since Puerto Rico is a small island, the effects of the sea breeze are felt over an appreciable part of its area.

The sea and land breezes are also important to the fishing industry. The fishermen leave for their work during the night or at the first hours of the day, taking advantage of the land breeze, and return during the day, favored by the sea breeze.

Another type of breeze, very local in character, is that of valley and mountain. Early in the day the mountain slopes, exposed to the sun rays, warm rapidly while the valley at their feet, protected by the mountains, remains relatively cool. As a result an area of high pressure arises in the valley and of low pressure on the mountainside, causing the cool air to rise along the slopes. The opposite occurs during the night; the mountain cools off more rapidly than does the valley, so reversing zones of high and low pressure, and the cooler air from the mountain descends into the valley. In both cases, the tendency is to equalize temperatures on the mountain and in the valley.

The phenomenon is quite pronounced in several valleys of the Cordillera Central. In the south, and probably the west, along the short and protected valleys which descend from the Central Range, the winds which blow from the lower to the higher parts in the first hours of the morning and descend more strongly at nightfall are clearly noticeable.

PRECIPITATION (REFER TO TABLE 7.2)

Two forms of precipitation occur in Puerto Rico, rain and hail.

Causes of rain. Rain is caused by five principal factors: relief or topography, convection, easterly waves, frontal zones, and hurricanes.

The relief gives rise to the so-called "orographic" rains. These occur primarily on the windward slopes of the mountain systems and their corresponding piedmonts, since the moisture is condensed out of the trade winds, to fall as rain, as the winds reach the mountains and are forced to rise. The rain falls not only on the mountains as such, but also on the terrain below them, on the windward side. The other side, the leeward, does not normally receive precipitation from those winds.

The so-called "convection" rain is caused directly by high temperatures. When the air near the land is very warm, which happens during the hours of maximum insolation, it grows lighter and rises, loaded with humidity. On rising, the air is chilled and the humidity condenses to form the clouds which are very common in Puerto Rico about noontime, especially in summer; they resemble enormous masses of cotton, some shaped like great towers, several miles high. The towers are produced by currents of warm air, rising within the clouds, which belong to the "nimbus" and "cumulonimbus" group. When the clouds finally break into rain, the latter is torrential but of short duration.

Convectional and orographic rains result from the chilling of air masses loaded with humidity. They differ in that in the former the air rises because of heat while in the latter it rises because it has reached a mountain slope. The result is the same in both cases, but in the case of orographic rains the clouds are usually not very high above the earth and the rain

Table 7.2. Monthly and annual averages of rainfall
(in inches)

Station	Altitude (feet)	Jan.	Feb.	Mar.	Apr.	May	June	July	Aug.	Sept.	Oct.	Nov.	Dec.	Year
Aguirre (Cambalache)	10	1.43	1.49	1.22	2.05	4.43	4.53	4.26	4.93	5.91	5.80	4.62	1.92	42.59
Arecibo	50	4.92	3.44	3.46	3.77	6.46	3.79	4.66	4.82	5.08	5.00	7.49	5.37	58.26
Cabo Rojo	250	2.27	2.39	4.03	4.08	8.51	3.98	6.04	8.99	8.99	7.61	5.50	3.43	65.82
Caguas	250	3.80	2.36	2.65	3.72	5.82	5.98	6.42	6.47	7.32	6.58	6.35	4.72	62.19
Cayey	1,400	3.31	2.64	2.57	3.64	5.63	5.47	6.08	6.65	6.81	6.43	5.80	3.71	58.74
Cidra	1,400	6.07	3.76	3.73	5.12	7.86	6.76	8.06	9.27	7.70	6.54	6.99	6.24	78.10
Coamo	200	1.31	1.24	0.78	2.10	5.84	4.09	2.91	6.24	5.75	6.75	4.23	1.29	42.53
Coloso	35	2.20	2.15	3.18	5.00	10.82	11.75	9.50	10.80	10.20	8.13	5.94	2.47	82.14
Corozal	400	5.12	4.06	4.06	5.89	8.12	5.53	7.40	8.22	7.41	7.29	8.62	6.77	78.49
Culebra (Naval St.)	50	1.89	1.45	1.26	2.61	4.75	4.69	3.75	4.00	4.44	4.57	5.96	2.54	41.69
Ensenada	10	0.83	1.23	1.37	1.92	3.77	2.46	1.94	3.17	4.27	4.36	3.68	1.46	30.68
Fajardo	40	3.56	3.83	2.82	3.81	6.85	5.58	5.62	6.19	7.30	8.17	7.95	4.62	65.30
Guayama	200	2.49	2.05	1.64	2.65	6.18	5.93	5.20	5.64	7.27	6.71	5.80	2.93	54.49
Humacao (C. Ejemplo)	90	4.52	3.32	3.32	4.59	9.54	9.14	8.26	8.89	9.96	9.66	8.99	5.16	85.35
Isabela (Mora Camp)	275	3.46	2.80	2.90	3.78	6.66	4.94	4.03	5.50	5.67	5.52	6.99	4.29	56.54
La Mina (El Yunque)	2,300	14.89	10.16	7.23	9.54	20.51	18.52	13.59	19.08	14.84	16.40	20.19	15.94	180.89
Lares	1,200	2.96	3.38	4.35	8.33	14.08	9.37	8.13	10.54	11.92	12.15	8.18	4.49	97.88
Maricao	1,500	2.19	3.05	5.11	7.92	12.41	8.70	11.60	14.16	15.14	14.96	8.17	3.71	107.12
Mayaguez	80	2.05	2.04	3.81	5.08	8.46	8.74	10.50	11.18	10.86	9.32	5.81	2.56	80.41
Ponce	40	1.09	1.13	1.17	2.12	4.05	3.40	2.68	4.43	5.01	5.77	4.12	1.13	36.10
Represa Dos Bocas	198	2.48	3.17	3.57	5.63	12.01	7.41	5.69	10.08	9.26	8.69	8.58	3.77	80.34
Represa El Guineo	2,250	4.11	4.72	4.25	7.12	17.13	7.61	7.22	13.48	13.54	15.91	8.37	4.68	108.14
Rio Blanco	500	7.76	6.08	5.36	7.27	15.23	14.14	11.94	13.66	14.22	13.49	13.65	10.85	133.65
Rio Grande	350	6.60	5.95	5.10	5.50	7.30	7.70	12.30	8.10	9.20	7.90	10.30	9.70	94.80
San German	350	1.18	2.08	2.45	2.94	7.56	2.92	3.89	6.35	8.09	9.29	6.73	3.00	56.48
San Juan (Neg. Tiempo)	50	4.34	2.58	2.75	4.13	6.07	5.35	5.73	6.16	6.08	5.60	6.72	5.10	60.81
Puerto Rico	—	73.6	73.5	74.2	75.7	77.7	78.7	79.0	79.5	79.3	78.7	77.4	75.0	76.8

Source: Charles L. McGuinness, "Ground Water Resources of Puerto Rico;" Puerto Rico Aqueduct and Sewer Service, in cooperation with the Geological Survey of the U.S. Department of the Interior, 1948, p. 88.

tends to fall in small drops, resembling a long, intermittent drizzle; the clouds producing convectional rains are found at high altitudes and the drops, uniting with one another in their downward course, fall to earth in fat drops in a heavy, violent storm of short duration, usually in the last hours of the morning or the first in the afternoon.

Other factors producing rain are the easterly waves and cold fronts. As stated above, the air ascends east of the axes of the easterly waves. If that air contains moisture, which is normal in Puerto Rico, it condenses to form clouds which eventually turn into rain. The rains resulting from easterly waves are commonly characterized by their long duration, often an entire day and even two or three, and by the large areas affected.

The rains caused by cold fronts are as usual as those caused by the waves, but the total is smaller. They occur principally in winter.

The hurricanes draw toward themselves enormous air masses in the lower atmosphere; they gyrate in ascending whirlwinds and reach great altitudes. Those air masses are loaded with humidity which condenses on rising and cooling to form the heavy, gray rain clouds which accompany hurricanes. Since hurricanes are relatively rare occurrences, the rains resulting from them are on the whole smaller than those caused by other factors, but their effects are disastrous.

Each of those types of rainfall, according to the form of its origin and the circumstances of its occurrence, affects various of the island's regions with varying effectiveness. The amount of precipitation throughout the year varies with the seasons and with variations in the factors causing it. But it is difficult to determine precisely what part of the rain at any one place is caused by any of the factors described above.

Hail occurs so infrequently in Puerto Rico that it is an object of curiosity. The records show that it has fallen on various occasions in all parts of the island, but more frequently in Las Marías, Coloso, Lares, and Maricao. It is produced by intense convection, usually in summer.

Seasons and fluctuation. The island's regimen of precipitation shows certain clear characterizations. Rainy seasons, humid seasons, and less rainy, or dry, seasons occur everywhere.

The dry season, or that of diminished rain, lasts four or five months. The first four months of the year are always relatively dry except on the west coast and the western and central parts of the mountains, where April is already wet. In those regions and along the south coast, December is also dry; there are always four months of low precipitation and the south coast sees five very dry months.

The rest of the year is rainy but with certain differences according to location. Almost everywhere the rainy season includes two peaks, except for the west coast which has only one, and the Sierra de Luquillo, with three. The first peak occurs at the beginning of the rainy season, in May or June, and the second in November wherever December is a rainy

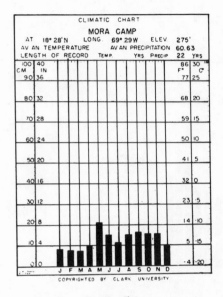

Figure 7.6.

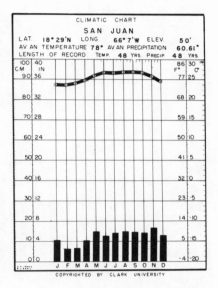

Figure 7.7.

only February and March can be considered dry. The last seven months are rainy. The rain diminishes in June and July, though not as greatly as in region I; it builds up again toward a maximum in November. San Juan is a typical station (Fig. 7.7). Manatí illustrates a transition zone between regions I and II; Canóvanas represents the more humid conditions toward the east and the interior.

No. III is the rainy region of the Sierra de Luquillo. It includes the Río Grande and Luquillo part of the coastal plain and all of the Luquillo Range. The precipitation varies between 90 and 200 inches (Fig. 7.8). It is abundant throughout the year though somewhat lower the first four months, with March as the driest. On the coastal plain (Río Grande, 94.80″) July and November are the wettest months. In the mountains (La Mina, 180.89″) they are May, August, and November. In the southern part (Río Blanco, 133.65″) May and August are the wettest.

This region typifies orographic rain. The east winds, loaded with moisture, are forced to rise over the Sierra de Luquillo and to drop a large part of their moisture on the slopes and peaks of the range. The higher peaks, like el Yunque, are almost always enveloped in clouds, dropping the fine mists of orographic precipitation. The low areas on both sides, such as Río Blanco and Río Grande, also benefit from the rain induced by the chilling of the clouds, but there the rainfall is less heavy. The highest rains on the island have been observed in this region (La Mina, 254.79″).

No. IV is the northeast subhumid region. Precipitation varies between 40 and 70 inches, diminishing from west to east. The region includes the

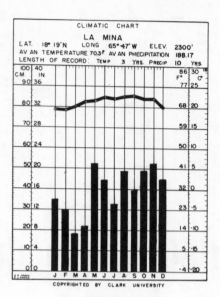

Figure 7.8.

Fajardo coastal plain as far as Ceiba as well as the islands of Vieques and Culebra. Actually Vieques and Culebra comprise a semiarid subregion within the semihumid region. The rain at Fajardo is 65.30″, but Vieques receives only 46.74″, and Culebra 41.69″. The first four months of the year are dry, with lows in February and March, except in Vieques where March and April show the lowest precipitation. In Fajardo the rest of the year is rainy, with maximums in May and October, but on the islands only September, October, and particularly November are truly humid (Fig. 7.9).

Fajardo is in the region which is unaffected by the orographic rains of el Yunque. On the contrary, the trade winds across the coast freely with their convection clouds which yield the most rain in summer. Culebra and Vieques are small islands with moderate relief which cannot produce much orographic rain or keep back many of the clouds to give them convection rains.

No. V consists of the humid valleys of the east, with 70 to 90 inches of rain, including the coastal valleys from Naguabo to Maunabo. The rain is well distributed, as in region II, but the first four months, especially in February, are driest. The rest of the year is humid, with a maximum in May or June and another in September, October, or November. The typical station is Naguabo with 84.54″ as the average annual (Fig. 7.10).

No. VI is the arid coastal plain of the south. It divides into two subregions, No. VI-A in the west, which is the more arid of the two, and No. VI-B in the east.

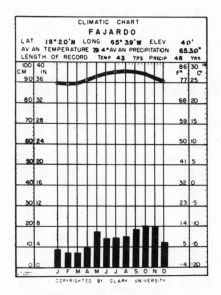

Figure 7.9.

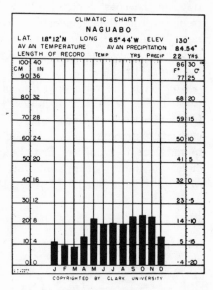

Figure 7.10.

Subregion VI-B extends from Patillas to Salinas, with 40–60 inches of rain. The first four months of the year, plus December, are dry, with March the driest (Fig. 7.11). In Guayama (54.49″) the remaining months are humid, with maximums in May and September; in Aguirre (42.59″) only August, September, and October can be regarded as truly humid. Altogether, there are again two peaks, a small one in June and one slightly higher in September. The rain diminishes toward the west but increases toward the interior, with 66.17″ at the Patillas reservoir.

Subregion VI-A extends from Salinas to Boquerón. Only three or four months of the year are humid. December and the first four months are very dry. May is relatively humid but another drought occurs in June and July. The months from August to November are somewhat humid, with peaks in September and October. Aridity increases toward the west, Santa Isabel (36.61″) and Ponce (36.10″) are representative of the middle part while the San Francisco sugar mill south of Yauco, with 34.67″, and Ensenada, with 30.68″, represent the extreme conditions in the southwest. Precipitation increases toward the interior and the west coast. Yauco has 39.51″ and Lajas 47.61″.

The idea that the aridity of this region is caused by its location on the leeward side of the Central Range and the Sierra de Cayey stems from the common concept of the trade winds as always coming from the northeast. But the fact that in those latitudes the trade winds almost always blow from the east makes it impossible for the south coast to be on the "leeward" side of the mountains. The fact that the trade winds freely traverse the coastal plain probably means that they are not prevented from carrying their convection clouds, so diminishing the possibility of rain. On the other hand, when the trade winds come from the southeast, in summer, they must drop a certain amount of orographic rain on ascending the south slopes of the mountains.

No. VII is the wet-dry region of the western coastal valleys, with 65 to 90 inches of rain. It includes the lower parts of those valleys, from Guanajibo to Culebrinas, and the intervening hills. As opposed to the east coast, precipitation occurs eight months a year, with a single maximum. December and the first three months are extremely dry but a decided maximum occurs from July to September. The typical station is Mayagüez with 80.41″ (Fig. 7.12). Cabo Rojo in the transition area

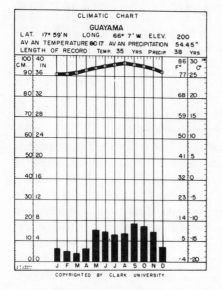

Figure 7.11.

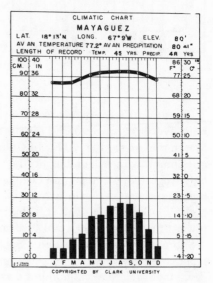

Figure 7.12.

toward region VI, is more arid, with 65.82″, including two maximums, one in May and the other in August and September. Coloso (82.14″) is wetter than Mayagüez but its regimen also differs from the typical in that it includes two maximums, one in May-June and the other in August-September.

The western valleys are in the typical zone of convection rains. Screened from the trade winds by the central mountains and their westward spurs, the convection processes have ample chances to develop in summer. In Mayagüez rain generally falls in the afternoon, at the warmest time of day. Convection is retarded in winter and the rains abate. The dry months in Mayagüez rival in aridity those of the south coast.

In summer the west coast occasionally experiences water-spouts, which seem to be related to the free and intensive development of convection conditions. These occur on land as whirlwinds though they should more properly be called tropical tornados. They are violent eddies of air, beginning as masses of air, which descend toward the earth from rain clouds to meet other currents, loaded with humidity, which rise from low-pressure areas. They don't always touch the earth, but when they do the centrifugal force of the wind and the low pressure is enormous and can cause great destruction to houses and fields, though over a limited area. Tropical tornados and water-spouts are familiar spectacles to the inhabitants of western cities such as Mayagüez and Aguadilla. In that region precipitation in the form of hail occurs often.

No. VIII is the humid region of the northern hills. It includes the hills and valleys between Moca and a point south of Río Piedras and receives between 70 and 100 inches of rain. December and the first three months are dry in the west, while in the east December is rainy and the more or less dry months are from January to April. The rainy months offer two maximums, one in May and the other in October, with a diminution of precipitation in June and July. Rainfall lessens from west to east, with 97.10″ in San Sebastián, 85.06″ in Bayaney, 80.34″ in Dos Bocas, and 78.49″ in Corozal (Fig. 7.13). However, advancing eastward, the precipitation becomes more evenly distributed throughout the year; in Corozal, for instance, there is no truly dry month. The regimen in those northern hills resembles that of the north coast, but the region is more humid because the higher and less regular relief offers more opportunities for orographic rains.

No. IX is like the other side of the coin. It comprises the *semiarid hills of the south,* with annual precipitation between 40 and 70 inches, extending along the southern slopes of the Central Range and over a part of the southern piedmont hills. It is wetter toward the west, with 67.07″ in San Germán, but in Sabana Grande the precipitation is only 56.48″, in Peñuelas 53″ or 54″, and in Coamo 42.53″ (Fig. 7.14). The rainfall increases toward the mountains, with 56.29″ at the Guayabal reservoir. In the west, December and the first three months are dry, with a minimum in January. Farther east the dryness continues into April. The rainy season includes two maximums in May and October, and a period of less rain in June or July. The dry season is very marked, as on the coast, greatly affecting the pastures which, however, recover rapidly in the rainy months.

No. X is the rainy region of the western mountains, including some of those in the central part. It is Puerto Rico's coffee region with an average annual rainfall of 70 to 120 inches. It is also the highest part of the island where the orographic rains are very important. Lares, at 1,200 feet, has 97.88″, annually; Maricao and Adjuntas, at more than 1,500 feet, have 107.12″ and 85.99″, respectively (Fig. 7.15). The difference is due to the

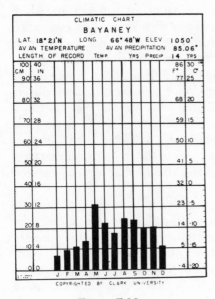

Figure 7.13.

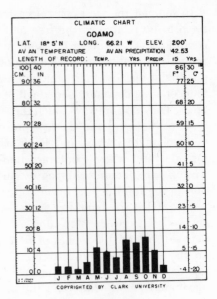

Figure 7.14.

fact that Adjuntas, lying in a sheltered valley, receives less orographic rain than does Maricao. The same thing occurs in Utuado (76.90″) and Orocovis (74.10″), which is less humid.

The dry season is from December to March, when the rain diminishes to 2 or 3 inches as against 12 or 15 inches during the rainier months from May to September or October. The maximum of May is pronounced in this region.

No. XI, the humid region of the eastern mountains, is Puerto Rico's tobacco region with an annual precipitation between 50 and 80 inches. There seems to be less orographic rain, perhaps because of the region's lower altitude, and also because a large part of it lies in the lee of the Sierra de Luquillo where the winds can't bring it much moisture. The phenomenon is even more noticeable in high, sheltered valleys where convection is less important, as at Cayey (58.74″).

This region, however, presents a few problems which are not easily explained. Cidra (78.10″) is located on an elevated plain at almost the same altitude as Cayey, but without the latter's shield of mountains, while Aibonito, in a similar setting and at a higher altitude has only 60.48″ (Fig. 7.16). On rising from Cidra to Aibonito the clouds may well drop their moisture on the mountain slopes; on arriving on the peneplain they stop rising while not being sufficiently chilled to continue producing abundant precipitation. On the other hand, while Caguas (62.19″) and Juncos (59.57″) are located in a relatively sheltered valley, leeward of the Luquillo Range, San Lorenzo, a little farther south and virtually at

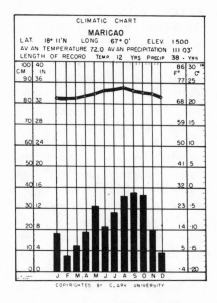

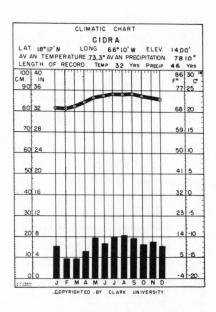

Figure 7.15.   Figure 7.16.

the same altitude, receives 74.54″. Being close to the northern slope of
the Sierra de Cayey, San Lorenzo may well benefit from the orographic
rains produced by that range.

The regimen is variable. Annual precipitation of some 120 inches has
been produced (San Lorenzo-Espino). January to April are generally
relatively dry months except in Cidra, where January is humid. December
is relatively dry in Cayey and Juncos, and humid elsewhere. The remaining months are humid, with a small maximum in May and one somewhat
larger in any month from August to October.

Effects on Farming. Water is indispensable to life. Animals and man
generally move toward sites where the vital water is available or build
artificial systems for bringing it from afar. But the greater part of the
plants, fixed to the soil by their roots, must depend on the soil's humidity
which, in Puerto Rico's climate, is brought by rains. Thence stems the
importance of rainfall to farming.

The rain must come in sufficient quantities. High temperatures throughout the year result in high evaporation of moisture accumulated in the
soil. According to Roberts,[5] 30″ of rain in Puerto Rico is the equivalent
of 15″ in the United States, for instance on the Western Great Plains under

5. R. C. Roberts, *Soil Survey of Puerto Rico*, U.S. Department of Agriculture,
Bureau of Plant Industry; University of Puerto Rico Agricultural Experiment Station
(Washington D.C., 1942), p. 53.

markedly arid conditions. Even a precipitation of 45″ tends to create semiarid conditions in Puerto Rico. For most farming only 60″ and more can be considered enough.

The map of mean annual rainfall (Fig. 7.17) shows that a considerable part of the islands northwest, Region I, receives less than 60 inches. The region is therefore classed as subhumid. Region IV is also subhumid while regions VI and VIII are arid.

The annual total precipitation alone is not enough. The slope of the land must also be considered since flat land retains more moisture than does land at a slope. Drainage conditions also affect the situation since lands toward which waters converge, such as valley bottoms, are more humid than the uplands along the divides. In the regions of karst topography, the bottoms of the sinkholes are wetter than are the haystacks. The physical character of the soil is an important factor. Sandy or rocky soil is permeable and much drier than clayey soil although the two receive equal amounts of rain. Varying degrees of insolation play their roles in determining if a given quantity of rain is more effective or less effective. Often the soils on the south slopes of a hill, exposed to more insolation, are drier than those on the north slopes. These, however, are secondary and local factors. The amount of annual precipitation and its distribution are basic in determining whether or not certain kinds of agriculture are possible.

Each of the distinctive kinds of farming practiced in Puerto Rico has its maximum and minimum limits (since an excess of rain can also damage crops) and an optimum under which the plants grow better and produce more.

If sugar cane, for instance, depended exclusively on rain, its commercial cultivation would be virtually impossible wherever the annual precipitation did not reach fifty inches. Production is possible between 50 and 60 inches, but even with other factors also favorable, the farmer can count on a good crop only where there are more than 75 inches of rainfall.

For coffee, bananas, and plantains, adequate rainfall begins at 80 inches; with less, the yield is poor. Cotton, on the other hand, yields best when precipitation is below 60 inches. Corn is also a preferred crop in the arid regions, not only because it produces more with less rain but also because of its rapid growth which yields a good harvest in a short humid period. Tobacco, though tolerant of varying conditions of humidity, develops different types of leaves according to the climate.

The importance of rainfall to Puerto Rican farming is so great that certain coincidences can be seen between the map of precipitation and one showing the distribution of various crops. Only where man has supplemented rainfall with irrigation does the influence of precipitation diminish.

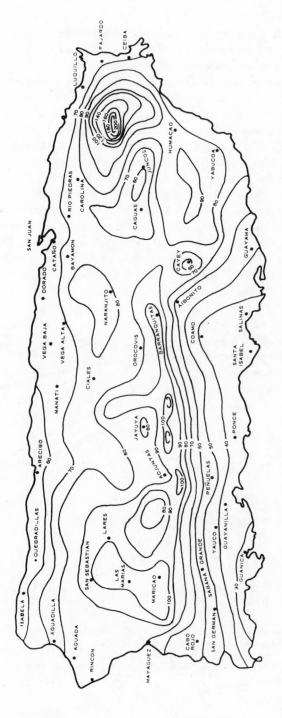

Figure 7.17. Average Annual Rainfall in Inches. (Source: Puerto Rico Water Resources Authority.)

169

HURRICANES

Hurricanes are common weather elements in the Caribbean during the warmest months, from June to November (Fig. 7.18).[6] The popular concept of a hurricane is that of a mass of winds, clouds, and rains, which moves over the earth's surface at elaborate velocities in such a way that observers at a given point see it as something which approaches, passes the point, and goes on, leaving behind a wake of destruction.

If we could see a hurricane from a satellite in space, we would observe that this mass of air moves in a circular manner like a great, spinning disk. It spins counterclockwise in the northern hemisphere and clockwise in the southern.

Actually, a hurricane is an enormous whirlpool in the air which, like all whirlpools, has its vortex, or axis of the spinning movement. The atmospheric pressure is very low in that vortex, and the winds, attracted by the low pressure, stream toward it from all directions. Because of the earths' rotation, they don't flow directly but in a spiral movement, gathering speed as they approach the vortex. The winds which are nearest

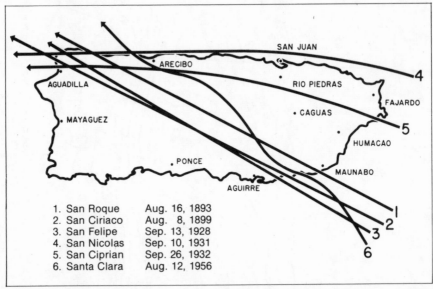

1. San Roque	Aug. 16, 1893	
2. San Ciriaco	Aug. 8, 1899	
3. San Felipe	Sep. 13, 1928	
4. San Nicolas	Sep. 10, 1931	
5. San Ciprian	Sep. 26, 1932	
6. Santa Clara	Aug. 12, 1956	

Figure 7.18. Route Followed by Most Important Hurricanes Affecting Puerto Rico since 1893. (Source: U.S. Weather Bureau in San Juan.)

6. *Translator's note:* Unlike today's Weather Bureau, which identifies observed hurricanes with the given names of women in alphabetic order (so enraging members of the "Women's Lib" movement) the Puerto Ricans have long, as though in rebuke, named the hurricanes which damaged their island after the saints on whose days they occurred.

the vortex are those which are the fastest, most powerful, and more destructive.

On the other hand, within the vortex itself, the center of the hurricane, an absolute calm prevails, despite the very low pressure. That zone of calm tends to be small, a few miles in diameter, but around it is a ring of destruction whose winds frequently gyrate at speeds between 100 and 200 m.p.h. The vortex has no clouds, rain, or winds. On looking up, one sees blue sky in the daytime and stars at night. But in all directions on the horizon is the enormous, threatening wall of dark clouds in agitated motion, containing all of nature's violence and destructive forces. The vortex of the hurricane is at one and the same time a magnificent and terrible spectacle.

Since the hurricane, in general, follows the path of the trade winds, the winds in its northerly half usually exceed in velocity those in the southern half by fifteen or twenty miles per hour.

In Puerto Rico the highest wind velocity reached by a hurricane was 150 miles per hour, during San Felipe in 1928.

In addition to its gyratory movement, a hurricane moves forward in a certain direction. While the gyratory movement is rapid and the cause of all destruction, the forward movement is slow, usually, 15 to 20 m.p.h., the average speed of the trade winds. As a result of the forward movement, the hurricane's destructive power is carried from place to place, permitting one hurricane to damage a large area along its route. Though the storm's movement is slow, the damages are enormous.

In the Caribbean the typical hurricane path is shaped like a parab la toward the west and north. Though, in general, the cyclonic path runs east–west across the Atlantic and Caribbean, various paths have been observed to undergo sinuous changes of up to 50 miles. On arrival at the Bahama Islands, they begin to veer toward the north, but at times soon change eastward across the North Atlantic, occasionally arriving at the coasts of Europe.

Other hurricanes move directly westward without veering, to strike the coasts of Central America and Mexico.

Since the forward movement is slow, the meteorologists—after determining the position of the vortex, the course it has followed, the pace of the forward movement, and the barometric pressures at the west and northwest of the phenomenon—are able to predict fairly accurately when it will affect a specific place, and so give warning to permit all possible precautions. Nevertheless, it is difficult to predict the exact path. The abundance of meteorological stations in the Caribbean area, the use of aircraft, radar, and artificial satellites, help to improve the system of prediction and warning; as yet, however, there is no way of foreseeing with any degree of precision when a hurricane will take an abnormal path.

The basic problem is to determine precisely the direction and speed of the wind current which is moving the storm. The current is an integral part of the entire earth's planetary circulation and is an atmospheric aspect which is still very difficult to observe and predict.

Although hurricanes can appear any time after June, the most dangerous time for Puerto Rico is between August 15 and October 15, and September is the month of greatest frequency. More than 60 per cent of the hurricanes which struck Puerto Rico between 1899 and 1932 came in that month, among them the two most violent and of saddest memory: San Felipe and San Ciprián.

It is now believed that most hurricanes originate in the eastern part of the North Atlantic, west of the Cape Verde Islands. Others, of lesser intensity, arising at the beginnings or ends of the cyclonic seasons, are incubated north of Panama and affect parts of Central America, Mexico, Cuba, and the southern United States. The hurricanes which scourge Puerto Rico usually originate in the Atlantic, between Africa and the Lesser Antilles. They begin as wide low-pressure areas which contract until they form whirlwinds, growing in intensity as they are fed by the warm waters of the Atlantic.

What causes hurricanes still puzzles meteorologists. Some are formed in late summer and early autumn, east of Africa, because the belt of equatorial calms in the intertropical front reaches that far at that time of year. The warm air rises and constantly forms a large belt of low pressure which—its vortices accentuated and transported by the trade winds—arrives at the Windward or Leeward Islands within some days in the form of destructive hurricanes, ready to sow desolation in the Caribbean. The hurricanes which are formed in the tropical Atlantic usually result from intensifications of the easterly waves while those which arise in the western Caribbean, north of Panama, originate from cold fronts.

To observers on the ground the hurricane, coming from the east, goes through three stages in its passage: the beginning, when the wind comes from the north and east; the calm when the vortex passes the affected point; and finally the "turn-over," called "revirá" or "virazón" in Puerto Rico, which comprises the strong winds from the south or southeast, following the passage of the vortex.

Many people believe that the "virazón" means another passage of the hurricane over the same spot. This belief is absolutely not true. The famous and dreaded "virazón" is caused exclusively by the winds in the hurricane's rear, flowing toward the low-pressure center which has already passed to the west of the affected spot. However, a few cases are known in which a hurricane returned to go over the same spot; one such occurred in northwestern Cuba, but was caused by very exceptional barometric conditions.

A hurricane's destructiveness varies with the proximity within which the vortex passes over the affected spot. The places traversed by the vortex always experience the greatest destruction. There are moreover two belts, along the two sides of the vortex's path, where the destruction is less, being in inverse ratio to the distance traveled by the vortex. The width of those belts varies with the diameter of the hurricane. A large hurricane may have a diameter of 200 to 300 miles; a small one seldom exceeds 50–100 miles. One of the disadvantages of Puerto Rico's small size is that a hurricane like San Ciriaco, or San Felipe, which passes along the island's center, affects it totally. However, the size of the hurricane has no relation to its destructiveness which stems much more from the low barometric pressure in its center.

San Roque, San Ciriaco, San Felipe, San Nicolás, San Ciprián, and Santa Clara. Recent decades have seen six hurricanes whose vortices passed directly over Puerto Rico and which therefore caused major destruction. These were the famous hurricanes of San Roque, San Ciriaco, San Felipe, San Nicolás, San Ciprián, and Santa Clara (Fig. 7.19). Table 7.3 gives data on those storms.

Table 7.3. Hurricanes that have struck Puerto Rico

Name of Hurricane	Date	Hours, Center over Island No.	Minimum Pressure in San Juan (Inches)	Maximum Wind in San Juan (M.p.H)	Deaths (No.)	Estimat. Damages (Dollars)
San Roque	8/16/93	7	29.17	—	4	—
San Ciriaco	8/ 8/99	6	29.23	75	3,000	20 million
San Felipe	9/13/28	8	28.74	150	300	50 million
San Nicolás	9/10/31	6	29.17	90	2	200 thousand
San Ciprián	9/26/32	7	28.95	120	225	30 million
Sta. Clara (Betsy)	8/12/56	3	29.61	90	11	40 million

Climate and Man in Puerto Rico

Early in this century most North American and German geographers subscribed to the "determinist" theory, which held that man is a docile doll in the hands of natural forces, principally climate. Heavy emphasis was placed on climates which were favorable or unfavorable to civilization and progress. The temperate climate, moderately humid, was regarded as optimum for higher efficiency and progress in all branches of human endeavor. Extremely cold or hot climates, humid or dry, were harmful to human activity. Puerto Rico's climate was classified among the hot and humid.

Figure 7.19. Destruction Caused by the Hurricane Santa Clara, August, 1956.

It was said that the island's climate, montonous and almost unvaried, failed adequately to stimulate the intellectual faculties. The excess of heat and the absence of cold as well as of marked changes in temperature, were said to eliminate the need for additional efforts toward acclimatization, a situation which was thought to be detrimental to health and physical vigor. Similarly, Puerto Ricans can cultivate the soil the year round without providing for winter and have no incentive for producing and earning more in order to have foodstuffs when the soils fail to yield them and in order to pay the cost of heavy clothing for winter and fuels for heating houses. The absence of those stimulants of human activity to which men are subjected in the temperate zones, was said to have created, in Puerto Rico, an indolent and lazy people, loving the hammock and the "siesta," suffering from tropical inertia and the kind of lethargy which the Puerto Ricans call "aplatanamiento." Under those conditions, the only qualities thought to be susceptible to great development were the imagination, passions, and vices. Even Puerto Rico's own Don Antonio Pedreira, in his great work *Insularismo*, ascribed the lethargy of the Puerto Ricans to the climate.[7]

7. "The climate robs us of our will and causes the rapid deterioration of our psychology. The national characteristic which we call *aplatanamiento* results from the debilitating pressure of heat on man. In our country, to *aplatanar* oneself is a kind of inhibition, of mental drowsiness, and lack of aggressiveness. It means to follow, without rushing, comfortably and routinely, the course of one's life, without changes or worries, scuttling our aspirations, and indifferent in the face of the future. . . ." Antonio S. Pedreira, *Insularismo* (Madrid: Tipografía Artística, 1934), pp. 39–40.

While the foregoing is a comfortable way of explaining some few human characteristics, it is unacceptable in so exaggerated a form. A few extreme tropical regions have conditions adverse to human habitation, but they are very small. Actually, there is no such thing as an ideal climate. While Puerto Rico's climate aids human life in some ways, it imposes difficulties in others and so stimulates efforts to overcome those difficulties.

The absence of truly low temperatures eliminates the need for expensive winter clothing, but the warm months demand many changes of clothing. It is therefore hard to say whether the hot weather reduces the cost of clothing. Certainly, the climate eliminates the need for heating houses in winter, though it also calls for more expenditures for cooling them in summer.

Many of Puerto Rico's deficiencies can be explained in terms of its small size and poor area, political, social and economic factors, habits of life, historic conditions, and other physical and human factors which have nothing to do with climate. While there are loafers everywhere, the island's country people are on the whole industrious and hard-working. If it is true that they lack the stimulation of winter, they do have the stimulation of an overpopulated land on which the last acre must be made productive.

It is extremely difficult to prove the theory that climatic changes influence intellectual powers. In the so-called temperate lands, the often excessive summer heat is at times detrimental to the intellectual and physical faculties; however, the people of Puerto Rico, accustomed to their warm but never oppressive temperatures, find that the summers do not materially affect their powers to think and act.

There can be no doubt that the island's relatively warm winters benefit the tourist industry.

Some disadvantages, however, seem to stem from the high temperatures. The average temperature, nearly 80 degrees, is precisely the optimum for the development of animal and vegetable life, which calls for an incessant struggle against all types of harmful insect pests, noxious weeds, and other stubborn plagues. The temperate-zone farmer is able to rest in winter or leave home to amuse himself elsewhere. The heat and humidity also favor the development of disease-bearing germs. At the same time, the absence of winter means that many crop-plants are not forced to store up certain nutritional substances, which may be the reason why temperate zone crops are more nourishing than are those of the tropics.

Recent studies have shown certain relations between climate, mainly temperature and humidity, and the physical and mental output of individuals, but these seem to be influencing factors rather than determinants. To be sure, some degrees of temperature and humidity are best for human comfort and activity. Where those, known as T-H, are too high or low, man turns to heating or air conditioning.

Another negative aspect of Puerto Rico's climate is the extreme inequality and irregularity of the precipitation. The year without a period of drought adversely affecting agriculture, is rare, especially on the south coast. Periodically, those periods become aggravated, calling for federal aid in some cases and Commonwealth aid in others.

In addition to such droughts, Puerto Rico experiences heavy flood in the lowlands near rivers, especially during the hurricane seasons.

On the matter of man and the tropical climate, it is interesting to note the opinion of Earl Parker Hanson, distinguished professor, geographer, and explorer of the tropics. According to Hanson,[8] the essential requirements for a healthy and normal life in hot countries are, primarily: "good psychological adjustment of which the ability to laugh is almost invariably a favorable symptom; second: physical labor or participation in sports; thirdly: a balanced diet; and finally: medical and sanitary care." Summing up, Hanson insists on the importance to health of living a so-called "normal" life, in the tropics as well as everywhere else. Some years ago, Dr. Antonio Fernós Isern wrote: "The climate is a factor but civilization makes it a far less important factor today than formerly. Civilized man can live in almost any climate: he knows how to create his own climate to his liking."[9]

A tropical people can become every bit as cultured, healthy, and active as a people of the temperate zones. The question of becoming outstanding in certain fields hinges on many other matters, such as the ability to exploit natural resources. Puerto Rico is at a disadvantage through the relative poverty of its mineral, forest, and fishing resources, and its relative scarcity of good soils. However, it does enjoy a good climate, cool in the highlands and not too warm—without drastic winters—in the lowlands.

The apparent disadvantages of relative aridity in certain regions are simply climatic challenges which the island's people have learned to meet. Where nature is ungenerous in the matter of sufficient rain for agriculture, man has built impressive engineering works to bring water from places where it is found in excess. Lands which formerly, because of their aridity, could be used only for pasturing cattle have by such means transformed into fertile countrysides. Elsewhere, excessive rains seemed like a curse because they washed cultivable soils from the mountains and carried them to the sea in heavy streams. Today that force is being regulated and put to man's service by generating low-cost electric energy to bring the light of civilization to the island's farthest corners. That great, collective effort is discussed in Chapter 4.

8. Earl P. Hanson, "Are the Tropics Unhealthy?," *Harper's*, October 1933.
9. A. Fernós Isern, "The White Man and the Tropics," *Puerto Rico Health Review*, October 1926.

The Natural Vegetation

The Original Vegetation and the Natural Vegetation

The term "original vegetation" is generally used for that which existed before the advent of man and was therefore influenced in its development only by such environmental factors as climate and soil. It is also called the "primitive" vegetation. Immediately after his arrival man begins to modify the original vegetation, cutting down trees for building his homes and making tools or clearing the land for the agriculture through which he substitutes cultivated species of plants, often imported from elsewhere, for those which had sprung up spontaneously.

The main problem in the study of primitive vegetation is the scarcity of sites where it has been preserved. There is also debate over the "primitive" nature of vegetation in thinly populated regions. Even in the Amazon basin, without a doubt one of the greatest regions of original vegetation in the world, the inhabitants, though relatively few, have actively modified the primitive vegetation with their "milpa" system of agriculture which consists of clearing certain forested areas, cultivating them for two or three years until the soil's fertility is exhausted, and then moving to another part of the forest to repeat the operation. The trees which grow again in the abandoned clearings differ from those of the original forest cover, not only in their characteristics but even in their species. In that manner, little by little in the course of centuries, the primitive vegetation of that vast and little known region has been changed along the main stream and its tributaries, though maintaining its original character in the less accessible regions.

If that happens to the vegetation in the vast Amazon basin, with its sparse and scattered population, what has happened in Puerto Rico which has been inhabited for centuries? Virtually all of the island's lands have been cultivated repeatedly, innumerable times, and the primitive vegetation has practically disappeared. Only a few specimens remain in certain areas where the original vegetation was allowed to stand, or suffered only minor modifications, because those regions have not lent themselves to agricultural exploitation of any kind. Those sites include parts of the forest reserves in Luquillo, Carite, Toro Negro, and Maricao, as well as some swamps on private lands.

However, while not much is left of Puerto Rico's primitive vegetation, natural vegetation *does* exist, arising from the actions of natural environmental factors and consisting largely of indigenous vegetation species which grew spontaneously in the region.

In the study of natural vegetation, the geographer is interested more in groups and associations formed by plants than in the plants themselves; more than the tree, he is concerned with the forest. He differs from the botanist in that manner, and also in the fact that his interest lies more in the forms of trunks and leaves rather than in the reproductive processes which are paramount for the botanist.

It is self-evident that certain plants adjust better than do others to such environmental conditions as sunlight, humidity, temperature, soil, the regimen of winds. In any one region, certain kinds of plants predominate according to specific, existing environmental conditions; by the same token, others are excluded. The plants which prosper in such a region tend also to appear in other regions with similar environmental conditions. The various species which adjust to the same conditions from what is known as a plant association. In mature associations the plants compete so intensely for the resources of light, water, and minerals that other species or individual plants which are less well adapted or weak are excluded from the association.

The plant associations are not stable, being gradually modified through changes in climate and soil, as well as through evolutionary trends within the vegetable kingdom wherein certain plants come to adapt themselves better to other types of environment which they can then invade successfully. However, such changes are extremely slow and create no great obstacles in the description of a plant association. The changes in natural vegetation following its destruction or modification, by man or through natural catastrophies, are far more rapid. Every modification of the vegetation or its environment favors the plants best adapted to the new environment as against those best adapted to former conditions. If the modification is not basic or permanent, the former vegetation gradually returns and the former plant association again takes over. That process is called plant succession and proceeds toward a stable association, in consonance with climate and soil, which is called climax vegetation.

Geographic Distribution of the Principal Plant Associations in Puerto Rico

While the present discussion is concerned primarily with conditions which exist today, a clear understanding demands projections, first into the past, to the days preceding not only discovery but even the advent of the Indians, and then into the future, imagining Puerto Rico's condition some time after its hypothetical abandonment by its entire population. Conditions to be considered for the present are the relief, the climate, the soils, the remains of vegetation which can be regarded as primitive still encountered in various parts of the island and the knowledge on hand as to the indigenous or spontaneous nature of certain plants which abound beyond the cultivated zones. Certain historic considerations are also relevant.

With all that in mind, Louis S. Murphy of the United States Department of Agriculture described four regions of natural vegetation in his study "The Forests of Puerto Rico, Past, Present, and Future."[1]

Subsequently, Leslie R. Holdridge made studies to delimit the areas of natural vegetation on the island. The natural vegetation, including the forests and plant successions, have also been described by H. A. Gleason and M. T. Cook.[2]

Until 1964, Murphy's work, written in 1916, was unquestionably the most complete available on the natural vegetation of Puerto Rico. But the appearance of the excellent work "Common Trees of Puerto Rico and the Virgin Islands," by Little and Wadsworth,[3] resulted in a much more complete understanding of the natural and imported vegetation, as well as in a new delimitation of regions which is followed in this chapter (Fig. 8.1).

The eight types of virgin climax forest delimited in Puerto Rico in that classification are described below, with their principal characteristics and most common trees.

Forests of the Plains and Hills

Along the wind-swept seacoasts was a low, scrubby, littoral woodland, so narrow and so small in area that it is not shown in Figure 8.1. Little and Wadsworth wrote:

> Most of the trees in this woodland were small and of poor form due to extreme exposure to salt winds. On dry, rocky slopes facing the southern or southwestern coasts, on Anegada, on Mona, and on other small, outlying islands, the littoral woodland assumed the form of cactus scrub [Fig. 8.2].

1. Louis S. Murphy, "The Forests of Puerto Rico, Past, Present and Future, and their Physical and Economical Environment" (U.S. Department of Agriculture, Bulletin No. 354) (Washington, D.C., October 20, 1916).

2. H. A. Gleason and M. T. Cook, "Plant Ecology of Porto Rico," in the *Scientific Survey of Porto Rico and the Virgin Islands* (New York: New York Academy of Sciences, 1927), vol. 7, p. 1.

3. Elbert L. Little, Jr. and Frank H. Wadsworth, "Common Trees of Puerto Rico and the Virgin Islands" (Agricultural Handbook No. 249) (Washington, D.C., U.S. Department of Agriculture, Forest Service, 1964).

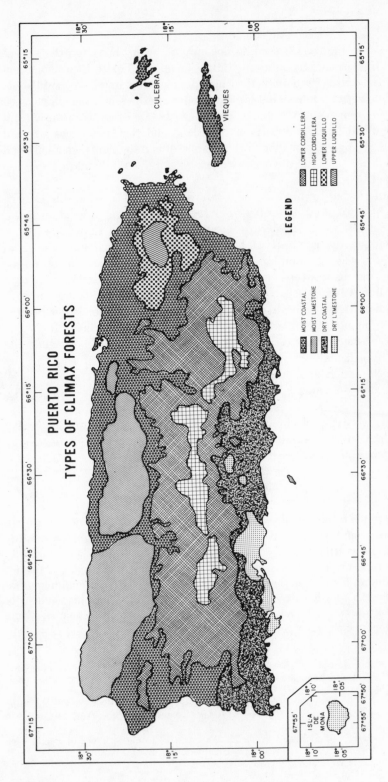

PUERTO RICO
TYPES OF CLIMAX FORESTS

LEGEND

MOIST COASTAL
MOIST LIMESTONE
DRY COASTAL
DRY LYMESTONE

LOWER CORDILLERA
HIGH CORDILLERA
LOWER LUQUILLO
UPPER LUQUILLO

CULEBRA

VIEQUES

ISLA DE MONA

Figure 8.1. Original Vegetation of Puerto Rico. (Adapted from map prepared by F. H. Wadsworth.)

In the more protected locations, particularly on the north coast of Puerto Rico, grew trees of good timber species such as maría (*Calophyllum antillanum*), ausubo (balata—*Manikara nitida*), roble (white cedar—*Tabebuia pallida*), and tortugo amarillo (false-mastic—*Mastichodendron Foetidissimum*). One of the most prominent species near the shore was uva de playa (sea grape—*Coccolobia uvifera*).

Along the shores of protected bays, lagoons, and estuaries, in an area too restricted to be shown [in figure 8.1,] were dense stands of mangrove. . . . Five public forests bordering the coast . . . still contain mangroves. In the water itself was mangle colorado (red mangrove) . . . On the adjacent area normally subject to tidal flooding were mangle blanco (white) . . . and mangle negro (black). On the landward side was mangle botón (button mangrove) . . . The strong, durable timbers of mangle colorado and mangle botón were much used for construction.

On the coastal plain and lower slopes, up to an elevation of 500 feet or more . . . grew a dry forest which was largely evergreen but with some deciduous species, particularly in the drier coastal areas. At its best development, on the northern coastal plain . . ., this forest attained 80 feet or more in height. Elsewhere, in the moist limestone region and on the south coast . . ., it was apparently shorter, from 40 to 60 feet tall. This forest consisted of two or three stories, each composed of distinct species. The lower story constituted a forest within a forest and depended on the upper canopy for its existence. The vegetation varied from place to place but it was everywhere a mixture of species. At least 200 tree species were present somewhere within the natural distribution of this forest.

Within the area described are four distinct forest regions or ecological provinces. These regions or provinces, designated as moist coast, moist limestone, dry coast, and dry limestone, are shown [in figure 8.1] (pp. 12–13).

MOIST COASTAL FOREST

Among the more common species in this ecological province are the corozo (*Acrocomia media*—prickly palm), mago (*Hernandia sonora*—called Jack-in-the-Box in Barbados), algarrobo (*Hymenaea courbaril*—West Indian locust), moca (*Andira inermis*—cabbage angelin), tortugo amarillo (*Sideroxyon foetidissimum*–false-mastic), maría (*Calophyllum brasiliense*), ausubo (*Manilkara bidentata*—balata), roble blanco (*Tabebuia heterophylla*—white cedar), laurel avispillo (*Phoebe elongata*—Jamaica nectranda, laurel), and palo de pollo (*Pterocarpus officinalis*—chicken tree) (Fig. 8.3).

MOIST LIMESTONE FOREST

This forest was similar to that along the coast and had many of the same species. The chief differences are due to the drier soils on the well-drained limestone hills and the great humidity in the protected areas between the hills, especially in the southern part which is close to the

Figure 8.2. Cactus. These plants appear even in the humid coastal belt where steady winds go hand in hand with extreme porosity of sandy soils. This photograph was taken near Arecibo. (Courtesy of the Government of Puerto Rico.)

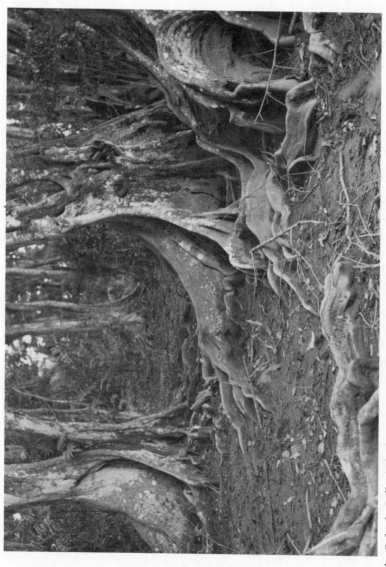

Figure 8.3. *The Palo de Pollo* (Chicken Tree, Swamp Bloodwood, *Pterocarpus Officinalis*). Characterized by its plant-like buttresses, it is among the typical trees of the humid coast. The above-shown specimens of that endemic specie are located in a freshwater swamp near Añasco. (Courtesy of the U.S. Forest Service.)

Cordillera Central. The most common species in the moist limestone forest include, among others: the palma de coyor (*Aiphones acanthophylla*—coyure ruffle-palm), la uvilla (*Coccoloba diversifolia*—doveplum or pigeon-plum), el moralón (*Coccoloba pubescens*—grandleaf sea-grape), cedro hembra (*Cedrela odorata*—Spanish cedar), cupey (*Clusia rosea*—monkey-apple), tortugo amarillo (*Sideroxyon foetidissimum*—mastic jungle-plum), úcar (*Bucida bucerus*—oxhorn bucida or black olive), canelilla (*Licaria salicifelia*—canela), almácigo (*Bursera simaruba*—turpentine tree or gumbo-limbo), cedro macho (*Hyeronima clusioides*—known only in Puerto Rico), and maga (*Montezuma speciosissima*—native only in Puerto Rico).

DRY COASTAL FOREST

On the dry, southern side of the island, adverse moisture conditions excluded many of the tree species common on the north side. In their places grew a few other species especially adapted to such conditions. The trees of the dry coastal forests include: calambreña (*Coccoloba venosa* —chicory grape), cóbana negra (*Stahlia monosperma*—coabanilla), genogeno (*Loncho-carpus domingensis*), tachuelo (*Pictetia aculeata*—fustic), guayacán (*Guaiacum officinale*—common lignumvitae), úcar (*Bucida buceras*—oxhorn bucida or black olive,), árbol de violeta (*Polygala cowellii*—violet tree), ceiba (*Ceiba pentranda*—silk-cotton tree), burro prieto (*Caparris cynophallophora*—Jamaica caper or zebrawood), and capá colorado (*Cordia nitida*—red manjack).

DRY LIMESTONE FOREST

In the dry limestone region of the south coast, as on the north coast, excessive soil drainage accentuates the dryness of the environment to a point where some species of trees cannot exist. They are replaced by others which are more hardy. The trees of the dry limestone forest include, among others: corcho bobo (*Pisonia albida*), guayacán blanco (*Guaiacum sanctum*—holywood lingumvitae), higüero (*Crescentia cujete* —calabash-tree), úcar (*Bucida buceras*—oxhorn bucida or black olive), guayacán (*Guaiacum officinale*—common lignumvitae), almácigo (*Bursera simaruba*—turpentine-tree gumbo-limbo, yaití (*Gymnanthes lucida*—oysterwood), tachuelo (*Pictetia aculeata*—fustic), and aleli (*Plumeria alba*—milktree).

Mountain Forests

Typical mountain forests are found in Puerto Rico between 500 and 2,000 feet altitude in the eastern mountains known as the Sierra de Luquillo, and to 3,000 feet in the Cordillera Central, slightly higher on the south slope than the north. These mountains harbor the most magnificent forests in Puerto Rico. Much of the original vegetation of this area is described as tropical moist forest; in the wettest part it is tropical rain forest. At its maximum development it reached 110 feet in height, with trees up to eight feet in diameter. Three forests of distinct size and composition grew together here, each forming a separate story of vegetation. Throughout the range of this type of forest there were probably about 170 species of trees.

Within that large mountain area are two forest regions or ecological provinces, and correspondingly distinct forest types. They are designated as Lower Cordillera and Lower Luquillo. Fig. 8.1 shows that the Lower Cordillera province includes both the north and south lower slopes of the central mountains, the Sierra de Cayey, as well as the upper slopes of the disconnected Sierra de Atalayain in the northwest.

LOWER CORDILLERA FOREST

The trees of the lower Cordillera include the following: yagrumo hembra (*Cecropia peltata*—trumpet-tree), laurel geo (*Ocotea leucoxylon* —laurel, or false avocado), nuez moscada (*Ocotea moschata,* known only in Puerto Rico), guamá (*Inga laurina*—"sweetpea"), moca (*Andira inermis* —cabbage angelin), tabonuco (*Dacryodes excelsa*—candlewood), guaraguao (*Guarea trichilioides*—American muskwood), ausubo (*Manilkara bidentata*—balata), granadillo (*Buchenavia capitata*—wild olive), capá prieto (*Cordia alliodora*—onion cordia), yagrumo macho (*Didymopanax morototoni*—matchwood), hueso blanco (*Linociera domingensis*—white rosewood), higüerillo (*Vitex divaricata*— white fiddlewood).

LOWER LUQUILLO FOREST

The forest of the lower slopes of the Luquillo Mountains is similar in general appearance to that in the Cordillera, but, because of greater precipitation and higher humidity, it is somewhat more luxuriant; several tree species exist only there. The trees of this province include the following: helecho gigante (*Cyathea arborea*—tree-fern), yagrumo hembra (*Cecropia peltata*—trumpet tree), guaraguao (*Guarea trichilioides*—American muskwood), tabonuco (*Dacryodes excelsa*—candlewood), cacao motillo (*Sloanea berteriana* —petit coco), ausubo (*Manilkara bidentata*—balata), nuez moscada (*Ocotea moschata*—known only in Puerto Rico), masa (*Tetragastris balsamifera*—palo de aceite or oil tree), palo de matos (*Ormosia krugii*), guano (*Ochroma pyramidale*—balsa), and roble blanco (*Tahebuia heterophylla*—white cedar) (Fig. 8.4).

HIGH CORDILLERA FOREST

Farther up the slopes, extending to near the tops of the peaks, was a subtropical rain forest. Here the temperature is lower and rainfall varies between 100 and 200 inches annually creating swampy conditions and

Figure 8.4. Original Forest in the Sierra de Luquillo. (Courtesy of F. H. Wadsworth.)

highly leached soils. The result was a comparatively poor forest about 60 feet tall, containing some 60 tree species.

The upper mountain forest of the Cordillera differed from that of the Sierra de Luquillo, primarily because of the moist conditions in the latter. The common or characteristic tree species of the upper Cordillera forest include: helecho gigante (*Cyathea arborea*—tree fern), palma de sierra (*Euterpe globosa*—sierra palm), jagüilla (*Magnolia portoricenses*—known only in Puerto Rico), nemocá (*Ocotea spathulata*—known only in Puerto Rico), palo colorado (*Cyrilla racemiflora*—swamp cyrilla), justillo (*Calycognium squalulosum*—known only in Puerto Rico), haya minga (*Guatteria blainii*), cupéillo (*Clusia krugiana*), caimitillo (*Micropholis chrysophylloides*—wild star-apple) and achiotillo (*Alchornia latifolia*—dove-wood) (Fig. 8.5).

Figure 8.5. "Colorado" Type of Forest Growing in the Alluvial Soils of the Hicacos River Valley. (Courtesy of the U.S. Forest Service.)

UPPER LUQUILLO FOREST

The forest of the Upper Luquillo Mountains is similar to that of the Cordillera, but there are additional species which are found only on the Luquillo Mountains. In the western part of the Cordillera and near El Yunque peak in the Luquillo Mountains grows Puerto Rico's only arborescent gymnosperm, the caobilla (*Podocarpus coriaceus*—podocarp—wild pitchpine).

The most common tree species of the upper Luquillo Forest include the following: helecho gigante (*Cyathea arborea*–tree-fern), laurel sabino (*Magnolia splendens*–known only in eastern Puerto Rico), nemocá (*Ocotea spathulata*–known only in Puerto Rico), palo colorado (*Cyrilla racemiflora*–swamp cyrilla), sabinón (*Croton poecilanthus*–known only in eastern Puerto Rico) and caimitillo verde (*Micropholis garciniaefolia*– known only in eastern Puerto Rico).

One of the most prominent species in these upper mountain forests is the sierra palm (*Euterpe globosa*) which forms extensive, nearly pure, stands on unstable soils.

On mountain peaks, above 2,500 feet, the forest is dwarfed to 20 feet or less in height. Little or no valuable timber is present in this forest but tree species of interest include oreganillo (*Weinmannia pinnata*–wild brazilletto) and palo bobo (*Brunellia comocladifolia*–West-Indian-Sumac).

History of its Destruction[4]

Little of the primitive vegetation remains today. At the time of discovery nearly all of the island was covered by forests. The deforestation had begun in pre-colombian days as the Indians cleared small patches for their crops, but the changes experienced by the vegetation were small because of the small population.

There were some clearings along the south coast but all the rest of the island was covered by trees and shrubs. Little by little, the colonists destroyed the forest cover to clear the land for crops; the practice gave rise to the term "tala" (felling), which is still used for such plantings. Unfortunately very few of the trees so cut down were used for their timber. Most of them were burned on the spot and others simply rotted away with time.

The clearings spread to all parts of the island after the arrival of the European colonists whose main occupation was agriculture. The history of population growth, the concessions of uncultivated lands by the Spanish Crown and the use of the land for agriculture, indicate the pace of deforestation.

There are indications that by 1830 approximately one half of the territory of the island had been ceded to the colonists; the other half remained in the hands of the Spanish Crown. The untouched forests, covering a considerable area, remained largely on Crown lands. The situation is explained by the sparse population during the sixteenth, seventeenth, and

---

4. In this section, full use is made of the excellent article by Frank H. Wadsworth, "Notes on the Climax Forests of Puerto Rico and their Destruction and Conservation prior to 1900," *Caribbean Forester* (January 1950), pp. 38–47.

eighteenth centuries; even at the beginning of the nineteenth it was barely 155,000 inhabitants. No matter how many trees were cut down by so small a population, it was easy to preserve large areas of primitive vegetation. In 1828, 72 per cent of the island was still covered by forests. According to Flinter, quoted by Murphy, 44 per cent of the total was still Crown territory; 28 per cent was owned privately.

The population grew rapidly in the course of the nineteenth century, and the situation was changed completely. At the close of the century the population had reached a million inhabitants, and perhaps 9/10 of the land owned by the Crown in 1830 had been ceded to settlers. The trees suffered from the impact of that growth of population, with the result that, by 1900, only 4 per cent of the land supported government-owned forests while 21 per cent was in privately owned forests. The larger part of that land was located in the mountains and, while exploitable for its forests, had small utility for agriculture.

The following table (Table 8.1) gives the forested areas in relation to those used for other purposes, in six significant years:

Table 8.1. Relative distribution of forested areas and those used for other purposes

| | Per Cent of Total | | |
Year	public forests	private forests	other uses
1828	44	28	28
1900	4	21	75
1912	2	19	77
1935	3	17	80
1950	4	5	91
1965	5	14	81

Source: L. S. Murphy, "Forests of Puerto Rico, Past, Present, and Future." The figures for 1935, 1950, and 1965, were calculated by Frank H. Wadsworth of the Forest Service, U.S. Department of Agriculture.

Note: Cultivation and pasture are the most important among "other uses." After 1912, the figure for cultivation surpassed that for pastures. Although arboreal in nature, coffee is included among "other uses."

The destruction continued until it reached the level of 1912, which was more or less the same as that of 1935, when 20 per cent of the total area was forested, 3 per cent government-owned and 17 per cent privately owned.

The most encouraging aspect of this picture is the government campaign to create and increase the forest reserves. It began at the turn of the century and was carried forward by Murphy, with the cooperation of the Puerto Rican and Federal governments as well as of such rehabilitation agencies as the Puerto Rico Reconstruction Administration (PRRA).

The task of conserving and enlarging the forests is primarily up to the government. It is difficult to gauge the situation of the privately owned forests. Most of them are in the coffee zones where, until 1950, many coffee plantations were destroyed to make room for sugar cane and other crops, so tending toward the diminution of private forests. The growth of private forests between 1950 and 1965 is not entirely encouraging, since it occurred in large measure on lands abandoned after World War II, in the Northern Limestone Region as well as the Central Range. Those terrains are today protected by a forest cover which is quite low in productivity.

What is encouraging is the fact that in 1964 about 1,500,000 small trees were distributed for planting on private farms and that a new nursery was established at a cost of more than $200,000, which will permit the figure to reach 6,000,000 annually (Fig. 8.6). Together with the tendency to prefer level lands for cultivation, because of their higher yield, that development will accelerate the trend toward using the mountainous regions for pastures and forests. The government agencies which lead the conservation campaign are: the Forest Division of the Commonwealth Department of Agriculture; the U.S. Forest Service; the personnel of the Agricultural Extension Division of the University of Puerto Rico; and the U.S. Soil Conservation Service.

Between one-fourth and one-fifth of the island is still covered by trees, including not only exploitable species, but also fruit trees in plantations and shade covers in the coffee regions. Timber trees are found only in government reserves and in the less accessible parts of some farms where the primitive vegetation still exists.

The record of efforts at conservation made before 1900 consists almost exclusively of a list of laws. Puerto Rico evidently had progressive forestry legislation during the nineteenth century, but the extent and condition of the island's forest resources as described at the end of that century testify to the fact that conservation efforts were not very effective.

The Conservation and Enlargement of the Forests

COMMONWEALTH AND FEDERAL FORESTRY SERVICES

After the change of sovereignty, the first important step toward forest conservation was the Presidential proclamation of January 17, 1903, creating the Luquillo Forest Reserve, which later came to be called the Caribbean National Forest. Today this forest has an area of 28,716 acres.

The Puerto Rican Forestry Service was established in 1917, and the first federal Forest Supervisor arrived on the island the following year. In that same year of 1918, the various mangrove swamps of the island were declared public forests, and the forests of Guánica, Maricao, and La Mona were added to them the following year. In 1920, the total area in forests

Figure 8.6. Santa Catalina Nursery on the North Slope of the Sierra de Luquillo. Nurseries play a role of incalculable value in reforestation and soil conservation. In the foreground are seedlings of the *guamá venezolana,* a fast-growing Puerto Rican tree greatly in demand for shade. In the background are eucalyptus trees about six years old. (Courtesy of the U.S. Forest Service.)

was approximately 39,000 acres. In 1931, new lands were acquired for public forests and four years later, in 1935, the Toro Negro Forest was established as a part of the Caribbean National Forest. In 1962 it was transferred to the Forestry Division of the Department of Agriculture (formerly the Puerto Rican Forestry Service), in exchange for lands near the Luquillo Forest. Today the Toro Negro Forest comprises a total of

7,000 acres, divided into several irregular parts which form a semicircle along the mountain peaks from La Punta in the west to Lake Matrullas in the east. Its functions include protecting the region of the El Guineo and Matrullas Lakes against erosion and the deposit of silt and helping to maintain the flow of water in their drainage basins.

In 1935, during the most active period in the development of public forests, the Federal Puerto Rico Reconstruction Administration (PRRA) added the forests of Carite, Río Abajo, Guajataca, Guilarte, and Susúa to the system. In 1943 these were transferred to the Forestry Service of Puerto Rico, while the island of La Mona was taken over for military purposes. The forests of Carite, Río Abajo, Guajataca, Guilarte, and Susúa provide partial protection to the drainage basins of the Carite, Dos Bocas, Guajataca, Garzas, Río Loco, and Yauco hydroelectric projects.

The Forestry Service estimates that about 500,000 acres, or more than 22 per cent of the total area of the island, is suitable for forest uses. That is the final objective of the Federal and Commonwealth Forest Services which today control 89,000 acres, or 5 per cent of the total area. Although it will be difficult to achieve that ambitious goal, it is significant that the forest areas have grown from 75,000 acres to 89,000 since 1950.

The Luquillo Forest, with almost exactly one-third of the forested area, continues to be the largest. Although it is today not cut for lumber, the reforestation being carried out there assures it a future as a valuable source of lumber. Through the former activities of the Civilian Conservation Corps (CCC) and the PRRA and the current labors of the Institute of Tropical Forestry and the Commonwealth's Parks and Public Recreation Administration, the Luquillo Forest has been converted into the finest outdoor recreational area in Puerto Rico (Fig. 8.7). It is served by an excellent, paved highway which crosses the entire Sierra from the village of Palmer on the north coastal plain to Naguabo in the eastern valleys. Other paved roads lead to various sites of interest, among them the peaks of El Yunque and Britton; there are footpaths, cabins, swimming pools, a restaurant, paking areas, and other facilities which, added to the natural beauty and the always pleasant temperature, weekly attract hundreds of visitors to the region from all parts of the island and from abroad.

It is estimated that in the "La Mina" recreation area, in the Luquillo Forest, "every acre developed for public recreational use returns more than $10,000 per year to the community,"[5] and that by the year 2,000 the number of visitors will reach some 3 million annually, or six times the present number.

Such growth, though at a slower rate, is also observed in the other forests such as Guavate, Toro Negro, Maricao, and Río Abajo (Fig. 8.8).

5. F. H. Wadsworth "Los bosques de Puerto Rico" [The forests of Puerto Rico] *Revista del Café* [Coffee Review] 20, no. 12 (October 1965).

Figure 8.7. Cascade of the Espíritu Santo River.

Figure 8.8. Recreation Area on the Jobos River, in the Public Forest of Río Abajo. The growth of Puerto Rico's population will demand the development of more such recreation areas. (Courtesy of the U.S. Forest Service.)

Table 8.2 and Fig. 8.9 indicate the present state of the forests of Puerto Rico.

The Economic Value of the Reserves

The fact that Puerto Rico imports millions of dollars worth of lumber and wood products lends considerable value to the forest reserves. In 1939–40, which can be regarded as a year of normal prices, the imports of wood and its derivatives exceeded $6 million. In 1946–47, with inflated prices, the total came to $16,236,000, of which more than $6,500,000 was for paper. During fiscal 1969 the imports of lumber, paper and their by-products were valued at more than $80 million. Virtually all the imported lumber and paper come from the United States or Canada, which have large forest reserves.

Murphy calculated that between 1910 and 1912 the per capita annual consumption of wood in Puerto Rico was about 23 cubic feet. In 1950

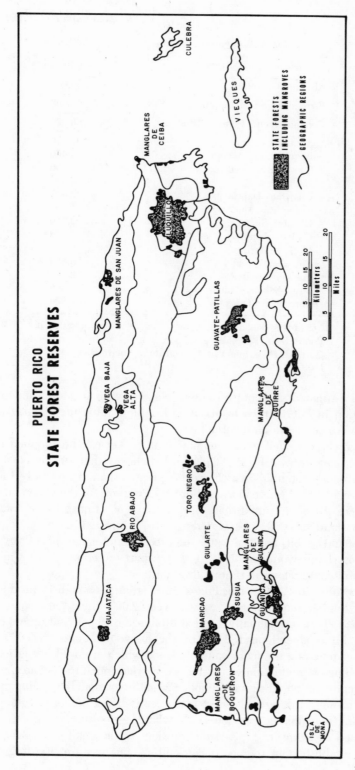

Figure 8.9. Forest Reserves of Puerto Rico. (Superimposed on the Geographic regions of the island.)

Table 8.2. Government forests in Puerto Rico

Name and Location	Area in Acres
All Forests, Total	89,000
Federal Forest of Luquillo	28,600
Commonwealth Forests, Total	60,400
Aguirre-Guayama	2,300
Boquerón-Cabo Rojo	3,400
Cambalache-Arecibo	1,500
Carite-Cayey	6,900
Guajataca-Isabela	2,300
Vega-Vega Alta	1,500
Guánica-Guánica	9,900
Guilarte-Adjuntas	3,600
Maricao-Maricao	10,300
Río Abajo-Utuado	5,800
Piñones-Carolina	2,600
Susúa-Sabana Grande	3,300
Toro Negro-Orocovis	7,000

Source: Benjamín R. Seda, "Los recursos forestales de Puerto Rico" [The Forest Resources of Puerto Rico], mimeographed, Department of Agriculture of Puerto Rico, October 1965.

it was estimated as about 50 cubic feet, bringing the total annual consumption in Puerto Rico to about 110 million cubic feet. Today it may well be some 200 million cubic feet.

What share of that enormous potential market can be supplied by the island's own forest? F. H. Wadsworth believes that the native lumber industry has potentials which are far greater than is generally thought. In his work "Suggestions for the Forestry Program for the Commonwealth of Puerto Rico" he stated that approximately one fourth of the total area of the island, 500,000 acres, would need to be forested in order adequately to protect the soils and the water resources. Maintenance of a forest cover on those lands would minimize the transport of sediments by the rivers and prolong the flows in time of drought.

According to Wadsworth, Puerto Rico is large enough to produce "all of its lumber requirements." In the year 2,000, their total value could reach $130 million annually. Of that total, some 48 per cent or $62 million could be produced on 180,000 of the above-mentioned 500,000 acres, without touching the more valuable lands which are used for agriculture. The value of production would reduce by that much the island's external payments and could provide about $20 million annually in employment.

At present, the area of forest resources is being enlarged through the planting of valuable trees on lands whose agricultural productivity has declined as a result of disastrous erosion, while small groves have also been established in regions of agriculture and pasture. Existing forests are being developed through the elimination of less valuable and defective trees by selective cutting, to give the remaining trees better chances for full growth.

The regions of new forests have been planted with fast-growing trees (eucalyptus, swamp oak, teak, and, more recently, Honduran pine) which soon became useful on the farms, for instance, for fence posts, housing, tool handles, firewood, and charcoal (Fig. 8.10).

Figure 8.10. Teak Trees from Southeastern Asia. Teak is among the imported trees that produce excellent lumber, immune to tropical insects. The forest shown above is about thirteen years old and is located near the Patillas Dam in the public forest of Carite. (Courtesy of the U.S. Forest Service.)

It is also possible that a small part of the paper and pulp now imported will in the future be produced from the Honduran pine (*Pinus caribaea*) which was introduced in recent years, grows rapidly, and adapts itself readily to the poorer soils. The species also yields good construction lumber and could be a good substitute for imported coniferous Christmas trees.

Utilization of the Forest Products

In 1950, the uses to which the forest products of Puerto Rico were put were highly varied. When amplified to include all natural vegetation, the list of uses grows larger and even more varied.

By 1966, industrial expansion and technical advances had substantially changed the uses for forest products, as indicated by comparison between the present situation and the extreme range of utilization in 1950.

1. Charcoal and Firewood. This was perhaps the largest forest-based industry in Puerto Rico. In 1945, the annual consumption was estimated[6] at about one million cords.[7] In addition, a small quantity, approximately 825 cords, was imported from the Dominican Republic, Cuba, and the British Antilles.

Because the market for charcoal fluctuated widely, its scientific production in modern retorts was very small. Since World War II there has been a decided slump in consumption, as a result of which only a few small producers of charcoal remain. The growing use of electricity, gas and other modern fuels, has resulted in the almost total disappearance of what was formerly the largest industry in Puerto Rico based on forest products.

2. Furniture. The furniture industry of Puerto Rico is small. But in recent years it has developed to the point where it turns out a product which, since it is made of tropical woods and is more resistant to time and insects, is as good as, or better than, imported furniture. It utilizes small quantities of such local woods as tabonuco (candlewood), laurel, and capá (a fast-growing tropical evergreen, widespread in the Antilles and tropical mainland America). Mahogany and laurel predominate among the imported woods. According to the 1939 Census of Manufacturers, the furniture industry employed 687 workers in that year and ranked fifth from the top in terms of employment. In 1949, the number of workers and employees in the industry was 1,727; in 1958 it was 2,867; and in 1967, 3,458.

3. Construction. Formerly the typical house of the rural areas was built of logs; all of its structural elements were of unsawed wood. The only material still needed for completing the house was straw for covering the sides and the roof. The "yagua," or broad sheath, of the royal palm was also used.

As wood for such uses became scarce, many substitutes were sought. Experiments were carried out with clay or earth for building houses, as well as with poured concrete and cement blocks. The Puerto Rico Industrial Development Company is experimenting with bagasse, the fibrous end-product of grinding sugar cane, for making boards which might serve as partitions and perhaps for roofs and outside walls. In the "mutual aid" program for building rural homes, cement blocks have been substituted for the primitive vegetation.

4. Fibers. The fiber, or rather the leaf, of the "yarey" or "hat" palm was used for making brooms, hats, and other objects for domestic or personal

---

6. L. V. Teesdale, and J .W. Girard, "Wood Utilization in Puerto Rico" (Washington, D.C., U.S. Department of Agriculture, Forest Service, 1945).

7. "Cords," a rectangular pile of wood, generally four feet wide by eight feet long and four feet high, with a net volume of 80 cubic feet.

use. The industry obtained its raw materials from the more arid zones where the palm grows: the northwest corner of Puerto Rico between Aguadilla and Isabela and the southwest corner in the vicinity of Cabo Rojo. The factories were concentrated in those regions. In Cabo Rojo the palm was used primarily for making hats. In Aguadilla it was used more for making brooms, since all the required raw materials were found locally: The fibers came from the palms while the handles from the "haystack" zone in the hills of Los Puertos, in the south. Though the construction of the Air Base of Punta Borinquen (Ramey Field), covering almost the entire area where the palm was found, seemed to deal a death blow to the industry, it held on tenaciously. As the availability of raw materials declined, the country people turned increasingly from making low-cost brooms to producing trays and baskets, center pieces for tables, place mats, carrying bags, in short, a wide variety of luxury items which demand fewer materials and command higher prices than brooms. The skill shown in the manufacture of such articles by the people of Aguadilla and Isabela is astonishing, as is their artistic feeling. The broom industry persists on a limited scale; for a time, the large part of the fibers used in it were imported from Cuba and the Dominican Republic, though trade with the former is now suspended.

5. Pastures. Many grasses native to Puerto Rico can be, and are being, used for pasture. Among them are "matojo" and Bermuda grass. Nevertheless, imported grasses like guinea grass, para grass ("matojillo"), pangola, and star grass, predominate on the best pasture lands. The planting of pangola, star and buffel grasses, which are more nutritious than others, is today encouraged through a program of incentives. In the hills surrounding the Valley of Caguas, and in other parts of the island, fields covered by such improved pasture grasses are today extensive.

6. Shade and Windbreaks. Some trees, especially the "guaba" and "guamá," are widely used in the coffee regions to provide the shade required by the coffee trees, while also helping to conserve the soil. Other trees are used as windbreaks to protect certain crops. The Australian pine (casuarina) is widely used for that purpose because it grows rapidly. Others are Siamese "casia" and mango trees.

7. Medicines. Plants form an important source of medical products, not only for the home remedies which the Puerto Rican country people know well but also for those which are accepted by the medical and pharmaceutical professions. The School of Tropical Medicine of Puerto Rico has experimented with many of these, but their commercial value is limited.

8. Recreation. In addition to the above-mentioned functions, trees serve an esthetic function by beautifying landscapes. Some forested regions, like that of El Yunque, described above, are fine recreation areas. The forest reserves of Río Abajo, Carite, Toro Nego, Maricao, and Susúa have also been improved for recreational purposes and attract visitors and residents.

The number of visitors per year shows that such utilization of forests is increasing at an astonishing rate. The figure was tripled between 1956 and 1965, when it reached 282,000. It should be remembered that the La Mina (El Yunque) area alone is expected to receive 3 million visitors in the year 2,000. The conservation program is aimed not only at the intelligent utilization of forest products, the protection of soils and water, and the conservation of wild life, but also at the promotion of recreation in the public forests.

9. Conservation and Enrichment of the Soils. Trees play a powerful role in those matters. Their foliage lessens the impact of rain, while their roots, as well as the leaves and branches which fall to the ground, impede erosive washing away of the soils. The coffee plantations are well protected by their complete tree covers. In other deforested regions certain imported grasses, like kudzu, are used to control erosion. The trees and leguminous plants also help to fertilize the soils through the ability of their roots to fix free nitrogen from the air and make it available to other plants. The most important leguminous trees in the coffee regions are guamá and guaba.

Greater emphasis on reforestation would prevent the formation of gulleys and rivers by reducing erosion, both sheet and gulley. It would also assure the provision of water for the growing needs of the rural as well as the urban populations. The contrast between the year-round clean and flowing waters of the Luquillo Forest and the dirty character of rivers and streams whose basins have been cleared for farming is striking. The task of conservation by all available means, to protect the waters received every year through copious rainfall, is imperative, since water is always a limiting factor in the development of natural resources and the general economy.

The Soils

Studies Accomplished

THE SOIL SURVEY OF PUERTO RICO

Knowledge of Puerto Rico's soils stems largely from the studies begun in 1928 by the Division of Soils of the U.S. Department of Agriculture, in cooperation with the Agricultural Experiment Station of the University of Puerto Rico, resulting in the publication, in 1942, of *Soil Survey of Puerto Rico*.[1] Work in the field began in the winter of 1928 and continued for nine years, from January to June in each year. The final result, following some years of computing and evaluating the field observations, proved to be one of the most complete and detailed soil studies ever made anywhere at that time. Although the work had been preceded by many soil surveys in the United States, it had the advantage of being done at a time when the standards and new ideas of the young soil science had recently crystallized; the Puerto Rico report became the last word on the subject.

April 1965 saw the publication of a new and important study of the soils in the Lajas Valley region.[2] That, though confined to the area mentioned, resulted in the first official revision of the map published in 1942 (Fig. 9.1).

In addition to the known soils, new ones were discovered, each of whose profiles and other characteristics were studied. Aerial photographs were used for the precise determination of locations and distributions. The resulting detailed map of the region had the advantage over Roberts'

1. R. C. Roberts, *Soil Survey of Puerto Rico*, U.S. Department of Agriculture, Bureau of Plant Industry; University of Puerto Rico Agricultural Experiment Station (Washington, D.C., 1942).
2. "Soil Survey, Lajas Valley Area," U.S. Department of Agriculture, Soil Conservation Service, in cooperation with the University of Puerto Rico Agricultural Experiment Station, 1965.

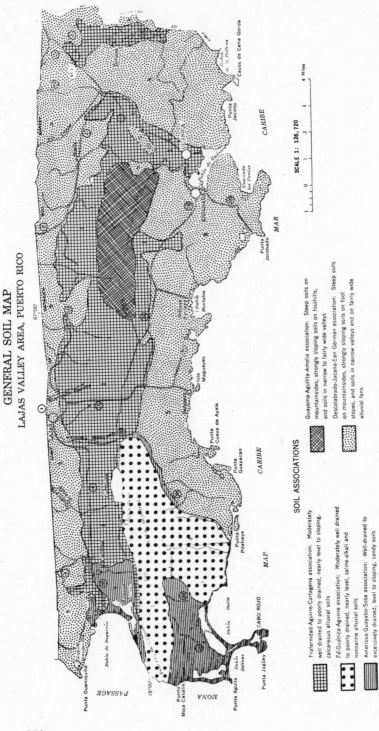

GENERAL SOIL MAP
LAJAS VALLEY AREA, PUERTO RICO

SCALE 1: 126,720

SOIL ASSOCIATIONS

Fraternidad-Aguirre-Cartagena association: Moderately
well drained to poorly drained, nearly level to sloping,
calcareous alluvial soils

Fé-Guánica-Aguirre association: Moderately well drained
to poorly drained, nearly level, saline-alkali and
nonsaline alluvial soils

Americus-Guayabo-Sosa association: Well-drained to
excessively drained, level to sloping, sandy soils

Guayama-Aguilita-Amelia association: Steep soils on
mountainsides, strongly sloping soils on foothills,
and soils in narrow to fairly wide valleys

Descalabrado-Jacana-San Germán association: Steep soils
on mountainsides, strongly sloping soils on foot
slopes, and soils in narrow valleys and on fairly wide
alluvial fans

Figure 9.1.

classic volume of being based on recent photographs which, among other things, showed such cultural features as highways, roads, and canals.

Modern soil science, also called pedology, had its start near the end of the nineteenth century in Russia primarily and in Germany. Until then the soil was commonly regarded as the cover of the earth's stony crust, able to sustain and nourish plants, which resulted from the decomposition of the underlying rocks and was studied only for its chemical and physical properties. Soil maps were more or less the same as those showing the distribution of surface rocks. Two classes of soils were recognized: those which resulted from the disintegration and decomposition of the under- lying rocks which they greatly resembled in nature and those which had been transported from elsewhere through such processes as river sedi- mentation, resulting in alluvial soils.

Scientists then found a veritable natural laboratory on the vast Russian plains with their enormous variety of soils and environmental conditions. The Russians noted that, from north to south, the types of soil changed gradually, far more in harmony with climate and natural vegetation than with the nature of the underlying rocks. New theories appeared, explain- ing soil formation by the *interaction* of various environmental factors; cli- mate and vegetation were the most important of these, followed by relief, the rocks, and, in some cases, even the fauna. Those ideas were developed in the United States during the century's first quarter, largely as a result of the work of C. F. Marbut of the U.S. Soil Survey. The United States also offered a great natural laboratory with excellent gradations of soil types. A group of disciples of Marbut arose little by little and, together with their master, devoted themselves eagerly to the study of their coun- try's soils, so laying the foundations of the modern American soil science.

Those studies converted the soil into a living thing, almost an organism. It lives because of its content of vast numbers of living organisms, micro- scopic plants and animals, insects, worms and the like. Moreover, the soil itself resembles such living organisms because, like them, it develops from its original state through such steps as youth, maturity, and old age.

The key to the recognition of such development arises from the study of the soil's profile to reveal the physical, chemical, and biological nature of each of its several mantles as revealed in a vertical section (Figs. 9.5 and 9.6). In a typical, well-developed soil those mantles comprise three horizontal layers, designated from top to bottom by the first three letters of the alphabet, differentiated by the varying degrees to which they have been affected by the soil-forming processes. As a result of those processes the top mantles, also called horizon A, are enriched in oxygen and humus but impoverished in soluble minerals, especially the fine-grained. The intermediate mantles, known as horizon B, are enriched in those min- erals and particles, brought by the infiltering water. If much water in- filters, horizon B, also, is deprived of soluble minerals. The lowest layers, horizon C, are least affected by those processes, as indicated by their greater resemblance to the original rock. The three horizons vary in thickness, though C is generally the thickest while B is the most important for study and classification.

Marbut divides the well-developed soils into two large groups: *pedocals* whose horizon B is rich in carbonate of calcium and *pedalfers* whose horizon B is rich in compounds of iron and aluminum. The first are characteristic of dry regions where the small rainfall cannot leach more calcium carbonate out of horizon B, but may enrich that layer by bringing the substance from horizon A. The *pedalfers* are characteristic of humid regions where the water has deprived the soil of its soluble minerals, leaving only the insoluble, such as compounds of aluminum and iron.

The *pedocals* are subdivided, according to the characteristics of their profiles, into chernozems, prairie soils, chestnut-colored soils, brown soils, and desert soils. The *pedalfers* are divided into podzols, podzolic soils, lateritic soils, and laterites. There are also the imperfectly developed soils which are divided into the *intrazonal* (rendzinas, planosola, bogs) and azonal (without horizons) which include the alluvial soils, sands, and lithosols.

It was long believed that Puerto Rico's zonal soils had to fall largely into the lateritic group which is typical of tropical warm and moist climates. But the studies of Roberts and his colleagues reveal that almost all of the large soil groups are represented on the island, where the laterites and lateritic soils occupy barely a fourth of the area. Naturally, the pedalfers dominate in almost all of the humid regions, and the pedocals in the arid and semiarid parts of the south of Puerto Rico.

Within those large groups, the soils are subdivided according to similarities in their profiles and their physical and chemical properties. The soils which most resemble each other form a *series*, commonly named after the place where it was first recognized or where it appears in its purest form. Accordingly, in Puerto Rico are found the series called Bayamón, Cataño, Ponceña, Vieques, and many others, up to a total of 115. Within any one series, one or more types are recognized, according to variations which may occur in the topsoil. Within the Paso Seco series, for instance, are found Paso Seco clay, Paso Seco loam, silty loam, silty clayloam, and silty clay. Moreover, at times some types of soil show distinct phases or special characteristics, such as smooth phase, broken, mixed, eroded, imperfectly drained phases. Altogether, including such phases, 352 types of soil are encountered in Puerto Rico.

In 1951 work began in the United States on a new classification of soils, defined primarily in terms of the intrinsic properties according to which a soil series may be included in higher categories. The soils are grouped in orders which are immediately subdivided until the individual types are arrived at. The classification was adopted in the United States in January 1965 and began to be used in Puerto Rico a year later. No map of the island has yet been drawn using that new classification, which is still being studied.

Main Soil Series

It would be impossible, here, to undertake a detailed description of Puerto Rico's 352 types of soil, as was done by Roberts who gave more than half of his book to the task (Fig. 9.2). Bonnet[3] selects 24 important series and unites them into eleven groups representing general conditions over a large area, so giving an idea sufficiently representative of the characteristics of Puerto Rico's main soils. Below are discussed some of the most important groups and series, selected and studied according to Bonnet, beginning with the two major regional divisions: *Soils of the humid and subhumid regions,* and *Soils of the arid and semiarid regions* (Fig. 9.3). The first are subdivided into: soils of the mountainous regions, soils of the northern limestone region, soils of the alluvial fans and terraces as well as of the interior plains, alluvial soils, sands, and bogs. The second are divided into soils of the southern limestone hills, soils of the south's nonlimestone hills, alluvial soils, and sands.

SOILS OF THE HUMID AND SUBHUMID REGIONS

I. The soils of the *humid mountain regions* are principally derived from igneous, metamorphic, and sedimentary rocks of the Cretaceous period. The first include the series called Los Guineos-Catalina-Alonso and Múcara-Naranjito; the second is the series known as Rosario-Nipe.

A. The soils of the Los Guineos-Catalina-Alonso series are typical of the coffee zone in the western half of the Cordillera Central, though they also appear in smaller pockets in the eastern part of the Cordillera Central and throughout the Sierra de Luquillo. They developed under rains of more than 76 inches. The soils are quite deep and reddish in color, at times nearly violet. Though poor in themselves, these soils can be made quite productive by the use of fertilizers. They are found in regions of rough or undulating relief, as well as on rocky sites void of vegetation. These soils cover about 10 per cent of Puerto Rico's total area but, as may be seen on the map, they are representative of much more extended soil types. Within the general classification of soils, those of Catalina and Alonso belong to the lateritic group, and the Los Guineos to the podzolic (Fig. 9.4).

3. Juan Amedeé Bonnet, "Series importantes de suelos de Puerto Rico" [Important Series of the Soils of Puerto Rico], in *Almanaque agrícola de P.R.* [Agriculture almanac of Puerto Rico] (San Juan,: Department of Agriculture and Commerce, 1944), pp. 83–90.

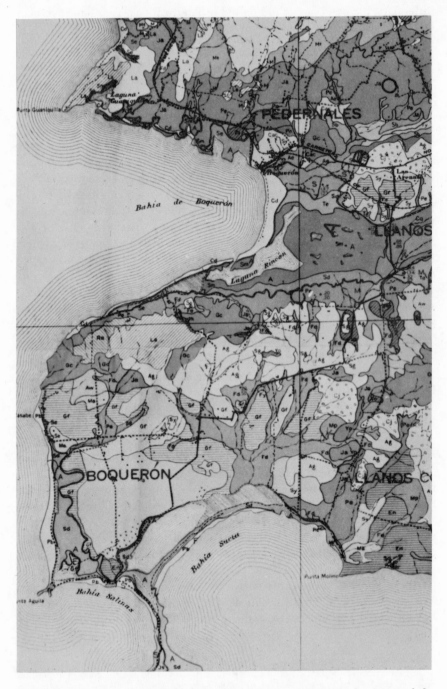

Figure 9.2. Section of the Soils Map of Puerto Rico. (Published as part of the U.S. Department of Agriculture, *Soil Survey of Puerto Rico*, in cooperation with the University of Puerto Rico.)

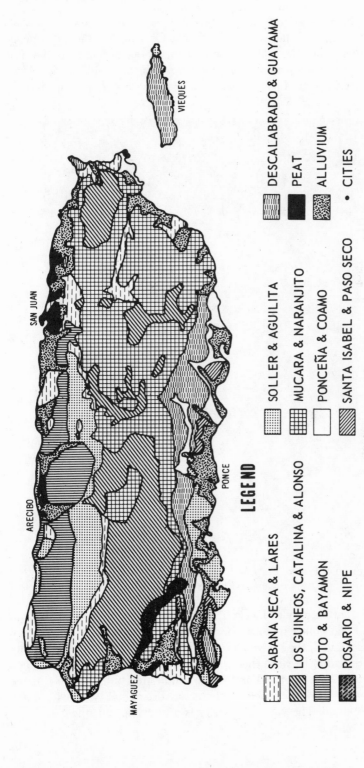

LEGEND

SABANA SECA & LARES		SOLLER & AGUILITA	DESCALABRADO & GUAYAMA
LOS GUINEOS, CATALINA & ALONSO		MUCARA & NARANJITO	PEAT
COTO & BAYAMON		PONCEÑA & COAMO	ALLUVIUM
ROSARIO & NIPE		SANTA ISABEL & PASO SECO	• CITIES

Figure 9.3. Groups of the Most Important Soil Series. (Courtesy of Dr. J. A. Bonnet, Director of the Soil Department of the Agricultural Experiment Station of the University of Puerto Rico.)

B. The Múcara-Naranjito soils are most common in the tobacco region in the middle part of the eastern Cordillera Central, but they also penetrate somewhat into the coffee zone and to various points near the east and west coasts. They were formed under rainfalls of 65–100 inches. They are shallower than the Los Guineos-Catalina-Alonso soils and are largely

Figure 9.4. Profile of a Los Guineos Soil. (Courtesy of the Soil Conservation Service.)

dark in color, often gray or black. They are on the whole less fertile than are those of the coffee regions. Susceptible to erosion, especially where the relief is rugged, they have the good quality of being able to rapidly renew their fertility because the rocks so exposed are rich in bases. They occupy about 17 per cent of Puerto Rico's total area but, like most of the series here described, they include characteristics of soil types with much wider distribution. The Naranjito series is a podzolic soil; the Múcara is a lithosol.

C. The Nipe-Rosario soils were formed exclusively by the decomposition of serpentines in the island's southwest. They occupy 1.3 per cent of the total area and are the true laterites within the general classification of soils. In fact, as explained in the chapter on minerals, they are also iron ores and may be worth more as such than cultivated. Precipitation varies between 80 and 100 inches. The soils are relatively deep, quite reddish in color, rich in aluminum and iron but poor in potassium, nitrogen, phosphorus, and lime. Fertility is very low and the soils are covered largely with shrubs and trees, as can be seen in the Cerro de las Mesas and in the Maricao forest.

II. The soils of the *northern limestone region* include, among others, the Coto-Bayamón, Soller, and Tanamá series.

A. The *Coto* series is typical of the northwestern part of the Quebradillas plain. The *Bayamón* series is the equivalent of the *Coto* in the eastern part of the north coast but, since this part is wetter, its soils have an acid reaction (Fig. 9.5). Both derive from the Tertiary limestones, especially the Aymamón formation. The area's precipitation varies between 50 and 78 inches. The Coto soils are dark yellow and relatively shallow while the Bayamón soils are dark red and much deeper. Both are rich in iron and aluminum and poor in nitrogen and phosphorus. Their fertility is average. These two series occupy a little more than 1 per cent of Puerto Rico's area. They belong to the group of lateritic soils.

B. The *Soller* series was named after the sugar mill of that name. It belongs to the Cibao Formation and the Lares limestone, but is also found in other parts of the island. It is generally shallow, black, with a high

Figure 9.5. Profile of a Soil of the Bayamón Series, on the Highway between Vega Alta and Bayamón. (Courtesy of the Soil Conservation Service.)

content of organic matter and with a clayey texture. Not very fertile, it erodes easily under cultivation. It belongs to the rendzina group and covers about 2 per cent of the island's total area.

C. The *Tanamá* series is another group of lithosols, found among the "haystacks" of the Aymamón, Aguada, and Lares formations, or among the hills of Los Puertos and Lares. Stony and very shallow, it is reddish and quite infertile, occasionally cultivated but generally covered by brush and forest (Fig. 9.6). It occupies about 5.2 per cent of the total area.

Figure 9.6. Profile of a Soil of the Tanamá Series. (Courtesy of the Soil Conservation Service.)

On the soil map the Tanamá series seems joined to the Coto-Bayamón.

III. The soils of the *alluvial terraces* and *interior plains* are typified by the *Sabana Seca* and *Lares* series. The former are found on the north coastal plain, in the east and west and in the Caguas Valley; the latter appear largely between the limestone and volcanic zones, in the middle and upper parts of the Culebrinas River Valley, and in the regions of undulating relief, reaching inland from the north coast to the vicinity of Bayamón and Río Piedras. Their thickness is average and their subsoil is hard, forming a crust; working them is generally difficult. Their color varies from dark gray to reddish. Acid soils, poor in nitrogen, phosphorus, and calcium, they are rich in iron oxide and aluminum. Some of them are related to the laterites without being laterites because the subsoil crust impedes the good drainage characteristic of the lateritic soils. The Sabana Seca soils belong to the intrazonal planosol group, while the Lares soils belong to the podzol group. Their total area is a little more than 1 per cent of the island.

IV. The *alluvial soils* in these humid and subhumid regions belong principally to the *Toa* and *Coloso* series along the north, east, and west coasts, from the valley of the Guanajibo to that of the Maunabo. The average rainfall is about 80 inches. They are transported soils, quite deep, dark to dark gray in color, slightly acid and generally very fertile, some 85 per cent of them supporting fields of sugar cane (Fig. 9.7). They occupy less than 4 per cent of Puerto Rico's total area.

V. *Sands and Bog Soils*

A. The *sandy soils* of the humid and subhumid regions are typified by the *Cataño* series. They are largely sandy beaches, at times supporting coconut plantations but with little agricultural value, though they are cultivated here and there. They cover a little more than 0.6 per cent of the total area.

B. The *bog soils* of those regions are found along the coast, or quite near it, all around Puerto Rico, in the swampy areas covered by mangroves, as, for instance, near Arecibo, Manatí, and Canóvanas. They are young soils, composed of recently decomposed organic matter, rich in humus but poor in minerals, and generally salty. Their color is generally very dark. Normally they are very poor, but can be used for sugar cane and pastures when well drained. They occupy a little more than 1 per cent of the total area.

SOILS OF THE ARID AND SEMIARID REGIONS

I. *The soils of the southern limestone hills* belong mainly to the *Aguilita* series which corresponds to the *Tanamá* in the north. They are very shallow, dark gray in color, and quite poor. They occupy about 2 per cent of the island's area.

II. *The soils of the nonlimestone hills in the south* comprise the lithosol series *Descalabrado* and *Guayama* (Fig. 9.8). They are also found in large parts of Vieques and Culebra. The annual rainfall varies between 25 and 65 inches. They are derived from tufas and shales and have very little depth. Being poor, they are largely used for pasture. They occupy about 5 per cent of the island's area.

III. *The alluvial soils of the arid and semiarid regions* belong to the *Ponceña-Coamo, Santa Isabel-Paso Seco,* and *San Antón* series.

A. The *Ponceña-Coamo* soils, true chernozems, are found in the interior plains of the south coast, on terraces and banks. The annual rainfall varies between 45 and 60 inches. They are very fertile, average in thickness, and are dark, almost black, in color. The moderate precipitation has permitted the development of vegetation and the enrichment of the soil with humus, without leaching the nutritive minerals from the subsoil; as a result, these are Puerto Rico's best soils. The same factor which enriched them, the paucity of rain, seems to prevent their complete agricultural utilization; however, since the introduction of irrigation, large parts of these soils have produced excellent crops of sugar cane. When not planted to sugar, they

Figure 9.7. Alluvial Soil of the Toa Series. Note the "haystacks" in the background. (Courtesy of the Soil Conservation Service.)

produce Guinea grass of the finest quality. Unfortunately, they occupy only 12,700 acres, much less than 1 per cent of the island's total.

B. The planosol series, *Santa Isabel* and *Paso Seco,* are found in the alluvial fans south of the *Ponceña-Coamo* soils. They are somewhat younger than the latter and very fertile. Annual rainfall varies between 35 and 40 inches. The B horizons of the Paso Seco soils lack the accumulations of lime which characterize the Santa Isabel soils and occasionally, due to dryness and their proximity to the sea, they are charged with salt. Both are generally dark in color. When irrigated, they produce excellent crops of sugar cane, and are used for pasture where they cannot be irrigated. They occupy nearly 1 per cent of the island's total area.

C. The *San Antón* series comprises the alluvia most recently deposited by southcoast rivers and were formed under an annual rainfall of about

Figure 9.8. Jacaná Soil. This soil has been found to be often associated with the Descalabrados. (Courtesy of the Soil Conservation Service.)

30 inches. Dark in color, their subsoil is alkaline and rich in bases. They, too, are generally very fertile and are widely irrigated, yielding large crops of sugar cane. They are found near the rivers, especially toward the coast. Their total area is a little more than 1 per cent of Puerto Rico's.

IV. *The sand soils of the arid and semiarid regions* are principally of the *Meros* series, sands which abound on the south coast beaches such as that of Ponce. Occasionally they are covered by coconut groves but their agricultural value is even less than is that of the sands of the humid coasts. Their area is hardly 0.2 per cent of Puerto Rico's.

Productivity of the Soils

The *Soil Survey* includes a detailed study of the productivity of Puerto Rico's soils. For each soil type the average yield is determined which might be expected of each of the island's principal crops, considering the agricultural practices in use. The soils are classified as to productivity on a scale ranging from 1 to 10, in which 1 denotes the most productive and 10 the least. The soils classified as 1 can produce 60 tons of sugar cane per well-cultivated acre; 18 hundredweight of tobacco; 6 hundredweight of coffee; 20 of corn; 10 of cotton; and so on for the remaining crops. Those norms are relatively high when one considers, for instance, that the island's average yield of sugar cane is between 30 and 35 tons per acre. A soil which produces 30 tons of cane per acre should have a classification of only 5.

The soils classified as 1 barely total 129,000 acres, or approximately 6 per cent of the island's area. They are located principally along the south coast in the Santa Isabel and Paso Seco series, as well as, to some extent, in the Ponceña, Coamo, and San Antón series. Elsewhere on the island they are found only in certain types of alluvium, among others in parts of the Coloso and Toa series. All of those soils are recent or old alluvia.

The soils classified from 1 to 5 cover 28 per cent of the island's total area. The remainder, about 72 per cent, are classified from 6 to 10. Those poorer soils are found largely in the mountainous areas and in regions of rugged relief. In other words, almost three quarters of the island is covered by inferior soils. Table 9.1 gives the productivity of each of 26 series, including that of its various types.

Problems of Conservation and Improved Utilization

Topography and climate are among the most important factors which influence soil productivity. Most of the poor soils are found in the mountain regions. The influence of topography works largely through the climate. The soils of the south are fertile in part because of the dry climate which, in turn, results from the topography. The relief also determines

Table 9.1. *Productivity of soil types belonging to 26
important soil series of Puerto Rico*

Series	Area (Acres)	Productivity
Santa Isabel	11,520	1
Paso Seco	9,856	1
Ponceña	3,264	1, 3
Coloso	41,728	1, 2, 6
San Antón	25,664	1, 4, 5
Coamo	9,408	1, 5
Toa	40,640	1, 6, 8
Coto	13,376	3, 4
Lares	22,400	3, 4, 8
Soller	61,632	3, 8, 9
Guayama	33,536	3, 10
Catalina	118,848	4, 5, 6, 7
Alonso	25,472	4, 5, 6, 9
Bayamón	13,568	5, 6
Sabana Seca	17,472	5, 6
Naranjito	14,784	6, 7, 8
Cataño	12,700	6, 7, 8, 10
Los Guineos	70,528	7, 8
Múcara	343,296	7, 8, 9
Tanamá	113,000	8, 9, 10
Nipe	2,880	9
Descalabrado	96,960	9, 10
Rosario	25,024	10
Aguilita	44,352	10
Meros	4,224	10
Turba	24,640	10

Source: R. C. Roberts, *Soil Survey of Puerto Rico*, Table 14,
pp. 392–407.

whether a region is one of deposition, receiving alluvial soils, or of poor
soils like those of mountains and rugged hills.

Relief and climate alone, however, were not sufficient to produce the
island's poorest soils. Man has also played an important role by removing,
with his clearing and destruction, the vegetable covers which protected
the soil, and by so exposing it to erosion. Especially during the past century and a half, the constant intensification of agriculture, as in tobacco,
corn, and minor crops which demand that the terrain be kept clear of all
other vegetation, has resulted in accelerated soil erosion.

There are two main kinds of erosion: "gully erosion" which forms
large ditches in which the water is concentrated, rapidly destroying and
carrying away the soils, and "sheet erosion" in which the water flows over
the terrain without forming gullies, as on a large plain, carrying away only
the top layer of soil. The first kind of erosion, which is the most destructive,
is rare in Puerto Rico and is found mostly in the granitic zones and on

the dry hills and terraces (Fig. 9.9). Sheet erosion is far more common but can at times be beneficial by carrying away the top layer of soil, which may be the poorest and most exhausted, and permitting the lower, more fertile layer to come to the top. However, sheet erosion has also played an

Figure 9.9. Gully Erosion between Juana Díaz and Coamo. (Courtesy of the Agricultural Extension Service.)

important role in the impoverishment of some of the mountain soils, as in the tobacco regions where the rocks have been exposed on the surface in many places (Fig. 9.10).

With its high density of population and scarcity of cultivable lands, Puerto Rico cannot afford the luxury of letting its soils be impoverished, little by little, through erosion. On the contrary, what the island needs is to have its soils produce constantly more.

The Soil Conservation Service of the United States has developed a series of techniques for preventing, or lessening, the erosion of the island's soils. In order to determine the applicability of the major means of combatting erosion, the Service has classified the various conditions of erosion in Puerto Rico, indicating where it is intense and where it is less. In the regions covered by trees, as in the coffee zone, it is minimal. Various degrees of erosion, classified by the Soil Conservation Service, are shown in Table 9.2.

The table shows that on about 28 per cent of Puerto Rico erosion is either minimal or undetectable. Between 30 per cent and 40 per cent of the island's lands present no serious conservation problems. About 50 per cent are inferior soils which do present conservation problems. Many

Figure 9.10. Sheet Erosion near Trujillo Alto. Note the uncovered roots of the tree. (Courtesy of the Puerto Rico Department of Education.)

Table 9.2. Soil erosion in Puerto Rico

Degree of Erosion	Percentage of All Soils
All soils	100.0
No apparent erosion	14.76
Light erosion, less than 25% of the topsoil removed	13.09
Moderate erosion, removing between 25 and 75% of the surface layer	9.49
Severe erosion, removing more than 75% of the surface layer and less than 25% of the subsoil	47.73
Extremely severe erosion, removing all of the surface layer and more than 25% of the subsoil	0.38
Limestone and rocky regions, used principally for forests, where the degree of erosion cannot be estimated	12.09
Urban areas, parks, lakes, etc.	2.46

of those lands are cultivated and produce, but at a cost of great labor and the application of capital in the form of fertilizers, machinery, and soil conservation programs. Whatever is won from those lands is done so at the cost of man's struggle to wrest as much as possible from nature.

In part toward the end of stemming erosion, studies have been made to determine the best uses to which the island's lands can be put without deteriorating. Table 9.3 summarizes the situation according to the findings of the Soil Conservation Service. After a detailed analysis of the problem, the Service concluded that the soils should be used as indicated in the table: only the soils of the first four groups should be cultivated; the following three groups should be used for pastures and forests; the last group should not be put to any agricultural or forestry uses whatever. The last-named are sterile beach sands, grounds covered by roads

Table 9.3. Productive capacity of the soils of Puerto Rico

Class	Description	Area (Acres)
	All lands	2,184,591
	Lands fit for cultivation	
I	Without special conservation practices	56,068
II	Requiring light conservation practices	181,204
III	Requiring complex or intensive ' conservation practices	366,283
IV	Occasionally requiring complex or intensive conservation practices	91,683
	Lands unfit for cultivation, but useful for pastures or forests	
V	Are not eroded and do not require special conservation practices	62,293
VI	With moderate restrictions and simple conservation practices	460,574
VII	For strongly restricted use and light conservation practices	882,328
	Lands unfit for productive vegetation	
VIII	Lands unfit for any kind of agricultural or forest use	23,424
	Miscellaneous (towns, roads, lakes, etc.)	53,734

Source: U.S. Department of Agriculture, Soil Conservation Service, 1948.

and buildings, and areas of bare rock where neither pastures nor forests can grow, let alone crops. Lands completely useless for agriculture total about three per cent of the island's area.

Table 9.3 shows that the area which can be utilized is quite large when compared with those of other countries, totalling about 97 per cent of the island and divided into two groups: 39 per cent can be used for crops and 58 per cent for pastures and forests.

However, the Soil Conservation Service established some restrictions with regard to the cultivated lands. The soils which require no special conservation practices are extremely limited in area, some 50,000 acres. The rest demand conservation practices—simple, complex, or intensive—or should be cultivated only occasionally (Figs. 9.11 and 9.12).

A comparison between those recommendations and what is being done today reveals the critical situation of the island's soils and their utilization. According to a study made by the Division of Scientific Land Use of the Puerto Rico Department of Agriculture, the area cultivated in 1951 was about 876,545 acres (39.24 per cent). That area included the acres which had been farmed the previous year, those which had been cultivated during the year in question and had been harvested at the time of the survey, those whose crops had failed, and some which had still to be harvested, like, for instance, sugar cane.

In addition to the 876,545 cultivated acres, a total of 101,570 were in rotation, being in pasture at the time of the survey. The figures give a total of 916,570 acres when the experts of the Soil Conservation Service had stated that the total usage should never exceed 845,000 acres. Puerto Rico, in other words, had exceeded the acreages fit for cultivation and had spilled into areas which, according to the experts, should not have been farmed. The latter included hills on which tobacco had been planted on slopes of 45 degrees or more, greatly accelerating erosion because the young tobacco plants were unable to hold the soil. But the pressure of population on the land makes it difficult to obey the recommendations of the experts in that field. Even with nearly 1,000,000 acres under cultivation at some time, Puerto Rico must constantly increase its agricultural production. From the economic point of view, if Puerto Rico farmed only the areas recommended by the Soil Conservation Service, the production would have to be optimum in the sense that each of the 800,000 would have to yield a maximum. However, the island has passed that point and has reached the point where the yield is disproportionate to the efforts expended. The island's soils have been farmed beyond the point of prudence. Instead of continuing the expansion, which is ruinous in the long run, Puerto Rico should cultivate the good soils more intensively, while combatting erosion by modern means.

In 1961 the Agricultural Extension Service of the University of Puerto Rico, together with the U.S. Department of Agriculture, published an inventory of the needs for conserving soils and water.[4] Based on a statistical sample, the inventory explains the conservation needs in terms of acres which require treatment in order to maintain production at the level required for national interests. The study traces the changes in land use expected by 1975 and makes recommendations regarding the desirability of converting soils which are currently being cultivated into areas of forests or pastures, or vice versa.

4. "Puerto Rico Soil and Water Conservation Needs Inventory," The Puerto Rico Conservation Needs Committee, 1961.

Figure 9.11. Barriers for Soil Conservation. (Courtesy of the Agricultural Extension Service.)

Figure 9.12. Tobacco Planted along Contours between Barranquitas and Comerío. (Courtesy of the Agricultural Extension Service. Photo by Atiles.)

221

Recently there appeared a study of the Mayagüez area, containing an analysis of the region's soils and recommendations for their best use, not only from the agricultural point of view but also from the commercial, industrial, and residential, with a detailed analysis of the limitations of the various areas in the light of such purposes.[5]

5. "Soils and their Interpretation for Various Uses, Mayagüez area, Puerto Rico," U.S. Department of Agriculture, Soil Conservation Service.

10

Population and Land

History of Development under Spanish Sovereignty

Puerto Rico's aboriginal inhabitants called the island Boriquén. The Spaniards named it San Juan Bautista (St. John the Baptist). Soon, however, the Spanish name came to designate the capital and the capital's name, Puerto Rico (Rich Port), was in turn applied to the island. According to the historian Cayetano Coll y Toste the indigenous population did not number more than 60,000, and modern investigators place it between 25,000 and 30,000. As mentioned in chapter 1, the Boriquén Indians were of the Arawak stock which had migrated to the lesser islands from South America, and probably from Florida to the Greater Antilles. Puerto Rico's Indians were peaceful people, somewhat more civilized than were the region's other natives, such as the Caribs of the Lesser Antilles who attacked Boriquén for loot and to capture women.

Columbus discovered Puerto Rico in 1493, between November 17 and 19. Fifteen years later, in 1508, Juan Ponce de León, who had accompanied the Great Admiral on his second voyage, arrived from Spain to start the island's colonization. Interest in the early settlement was heightened by the discovery of gold in the rivers as well as by the island's location near Hispaniola which in those days was the seat of Spain's imperial power in the Americas.

After some preliminary exploration, Ponce de León selected a site in the vicinity of the present capital. The first Spanish settlement, called Caparra, was founded May 10, 1509 (Fig. 10.1). About 1515, the city had a population of some 35.[1]

Some years later, the people of Caparra requested that the settlement be moved because the site was unhealthy and too far from the harbor. Ponce de León opposed the move but in 1521, during his absence from

1. Cayetano Coll y Toste, *Reseña del estado social y económico de la isla de Puerto Rico al tomar posesión de ella los Estados Unidos* [Review of the social-economic state of the island of Puerto Rico at the time of being taken over by the United States] (San Juan: "La Correspondencia," 1889), p. 26.

Figure 10.1. Ruins of Ponce de León's House in Pueblo Viejo, Caparra.

Figure 10.2. The Porta Coeli (Gate to Heaven) Church, in San Germán. Built in 1621, today it houses a museum of religious art.

Puerto Rico, the city was shifted to the small island on which it is still located.

While Ponce de León founded Caparra, Cristóbal de Sotomayor colonized the island's south. He founded Guánica in 1510 but was soon forced to abandon it because of the mosquitoes which bred in a nearby lagoon.

Near the end of 1510 Sotomayor moved to the port of Aguada where he founded the town of Sotomayor, which was burned and razed by Indians the following year. The same year (1511) it was replaced, on the banks of the Guaorabo River, by a town which came later to be called San Germán.[2] In 1528 it was sacked and burned by the French while the Indians did the same to the Convent of El Espinar which the Franciscans had built in Aguada. San Germán was rebuilt but its location near the harbor made it so accessible to the enemy that it was repeatedly burned and looted. In 1570 it was moved several leagues inland to its present location (Fig. 10.2).

During the first half of the sixteenth century the Carib Indians destroyed several other towns shortly after they were established, among them Santiago, today Naguabo near the Daguao River and Canóvanas. Colonization was further impeded by the scourge of hurricanes, three of

2. Salvador Brau, *Historia de Puerto Rico* [History of Puerto Rico] (New York: Appleton-Century-Crofts, 1904) pp. 27, 45.

which wrecked the colony in 1530 and another three in 1537, leaving desolation and misery in their wakes.

Salvador Brau describes the island's urban development during the first hundred years as follows:

> The slow pace of urban progress during the first century is explained by the prevailing poverty and the instability of production. The incomplete statistics of 1590 reveal only 2,500 white inhabitants . . . . only three towns existed in 1600. . . . The capital had 170 inhabitants and San Germán a hundred families. San Blás de Illescas, today's Coamo, had two or three dozen families. Those were the only towns which were officially recognized at the end of the sixteenth century.[3]

However, other settlements had been founded in addition to those three. On the north coast, by the Abacoa River, a group of settlers established what came soon to be known as Arecibo which, in 1570, already contained 30 families. Not until 1616 was it granted formal recognition under the name of San Felipe de Arecibo. By then it housed some 80 families.[4]

While the discovery of gold had heightened interest in the island's colonization early in the sixteenth century, its early exhaustion at the rivers' placer sites changed the settlers' interests and affected the colony's population. At the same time, the discovery and conquest of the rich empires of Mexico and Perú resulted in migrations from Puerto Rico to those countries. The Spanish Crown had to stop these migrations to prevent the island's depopulation.

To stay alive after the gold's exhaustion, the inhabitants had to begin cultivating the land. Very few Indians—their numbers reduced by forced labor, attacks by other Indians from the Lesser Antilles, and diseases—were left by the middle of the sixteenth century. The Indians who managed to survive until the nineteenth century were mixed with Negroes and white countrymen. As an ethnological component of Puerto Rico's population, the Indians virtually disappeared during the sixteenth century. They began to be replaced, as agricultural workers, by Negro slaves imported from Africa. In 1501, the Spanish Crown authorized Nicolás de Ovando, Governor of the Indies, to introduce such slaves.

Ruiz Arnau wrote as follows about the social-ethnologic development of Puerto Rico:

> During a large part of the sixteenth century, and all of the seventeenth, the conquest and colonization of Mexico impeded population growth in the

---

3. Ibid., p. 117.
4. Ibid., pp. 118–119.

Antilles, and Puerto Rico suffered serious setbacks in its demographic and social development.[5]

Three more towns, Aguada, Ponce, and Arecibo, which began to be formed during the preceding century, were officially founded during the seventeenth century.[6] The population of the capital was 500 in 1646, that of San Germán 200, and those of Arecibo and Coamo were about 100 and 80, respectively.[7]

The homes and other structures in the towns were wooden, except in San Juan where they were largely built of bricks, and many had two floors (Fig. 10.3). In the rest of the island, stonework construction did not begin until the eighteenth century.

Ruiz Arnau continues:

The eighteenth and nineteenth centuries saw a veritable rebirth through several immigration movements which first brought Biscayans, then Catalonians, and, during the final third, Asturians and Gallegos, ending with people from Mallorca. This became the most important ethnological movement of the Caucasian race and its evolution on Puerto Rican soil . . . .[8]

Thirty-one new towns were founded, chiefly during the second half of the eighteenth century.[9] Immigration continued while emigration stopped. In 1765 the colony had 44,833 inhabitants and at the century's end the population was 155,426, indicating a growth of more than 300 per cent in 35 years.[10]

During the first three centuries of colonization, the population distribution was determined largely by physical factors. In the early years, population growth occurred on the coast. Despite the south coast's greater advantages in the form of harbors, that of the north was more densely populated in the eighteenth century. The large number of rivers with auriferous sands, and the abundant precipitation, favored the north, while colonization was impeded along the south coast by the arid climate and the small flow of rivers in the dry seasons. In the number of inhabi-

5. R. Ruiz Arnau, *Desarrollo étnico social del pueblo puertorriqueño en el Cuarto Centenario de la Colonización de Puerto Rico* [Puerto Rico's ethnic and social development during the Fourth Centenary of the Island's Colonization] (publisher and date of publication unknown), p. 102.

6. Puerto Rico Planning Board, *Mapa de municipios y barrios* [Map of municipios and barrios] *Memoirs* 27, 31 (1953), and 55 (1955), San Juan, Puerto Rico. Note: In Puerto Rico a *municipio* is an administrative area, resembling a county. A *barrio* is a delimited administrative subdivision, resembling a precinct but either rural or urban in nature. For lack of precise translations, the two terms are here used in Spanish.

7. C. Coll y Toste, *op. cit.*

8. R. Ruiz Arnau, *op. cit.*, pp. 102–3.

9. Puerto Rico Planning Board, Map of Municipios and Barrios.

10. U.S. War Department, Census of Puerto Rico (Washington, D.C., 1900).

Figure 10.3. Restored Building. The construction is typical of
Spanish Architecture.

tants, the west coast came second to that of the north. Because of the
inaccessibility of the interior mountains, especially in the west, the mountainous regions were sparsely populated in the eighteenth century. Near
the end of the century, the population had expanded toward the west
coast and as far as the Caguas Valley on the interior plains.

The nineteenth century was marked by growth and development.
Largely during the century's first third, the population was enriched by
the immigration of Venezuelans, Frenchmen, Dominicans, and Spaniards
loyal to the Crown who fled from the revolutionary movements in Spain's
American possessions and were drawn to Puerto Rico by the island's political stability. During the period 1800 to 1834 the population increased
considerably, from 155,426 to 358,157 inhabitants.[11] In 1828 there were
3,111 houses and 2,392 huts in the towns, and 13,548 houses in the coun-

11. Pedro Tomás de Córdoba, *Memorias de la isla de Puerto Rico* [Record of the
Island of Puerto Rico] (Office of the Government, 1831).

try, together with 20,846 huts.[12] Although the statistics did not differentiate between urban and rural populations, the numbers of dwellings in the two zones indicate that the population was largely rural. One third of all the urban houses were located in the capital.

In 1765 the King abolished the payment of duties and taxes on African slaves brought to the Antilles. Between that year and 1845 the number of slaves in Puerto Rico increased greatly. However, while there were 41,818 slaves in 1834, there were only 31,600 in 1872. The reduction was caused by various government decrees and the rapid, worldwide spread of anti-slavery sentiments. The Puerto Ricans were prominent leaders in the movement for abolition. In March 1873, at the instigation of the Puerto Rican representatives some of whom were slave owners, Spain's National Revolutionary Assembly abolished slavery forever on the island. It should be noted that the Puerto Ricans were ready to accept abolition even without compensation.

Despite the cholera epidemic of 1855, which caused some 30,000 deaths, the population continued to grow as a result of immigration and births. At the end of the nineteenth century the census showed a total population of 953,243, which was 83 per cent rural.

The island's interior was colonized during the nineteenth century. The introduction of coffee helped to populate the region, especially in the west where natural conditions for cultivation of the crop were best. Coffee culture helped to develop the ports of Ponce and Mayagüez which were nearest to the coffee regions.

During the nineteenth century, the demographic and economic expansion of the island was aided considerably by a program of permanent public works. The capital's lighting system was inaugurated in 1820. Construction of the highway to cross the island from north to south, via the Cordillera Central, was begun in 1813 and completed in 1886. Before the end of the century, railway communication was established between San Juan and Río Piedras as well as between Cataño and Bayamón. In addition, the ports of Ponce, Mayagüez, Cabo Rojo, Aguadilla, and Fajardo were opened to commerce.

Development Under the United States of America

In 1898 Puerto Rico was ceded to the United States as one of the terms of the Treaty of Paris that put an end to the Spanish-American War. The island was ruled by American governors appointed by the U.S. President until 1948, when the first Puerto Rican, Jesús T. Piñero, was appointed to the governorship. The Island's Legislative Assembly was partly elected until 1917 and since then fully elected by popular vote. In 1952 Puerto

12. *Ibid.*

Rico became a Commonwealth with its own Constitution but voluntarily associated to the United States under the provisions of Public Law 600.

In 1899 the first census under the new regime showed a total population of 953,243. Since that date, the island's basic ethnic composition has remained the same, as the population has not been subject to large immigration movements. Race composition consists of Antillean Indian, African Negro, and European, predominantly Spanish. In 1970 the inhabitants numbered 2,689,932[13] a growth of 300 per cent since 1899. Between the present century's beginning and 1940, the rate of population growth increased, reaching 18.3 per cent during the last decade. That rate was due primarily to the decrease in the death rate. The birth rate remained at about 40 per 1,000 inhabitants until 1950, when it began to decline. In 1970 there were 23.7 births for every thousand inhabitants. But the decline in births was more than offset by that in deaths, which decreased from 31.4 per 1,000 in 1899 to 6.2 in 1970. As a result of improvements in the education of people of child-bearing age, the decline of the birth rate is expected to continue.

The percentage rate of population increase has diminished since 1940, to the point where the population of 1960 was only 6.3 per cent larger than that of 1950. The main reason for the decline in the rate of growth was heavy migration to the United States during the decade. Between 1960 and 1970 the average rate of population growth was some 14.5 per cent, an increase of more than 130 per cent over the 1960 census. The increase resulted from an excess of births over deaths as well as from changes in the migration movement to the U. S. mainland.

Population Distribution by Areas

In 1899, Puerto Rico's west and northwest—many of whose *barrios* (see footnote 6) contained more than 250 people per square mile—had the greatest densities of population. In the east central part, despite the fact that it began to be populated before the west, the density was about the same as in the west. Figs. 10.4 and 10.5). In 1899 almost the entire metropolitan area of San Juan contained fewer than 250 per square mile. It therefore seemed that the island's future growth of population would be concentrated in the northwest and west.

In 1899, the southern zone included a large number of *barrios* with 100 or fewer people per square mile. The situation reflected the region's aridity, but the subsequent creation of irrigation systems came to permit agriculture and so stimulated immigration from other regions. Nevertheless, in 1960 there were still a number of *barrios* in the south with densities below 100 per square mile.

13. According to preliminary figures of the 1970 U.S. decennial census.

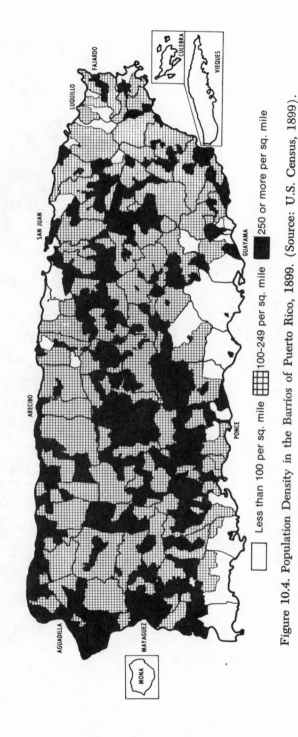

Figure 10.4. Population Density in the Barrios of Puerto Rico, 1899. (Source: U.S. Census, 1899).

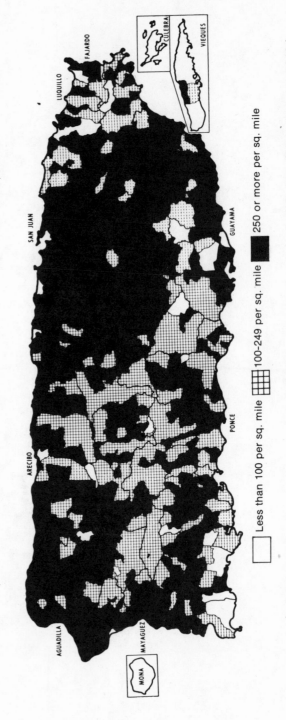

Figure 10.5. Population Density in the Barrios of Puerto Rico, 1960. (Source: U.S. Population Census, 1960.)

Less than 100 per sq. mile   100-249 per sq. mile   250 or more per sq. mile

Puerto Rico's most sparsely populated regions, with fewer than 100 per square mile, are those in which large areas are cultivated intensively, as for sugar cane, those covered by forests, and those which are too arid to permit intensive cultivation.

Urban Geography

Today, Puerto Rico's population is changing from rural to urban. In 1899 an estimated 138,707, persons, or 14.6 per cent of the total, lived in towns or cities. By 1970, the urban population came to 1,492,713 or 55.5 per cent of the total (Fig. 10.6). In 1970 there were 21 towns and cities whose metropolitan areas included more than 10,000 inhabitants, with a total of 1,248,229 or 83.6 per cent of the island's urban population. San Juan and Bayamón were the most densely populated, with 444,952 and 146,363, respectively. The municipalities which comprise the capital's metropolitan area (San Juan, Carolina, Guaynabo, Cataño, Bayamón, Trujillo Alto, and the Levittown Village of Toa Baja) had a total population of 814,286 in 1970, of whom 760,501 lived in their urban zones, and comprised 51 per cent of the island's total urban population. The concentration of people in metropolitan areas is today a worldwide phenomenon: it is expected that 64 per cent of Puerto Rico's total population will live in urban areas by 1975.

In 1970, the island's density of population was 787 per square mile. The agglomeration is, of course, greater in certain such urban zones as Santurce (a part of San Juan), where one finds 37,000 per square mile. In its slums the density reaches 75,000 per square mile.

The natural growth and the population's concentration in certain areas give rise to serious economic and social problems. Human crowding

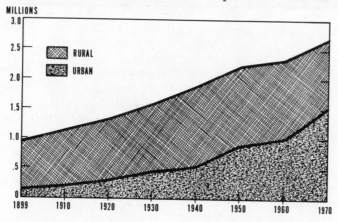

Figure 10.6. Urban and Rural Population 1899-1970.
(Source: U.S. Census Bureau.)

creates conditions unfavorable to health and conducive to contagion and tends to create scarcity of light and pure air. Puerto Rico's cities, like those in other countries, include industrial zones which create such problems as traffic congestion, noise, polution and the like, which make life disagreeable (Fig. 10.7). Family life is affected in the large urban centers where the human relationship and co-existence of the small town give way to mass anonymity. Urban life, moreover, creates problems for the government, such as the need to provide housing for people with low incomes and the extension and maintenance of public services.

Figure 10.7. Traffic on the Modern Baldorioty de Castro Avenue and Adjoining Streets.

Many urban problems result from the ignorance of basic planning concepts which has on occasion led to great disasters. During the Middle Ages cities were abandoned after being invaded by epidemics like the "Black Death" which took one third of Europe's population. While the rapid growth of modern cities has given rise to serious problems, the conditions of life and development in them have nevertheless been greatly improved through the use of modern planning.

Planning has been applied in Puerto Rico since the beginnings of Spanish colonization but the present system, dating from 1942, is characterized by its democratic and integrated processes. Physical, fiscal, economic, and social planning are brought into play in an atmosphere of democracy. The results are apparent not only in the physical improve-

Figure 10.8. Urban Housing Development for Low-Income Families in Aguadilla.

ment of the cities but also in that of the economic and social life of their inhabitants. (Fig. 10.8).

Socioeconomic Problems and Their Geographic Base

Despite Puerto Rico's small size, its people display a high degree of mobility for internal migration. As elsewhere, that geographic mobility stems primarily from the better social-economic opportunities offered by one region in comparison with others. In 1960, 25 per cent of Puerto Rico's inhabitants did not live in the places of their births. In San Juan's metropolitan area, which showed the greatest increase in population, 54.4 per cent of the inhabitants had come from other municipalities.

The outward mobility of the Puerto Ricans has increased during the past three decades. Between the century's onset and 1940 the total net emigration comprised 70,000 persons. After World War II, near the end of the 1940's, the average annual emigrants rose to 35,000, most of whom moved to the United States. During the first half of the 1950's, the rate of emigration averaged 49,000 annually, but the figure was reduced to 40,000 during the second five years. The period 1960–63 saw a drastic reduction in emigration, with a departure of only 9,000 migrants annually. The net emigration in 1964 comprised 4,366 persons, the lowest in 22 years. During the four-year period 1966 to 1970 the net loss was 132,753, a high average.

Immigration was dominated by people born in Puerto Rico or of Puerto Rican descent. During the first half of the 1960's the immigration consisted of: 77 per cent Puerto Ricans; 9 per cent people born in the United States of non-Puerto Rican origins; and 14 per cent foreigners (Table 10.1). Among the foreigners, about 10 per cent of the total immigrants were Cubans; before 1960, the majority of foreigners were from the Dominican Republic.

Table 10.1. Composition of immigration
(years ending in March)

| | 1960–65 | | 1965–66 |
	number	Average Annual	number
Born in Puerto Rico or of Puerto Rican descent	143,100	28,620	35,800
Born in the United States, not of Puerto Rican descent	17,200	3,440	5,400
Foreign-born, not of Puerto Rican descent			
Cubans	18,900	3,780	3,200
Others	8,000	1,600	5,200
Totals	187,200	37,440	49,600

The interchange between in and out migrations prevents the movement of people to the island from having cumulative effects. There have been periods when immigration fell below emigration. In 1967, when work opportunities for Puerto Ricans were high in the United States, net emigration exceeded the inflow of people.

The majority of emigrants are rural young people in search of better economic opportunities. About 64 per cent of those who leave the island have family incomes of below $2,000 per year, and most of them are men.

Were it not for emigration and the decline of the populations' natural growth, Puerto Rico's population would today exceed 3,000,000 as compared with approximately 2,700,000, and the population problem would be even greater.

The sizes of families reflect the population's proportional reduction. In 1940 the island's homes contained an average of 5.2 persons each, which fell to 4.79 by 1960. In the latter year, urban families consisted of an average of 4.36 members and those in the rural areas of 5.19. The average size of Puerto Rican families was 4.5 in 1970.

The decline in the sizes of families during the past two decades helps the distribution of incomes. In 1940, 2.9 per cent of all Puerto Rican families had annual incomes of $1,000 or more; by 1963, the figure had risen to 83 per cent. It is expected that, by 1975, the great majority of the island's families will enjoy incomes of $2,000 or more; in 1965, only 56 per cent of the families had reached that point. (Fig. 17.5; Appendix R).

Improved education has enabled the population increasingly to take advantage of new opportunities arising from the country's progress. In 1940, about 50 per cent of the school-age population attended public or private schools. In 1966, more than 86 per cent of the children between six and eighteen years of age were in those schools; in the United States the figure was 90.8 per cent. In 1940, 49,340 pupils attended secondary schools (grades 7 to 12); the figure exceeded 255,000 in 1970 (Fig. 10.9). The lunchrooms of public and private schools served more than 429,489 children in 1970, as contrasted with 54,000 in 1940. The school-lunch program has not only benefited the children's health but has also improved dietary habits and fostered democratic co-existence.

University education has been diversified and intensified. Among today's several centers of higher learning, the University of Puerto Rico is the most important, with its College of Agriculture and Mechanical Arts in Mayagüez, its Schools of Medicine and Odontology in San Juan, its university College in Cayey, and regional colleges in Humacao, Arecibo, and Ponce. In 1940, about 5,000 students attended the university; by 1970 the student body exceeded 42,500 (Fig. 10.10). The Inter American University is located in San Germán but maintains several campuses in other parts of the island. Its student body numbered 10,000 in 1970. There is also a "Colegio del Sagrado Corazón" (Sacred Heart College) in Santurce, a part of San Juan, the Puerto Rico Junior College in Río Piedras, and the Catholic University (Regina Cleri) in Ponce. The latter has an enrollment of some 7,150 students. The total enrollment in Puerto Rican universities and colleges had risen to 64,450 by 1970. As the universities grew, new subjects of study were added and teaching methods were improved. The studies of medicine and odontology did not exist in 1940, nor did those of public administration, cooperatives, and labor relations, which are offered by the universities today.

One-fourth of Puerto Rico's population attends school today; in the United States the figure is one-fifth. In Puerto Rico approximately one child is in school for every worker while in the United States there are two workers for every school-child. Moreover, the worker in the continental United States enjoys a higher income than does his Puerto Rican counterpart, indicating that Puerto Rico's efforts in education are considerably greater than are those of the United States. Illiteracy has been reduced in Puerto Rico from 31.5 per cent in 1940 to below 12 per cent in 1970.

The condition of the island's homes reflects dramatically the population's social-economic levels. In recent years the construction of homes, private as well as public, has very greatly accelerated. Generally, they are now built of reinforced concrete or cement blocks. The traditional

Figure 10.9. Modern Secondary School in a New San Juan Community.

Figure 10.10. The University of Puerto Rico in Rió Piedras.

use of wood, bricks, and rubble, as construction materials, has been largely eliminated. The growth of urban zones, with the increased demand for adequate housing, has created serious problems. The people's social mobility, resulting in an increase of 473,000 urban inhabitants during the past two decades, created a need for 100,000 new homes.

In 1957, the Planning Board estimated that 60 per cent of the population lived in 278,000 homes which were inadequate, unsanitary, flimsy, and located in bad environments. Most of those homes, some 56 per cent, were found in the rural areas inhabited by families with low incomes. Migration to the rural towns and settlements intensified the problem. More than 70,400 new homes were built during the decade 1940–50, and 71,450 during the ensuing ten years. The cost of those homes, without lots, averaged $6,000 each, which was far too high for most families in need of lodging. About 88 per cent of those families had average incomes of less than $2,000. The slums grew primarily from the people's economic condition and the resulting imbalance between supply and demand. Between 30 and 40 per cent of the urban inhabitants live in slums. In San Juan's metropolitan area, where the condition is most serious, some 36,000 families live in slums and about 2,000 more are added annually to that population.

The average annual increase in the construction of private dwellings has been about 17 per cent in recent years. As a result, Puerto Rico is among the countries with the highest percentage of owner-occupied homes. In 1963 about 70 per cent of the island's families owned their homes. In San Juan's metropolitan area the rate was about 62 per cent; in the rest of the island it was some 74 per cent.

The rapid and expensive clearing of slums is an extremely difficult task. The Urban Renewal and Housing Corporation ("Corporación de Renovación Urbana y Vivienda," known as CRUV) has done much to move people who live in slums into economic and hygienic homes. By June 1967, the corporation had built 54,095 housing units at a cost of $292 million, 60 per cent of them in San Juan's metropolitan area. Since incomes of $2,000 per year forbid the acquisition of houses costing an average of $6,000, it is impossible to depend exclusively on private initiative for the construction of homes. To date, technological methods have not reached the point where adequate urban homes for families with incomes of $2,000 can be built for $3,000 to $3,500.

Thanks to various Commonwealth and Federal programs, rural housing has improved greatly. As a result of those programs, more than 80,000 rural families have moved to family-sized farms or new rural communities. One of the agencies involved is the Social Programs Administration of the Department of Agriculture which distributes farms toward the end of improving life and providing minimum incomes for rural familes. Some 11,667 such farms have been established where the farmer and his family receive instruction in adequate agricultural methods. The size of such farms varies with the soil's fertility, but all are designed for a potential production of at least $2,000 net per family.

The rural families which lack access to such farms, or are not qualified to work them, are moved into rural communities, located in regions which offer opportunities for employment, access to schools and roads, and use of public services. In addition, the communities provide common pastures, recreation fields, religious centers, and the like. Some 385 such communities, inhabited by more than 70,185 families, have been established to date under that program (Fig. 10.11).

The provision of good housing for rural families is accelerated by the Social Programs Administration's programs of mutual aid and self-help (Fig. 10.12). Under that system of community action, the families donate their labor, working together on the construction of concrete homes, each containing at least two bedrooms as well as basic facilities. The government gives advice and technical assistance, and makes loans for the value of the construction materials.

Such community action makes it possible to build homes at a cost of between $475 and $575 each. The family repays the cost, without interest, in monthly installments of $3.00. In that manner, 28,339 homes have been built in the island's various communities. The greatest benefit gained from the mutual aid, self-help, program may well be the growth of a spirit of integration and social cohesion among the families of the communities, resulting in a marked improvement of rural life. The government's aim is to help every Puerto Rican family to own an adequate home. In the public housing projects in which families live either temporarily or permanently, efforts are made to provide the various apartments with facilities which resemble those of privately owned homes.

The government's policy for improving rural life does not stop with the reestablishment of poor families. Among the programs which contribute considerably to that improvement are those under which the government provides and extends such public services as electrification, the building of roads and highways, the distribution of potable water, and the installation of rural telephones. According to the 1970 Census there were 278,000 rural families in Puerto Rico. Potable water has been brought to more than 200,000 of these families. Most rural families have by now been provided with electric light and power, and it is expected that the program of rural electrification will reach all of the island's rural families very soon. Not only does the extension of those services improve rural life, but it also reduces the isolation of rural families and, in turn, the migration to urban areas (Fig. 10.13).

The island's vital statistics indicate notable improvements in the people's economic and general well-being. During the period 1940 to 1970, the life expectancy of the average Puerto Rican rose from 47.1 to 70.4

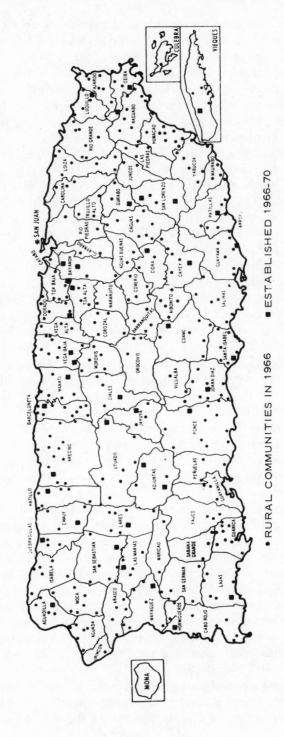

● RURAL COMMUNITIES IN 1966 ■ ESTABLISHED 1966-70

Figure 10.11. Rural Communities Established under the Auspices of the Commonwealth Government. (Source: Social Programs Administration, Department of Agriculture of Puerto Rico.

Figure 10.12. Home for a Low-Income Family. The house is being built by mutual aid and self-help.

years, while the death rate fell from 18.2 per thousand inhabitants to a little more than 6. Today, life expectancy is 70 years, equal to that in the United States. Between 1940 and 1963, Puerto Rico's life expectancy rose 22.8 years, while that in the United States rose only 7 years. The fact that Puerto Rico's people live considerably longer than they did results in a marked decrease of annual deaths. The death rate compares favorably with that of a highly developed country.

The improvements in health are in large measure due to progress in education and medical care. During the past two decades the number of doctors doubled. The disease rate was greatly reduced in such ailments as tuberculosis and gastroenteritis while others, notably malaria, have been completely eliminated. Major attention is given to the public health services which receive approximately 15 per cent of the island's total budget. The improvement of hospital facilities plays a major role in the matter of public health. It is expected that by 1975 the public health service will offer 3.5 beds per thousand inhabitants.

Improvements in diet have been fundamental in bettering the people's health. At the beginning of the 1940's the general diet contained a high proportion of starches. By the end of the decade of 1950, the annual consumption of starches had been reduced to 166 pounds per capita. The same

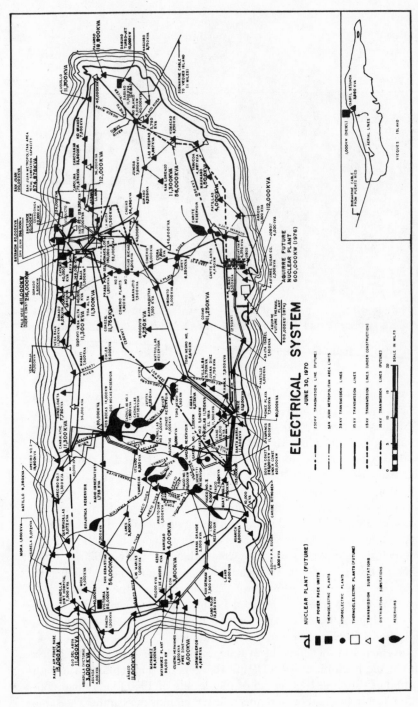

Figure 10.13. Electrical System of Puerto Rico Operated by the Water Resources Authority. (Source: Prospectus for $60 million bond issue by WRA, January 1, 1971.)

244

period saw an increase to 265 pounds per capita in the consumption of such nourishing protein foods as milk, meat, fruits, and eggs. That dietary improvement is expected to continue, and by 1975 the Puerto Rican people may well consume one-third more milk, double the amount of meat, and three times as many eggs as are consumed today.

Puerto Rico's per capita consumption of such nourishing foods as meat and milk is considerably higher, for instance, than is that in the Dominican Republic, though as yet it is lower than in the United States. In 1969, the consumption of beef and pork rose to 89.9 pounds per capita, which was double that in the Dominican Republic but only more than half of the 155.5 pounds consumed in the United States. The per capita average annual consumption of milk is about 140 quarts in Puerto Rico, some 60 quarts in the Dominican Republic, and about 485 quarts in the United States. Technicians in the United Nations recommend a per capita average annual consumption of some 230 quarts of milk. Although it has improved greatly, the diet of the Puerto Rican people still remains deficient in the more nourishing items.

The planning of cities and communities has been another major factor in the island's development, as has the provision of parks and beaches for popular rest and recreation. Parks and playgrounds created since 1940 number 637, and every town has at least one. Such means have helped to make the people more aware of the need for good daily coexistence. The recreation fields, moreover, help to reduce juvenile delinquency.

11

The Economic Structure

A country's economic structure results from the interplay of the various productive sectors which comprise the economic order. It depends primarily on the availability of the basic factors of production (capital, land, and labor), on the degree of technology and specialization devoted to the utilization of those factors, and on the market for current production. The concurrence of those factors comprises the basis for all industry, as well as for the development of economic systems.

Basic Factors of Production

The basic factors of production are defined as those goods which do not in themselves satisfy human wants or needs, though serving to produce other goods which do satisfy those desires and needs.

LAND

In the broadest sense, the factor of land includes not only the physical area of terrain, but also its natural resources, the God-given riches such as its extent and quality, its natural vegetation, minerals, internal and external hydrography, and the like. In the quantitative sense, the natural resources are fixed. We may use a part or all of them, well or poorly, but we cannot alter their quantities. While the use of fertilizer and irrigation increases the land's yield, the land itself is fixed; increased production is the result of capital investment, while improved techniques permit the use of natural resources which had previously remained idle. Possibly, sunlight may in the future be used for the production of the energy needed for the operation of industrial plants, but it must be repeated that natural resources have their fixed limits. That fact led to Malthus' profound pessimism over a major future economic crisis,[1] which he expressed in his famous "Law of Diminishing Returns."[2]

In Puerto Rico's case it must be repeated that the natural resources are scarce, especially in relation to the density of population. In that important matter the island compares extremely unfavorably with the majority of the world's countries blessed with abundant natural riches. It is therefore imperative that the Puerto Ricans use their scarce resources to the utmost and with the greatest effectiveness.

Area. As stated above, Puerto Rico, with an area of 3,435 square miles, is the smallest of the Greater Antilles. The land area, after deducting the lakes and lagoons, is only 3,417 square miles, which is almost microscopic when compared with many European and American countries. That small area obviously has an inhibiting effect on opportunities for economic expansion, especially in view of a demographic density of 800 inhabitants per square mile, which places Puerto Rico among the world's most heavily populated countries.

It is estimated that some 40 per cent of the island's total area consists of mountains, 35 per cent of hills, and only 25 per cent of plains.[3] A large part of the country is hilly and rugged, a terrain unfavorable for agriculture. Moreover, only 25 to 30 per cent of the island's soils can be classified as good.

According to studies made by the Federal Soil Conservation Service, no more than 700,000 acres, or slightly over 30 per cent of the total, are fit for cultivation, and even some of those require careful measures for the control of soil erosion. The technicians recommend that the rest of the island, some 70 per cent, be used for pastures and forests and nonagricultural uses.[4] In 1968 land use in Puerto Rico according to the Commonwealth's Department of Agriculture was as follows: 35 per cent in pastures; 14 per cent in forests and woodlands; 20 per cent nonproductive or located in urban areas or military reserves; the remainder, about 31 per cent, is cultivated as follows: about 11 per cent for sugar cane, 8 per cent coffee, and 12 per cent tobacco, minor fruits, and so on (Table 18.1).

Minerals. Comparatively speaking, Puerto Rico is extremely poor in mineral resources. Iron, nickel, manganese, lead, and zinc exist in quantities known to be so small that their commercial exploitation is impossible by methods known today. Recent explorations, high prices, and new tech-

1. T. R. Malthus, *An Essay on the Principles of Population* (London: Reeves and Turner, 1872).

2. In its simplest sense, the law states that increased expenditures of labor or invested capital on a given area of land will result in the increase of resulting returns but that the time will come when the rate of production growth will fall below that of the increase of labor and capital.

3. Rafael Picó, *Geografía de Puerto* [Geography of Puerto Rico], Part I (Río Piedras: University of Puerto Rico Press, 1954), p. 16.

4. Ibid., pp. 212–16.

niques seem to permit the imminent working of low-grade copper ores in the island's interior. Only the "common," nonmetallic minerals are found in abundance, such as lime, marble, silica sands, limestone, and clay. These are important in several of the island's principal industries, such as construction, the manufacture of cement, bottles, and agriculture.

Sources of Energy. The use of such sources of energy as coal and oil is basic to modern economic activity. The increasing substitution of mechanical forces for human labor in the operation of factories is a dominant characteristic of the industrial revolution. Unfortunately Puerto Rico, having neither oil wells nor coal mines, has no sources of direct energy and has therefore had to labor for maximum development of its sources of hydroelectric energy. Until the beginning of the last decade that was the main source of electric energy. However, the enormous industrial development of recent years demanded so much energy that hydraulic sources proved insufficient. At present, only about 1/20 of the energy is produced hydraulically, the remainder from imported oils. Though that fact seems to limit the possibilities for economic and social development it has not constituted, to date, an insurmountable obstacle.

Hydrography. A large number of rivers, though most of them with limited flow, are found in Puerto Rico's interior. None are navigable or contain sufficient fish to constitute a mode of life. However, several of the rivers are used for the production of electric energy which has by now been developed virtually to its limits.

Regarding external hydrography, it should be repeated here that the resources of the surrounding seas are sparse. The coastal waters lack the conditions required for the creation of the fishing banks which are essential for the development of the industry on a commercial scale.

Capital. The factor of capital includes such goods as buildings, machinery, equipment, and the like, which are used for the production of other goods and services for the consuming public. Private concerns are the principal owners of such capital goods. The municipal governments as well as the Commonwealth, also possess such capital goods as office buildings, trucks, highways, and the like. All homes, most of them privately owned, also represent investments in capital goods.

Unlike the natural resources, whose quantities are fixed by nature, capital goods can be multiplied through investments. In fact, the accumulation of capital goods is the backbone of a country's development and economic progress. In that important matter, Puerto Rico has in recent years succeeded in maintaining a rate of capital formation which is at least 25 per cent of the gross product. This percentage compares favorably with most of the world's nations. That great accumulation of capital is demonstrated by the fact that toward the end of 1969 the Economic Development Administration had promoted, or helped to promote, about 1,785 modern factories. The accumulation of capital can also be observed in the improvements of means of communication and transportation; in schools, hospitals, and universities; in the extension and improvement of such public services as the distribution of water and light, which benefits almost the entire population. In addition to such general expansion, individual citizens have built modern homes and apartment houses in unprecedented quantities. During fiscal 1969, private investment in capital goods and homes reached $983 million and that by the government $107 million, which adds up to 26.6 per cent of the gross product. Consideration of the growth of inventory, some $145 million, reveals that Puerto Rico's gross domestic investment reached $1,235 million in 1969, or 30.2 per cent of the value of gross production. The cumulative total investment in new factories had by then reached more than $1.6 billion.

The Formation of Capital. In the process of capital formation, a part of a country's productive resources is used for the construction of factories, homes, roads, the acquisition of machinery and equipment, and the like, instead of being used to produce such consumer goods as foodstuffs, clothing, automobiles, and refrigerators. In other words, a part of the income is saved instead of being consumed. Directly or indirectly, through the banks and other financial institutions, the savings are soon channeled into investments for the multiplication of producer goods.

Naturally, the formation of capital is much easier in a rich and developed country like the United States than in one which is underdeveloped and poor in natural resources. In the United States a substantial part of current production can be used every year for adding to the producer goods, without undue restrictions on consumption. In underdeveloped countries, on the other hand, current production is often barely sufficient to provide for the people's minimal needs. Such a country is unable to save and so finds it impossible to use a considerable part of its resources for the creation of capital goods through which to increase its productive capacity and raise its population's level of living. Puerto Rico's case is therefore noteworthy. With few natural resources and little capital, the island has now reached the point where its economic system compares favorably with those of most of the world's countries, and especially the Latin American republics.

In the 22 years between 1947 and 1969, the investment in capital goods on the island was $7,906 million, nearly 54 per cent of which came from continental United States. The annual formation of capital was only $23 million in 1940; $1,404 million in 1971.

The Government's Role in Capital Formation. While private investments have played an important part in Puerto Rico's development, those of the government have also contributed notably to the island's high rate of capital formation. The essential public services, such as, roads, electric energy, aqueducts and sewers, public health, and education, have been improved and expanded remarkably. Of the $1,090 million invested in

capital goods in 1969, approximately $322 million were public invest-
ments; approximately $107 million were alloted to permanent improve-
ments such as schools and roads (Fig. 11.1); more than $46 million were
invested in urban public housing developments; and $170 million in phys-
ical plant, equipment and machinery by the public corporations of the
Commonwealth and its municipalities. Those considerable public investments have resulted in the fact that the quality and extent of government
services are today far greater than they were fifteen or twenty years ago,
a condition which has greatly facilitated the island's economic and social
growth during those years.

Puerto Rico's political and economic relations with the United States
are extremely important in the formation of capital. Its fortunate position
within the financial and credit structure of the United States facilitates
the acquisition of public financing and private capital. The fact that income derived from public bond issues is exempt from federal, state, and
local taxes is extremely important.

The Government Development Bank for Puerto Rico, since its establishment as fiscal agent (May 15, 1945) of Puerto Rico's public borrowers
and up to June 30, 1970, had obtained for the Commonwealth, its municipalities, and public corporations, financing to the extent of $4.2 billion of
which $1.8 billion was long-term credit for capital improvement projects.

All of those organizations and institutions have an unblemished debt
record; to date they have never defaulted or been delinquent in the payment of principal or interest on any of their financial obligations.

POPULATION AND LABOR

Labor constitutes the most important factor of production. Puerto
Rico's population grew from 1,859,000 in 1940 to 2,689,932 in 1970. During that period the birth rate declined from 39 to 24.8 per thousand inhabitants while the death rate went from 18.2 to 6.1 per thousand. The
average life expectancy, on the other hand, rose from 46 to 70 years between 1940 and today. According to the United Nations the world's population increased by more than 1,200 million during the past 60 years.[5]
Projections made by United Nations' experts indicate that the world's
population will increase by another thousand million in the course of the
next 15 or 20 years and that the greater part of the growth will occur in
the underdeveloped countries. The experts refer to a "population explo-
sion" by 1980. Projections for Puerto Rico indicate that the island's population will reach 3,643,000 by then,[6] resulting in a population density of
more than 1,000 per square mile as compared with today's 800. While the
population growth will certainly produce more workers, it will also pro-

5. World Population 1900: 1,608 million; 1959: 2,810 million.
6. Social Analysis Group, Planning Board, 1963.

Figure 11.1. Intersection No. 5, San Juan.

duce more people to be fed and more consumers to be satisfied, while the natural resources remain static.

The term "labor force" denotes all people who are working or seeking work, including the self-employed. Most of them are between 14 and 70 years old. A marked growth of the labor force began at the onset of the present decade. In 1970 the labor force had risen to 838,000, an increase of 213,000 since 1960 (Table 11.1). The growth was caused primarily by immigration and by the increasing number of women who enter the labor force every year.

The employment of women has increased at a higher rate than has that of men. In 1970, the force comprised 47 per cent of the civilian population, 14 or more years old, a proportion which has remained relatively stable since 1960. In addition to the labor force, Puerto Rico's population in 1969 included more than 923,000 persons, such as housewives, school and university students, and retired people, capable of doing productive work.

The productivity of the labor force does not depend only on its size; it also depends on its quality, namely skills and energy, and on the quality and quantity of other factors of production, such as capital goods, natural resources, and technological levels. Though the island's labor force is

Table 11.1. Average civilian population, (not in institutions) 14 years of age or more, and the labor force, 1950–1969 (in thousands)

Year	Civilian Population	Labor Force
1950	1,289	684
1951	1,286	713
1952	1,270	679
1953	1,268	646
1954	1,260	631
1955	1,300	637
1956	1,331	643
1957	1,338	636
1958	1,350	637
1959	1,374	637
1960	1,383	625
1961	1,401	639
1962	1,454	670
1963	1,513	695
1964	1,583	736
1965	1,646	769
1966	1,640	771
1967	1,665	783
1968	1,703	800
1969	1,731	808

Source: Puerto Rico Department of Labor.
Note: Figures revised on the basis of the 1960 population census.

large in comparison with other factors of production, there is a shortage of the skills and knowledge required for industrialization. A study of "The Unemployment Problem of Puerto Rico," made by the Economic Research Department of the Government Development Bank for Puerto Rico, revealed that among the main causes of unemployment are the abundance of unskilled labor, which in turn results from the density of population, and the rapid advance of industrialization.[7] Puerto Rico's labor force comprises less than 30 per cent of the population while that of the United States comes to 40 per cent. Since approximately 70 per cent of Puerto Rico's population does not belong to the labor force, and since more than 36 per cent of the population is younger than 14 years, the body of workers is expected to expand greatly in the next few years. Since the land cannot be stretched, the maintenance of the high rate of social-economic progress, and the attainment of the stated objectives, depend primarily on the accumulation of capital goods and the training of workers. Continued investments in the improvement of education and in vocational training is therefore imperative, as is the maintenance, year after year, of the high rate of capital investment. While the worker is the most important factor of production, he is only potentially so since he must be employed in order to produce.

Technique. Economists define technology as the art of combining the means of production to achieve maximum benefits from the avilable resources, by means of improved management and efficiency. It is impossible, in Puerto Rico, to measure the value of technology quantitatively or to estimate the rate of its progress through the years. Nevertheless, technological advances have clearly played an extremely important role in the island's economic progress. The close relations between private enterprise and the government on the one hand and those with the United States on the other have enabled the Puerto Ricans to adopt for their economy many of the most modern technical advances of the United States. Many North American enterprises, when establishing branches in Puerto Rico, bring to the island the most advanced knowledge and techniques.

One way of calculating technological advances quantitatively is to estimate the relations between production and labor according to the formula: production ÷ man-hours. The growth of that ratio is due partly to the increase in capital and partly to technology. In the sugar industry, for instance, 166.2 man-hours were required to produce one ton of sugar in 1946, while only 76 man-hours were needed in 1966. The decrease of 90

7. The number of workers per square mile was some 200 in Puerto Rico, compared to 20 in the United States, according to the study by Dr. Vernon R. Esteves and Vicente Guzmán Soto, "El problema del desempleo en Puerto Rico" [The unemployment problem in Puerto Rico] (San Juan: Government Development Bank for Puerto Rico, January 1963), p. 8.

man-hours, indicating a marked improvement in efficiency in the production of sugar in two decades, was undoubtedly due in part to increases in
capital investments and in part to technological advances.

To an extent Puerto Rican technology speaks for itself without re-
course to statistics. The island's progress in that respect is easily appre-
ciated through a visit to one of its refineries to see how, through the
investment of millions of dollars, vast quantities of crude oil are transformed into energy and other products with help from a very small group
of workers; or through comparison of the old home needlework with to-
days' clothing factories; or by comparing the various agricultural
processes used on the island's large farms such as the dairy farms and the
sugar plantations with the agricultural operations of twenty years ago
(Fig. 11.2).

Figure 11.2. Milking Machine on a Modern Dairy Farm.

Technical advances result from research and education. The island's
rate of progress depends basically on the research which constitutes one
of the determining factors in the attainment of progress. The research, in
turn, depends on the educational system without which there would be
no scientists for the laboratories or engineers and administrators for the
factories. Clearly, no country can hope to reach a rapid pace of social-
economic development without first and constantly improving and accelerating the people's education. Maximum investment in education is
therefore not only beneficial, but indispensable for continued social-

economic progress. Hence, Puerto Rico's government allots major priority to the intensification of education.

In 1970 students in the island's educational institutions numbered more than 814,000 of whom 65,000 attended universities. In that year, the people of Puerto Rico invested $350 million in the educational system, the equivalent of 8 per cent of the gross product and one third of the current budget.

The Government and Economic Development

The attitude and policy of the Puerto Rican government have been, undoubtedly, the most effective stimuli given to the factors of production. The government's contribution to economic development has consisted not only of aid in the formation of capital but also of taking the initiative in many aspects of the people's general progress. The success of various developmental programs, such as industrialization, aid to agriculture and commerce, and the development of cooperatives, results from the constant application of governmental planning programs as well as from the abilities and dedication of the public servants who participate in those programs. Public agencies have been established to serve various aspects of the economy, among them the Planning Board, the Economic Development Administration, the Commercial Development Company, the Land Authority, and the Government Development Bank. These stimulate and complement private activity in addition to contributing to economic growth through credit, subsidies, investments, buildings, and technical advice In addition, as in the case of the Land Authority, they may participate directly in the production process.

The creation of such agencies has resulted from an orderly, democratic, and integrated process of planning in the economic, fiscal, physical, and social fields. Undoubtedly, one of the main functions of the Planning Board is to advise. This government agency carries out also coordinating and regulatory functions such as regulating urban development and reviewing public works projects. The task of coordinating public works through construction programs, master plans, and the reveiw of projects, is an important function that avoids duplication of effort in Puerto Rico's public works. Moreover, it assures that the standards applied and the locations of projects are in accord with existing laws and the directives of the governor as the island's first executive. The mission of planning is to harmonize public and private action for the public's benefit.

Sectors of Production

Under "Basic Factors of Production," we discussed Puerto Rico's situation with regard to natural resources, the labor force, and capital. We showed the labor force to be abundant in relation to the island's area, though its productive potential is limited by the paucity of skills. The natural resources, on the other hand, are in general extremely limited. several important resources, such as copper and petroleum, indispensible for basic industries, are not exploited in Puerto Rico. Moreover, it is well-known that the cultivation of large parts of the island is limited by factors of area and nature which impede to a great extent the potential growth and expansion of the economy. While the factor of capital is regarded as small, we have shown that the high rate at which capital goods have accumulated in recent years, plus the government's orderly and integrated planning of the factors of production, have facilitated the maintenance of a rate of growth comparable to those of the world's most progressive countries.

In this section, we propose to clarify the structure of the island's economic system through the analysis of the several sectors of production, how the resources of production are used, and the manner in which they are distributed among the most important industires.

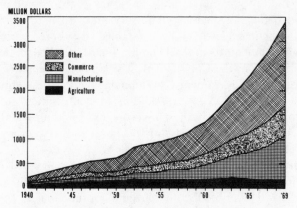

MILLION DOLLARS

Other
Commerce
Manufacturing
Agriculture

Figure 11.3 Net Income by Industrial Origin, 1940–1969. (Source: Puerto Rico Planning Board.)

Figures 11.3 and 11.4 and Appendices B and C compare the sources of the Commonwealth's income and the employment per economic sector in 1940, 1950, 1960, 1965 and 1970, indicating the relative importance of the six principal sectors of the economy. Fig. 11.3 and Appendix B show the contribution of each sector to the island's net income, while Fig. 11.4 and Appendix C reveal the average employment per sector. The charts bring out the economic transformation which has taken place during the time indicated, and especially since 1950.

Fig. 11.3 shows Puerto Rico's economy to have been preponderantly agricultural in 1940. In that year agriculture yielded $70.5 million, almost a third of the total net income, while providing 230,000 jobs, about 43 per cent of the island's total. Manufacturing brought in less than $27 million, or some 11.6 per cent of the total, and employed about 100,000 workers, of whom 45,000 did home needlework, an industry which was characterized by abysmally low pay. The other economic sectors, construction and mining, were insignificant, contributing only $3 million to the total net income. Commerce, central and municipal governments, transportation and other public utilities, finance, insurance, real estate, and the like yielded more than 57 per cent of the total net income and provided approximately 38 per cent of the employment.

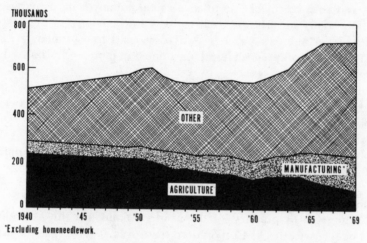

Figure 11.4. Employment by Industries, 1940–1969.
(Source: Puerto Rico Planning Board.)

By 1970 the situation was entirely different. Although the contribution of agriculture to the total net income had increased 250 per cent during the past 29 years, from $70.0 million to $184 million, the proportion of the total net income contributed by it was less than 5 per cent. In 1940 agriculture came first in employment. In 1970 it employed about 74,000 workers, or about 156,000 fewer than in 1940. On the other hand, wages and working conditions were much better than they were 30 years before. Meanwhile, during the period under consideration, the contibution to the total net income made by manufacturing grew by 2,400 per cent, or from $27 million to $953 million. In 1970 total employment was about 142,000. The growth in employment opportunities resulting from the factories promoted by the Economic Development Administration, providing more than 102,000 direct jobs, had been offset by the great reduction of employees in home needlework, amounting to some 46,000 between 1950 and 1969. Thousands of poorly paid workers were replaced by other thousands with much higher pay. In that sector of the economy a transformation occurred which is of vital importance to the economy and to the people's life.

Other economic sectors, such as commerce, construction, transportation and government services, also show extraordinary progress. The net value of goods and services produced by those sectors increased more than 517 per cent during the past three decades. In 1969, that value surpassed $2,320 million representing 68.2 per cent of the total net income. Twenty nine years ago, the corresponding figures were only $376 million and 61.2 per cent. Today those sectors employ 495,000 workers, or a little more than 68 per cent of Puerto Rico's total employment, as opposed to 178,000 workers and 34.8 per cent in 1940. In the course of the past two decades, Puerto Rico's economy was obviously transformed from one which was primarily agricultural into one far more industrialized and diversified.

The structural transformation experienced by the economy reflects the achievements of the economic development program and its success in establishing "core" industries which contribute to industrial integration in that their by-products serve as raw materials for other industries. The petroleum refineries on the south coast, whose by-products permit the manufacture of many things, form the base for a complete internal industrial structure. The Union Carbide Company, for instance, invested $28 million in a petrochemical plant for the manufacture of ethylene glycol from the by-products of the nearby Commonwealth Oil refinery. The Commonwealth Oil Corporation, now over 15 years on the island, has undertaken a vast program of investment and expansion in the Guayanilla and Peñuelas region, where its new factory for aromatics is regarded as the world's largest. The company also operates a factory which produces paraxilen, used in the manufacture of synthetic and laminated fibers. A factory for the manufacture of nylon threads, the Fibers International Corporation, was the first plant to be established in the petrochemical complex of the Phillips Petroleum Company in Guayama. Built at an initial investment of $60 million, that factory shall employ 1,450 workers when it operates at capacity; its annual payroll shall come to about $7 million, or some $4,000 per capita. The by-products of that industry comprise the raw materials for other enterprises, such as those producing plastic products and synthetic fibers.

The petrochemical industry was started in southern Puerto Rico in 1956, with the establishment of the Commonwealth Oil Refining Co. (CORCO) in Peñuelas. The industry began by refining crude oil imported from South America. Today there are several firms: among them, Commonwealth Petrochemicals; Commonwealth Oil Refining Company, Inc.; Union Carbide, Inc.; Phillips Petroleum; Puerto Rico Chemical Company. The Caribbean Gulf Refining Company, located near San

Juan, was Puerto Rico's first refinery of petroleum. New firms will begin to operate in the near future: among them Shell and Commonwealth Chemicals, Inc.; Corco PPG, Corco Grace; and the Sun Oil Company, with a refinery under construction in Yabucoa.

Once the petrochemical industries start operating at full capacity, they will represent total investments of more than $1.5 billion, and employ more than 60,000 workers. Already $726 million were invested by 1969. The interest in petrochemicals stems from the fact that more than 300 products can be produced from petroleum, such as plastics, paints, detergents, synthetic fibers, and artificial rubber. Products derived from petroleum have the advantage that the raw material is cheap and yields many by-products, while the cost of transportation is reasonable.

Another important industrial-agricultural "core" industry consists of the modern mills which produce wheat flour and at the same time animal feeds, but more so by being the nucleus for integrating many phases of economic activity. Not only does it stimulate the island's increasing production of beef and pork, but it affects directly, and favorably, a number of such industries as leather work, the extraction of soybean oil, breweries, tuna canneries, packaging plants, and others.

The establishment of such integrated, internal complexes forms the basis for the transformation of the economy into one that is predominantly industrial and increasingly diversified.

The Balance of Trade

The balance of trade is the difference in value between goods imported and those exported. Because imports exceeded exports, Puerto Rico has long had a debit balance. In 1969–70, the value of imports exceeded that of exports by $837 million. The resulting debit balance with the United States, excluding the Virgin Islands with which Puerto Rico has a favorable balance of close to $100 million, was around $430 million, and the remainder was with foreign countries. Recently, the imbalance with foreign countries was greater than that with the United States. The imbalance in foreign trade is caused largely by the importation of crude oils, materials, and other products. Increases in the rest of the imports are to be expected, since the island's continued development demands increases in investments and production. Capital goods imported in 1970 came to $465 million, an increase of $442 million over similar imports in 1950. In relative terms, 10 per cent of all imports in 1960 consisted of capital goods; in 1969 the figure was 18 per cent. The importation of consumer goods, reflecting higher income levels, has also increased but not as much. In 1970, $848 million worth of consumer goods were imported, (only $365 million worth in 1960), representing a proportional decline from 40 per cent to 33 per cent of total merchandise imported.

The Balance of Payments

The balance of payments brings out in detail the movement of external trade and counteracts that trade's imbalance. In addition to movements of merchandise, there are certain services and contributions which are know as "invisible" items that do not constitute physical merchandise. Those items consist of transportation costs, passenger fares, interest payments, profits, amortization of debts, federal contributions, donations, tourist expenditures, and the like, which also affect the balance with foreign countries.

In 1969–70, the imported goods were valued at $2,513 million which, added to $1,110 million worth of services received from overseas, brought the total to $3,623 million (Appendix J). In the same year, the export of goods and services amounted to $2,387 million (goods, $1,747 million; services, etc., $640 million). The difference between $3,623 million in imports and the exported $2,387 million, results, in the balance of payments, in a debit balance for Puerto Rico of $1,236 million. It is obvious that the debit balance is found in the item of services as well as in that of goods. Those $1,236 million of debit balance are compensated for by the following unilateral payments on Puerto Rico's favor: private remittances sent by Puerto Ricans living abroad to ther relatives in Puerto Rico, $66 million; payments by the Federal government to that of Puerto Rico, $230 million; payments by the Federal and State governments to individual and private corporations, such as to veterans, social security recipients, farmers' compensation for soil conservation, payments for the production of certain crops such as sugar, $29 million. The sum total of unilateral payments to Puerto Rico was $325 million. The difference between that $325 million and the above-listed $1,236 million, $902 million, represent the net long or short term capital movements in Puerto Rico from abroad after discounting Puerto Rican investments abroad, plus a deduction for statistical errors and unidentified omissions. Those net investments of $902 million were made in Puerto Rico by industrialists and investors and have contributed much to the island's progress; at the same time, they have also contributed to the increase of the export capacity of new products which today represent 70 per cent of the total exports and have increased at a higher rate than the imports of producer and consumer goods. The investments from outside are complemented by strong internal investments of fixed capital, which amounted to over $500 million in fiscal year 1970.

12

Traditional Agriculture

Except during the first years of colonization, agriculture was long the basis of Puerto Rico's economy. The colonists' first occupation was mining the gold deposits of the rivers. But the mining phase lasted only a few years; the gold gave out near the middle of the sixteenth century. The settlers were then forced to cultivate the land more intensively than for subsistence purposes. Since very few local agricultural products were available for export, they had to introduce new crops for the incipient farming and livestock economy.

Cattle were introduced from Santo Domingo early in the sixteenth century and ginger in the middle of the century. In those years the most important trade was that of the "dealers in ginger and hides," meaning those who produced ginger and cattle. Economically important until the middle of the seventeenth century, ginger cultivation began to fall off under the threat of a war with France and ceased when a royal order prohibited its cultivation.

The abandonment of ginger cultivation aroused the government's special interest in sugar cane. The crop had been imported from Santo Domingo early in the sixteenth century, and in 1581 some 187 tons had been harvested and converted almost entirely into molasses. Continuing to increase, the cultivation of sugar cane reached a peak in the nineteenth century. Its cultivation was stimulated by the export of sugar to the United States which had been made possible by the so-called *Cédula de Gracias* through which Spain gave up its trade monopoly and permitted the colony to deal commercially with other nations. At the beginning of the twentieth century, the export of sugar and other cane products amounted to $4.7 million.

Coffee was introduced from Haiti in 1736. By 1768 it was widely cultivated in Puerto Rico, and by the end of the nineteenth century it was one of the mainstays of the economy. The growth of the coffee industry until

261

1898 resulted from the demand for Puerto Rican coffee in European markets and especially Sapin and from the tariff protection which it enjoyed there. In 1897 more than 50 million pounds were harvested, valued at 12 million pesos or approximately U.S. $7 million. Production was greatly reduced in 1899 as a result of the "San Ciriaco" hurricane which destroyed some of the plantations. The rehabilitation of coffee was difficult because of the disorganization of the market when Puerto Rico came under United States rule. Unlike sugar and tobacco, coffee was given no tariff protection in the United States. Moreover, despite the excellence of Puerto Rican coffee, North American consumers continued to use that from other lands. In the face of their loss of markets, coffee farmers naturally lost interest in the improvement of their plantations.

Tobacco is native to Puerto Rico. Nevertheless, very little was planted before 1765, and the crop was almost entirely for the local market for cigars and chewing tobacco. Some 4 million pounds were produced in 1897, valued at more than one million pesos. During the present century its production has grown to the point where tobacco, as an agricultural product, has been second only to sugar cane in economic importance.

Mixed vegetables formed part of the indigenous diet, especially cassave, "yautía" (tanniers), sweet potatoes, and maize; and among the fruits, pineapple. Curiously, fruits which are as well known locally and thoroughly characteristic of the environment, such as coconuts, bananas, and plantains, came from the Old World.

Economic Importance

Until recently, the net income from agriculture surpassed that from all other economic activities in Puerto Rico. In 1940, of the island's total net income of about $225 million, agriculture contributed 31.3 per cent and manufacturing 11.6 per cent (Fig. 11.3; Appendix B). Agriculture's preeminence ended in 1955, when the net income from manufacturing was $169 million, one million more than that from agriculture. In 1970 the latter generated $184 million, and the former $953 million, of a total net income of $3,821 million. Commerce, which in 1940 contributed to the total an amount equal to that from manufacturing, surpassed the income from agriculture by some $25 million in 1957. However, since the net income from agriculture was almost 2½ times as large in 1969 as in 1940, its general situation is not as precarious as its relative importance. Its lag is due partly to the biological factor—less important in other industries—which slows down its response to change.

The value of agricultural products on the farm has grown from $84 million in 1940 to about $271 million in 1970. In 1940, sugar cane on the farm was valued at $43.3 million; in 1970 it was $52 million. Coffee is another Puerto Rican farm product of high value. In 1971 its production was 325,000 hundredweight, valued at $17 million (Fig. 12.4; Appendix M).

Tobacco, another of the island's traditional crops, yielded 260,000 hundredweight in 1950, 379,000 in 1965 and 55,000 in 1971. In 1950, the value of the tobacco was $5 million; in 1965, $14 million; in 1971, less than $2 million. The reduction of more than 300,000 hundredweight and $12 million of total value between 1965 and 1971 resulted from a drastic reduction, caused by a glut in the market of Puerto Rico's quota at that time. Moreover, the price of tobacco fell from $38.24 per hundredweight in 1965 to $30.70 in fiscal 1969.

Except for plantains, the production of starchy vegetables did not increase as rapidly as did that of other products. In 1950 about 100 million plantains were produced; the figure was more than doubled in the mid-sixties. Their value on the farm was $1.7 million in 1950 and $10.4 million in 1970.

The crops of the traditional agriculture are important in the export of foodstuffs, of which more than $128 million worth were exported in fiscal 1968. Sugar, exported to the value of $83.7 million, was by far the most important at that time. The value of exported starchy vegetables rose from about $500,000 in 1950 to more than $1.5 million in 1969. While the increase is considerable, it is possible to produce even more for the continental market. Puerto Rico has the advantage of producing certain tropical fruits which are sought abroad and of harvesting others in winter when they are scarce in the United States.

Geographic Distribution

PRINCIPAL CROPS

Sugar Cane. The geographic distribution of the island's principal crops resulted largely from the trials made by farmers in the course of four centuries, which determined the regions best suited for each crop. Among them, sugar has been the most diversified geographically, having been planted in the island's interior as well as on the coasts. Its culture was extended to the south coast early in the twentieth century, when the region's irrigation system was built. Today sugar cane occupies the largest part of Puerto Rico's cultivated areas, some 260,000 acres, largely on the coastal plains and in such interior valleys as that of Caguas.

The development of cane culture in the twentieth century grew largely out of the investment of United States capital, a protected market, the extension of credit, and the application of good techniques. Year after year until 1934, the production of sugar rose steadily and substantially from agriculture by some $25 million in 1957. However, since the net in- (Fig. 12.1; Appendix L). After 1934, the annual increase did not vary greatly; production reached its peak in 1952, with 1,359,841 tons of sugar. It declined in the ensuing years; in 1969, only 478,000 tons of sugar were produced and in 1970, around 455,000.

The rate of growth in the production of sugar went down after 1934 as

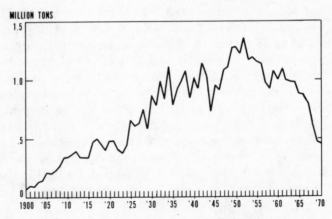

Figure 12.1. Sugar Production, 1900–1970. (Source: Department of Agriculture of Puerto Rico.)

a result of the quota system imposed by the United States on the recommendation of the U.S. Secretary of Agriculture. The quotas were suspended during World War II, but were reinstated in 1948 and restrictively applied in 1953. Since 1957, Puerto Rico has been unable to harvest enough sugar to fill its quota and it was found necessary to suspend the quota in the effort to increase the total crop. The decline of production after 1952 is attributed to climatic conditions, labor relations, lack of adequate mechanization, and the replacement of cane cultivation by other such agricultural pursuits as cattle raising, which offer greater stability and yield reasonable returns on the investments. It is estimated

Figure 12.2. Cattle Farm. Lands were cultivated to sugar cane up to 1957.

that urban growth, industrialization, and the growing cattle industry today use more than 75,000 acres which had previously produced sugar cane (Fig. 12.2). Moreover, some poor lands on which cane had once grown are now released for other purposes.

Analysis of tenure in sugar lands reveals that in 1968, around 7,700 farms were engaged in the production of sugar cane. The majority of these, some 92 per cent, are small properties on which fifty acres or fewer are harvested. The principal group of cane growers, with some 2 per cent of the farms, harvest more than 100 acres per farm, cultivate 57 per cent of the total area in sugar, and produce 72 per cent of the crop. One of the largest producers is the Land Authority of Puerto Rico, a public corporation, which harvested 27,790 acres and produced about 10 per cent of the island's total crop. On 41,000 acres in cane (12.51 per cent of the total) the Land Authority has eliminated the ownership of land by sugar corporations in excess of 500 acres, in violation of the Commonwealth's Constitution.

Between 1940 and 1969, the average number of laborers employed in the sugar cane industry (agricultural phase) went down from 124,000 to 23,000, that is, to much less than one-fifth.[1] The reduction was accompanied by an increase in wages but has created serious readjustment problems. The reduction of the labor force employed in sugar resulted from increased efficiency in production and the partial mechanization of work in the field. Such mechanization is inevitable if Puerto Rico is to continue competing with other cane growing regions which have been mechanized. The island, however, has not yet arrived at a degree of mechanization comparable to that in Hawaii and in the beet-sugar industry of the United States. In Puerto Rico, 10.2 man-days are required for the production of 1 ton of sugar, 2.4 in the beet-sugar industry, and 1.6 in Hawaii.[2] In Hawaii, the production of a hundred pounds of sugar requires 37.5 minutes; in Puerto Rico it takes 243.3 minutes. The cost of producing a hundred pounds in sugar in Puerto Rico is thirty per cent higher than that in Hawaii, despite the fact that Puerto Rico's wages are much lower than Hawaii's.

The difference stems largely from the fact that Puerto Rican cane is still cut to a large extent with "machetes," by hand, while in Hawaii it is cut and gathered by machines. Mechanization has reduced manual labor and has enabled the Hawaiian planters to pay much higher wages. It is estimated that in Puerto Rico some 56 per cent of the field operations have been mechanized (Fig. 12.3, a and b). The sugar mills have improved their machinery to the point where 16 mills today grind what required 40 mills some years ago. Another recent step in the mechanization

1. Puerto Rico Department of Agriculture, Bureau of Agricultural Statistics, Santurce, Puerto Rico.
2. Sugar Reports, September 1966.

Figure 12.3a Loading Sugar Cane with Machinery.

process which resulted in great economies for the industry is the shipment of sugar in bulk, where it had formerly been bagged.

According to the United States Department of Agriculture, some Caribbean islands which formerly produced sugar are now importing it. The
Department attributes that situation to pests, rains, and the low price
which sugar has commanded during the past 25 years. The average ratio

Figure 12.3b Spraying Fertilizer by Plane on a Sugar Cane Plantation.

between cane and sugar is ten tons of cane to one of sugar. In 1964, the per-acre yield of sugar was 3.5 tons in the Caribbean and 2.73 in Puerto Rico; Australia obtained 7 tons per acre, and Hawaii 10.45.

Interested in improving the industry, the government has recently proposed a plan for reforms and aid, to achieve greater efficiency in the agricultural and processing phases. The plan emphasizes mechanization. It is estimated that such mechanization of the industry will displace more than 10,000 workers for whom, under programs being prepared, employment will be created in other industries.

In general, the sugar industry is undergoing a period of reorganization toward the use of new techniques and the mechanization of the agricultural side; by such means it will undoubtedly achieve greater efficiency to permit it to compete with other industries which offer better economic opportunities to farmers and workers.

Coffee. The cultivation of coffee occupies about 180,000 acres, of which 160,000 are in production. While the crop requires an annual precipitation of about 80 inches, it also demands a dry spring for flowering. Such conditions are found at between 500 and 2,000 feet altitude in the Rainy West Central Mountains which have become the island's principal coffee region.

According to studies made by the Puerto Rican Department of Agriculture, fifty per cent of the 160,000 acres in production have slopes of 60 per cent or more. Some 30,000 acres, planted during the past 10 years, produce about 4 hundredweight per acre; 83,000 acres yield 2 hundredweight, while 48,000 give only 25 pounds per acre. The study also shows that the number of trees per acre goes down with increases in the land's steepness. The condition indicates the difficulties of cultivation in rugged terrains.

Coffee is produced largely on medium-sized farms of 100–200 acres, where the practice of diversified farming is common. About 30 per cent of the land may be in coffee, while the rest produces mixed vegetables, fruits (largely oranges), and some cattle. The coffee region produces about 75 per cent of the oranges harvested in Puerto Rico.

According to the region where the crop is grown, the coffee industry also faces problems of rugged terrain and infertile soils, as well as that of antiquated methods of cultivation and the scarcity of labor. Because of the low wages paid in coffee, in comparison with other industries, the growers have difficulties in obtaining the workers they need.

The problem of the scarcity of help during the harvest season is serious. During that season, September to January, many children in the coffee region stay away from school in order to pick coffee. In recent years the Department of Education, in the municipalities of Jayuya, Utuado, Adjuntas, Lares, Las Marías, and Maricao. has changed the period of annual vacations from May-August to the period from October 27 to January 7, to permit the children to pick coffee.

The variety of coffee most prevalent in Puerto Rico is "Coffee arabica" which requires shade for optimum production. In small regions where the sun penetrates directly to the ground, bananas, and plantains are planted until trees can be grown to give permanent shade. The variety of coffee requiring shade is affected by hurricanes which destroy the shade trees as well as the coffee trees. The Department of Agriculture provides insurance for the coffee growers who pay low premiums for the protection of their plantations and crops.

Puerto Rico's coffee culture has been affected adversely by the price of beans in the world market, which is today about $50 per hundredweight, compared with $80 which it reached during the first half of the fifties. The high price stimulated plantings in the producing countries; prices went down when the supply exceeded the demand. Since the yields of Puerto Rico's coffee plantations are low, the island's growers cannot compete on the basis of world prices. On exported coffee, the government therefore guarantees a bonus of $30 per hundredweight over the world market price. Through that step it is proposed to contribute to the improvement of the coffee plantations to the point where, to permit competition in the world market, the per-acre yield is no less than 500 pounds. The Department of Agriculture also has other programs for the renovation of the coffee regions through the intensification of cultivation. It promotes the cultivation of coffee without shade, with a shrub which produced earlier and much more than does the shaded coffee (Fig. 12.4). While the life of the new shrub is shorter than that of the one used traditionally, a yield of more than 25 hundredweight has been obtained on

Figure 12.4. Coffee Plantation without Shade.

the new plantations as against an average of 2 from coffee grown under shade. As a result of improvements on the coffee plantations, the average yield per acre rose from 230 pounds during 1940–50 to 260 pounds during the ensuing ten years.

The coffee harvest was about 300,000 hundredweight in 1966 and 260,000 in 1969 and 325,000 in 1971 (Fig. 12.5; Appendix M). Consumption of coffee in Puerto Rico is about 300,000 hundredweight annually. In years when production is higher than the local consumption, coffee is exported to the United States under the above-mentioned subsidy arrangement or to countries in Europe where Puerto Rican coffee is still esteemed.

Puerto Rico's domestic market is protected by a tariff under which the price is stabilized at $67.12 per hundred pounds. As a result, only about $700,000 worth of coffee is imported to the island annually, nearly all from the United States. By far the bulk of the imported coffee is the so-called "instant" kind, powdered and soluble. Future imports will be smaller because today two local factories make soluble coffee from Puerto Rican beans.

Tobacco. The tobacco industry is located largely in the Humid East Central Mountains where mild temperatures and relatively low humidity, especially during the harvest season from December to February, are propitious for the kind of tobacco grown on the island. The tobacco is used largely for cigar-filler. Small tobacco plantings, yielding about two per cent of the total crop and producing chewing tobacco, are also found in the subhumid northwest part of the northern coastal plain (Isabela) as well as west of the south coastal plain (Lajas), and in the semi-arid foothills of the south (Coamo).

In 1967–68, 5,000 farmers planted an average of an acre and a half each to tobacco. Planting and harvesting are almost exclusively family

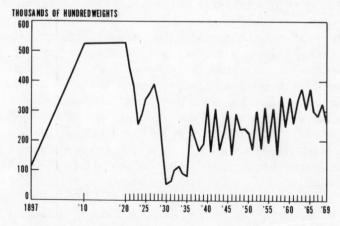

Figure 12.5. Production of Coffee, 1897–1969. (Source: Department of Agriculture of Puerto Rico.)

occupations. Planting, cutting, and binding the leaves for hanging in the drying sheds cannot be entirely mechanized and require much cheap labor, for which about 7,000 workers were hired in 1966 and 3,000 in 1969.

Since 1947, tobacco has been produced under a system of quotas determined by Puerto Rico's Secretary of Agriculture. While the production has generally increased, the cultivated area has been reduced from 36,000 acres in 1952 to 30,000 in 1965. The yield increased from 7.8 hundredweight to 12.64 per acre and in some areas 20 hundredweight were obtained. In 1965, 379,000 cwt. were produced on about 30,000 acres, and in 1969 about 80,000 on 6,000 acres. (Fig. 12.6). The 1971 crop was

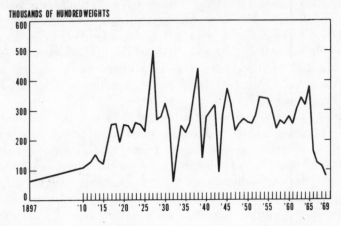

Figure 12.6. Production of Tobacco, 1897–1969.
(Source: Department of Agriculture of Puerto Rico.)

further reduced to 55,000 cwt. The reduction was attributed to an excessive inventory of tobacco and to the high prices for which Puerto Rican tobacco must be sold. The fact that, in the United States, the price of Puerto Rican tobacco is higher than that from other countries affects the consumption of tobacco from the island. The consumption of Puerto Rican tobacco has diminished in the United States. It fell from 37 per cent of total consumed during the first years of the 1950's to less than 32 per cent today. It should be noted that, while the consumption of foreign tobaccos has increased, that of domestic and Puerto Rican tobacco has gone down. Puerto Rican tobacco is used for fillers in cigars, for which purpose, together with Cuban tobacco, it is regarded as among the best. The United States' embargo on Cuban tobacco during the early sixties created a demand for that of Puerto Rico, raising the value of the island's production. However, during the past decade, methods were developed making it feasible to use tobacco of inferior quality produced in the United States and other American countries. The price of the inferior tobaccos is much lower than is that of the Puerto Rican product, despite the fact that a duty of $16.00 per hundredweight is imposed on tobaccos from all foreign nations except the Philippines, which pay $12.00. Competition from inferior tobaccos, plus the large inventory of the Puerto Rican product, have contributed to the lowering of the value of production on the island.

Figure 12.7. Manufacture of Cigars in the Consolidated Cigar Corporation Factory, Caguas, Puerto Rico.

The integration between the growing of tobacco and the manufacture of cigars has helped to keep the tobacco industry among the island's most important agricultural activities. Two manufacturers, the Consolidated Cigar Corporation and the General Cigar Company, are established in Puerto Rico. The Consolidated makes cigars in Caguas and Cayey and operates a factory in Comerío for preparing the raw materials (Fig. 12.7). The General Cigar Company has only one factory, in Utuado. In 1966, the Consolidated Cigar Corporation used about 90 per cent of the tobacco sold in Puerto Rico. The manufacture of cigars for export rose from about 690,000 in 1952 to over 1 billion in 1967 and 1968, which, in turn, raised the company's annual excise taxes from $7,000 to $9.5 million. The cigar industry is relatively stable because of the quality of the island's tobacco, skilled labor, and good promotion. Nevertheless, it is affected by abnormal inventories and by fluctuations in the consumption of cigars.

Figure 12.8. Sheds for Drying Tobacco. The town of Comerío in the background. (Courtesy of the Department of Agriculture of Puerto Rico.)

The Department of Agriculture offers the farmers technical assistance for the growing and processing of tobacco, provides seedlings and credit for drying sheds (Fig. 12.8). In addition, recent agricultural legislation provided means for subsidizing the farmers in the sale of the accumulated inventory of former years to the United States and Europe.

Food Crops. The island's food crops, including a variety of vegetables, come second in importance after the large commercial crops. Bananas and oranges are grown largely in the coffee regions which produce 85 per cent of the bananas and 75 per cent of the oranges marketed on the island. Corn and beans are produced in the tobacco areas: pigeon peas ("gandules"), tropical yams ("ñames"), tanniers ("yautía"), sweet potatoes, and plantains are harvested on small farms side-by-side with major crops (Fig. 12.9). The area producing small crops has been reduced from 320,000 acres in 1939 to fewer than 170,000 today.

The cultivation of local food crops entails certain difficulties. In the first place, the consumption of local starchy vegetables has in recent years gone down about 166 lbs. per capita per year. The number of workers in the rural zones has decreased, and the fact that wages have risen in commercial agriculture has adversely affected the planting of food crops. Fluctuations in the supply, within any one year or from year to year, have affected the regular consumption of starchy products. Such fluctuations are related directly to the instability of prices which in turn might be due largely to the fact that the producer has neither credit nor

Figure 12.9. Cultivation of Plantains in the Humid Mountains of the East. (Courtesy of the Department of Agriculture of Puerto Rico.)

price guarantees. Finally, market problems impede the products' distribution. With regard to that matter, efforts are now being made to establish a market for Puerto Rican food crops among the Puerto Ricans living in the continental United States. Modern marketing methods are being introduced and local markets are reorganized; prices are being guaranteed and agricultural service centers are being established under the auspices of the Commonwealth Department of Agriculture.

Problems of the Traditional Agriculture

Puerto Rico's geographic environment is propitious for the development of the traditional agriculture. However, the latter's continuity will depend on progress in various phases of production and marketing, the need for which grows out of the island's rapid social-economic development. One obstacle which must be overcome is the scarcity of agricultural labor, resulting from migrations from the rural to the urban areas and abroad, in search of better wages and higher levels of living than are found in the rural zones. As a result of that movement it is necessary to mechanize agriculture and so to lessen the dependence on large numbers of workers. Moreover, modern agriculture demands daily increases in the worker's production, to enable him to earn such wages as will permit him to live in conditions equal to those offered by nonagricultural occupations. For competition with other countries with similar products, the highest degree of mechanization is essential. For instance, the introduction of machinery for filling the sugar industry's haulage cars reduces the number of workers needed, so solving the problem of labor shortage while also increasing the output per worker. Machines for cutting sugar cane, to overcome the shortage of manual cutters and increase the output per man, are at present being adapted to Puerto Rican conditions. The government helps farmers to buy agricultural equipment, toward the end of achieving maximum mechanization of the work in the fields.

Experimental work is being done to improve the various crops and agricultural practices. Progress has been made, for instance, in the introduction of coffee varieties which don't require shade. In the matter of industrialization of agriculture, the integration of tobacco's agricultural phase with the processing has, among others, been achieved. However, the general lack of integration between production, processing, and marketing demands more thorough investigation. The required techniques are largely installed through government help and incentives.

Puerto Rico's agricultural production is limited by the fact that many farmers have lands with great potentials which they work extensively or inefficiently or both. The government is studying various means of remedying that situation, among them the adoption of a new system of land tenure. It recommends that the farmers, without losing ownership, contract for the services of experts to whom certain phases of the farm-work would be delegated. The individuals or entities so contracted for agricultural services might contribute knowledge and resources, or manage the farms, or do both. Installed in sugar cane, such a system would be expected to increase production and profits for the farmer. Among the great advantages offered by that form of tenure is that of bringing more capital for farm operation. Under the recommended new system, production costs would be much lower, especially in the use of equipment which could be utilized more intensively. The system offers the advantage of permitting integration in the administration of various farms or parts of farms for the cultivation of crops which need larger areas of given physical conditions. Naturally, the rights of farm owners must be respected and they should be permitted to rescind the contracts after a reasonable time, with a possible maximum of five years at a time. The ultimate goal of that new system of working the land is to train the farmer in efficient practices which he may soon apply directly to his lands. It certainly has educational value in that the farmer learns to manage his farm with more profit to himself and the community.

In addition to credit facilities offered by branches of the Federal Government, the Puerto Rican Government is concerned with credit problems, especially for small and average farmers. In past years, the Industrial Development Company and the Government Development Bank provided part of the credit, out of government funds, needed by certain farmers. Within the program of guaranteed agricultural credit of the Department of Agriculture, the commercial banks also meet some of those needs. The Agricultural Credit Corporation, in which the credit facilities offered by government agencies have been integrated, has contributed to the development of other industries, such as chicken and cattle cultures and coffee planting.

Among the purposes of Puerto Rico's program of industrialization is the utilization of agricultural products as industrial raw materials. Much has been achieved within the framework of the traditional agriculture, especially in tobacco where, as stated above, production and manufacture follow sugar in the matter of integration.

In the production of mixed foodstuffs, with the exception of pigeon peas ("gandures") and plantains, there are no industries which use them as raw materials. The industrialization of those products would permit processing during the months of abundance, stabilize prices, and provide incentives for increased production.

The present marketing system for foodstuffs products is very deficient. Various government agencies offer technical aid to the farmers toward the end of remedying that situation. Within the Department of Agriculture, the program for the production and distribution of foods offers farmers seeds, fertilizers, and working equipment at minimum cost, in addition to providing facilities for selling their crops. The program has established two centers for purchase and distribution, in Naranjito and Utuado, in which farmers can sell their crops wholesale. Reasonable prices are guaranteed for certain crops whose production should be increased, and, for certain times, fixed minimum prices have been established for pigeon peas ("gandures"), tropical yams ("ñames"), and other crops.

It is to be expected that efforts on the part of the government and farmers to improve the traditional agriculture will complement the development of the new agricultural industries.

13

A New Era in Agriculture

A new type of agriculture, which promises to revolutionize land utilization, has begun to be developed in Puerto Rico in recent years. The new era results directly from the economic and social changes which have taken place on the island during the past two decades. The growth of manufacturing as Puerto Rico's main industry, the internal migrations to towns and cities, and the external movement to the United States have reduced the number of agricultural workers to the point where, of the 230,000 such workers in 1940, only about 119,000 remained in 1965, and 74,000 in 1969 (Appendix C). The wages and living conditions of those workers are better today than they were in 1940. Statistics show that the number of agricultural workers continues to decrease under the impact of mechanization; those who remain in the rural areas are expected, soon, to constitute a reduced nucleus of specialized workers, earning wages comparable to those of their fellows in the urban regions.

The farm of the new era in agriculture is a unit of medium size which employs few workers, though it calls for high capital investments, and demands, in turn, operations with mechanized equipment. The most important products of the new agriculture are those resulting from the raising of cattle and poultry: milk, meat, chickens, eggs, all rich in proteins. There are also some farms which produce fruits and vegetables, but such production still remains, largely, to be developed on a commercial scale.

Most of the products of the new agriculture are sold in the domestic market which, as a result of the growth in income from such other occupations as manufacturing, tourism, and commerce, is much larger today than it was formerly. The new products are generally prepared for the market in pasteurizing plants, slaughter houses, packing plants, and other factories which improve their quality and facilitate their distribution. While the traditional agriculture of sugar cane, coffee, and tobacco is typical of colonial development in the tropics, that of the new era resembles much more that of the temperate zones which have attained high levels of living. Today's agriculture and its workers use such facilities as roads, electric light, potable water, telephones, and schools. Use of these facilities permit rural inhabitants to enjoy benefits which previously were available exclusively to the urban dwellers.

Production and Consumption

During the past decades, agriculture's farm values have not increased at the same rate for each product. In 1940, total farm value was $84 million; in 1969, $259 million; and in 1970, $271 million. Sugar cane had a value of $44 million in 1940 and $49 million in 1970. In other words, while the total value of agricultural and cattle products has more than tripled since 1940, that of sugar cane, after a great increase, dropped back to the 1940 level.

In 1940, the farm value of the products of cattle-and-poultry culture was about $16 million, in 1950 about $43 million, and in 1970 some $113.7 million. In 30 years, the value of that production has been multiplied by eight and more recently at an average annual rate of 5 per cent. The major part of that increase stemmed from the production of milk which in 1969 constituted some 58 per cent of the total value of cattle and poultry products. The production of milk was more than 385 million quarts, or 1 and 1/2 times that of ten years earlier.

The pineapple is the most important of the commercially produced fruits. The pineapple crop value was about $800,000 in 1940; by 1970 it had risen to $3.3 million. In pineapple culture, as in that of tobacco, agricultural production has been successfully integrated with industrial processing. In Barceloneta, near the town of Manatí, the Land Authority owns one of the most modern canning plants for pineapples, which ships almost its entire production to continental markets (Fig. 13.1). Pineapples, oranges, and other fruits are also processed by the Frozen Fruit Concentrates, Inc., in Bayamón, and the Federation of Orange Producers of the West, Inc., in Maricao.

New developments in agriculture parallel changes in Puerto Rico's diet regimen. The annual per capita consumption of such starchy vegetables as the sweet potatoes, bananas, tanniers ("yautías"), and taro has gone down by more than 160 pounds, while the per capita consumption of the more nourishing animal products increased more than 265 pounds.

Puerto Rico's per capita consumption of milk was about 412 pounds in 1957, higher than that in the countries listed in Table 13.1.

In recent years, the annual per capita consumption of protein-rich foods has increased by about thirty pounds, indicating that the diet has improved quantitatively as well as qualitatively. The value of those foods now exceeds $175 million per year. The production growth is expected to

Figure 13.1. The Land Authority's Pineapple Canning Plant at Barceloneta,
Puerto Rico.

continue in view of today's higher incomes and the growth of population.
It is estimated that by 1975 the consumption of milk will be 33 per cent
greater, of meat twice as high, of eggs three times, and of vegetables and
fruits 75 per cent higher than it is today.

Those changes in diet result from increases in family incomes. Today,
the expenditures for foods represent 32 per cent of those incomes as compared with 46 per cent in 1950. In the United States, where incomes are
much higher, the ratio is about 27 per cent; in Canada it is some 31 per

Table 13.1. *Estimated consumption of milk per capita in Puerto Rico and various
Latin American countries, 1957*

Country	Consumption of Milk, Pounds*
Puerto Rico	412
Costa Rica	300
Cuba	287
Venezuela	285
Honduras	240
Nicaragua	200
Guatemala	175

Source: Donald D. MacPhail, "Puerto Rican Dairying, a Revolution in Tropical
Agriculture," reprinted from the *Geographical Review* 53, no. 2 (1963) (New York:
American Geographical Society) pp. 224–46.
*Total milk equivalent to all dairy products consumed.

cent; in countries like Ecuador it is around 57 per cent. In Puerto Rico the consumption of foods and beverages has risen at an average of some 4 per cent per year; nevertheless, the proportion of income devoted to foods and beverages diminishes, as also happens in the United States, because of the increase of income which give rise to greater demands for durable goods and services. One instance of that relation is the consumption of fresh and processed milk in Puerto Rico and the United States. In Puerto Rico the per capita consumption of milk was 105.8 quarts in 1953, and in the United States 173. In 1963 the consumption in Puerto Rico was 220.3 quarts, while in the United States it was 157 quarts (Table 13.2).

Table 13.2. Per capita consumption of fresh and processed milk in Puerto Rico and the United States, 1953–1965
(Quarts)

Fiscal Year	Per Capita Consumption	
	Puerto Rico	United States
1953	105.8	173
1954	118.0	172
1955	121.6	173
1956	131.5	173
1957	152.5	170
1958	168.3	167
1959	171.2	165
1960	189.8	161
1961	189.8	157
1962	198.5	157
1963	200.3	157
1964	195.5	
1965	195.3	

Source: Caribe Consulting Service, "Analysis of Projections for the Milk Processing Industry in Puerto Rico," (Hato Rey, Puerto Rico: Banco Popular Center, September 26, 1966).

Rising demands and changes in the consumption of products tend to readjust the methods of production and the products themselves. Not producing all the foods needed by its inhabitants, Puerto Rico must import a large share of them. In 1940, about 30 per cent of imports totalling $107.4 million were foods and beverages; in 1950, these comprised about 25 per cent of a total of $345 million; in 1966, 17.5 per cent of $1,357 million. While the proportion of the value of imported foods and beverages, in relation to total imports, has decreased, the total value of imported foods and beverages has risen more than twelve times since 1940.

By value, animals and their products comprise the largest part of the imported foods. Imports of the products of the cattle-and-poultry industry have risen despite the growth of those industries in the island as a result of increases in per capita consumption. In 1955 the value of imported fresh and frozen meats was $20.1 million, and in 1969 it was $67 million. Beef comprised the largest share of those imports, amounting to $4.9 million in 1955 and about $30 million in 1969. In addition, the imports of various canned and processed meats came to $5.5 million in 1955 and about $29 million in 1966. The importation of milk and milk products from the United States rose from $15 million in 1955 to $34.4 million in 1966. The value of imported vegetable products also rose. That of imported grains, for instance, is twice as high today as it was in 1940. The nature of those imported foods indicates that the agriculture of the new era has plenty of room for expansion, although the scarcity of available land will prevent self-sufficiency in those products. Today the processing of foods employs some 23,100 workers in 485 industries, among which fish, fruits, and vegetables are important. The products of those industries have a total value, in the local as well as the external markets, of $131 million.

Exports of foodstuffs and beverages reached a value of more than $242 million in 1966, an increase of 57 per cent since the onset of the past decade. Among those exports, animals and animal products have increased the most. The increase in 1966 resulted largely from that of fish products. The four tuna fish canning plants exported more than $36 million, though it should be noted that their fish had been brought from far away. The canning of tuna fish is the largest of the food processing industries, producing more than 30 per cent of the tuna fish processed in the United States. As a center for canning tuna, Puerto Rico can now be compared with California, known until recently as the tuna fish capital of the western hemisphere.

Locally canned fruits and vegetables now have an annual sales value of more than $20 million. They are followed in importance by the products of bakeries and pastry shops of whose value—$20 million—some $18 million is that of bread. Those products are made largely for the local market, as are the beverages, including rum and beer, which are produced in the amount of $20 million annually.

The industries developed applying the techniques of the new agricultural era are discussed below.

THE DAIRY INDUSTRY

In terms of the value of agricultural production, the milk industry now ranks first in Puerto Rico. During the first half of the 1940's it produced a little over 114 million quarts of milk. Its production of about 152 million quarts in 1950 rose to some 384 million by 1970, more than doubling the production within twenty years. The increase of farm value was even greater, from $8.8 million to $69 million. The number of cows on first class dairy farms rose to correspond, from fewer than 100,000 in 1945 to about 270,000 in 1966. The production of milk per cow has risen more than 10 per cent during the past decade. The increase in quantity has been accompanied by corresponding improvements in quality resulting from improved pasteurization, homogenization, and the processing of milk products. It should be noted, however, that, despite such increases in local production, about $35 million worth of milk products are imported, corresponding roughly to 270 million quarts of milk and more than double the imports of 1955.

In value, more than 50 per cent of the imports consists of condensed, evaporated, and powdered milk, both whole and skimmed; about 40 per cent of the imported dairy products consist of butter and various kinds of cheese, while the remaining 10 per cent include baby foods and mixtures of various kinds.

All of the fresh milk consumed on the island is produced locally. The per capita annual consumption is 195 quarts, almost double that of 1950.

Dr. Donald D. MacPhail wrote as follows about the industry's development in Puerto Rico:

> The Puerto Rican dairy industry should serve as a model for other densely populated countries in the tropics that may be underdeveloped. Certainly, not all such areas will qualify, for conditions favorable to dairying are many; they include, in addition to a responsive market, active governmental support in finance, education, and technology. Any nation or region endowed with these potentials would do well to emulate the Puerto Rican example and begin its own revolution in tropical agriculture.[1]

Though the Puerto Rican dairy industry has expanded greatly, it still has a domestic market large enough to permit the growth's continuation. The industry's progress resulted not only from growth in the consumption of foods which were formerly very expensive for the average Puerto Rican but also from the improvement of milk cattle as well as help received from the government. Through its Office of Milk Industry Regulation, the government carries out several programs. Among these are the construction of buildings for the dairy industry, artificial insemination, the importation of vaccinated cattle, improvement of the pastures, and the industry's regulation and promotion.

The program for the construction of structures includes technical direction for building silos, tanks for molasses, deep wells, and milking sheds. Milch cattle have been improved through artificial insemination with imported semens of known quality. The program for the improvement of pastures brings to the farmers technical assistance as well as subsidies for grass improvement and erosion control. Some 300,000 acres

---

1. Donald D. MacPhail, "Puerto Rican Dairying: A Revolution in Tropical Agriculture," *Geographical Review* 53, no. 2 (1963), p. 246.

have been planted to pangola, guinea, and other grasses. Through the program for regulation, systems have been established for the utilization of surplus milk in springtime when the production is greatest, converting it into cheese, butter, and other products. Efforts are also made within that program to improve business relations between the producers and the processors of milk.

AVICULTURE

At the beginning of the 1940's nobody could dream that the poultry industry would reach its present importance. It began in the eastern humid mountains, mainly in the municipalities of Cidra, Aibonito, and Barranquitas (Fig. 13.2). In 1940 the production's farm value was estimated as $4 million; by 1970 it had multiplied six times, to $24 million. The products of aviculture are today high in quality and relatively low in price, which benefits the consumers greatly. Production of chickens for meat has increased from about 2.8 million pounds in 1940 to 25.7 million pounds in 1970. The local per capita annual consumption of chicken meat is about 29.9 pounds, of which 9.2 are produced on the island and the remaining 20.7 million pounds are imported. Those imports show that there is still much room for the industry's growth.

The industry for producing fresh eggs has also expanded greatly. In 1940 the value of that production was a little more than $1 million; in 1970 it was $12.4 million. The annual per capita consumption of eggs is about 132, as against some 335 in the United States in 1960. Imports of

Figure 13.2. Poultry Farm.

eggs and their edible products had a value of $6.8 million. Imported fresh eggs totaled 17.7 million dozens in 1969 while 21.2 million dozens were produced locally in 1970, so again showing ample room for expansion. The poultry-and-egg industry distributes fresh foods of high quality at low prices, produced locally by enterprises established under the program for industrial expansion.

BEEF

The production of high quality beef is relatively new in Puerto Rico but today it supplies about 48.8 per cent of the demand for meat and meat products, which comes to more than 90 million pounds. The fact that the local production, while rising, has not filled the entire demand, has caused corresponding increases in the imports of meat. The per capita annual consumption of beef has risen 9.4 pounds since 1956, to about 30 pounds. Of that consumption, 14.8 pounds are produced locally while 15.2 are imported. The value of imported fresh and frozen meats is a little more than $14.8 million, so again indicating a good margin for the increase of local production. The rise in local production stems from the fact that the Land Authority has imported good beef cattle such as Charollaise and Brahma and their interbreeds. The industry has also been helped by the programs for the improvement of pastures and by the credit facilities established to help breeders improve their stock through the purchase of good beef cattle (Fig. 13.3). Another important factor in

Figure 13.3. Charbray Beef Cattle of the Land Authority for Restocking Farmers' Ranges. (Courtesy of the Department of Agriculture of Puerto Rico.)

the production of good beef is the hygienic and well-equipped slaughter house which was built by the Industrial Development Company in Caguas and the new regional abattoirs now under construction. As may be seen in the island's modern super markets, the preparation and conservation of meats for sale to the consumers has improved greatly.

SPECIALIZED FARMING

Prospects for the export and local consumption of specialized crops are good. Among exported fruits are pineapples, coconuts, oranges, grapefruits, mangos, avocados, and acerola. Acerola is a cherry-like fruit, native to Puerto Rico, which is remarkably high in vitamin C. Pineapples are grown on more than 4,700 acres (Fig. 13.4). Fresh and canned pineapples are consumed locally and are exported. The export value of pineapples and their products was about $4.2 million in 1966. The Land Authority produces the fruit and has a large canning plant which aids the industry. The Authority also helps private farmers by teaching them the most modern methods of pineapple cultivation, which improve quality, as well as helping them to market their crops. Pineapple cultivation produces the highest gross income and agricultural wages and salaries per acre. In 1960, its gross income per acre was $390, as against $39 from beef cattle. Wages and salaries per acre in pineapples rose to $323; in beef cattle they were about $11.

Oranges and grapefruit, which constituted important export items some thirty years ago, are again beginning to interest farmers. Until today, oranges were largely by-products of coffee cultivation. The Department of Agriculture operates several nurseries for good fruit trees, principally oranges and grapefruit, which it distributes at nominal prices. In recent years it distributed more than 125,000 young trees. Several canning plants which produce natural and concentrated juices utilize the surpluses of those fruits and those which are not exported or sold in the local market. The fruit processing industries are in a position to continue their growth, since some $3 million worth of the juices of pineapples, tomatoes, oranges, canned fruits, and the like, are imported.

Vegetables have a fine potential among the crops of the new agricultural era. On the south coastal plain there are areas and physical conditions which favor the production of vegetables in competition with sugar cane. Libby, McNeill and Libby (Alimentos Borinqueños, S.A.) operates a farm of about 1,200 acres in Santa Isabel which produces tomatoes for canning as well as for sale fresh in the local and export markets. However, since 5,000 acres are required for efficient operation, the farm area is too small. Lack of production prevents meeting the demand for fresh tomatoes in the United States in wintertime. The Agricultural Experiment Station has developed varieties which are far better than the imported tomatoes, besides devising efficient production methods. Areas

Figure 13.4. Pineapple Cultivation in the Municipality of Manatí.

devoted to the cultivation of tomatoes are also found in the island's interior, as, for example, at Jayuya. However, those areas are not ideal for the crop which is inferior to that produced on the south coast. Nevertheless, it is harvested for the domestic market. The scarcity of land which affects adversely the tomato industry also prevents the large-scale production of such other crops as peppers, corn, and green beans.

The Lajas Valley

One of the best examples of the new agricultural era, and the island's most important multiple purpose project, is that of the Lajas Valley. Located in Puerto Rico's southwest, it is managed jointly by the Water Resources Authority, the Department of Agriculture, and agricultural agencies of the University of Puerto Rico. In addition to preventing floods caused by the Río Loco, it includes the eventual irrigation of 20,000 acres, the reclamation of salty lands, the provision of 6 and 1/2 million gallons of potable water annually, and the generation of 35,000 kilowatts for the region.

The Lajas Valley is a small T.V.A.,[2] providing integrated development which is immensely valuable to the country. In 1966, about 18,000 acres were irrigated and the project's remaining 2,000 acres are expected to be irrigated within the next few years. The area planted to sugar cane was expanded from 7,200 acres in 1951 to 17,000 in 1966. A good beef-and-poultry industry has begun to be developed, integrated into a cooperative for marketing eggs. The value of its agricultural production has quadrupled, from $2.4 million in 1951 to about $10 million in 1966.

The Lajas Valley project has encountered certain difficulties, especially that of the origins of the soil's saltiness. The greater part of the salted soil, however, has been reclaimed and is rapidly being improved. Everything seems to indicate that the project is a success, and in the near future it is expected to produce some $12 million worth of agricultural products annually.

The Future of Agriculture

Technological changes in the new era have resulted in reorganization, not only of farmers' methods but also of their whole economy. The continuity of the new agriculture demands higher production and improvements of the crop's quality, going hand in hand with greater efficiency in productivity. The fact that the production and marketing factors have not changed, so far, sufficiently to yield permanent results means that constant improvement is essential. Among those factors the increase in out-

2. Tennessee Valley Authority.

put capacity of the individual worker demands new techniques. The complete mechanization of agriculture, resulting in higher financial returns for farmers and workers while also preventing the abandonment of agriculture itself, has not yet been achieved. In several agricultural operations, such as the sugar cane cutting, adequate machinery adapted to our conditions, to compensate for the shortage of harvest workers is not yet generally available. In other cases, machinery adequate for mechanization is available but the size of the farm or its plantings doesn't justify its acquisition, since the machine would lie idle most of the time. That, however, is one of the minor problems, since it can be solved through coordinated use and the organization of machinery cooperatives.

Act No. 26 of 1941, known as Puerto Rico's "Land Law," authorized the reorganization of land tenure in the island. The law's objective was the acquisition and redistribution of lands held in excess of 500 acres by corporations, societies, and other juridical organisms. The Land Authority, created to carry out the law's aims, had acquired up to 1965 about 100,000 acres, devoted largely to sugar cane, pineapples and pasture.

Since then two substantial purchases have increased the public domain in agriculture. The Land Authority and the Puerto Rico Land Administration, two Commonwealth Government instrumentalities, acquired from Brewer Associates 10,000 acres of sugar cane lands and two sugar mills (Fajardo and Juncos) in the northeastern part of the island and in the Caguas Valley. A similar measure was taken more recently by the Commonwealth Government, when in 1970 it purchased for $3 million the largest sugar mill in the island, Central Guánica. Later, 13,000 acres of sugar lands and two additional sugar mills (Aguirre and Cortada) were expropriated in the southern coastal lowlands from the Aguirre Company for an initial payment of $11 million. These more recent measures were taken by the government in order to prevent the closing of the mills and corresponding field operations as a result of heavy losses incurred by their owners during several calamitous sugar cane crops. Governor Luis A. Ferré announced as official policy the early return of all of these properties to private hands as soon as conditions in the industry normalize.

While the law's social and economic aims have been achieved, the real problem of tenure, in the Authority's lands as well as in those of all other Puerto Rican farms, lies in attaining higher agricultural efficiency. The former director of the Office of Planning and Budget in the Department of Agriculture, expressed himself as follows: about the problem:

> This break with the traditional—always painful and usually slow—is one of the great difficulties which must be overcome in agriculture.
>
> In Puerto Rico, a certain disillusionment results from a study of the statistics which show that progress in agriculture lags behind that in other production sectors, principally manufacturing. . . . For development of the manufacturing sector we imported, during the 1950's, not only the needed

capital but also management skilled in modern techniques; in agriculture, on the other hand, our manager—that is, our farmer—has not only had to struggle without the sources of capital and credit which, in most cases, have never been established to meet his needs, but has also had to struggle with himself to change his personal, traditional attitudes in the modern day which demands adjustments on himself, radical changes whose achievement at times seems impossible.[3]

Considerable time is required to achieve the change from the traditional agriculture to that of the new era. The farmer, usually conservative regarding changes in the management of his farm, receives help from various government agencies which teach new methods and agricultural practices. He has opportunities to attend agricultural workshops; trips are organized to permit him to observe methods used in regions of more advanced agriculture; he is also helped directly in the management of his farm. The results achieved are remarkable when viewed in terms of the short time available for the introduction of new methods.

Agricultural production must be accompanied by efficient marketing as an incentive for progress in farming and cattle raising. When the farmer knows that he has a good market for his crops, he strives to increase and improve them. Today efforts are made to create markets for Puerto Rican crops in the United States, especially where there are concentrations of Puerto Ricans and Latin Americans. As regards the domestic market new methods are also being introduced such as the rural market in Naranjito where farmers sell their crops. The Department of Agriculture guarantees prices for certain products or maintains marketing centers where the farmer sells his crops for distribution to consumers. Various government agencies help farmers in sorting their products and preparing them for the markets. Such services further the optimum utilization of the production and marketing factors.

Capital is needed for making the best use of the other factors. In agriculture it is invested in machinery as well as in plants and animals. Most farmers don't have such capital and therefore must turn to the sources of credit. Several Puerto Rican and Federal agencies offer credit which, however, doesn't yet reach all the farmers. As stated in the preceding chapter, a few years ago the Commonwealth Department of Agriculture organized the Agricultural Credit Corporation which offers both direct credit and credit guarantees. It largely serves farmers who, for various reasons, cannot obtain credit elsewhere. While guarantees have a maximum ceiling of $15,000, the sizes of direct loans are determined by the farmers' needs. Since its inception, the corporation has made some 5,325

3. Pedro Negrón Ramos, "Reconstruction of Puerto Rican Agriculture—the Experience of the Past Ten Years," mimeographed. (Read at a meeting of the Puerto Rican Society for Economics and Statistics and the Puerto Rican College of Agronomists. Department of Agriculture, July 1963).

loans, totalling more than $12 million. The Federal Bank of Agriculture, established in Puerto Rico in 1922 through Congressional action, currently has some 2,800 loans outstanding with a value of about $46 million. Since starting operations, the bank has made 12,700 loans, totalling $115 million.

Among the most difficult immediate problems confronted by the modern agriculture are those of experimentation and the development of adequate machinery. Puerto Rico's agricultural experiment work depends almost exclusively on government financing. As work in agriculture is chained to the biological processes, the process of experimentation is slow and takes years to achieve results. It could be speeded up, however, if private enterprise were to help in all phases of experimentation. There is no doubt that Puerto Rico needs new varieties of sugar cane, coffee, and tobacco, as well as new types of cattle, together with new and improved agricultural practices. There is also need for the development of new kinds of agricultural machinery which, like the methods of cultivation, can be adapted to the island's soils.

In short, my criterion may be summarized as follows:

What We Need. The foregoing is a very condensed picture of the efforts being made in Puerto Rico to promote the new agriculture. However, that is not enough. Primarily, we need enterprising farmers, from here and elsewhere, to follow and accelerate the pace of the new agricultural era, as others are doing in manufacturing. We must establish individual, medium-sized farms—neither too large nor too small—that will result in efficient production units under the guidance and supervision of the Land Authority. We hould also modernize farming, possibly through service-contracts granted to organizations which are expert in that work. Once again, I stress the need for experimental work aimed at the development of new varieties as well as new methods. The urgent need for improving marketing efficiency, both local and external, is perhaps the most difficult immediate problem faced by our agriculture.[4]

4. Rafael Picó, *Puerto Rico: Planificación y acción* [Planning and action] (San Juan: Government Development Bank for Puerto Rico, 1962). p. 192.

14

Manufacturing

Manufacturing is a relatively new Puerto Rican industry. Before 1940 it was rather unimportant, consisting largely of processing such agricultural products as sugar cane and tobacco, canning fruits, and making rum. The others were light industries, like needlework, which was done largely at home.

Industrial Development, 1900–1940

The Census of 1909 showed that 939 manufacturing establishments existed in the island during the first decade of the century (Appendix D). In value of production, the sugar industry was the most important.[1] There were 108 sugar mills, employing about 5,000 workers out of the total of 15,582 in manufacturing. The value of all manufactured products came to $36.7 million, of which the sugar industry contributed $20.5 million. Workers' wages were $3.6 million, of which $1.2 million came from sugar.

There were 282 tobacco factories, devoted largely to making cigars by hand. The industry employed about 45 per cent of all workers in manufacturing, who earned wages totaling some $1.5 million (Appendix E). The tobacco industry outranked that of sugar in the matter of workers employed and their earnings. The other manufacturing industries were small affairs, such as shops, bakeries, shoemaking establishments, and produced for local consumption.

The sugar mills and cigar factories were located in the regions of their raw materials; the factories and shops producing for local consumption were largely in the centers of population. Sugar mills occupied several

1. Bureau of the Census, United States Department of Commerce, *Census of Manufactures, Puerto Rico, 1939* (Washington, D.C.: Government Printing Office, 1941).

coastal plains and interior valleys. Tobacco was processed in such towns as Caguas, Comerío, Cayey, Barranquitas, Aibonito, Bayamón, and San Juan.

Many small factories disappeared during the decade 1910–20; the number of manufacturing establishments was reduced to 619. The reduction was caused by the mounting importation of consumer products which eliminated a number of small factories and integrated others into larger and more efficient units. Nevertheless, the value of manufactured goods rose from $36.7 million in 1909 to $85.5 million in 1919. Those increases resulted from the rising prices of sugar and tobacco, caused by World War I, as well as by the growth of production. The number of workers employed in manufacturing rose only by some 400 during 1910–19. The newly established factories employed half again as many workers as the factories which existed before and paid wages which were more than twice as high as those of the preceding decade. The production of sugar almost tripled in value, from $20.5 million in 1909 to $56.4 million in 1919, surpassing in value the production of all other industries combined. The new cane plantings along the south coast, resulting from the construction of irrigation systems begun in 1908, contributed greatly to the growth of sugar production. During the decade, a group of sugar mills began to improve their physical plant and to integrate for the purpose of grinding cane for a number of planters since previously most of the larger planters had their own mills.

The shops for processing tobacco were reduced in number from 282 in 1909 to 183 by 1919. The industry employed 2,000 fewer workers than it had in 1909, but paid better wages which rose from $1.5 million to $2.3 million, during the decade. As was the case in cane grinding, the cigar industry began to be centralized in larger factories; shops of only two or three workers, in their homes, began to disappear. In the face of growing imports from the United States, the other industries for local consumption also began to decrease in number.

The needlework industry arose during the period 1910–20 as a result of World War I, which stopped imports of European textiles and embroideries. The markets of the continental United States began to promote the production of needlework in Puerto Rico and other Antillean countries.

The fact that Puerto Rico was a center for cheap hand labor led to the establishment of new industries and the abandonment of others during 1920–30. The sugar industry continued its growth and produced nearly 587,000 tons of sugar in 1929, compared to 406,000 in 1919.[2] The refining of sugar on the south coast and the canning of fruits on the north coast

2. Data on the value of production and the number of workers employed in manufacturing as a whole are not available for the end of the 1920 decade.

also began during the decade. The value of exported canned goods rose from $113,000 in 1922 to more than $1 million toward the end of the decade. Crude tobacco, imported from Cuba, was stripped in Puerto Rico for shipment to the United States. This industry reached new heights as a result of certain customs advantages enjoyed by Puerto Rico. Unstripped tobacco got 35 cents per pound on entering the United States while stripped tobacco got 50 cents; the difference favored stripping in Puerto Rico though the most important incentive was the fact that handwork was as cheap as, or cheaper than, in Cuba.

The decade saw the growth of the needlework industry, based solidly on the cheapest kind of labor. Contractors arrived from the continental United States to set up agreements with Puerto Ricans for the hand processing of goods from the United States. Wages in the needlework shops were abysmally low, and even lower were the 3 to 4 cents per hour paid for work in the homes. But the importance attained by the industry was attested by the rise of its exports, from about $3.8 million in 1922 to some $15 million in 1929. The exports value of the needlework industry exceeded those of the tobacco industry by half a million dollars.

The new industries, principally that of needlework, were located in the larger population centers such as Ponce, San Juan, Arecibo, and Mayagüez. The largest number of shops were established in Mayagüez which, until recently, was known as Puerto Rico's needlework center, favored by good shipping facilities and a large rural and urban population.

Capital for the development of the sugar and tobacco industries came largely from the United States, local sources contributed little. The report of the Brookings Institution states that during the first thirty years of the century outside capital contributed about $120 million to Puerto Rico's development, largely in the sugar industry[3] It is notable that during fiscal year 1966 alone private capital investments in Puerto Rico from the outside were almost four times as high as that figure, reaching $474 million. The slight importance of manufacturing in relation to the rest of the economy is reflected by the consumption of electric energy; in 1927 some 62 million kilowatt-hours were consumed for all uses; the figure is less than one-tenth of the present consumption by the manufacturing industry alone.

The predominance of the sugar industry in manufacturing continued during the decade 1930–40. In 1939 it employed close to 10,000 workers in the forty sugar mills then in operation. The value of its production was $67.8 million, compared to $43.7 million of the total nonsugar production.

About 1935, the manufacture of rum began to grow as an important new Puerto Rican industry (Fig. 14.1). It had existed on the island be-

3. Victor S. Clark et al., *Porto Rico and its Problems* (Washington, D.C.: The Brookings Institution, May 1930).

fore the passage of the Prohibition Act,[4] but its greatest growth did not begin until after the law was repealed.[5] Before 1940, the rum industry produced about 2 million gallons per year, of which more than half was exported, principally to the United States. In 1939–40 the industry paid $3,865,700 to the Puerto Rican treasury in both local and federal taxes, which were returned to Puerto Rico. The industry reached its greatest development during World War II when, in 1943–44, more than 10 million gallons were exported to the United States where a great shortage of alcoholic beverages was felt. Federal excise taxes on rum returned to Puerto Rico amounted to $68.8 million in that year.

Figure 14.1. The Bacardí Distillery in Cataño.

The decade 1930–40 saw the virtual disappearance of factories making cigars and cigarettes. Cigars were usually made in small shops. The value of production fell from $8.1 million in 1919 to $0.7 million in 1939. The industry employed 7,000 workers in 1909; 5,000 in 1919, and a mere 445 in 1939.[6]

The needlework industry suffered a decline no less spectacular than that of tobacco. In 1935 it employed more than 40,000 workers, 80 per cent of whom worked at home. Competition then set in from the Far East with its low wages, while the Federal Minimum Wage Act, fixing a minimum of 25 cents per hour for needlework, was applied in Puerto Rico in 1938. An industry which had been paying three or four cents per hour for

4. Organic Act of Puerto Rico, Chapter 145, Article 2, 39 Stat. 962 (March 2, 1917).

5. Acts of the second regular legislative session of Puerto Rico's Thirteenth Legislative Assembly (San Juan: Bureau of Materials, Printing, and Transportation, 1934), p. 131.

6. *Census of Manufactures, 1939,* op. cit., p. 8.

work in the homes could obviously not survive under that drastic manda-
tory increase. The effects of the law, together with mounting competition,
were catastrophic; exports were reduced from $20 million in 1937 to $5 million in 1940.[7] The industry would have disappeared entirely if a legislative appeal for special legislation on minimum wages had not been sent
to the Congress of the United States.[8] It became necessary to establish
a new system for setting minimum wages, arrived at through "industrial
committees" which studied each case individually on its merits and in relation to the island's general industrial and economic situation. Even so,
however, the minimum wage for needlework rose sharply, having been
fixed at 12.5 cents per hour, or half of the figure first set by Federal Act.
Although that wage was still extremely low, the industry felt the impact
of so considerable a rise in wages.

Among other industries of the 1930's were foundries which had long
been especially important to the sugar industry. There were also bak-
eries, fertilizer factories, and print shops.

Puerto Rico's industrial development reached a critical stage during
the decade 1930–40, as a result of the low price of sugar during the world
economic depression, which affected the other established industries and
inhibited the growth of industrialization. In addition, two violent hurricanes scourged the island in 1928 and 1932. Flaws inherent in an economy based on the monoculture of sugar made the situation especially serious in Puerto Rico. The direct consequences were reflected in the drop
of per capita net income from $122 in 1930 to $86 in 1935. There was partial recovery to $121 in 1940. The fact that it did not fall lower was due
to heavy aid from the Federal Government, which prevented a major
disaster during the decade.

Industrial Planning During 1930–40

Puerto Rico's serious economic situation during the 1930's spurred interest in industrial planning which laid the foundations for the development of that activity in subsequent decades. The 1930 report of the
Brookings Institution[9] must again be mentioned in that connection as the
first work of its kind. The book contains a series of political recommendations which were quite objectionable in that they were aimed at restrict-
ing still more the island's scant political autonomy. In the economic field,
however, the report is a careful analysis and offers important conclusions

7. Government of Puerto Rico, Department of Agriculture and Commerce, Division of Commerce, *Annual Book of Statistics,* Fiscal years 1936–37, 1939–40.
8. H. C. Barton, Jr. and Robert A. Solo, *The Effect of Minimum Wage Laws on
the Economic Growth of Puerto Rico* (Cambridge, Mass.: Center of International Affairs, Harvard University, 1959), p. 8.
9. Victor S. Clark et al., op. cit.

and observations. It analyzed various types of industries and factors affecting them, such as markets, raw materials, and labor. However, in saying that Puerto Rico was not equipped for the task of refining its own sugar, it made a recommendation which, in my opinion, was erroneous and unfortunate. The truth is that the island could then, and can today, refine all the sugar it produces if existing political restrictions were removed. Aside from the above, the Brookings Institution recommended the establishment of a number of promising industries, some of which have since then been created. It suggested, for instance, the utilization of the sugar industry's bagasse (the fibrous end product of grinding cane) for making wallboard (*Celotex*). However, that recommendation was not carried out in those days because of opposition from powerful conservative economic interests which feared that the new industry would result in an increase in Puerto Rican wages, so preventing the establishment of an important enterprise on the island.

The report indicated the desirability of promoting foundries as an industry needed by the sugar mills for producing machinery and went so far as to point to the desirability of manufacturing complete mills for sale abroad. It also recommended the canning of grapefruit and pineapples, and the production of concentrated and frozen orange juice, which was later carried out. In addition, it referred to light industries using the Puerto Rican's manual skills, including the manufacture of jewelry and fine needlework.

Another matter on which the report took a firm stand was that of urging the Puerto Rican Government to give direct aid to industrialization. Among other things, it proposed the return of customs duties paid by local manufacturers, the training of workers and operators, and a publicity campaign on industrialization in the United States to attract continental enterprises. However, it commited the error of opposing tax exemption for industry, without which Puerto Rico's industrial growth of the past two decades would have been impossible. Undoubtedly, this exemption has been the major incentive for the establishment of new industries on the island.

In the "Chardón Plan,"[10] one of the best examples of economic-industrial planning during the decade of 1930–40, the conclusion was reached that the island's population density demanded industrialization, making it impossible to depend solely on agriculture for development, and much less for the improvement of levels of living to the extent essential for modern civilization. The Chardón Plan noted the obstacles to such a goal and mentioned possible remedies. Lack of local capital and competition from mainland U.S. industries—often resorting to "dumping" or cheapen-

10. C. Chardón, R. Fernández García, R. Menéndez Ramos, *Report of the Puerto Rico Policy Committee* (Washington, D.C.: Department of the Interior, 1934).

ing the island's market by selling below cost—were obstacles difficult to
overcome, against which tariff protection was recommended. The report
pointed out the urgency of maximum development of hydroelectric
power generation as an unavoidable requirement for the establishment
of new industries and the expansion of those in existence. That recommendation led to the construction of the Garzas and Dos Bocas hydroelectric projects.

The plan recommended the establishment of free zones in the ports of
San Juan, Ponce, and Mayagüez, so anticipating the present day when
Mayagüez has its free zone, not in the port but near it. It also indicated
the need for repealing the Coastwise Shipping Act. Whether or not this
act should be repealed is, even today, an extremely debatable question.

The plan viewed the cooperative movement as an adequate instrument
for creating and distributing goods with maximum equity and justice and
recommended the creation of cooperatives, with centralized organizations to direct and guide the movement. Today there exists a government
body, the Cooperative Development Administration, to stimulate the establishment of cooperatives through incentives and other means.

Another important recommendation of the Chardón Plan was the creation of a "Division for Industrial Development Study and Research" to
be financed with $150,000 during its first stage, and later with $50,000 per
year. Today, the Economic Development Administration (EDA) fulfills
that need.

In the matter of creating new industries, the plan recommended that
first consideration be given to those which would use, as raw materials,
agricultural products which were, or could be, produced in Puerto Rico;
second consideration should be given to industries based on the cheap
and abundant hand labor resulting from the high density of population.
The report also mentioned the possibility of industries based on raw materials imported from neighboring countries, paying low customs duties.
It dealt with industries with voluminous, low-priced products whose cost
would be determined largely by transportation costs. Finally, it mentioned service industries as well as a few, small, miscellaneous manufacturing ventures.

One of the important results of the Chardón Plan was the creation of
the Planning Division of the Puerto Rico Reconstruction Administration,
established in 1935 by the Federal Government. The Division made a
series of economic and industrial studies which, beside providing impetus
for the creation of new industries, laid the foundation for much future
action in the island's industrial development. Studies were made of the
socio-economic problems of the sugar industry, of the possibilities for a
cement factory, and many others. The division, moreover, brought together a group of Puerto Rican technicians devoted to economic studies
and research, who later rendered valuable services to the country.

The Chardón Plan suggested the creation of certain industrial enterprises such as the cement plant which a short time later was built in the Municipality of Guaynabo, serving as an example for the cement factory built subsequently in Ponce. It recommended the creation of a cooperative for handling pork products; a plant for bottling orange juice, with wine and vinegar as by-products; the local refining of all sugar produced on the island; the canning of fruits and other crops; the manufacture of paper, rayon, and insulating boards from bagasse; the manufacture of nitrogenous feeds from molasses; the production of alcohol from molasses, to be mixed with gasoline for use as a motor fuel; the production of starch from cassava; the manufacture of matting and brushes from coconut fibers and of soap from coconut oil; the manufacture of shoes for local distribution; the weaving of straw hats and cotton textiles; a ceramic industry; and, finally, the manufacture of furniture from local or imported woods.

Many of the recommendations for important industries proposed in the Plan have been carried out, as for instance the canning of fruit juices by the Land Authority, the Parkhurst Company, and others; paper is, today, being manufactured from bagasse in Arecibo, by the International Paper Company; cotton fabrics are produced in Ponce and in other communities; in the manufacture of furniture, which has become an important Puerto Rican industry, a high degree of mechanization has been attained.

Industrial Promotion, 1940–1967

In the late 1930's and the early 1940's, the study of industrial planning coincided with the rise of a new political organization, the Popular Democratic Party (PPD), led by Luis Muñoz Marín, who was later to become Puerto Rico's first elected governor. In the 1940 election, the PPD party gained control of both houses of the island's legislature, though by a very narrow margin. The new political party maintained that Puerto Rico's most urgent and immediate task was the improvement of the island's social-economic conditions.

The industrial planning of preceding years now served as a basis for new plans and developments. In view of the density of population, industrialization seemed to be the only means of creating employment and raising levels of living. As a first step, the Puerto Rican government created in 1942 three organizations to stimulate and coordinate the industrialization program: The Puerto Rico Planning Board, the P.R. Industrial Development Company (PRIDCO), now reorganized within the Economic Development Administration, and the Government Development Bank for Puerto Rico.

The Planning Board studied and projected in broad terms the island's economic and social development (I was its first chairman, 1942–55).

From the beginning, the planning process was democratic and comprehensive, dealing with economic and social as well as physical aspects. The judicious use of all phases of democratic planning contributed to the government's success as well as to the improved utilization of the island's resources.

The Planning Board continued the earlier studies of industrial planning and in 1944 published "A Development Plan for Puerto Rico," a report prepared by the local office of the National Resources Planning Board (NRPB).[11] Actually the report started modern industrial planning. It discusses in detail possibilities for new industries and stresses the urgency of taking a firm stand on manufacturing. It recognizes the urgent need for supplementing the sugar economy with new industrial enterprises. It points out the importance of production for the local market as opposed to export. Among the possible industrial by-products of sugar cane, it mentions the manufacture of pressed wood from bagasse, as well as of alcohol, wax, and candies. The report refers to prospects for industries based on the products of the coconut palm, and such others as charcoal, textiles from Puerto Rican or imported cotton textiles, glass, and quality needlework.

The Puerto Rico Industrial Development Company (PRIDCO),[12] created in 1942, began with a capital of $500,000 for starting the program of "Operation Bootstrap." Three years later, in 1945, it was given $20 million and inherited from the PRRA the cement factory located in the Municipality of Guaynabo, across the bay from San Juan, valued at $2 million (Fig 14.2).[13] PRIDCO was organized for the purpose of studying the island's resources and experimenting toward the production, export, and sale of new products. It operated a laboratory for the study of the island's products and was authorized to create and operate manufacturing enterprises, as well as to make loans to producers, manufacturers, miners, commercial and even agricultural enterprises, provided they were related to industry.

The first step taken by PRIDCO was to engage a well-known firm, Arthur D. Little, Inc. of Boston, to prepare a kind of master plan for industrialization and its potentials in Puerto Rico.[14] Among other things the firm recommended the establishment of factories for cotton textiles, pressed wood from bagasse, glass for bottles and objects of art, the fer-

---

11. Puerto Rico Planning, Urbanization and Zoning Board. Office of Information for Puerto Rico for the Puerto Rico Planning, Urbanization, and Zoning Board, "A Development Plan for Puerto Rico" (Technical Paper No. 1) (San Juan: Insular Procurement Office, Printing Division, January 1944).

12. In Spanish: "Compañía de Fomento Industrial de Puerto Rico."

13. Economic Development Administration, "The Industrial Development Program, 1940–60" (San Juan: Office of Economic Research), p. 14.

14. Arthur D. Little, Inc., *New Industries for Puerto Rico* (Report to the Puerto Rico Industrial Development Company, San Juan, 1943).

Figure 14.2. View of the Cement Factory in the Municipality of Guaynabo.

mentations of molasses for industrial alcohol, cardboard containers, ceramics, bricks, oil refineries, and the manufacture of ammonia for fertilizers.

The recommendations were carried out without delay. The cement factory which PRIDCO had inherited was enlarged with the installation of another kiln; factories were built for making glass bottles and cardboard containers, as was a ceramics plant for making bricks, building blocks, and sanitary ware; finally, a plant for making shoes was established in Ponce.

The cement factory was a notable economic success, due largely to the growing local demand for its product and the cost of transporting cement from the United States. On the other hand, the glass and ceramics factories never showed profits. The main problem in the government operation of those industries was that of labor relations, similar to that found in laborite governments, or prolabor governments, which, as in the case of England, operate nationalized industries. Usually, such governments cannot cope with labor problems as effectively as private enterprise.

The above-mentioned factories had absorbed a large share of the $20 million in capital which had been given to PRIDCO, while employing only some 2,000 workers in 1947. A radical change in the emphasis and orientation of the industrial development program seemed therefore called for.

However, it must be stated that the results of those first efforts proved to benefit Puerto Rico greatly. In the first place, the program of developing industries to be run by the government taught valuable lessons in management, markets, industrial possibilities, and other aspects. Secondly, and this point was far more important, the experience taught private enterprise that industrialization was feasible, so decreasing the timidity which had previously prevented private capital from investing in new Puerto Rican industrial ventures.

Reorientation of the Industrial Program

The above-mentioned experiences reoriented the Industrial Development Company. A small but effective promotion campaign was organized in New York in 1945 to attract private entrepreneurs to invest in Puerto Rico's industrial development. Industrial buildings were constructed, to be rented to companies willing to establish themselves on the island. By 1949, it had been decided to stimulate the investment of outside capital in Puerto Rico's industrialization. The shoe factory in Ponce was in that year leased to the *Joyce* Company; *Textron* rented the textile factory in Ponce and set to work immediately. In that same year, the government invested considerable sums in the construction of the *Caribe* Hotel which was rented to the Hilton chain and has since been known as the *Caribe*

Hilton. In more ways than the purely economic, that transaction proved one of the most profitable to the people of Puerto Rico ever undertaken by the Development Company. The hotel yields an annual net of more than $2 million to the Industrial Development Company.

The basic change in the industrialization program's orientation occurred in 1950–51 when the factories established and operated by the Development Company were sold to the Ferré interests of Ponce; the price of $10 million was practically the sum which had been invested in them. The Puerto Rican government did not lose by the deal and the factories have continued to operate efficiently. They employ many workers, pay taxes, and contribute to the island's general economic expansion.

The Industrial Development Company was reorganized in 1950 as a subsidiary of the Economic Development Administration, known as EDA,[15] created that same year. The Administration is charged with promotion and industrial experimentation to be financed not by profits which might accrue from promoted factories, since in some cases there might not be such profits, but by appropriations from the island's general budget for promotion and services. In the beginning those appropriations were relatively small, not exceeding two per cent of Puerto Rico's operating budget. Under the new orientation, a vigorous promotion campaign was begun for the establishment of private industries. The new philosophy had its greatest impulse with the approval of the tax exemption act. Promotion offices were established in the United States. The P.R. Industrial Development Company continued to operate as a public corporation, empowered to make loans, build factories, lend and invest, and offer special incentives to industrial enterprises. It is also aware of the need for changes and adjustments in its program, as demanded by new developments.

Achievements of Industrial Planning

The success of the effort to industrialize the island, made by the Economic Development Administration and the government in general, is shown by the net income generated by manufacturing and by the number of factories established. In 1940, the net income from manufacturing was $27 million; in 1969 it was $908 million. In 1955, the net income from manufacturing for the first time exceeded that from agriculture; the figures were $169 and $168 million, respectively. Agricultural total income has not regressed that much, but manufacturing has grown much more rapidly.

In 1939, 798 manufacturing establishments existed on the island; by 1949 their number had grown to about 2,000 and in 1967 there were 2,367

15. In Spanish: "Administración de Fomento Económico."

(See Appendix D). When one realizes that the present number of factories produce much more and pay far higher wages, absolutely and relatively, than did the 798 factories of former times, that advance in a short time proves to be little less than revolutionary. In 1967, some 104,000 production workers earned $280 million in wages and the average wage in manufacturing was $1.41 per hour. A study made by the Economic Development Administration reveals that among the more developed countries of Europe only Sweden paid higher wages than did Puerto Rico in 1965. In that year Puerto Rico's average wage was $1.23 per hour while Sweden's was $1.52. The countries which trailed behind Puerto Rico were, in descending order, the United Kingdom with $1.22; Germany, $1.02; Holland, $0.81; Italy, $0.59 in 1964; and France, with $0.61 in 1965. In chemical and petrochemical industries Puerto Rico paid a little more than did Sweden. In 1964 the average wage in Puerto Rico's chemical industry was $1.46 per hour while Sweden's was $1.28. In June 30, 1971, the average industrial wage in manufacturing was $1.84 per hour.

In 1940, the total net income from manufacturing was about $27 million, of which $9.3 million came from the sugar industry, indicating that Puerto Rico's manufacturing consisted primarily of processing sugar. In 1966, the total net income from manufacturing was $611.6 million ($953 million in 1970) while that from sugar was $30 million, showing that today the manufacturing industry is vastly more diversified than it was twenty-six years ago.

The examples of tobacco and needlework indicate the changes which have occurred in industrialization. In 1909, some 7,000 workers processed tobacco in small shops. The number decreased to 5,000 by 1919 and virtually disappeared by 1939, when it went down to 445. However, as a result of the "Operation Bootstrap" efforts, the industry began to come back after 1949. In 1967 it employed some 7,000 workers, largely as a result of the operations of the Consolidated Cigar Company which came to Puerto Rico in response to efforts made by the Industrial Development Company and established factories in Caguas, Cayey, and Comerío. Later, the General Cigar Company opened a factory in the town of Utuado.

The needlework industry, which employed some 40,000 workers in 1935, most of them women who worked at home for abysmally low wages, virtually disappeared as a result of foreign competition and the application of Federal minimum wage laws. After 1940, the industry was transformed through the installation of factories for making cloth and wearing apparel. These factories are extremely important today. In 1967, for instance, there were 471 textile and apparel factories as compared with 136 in 1939 employing 40,000 workers, five times as many as the earlier establishments had used in their shops.[16] The new factories for

16. Data from the Industrial Development Company and the 1967 Census of Manufactures.

textiles and clothes produce several times more than the earlier ones and distribute $87 million in wages as compared with a little more than $1.5 million paid formerly.

The metals industry is one of the most important in the industrial development program. It has reduced its production costs to the point where it now enjoys a higher margin of profits. The value of annual production in the primary and fabricated metal industry exceeded $100 million in 1967. The group of those industries includes 218 firms which manufacture such products as aluminum doors and windows, steel bars and gratings, screws, kitchen appliances, and cans for the local and external markets. Among the metal working firms is the Ford Motor Company, which recently established a factory for precision ball bearings.

The transformation which has taken place, as shown by the examples mentioned above, has also manifested itself in fast-rising values of production, in wages received by the labor force as a whole as well as by individual workers, and in the total number of industrial workers. However, the geographic distribution of those benefits has not been uniform. The new industries tend to be located in the San Juan Metropolitan Area where some 40 per cent of the 2,367 manufacturing enterprises in existence in 1967 were established (Fig. 14.3). Because of the presence, in the Metropolitan Area, of such facilities as communications, transportation, and shipping, it is difficult to resist concentrating industries there. In its efforts to decentralize industries, the government offers special incentives to those located in other parts of the island. As a result, virtually every town now has at least one factory. The Economic Development Administration has set out to create at least one factory job per fifty inhabitants in each of the island's municipalities. In 1961, out of a total of 76 municipalities, 23 already showed that ratio between factory workers and inhabitants; by 1966 the number had increased to 43.

UNFAVORABLE INDUSTRIAL FACTORS

In general, the geographic environment has restricted Puerto Rico's industrial development, especially in the matters of raw materials and fuels. With the exception of copper, no commercially exploitable metals, which might also serve as bases for other industries, have as yet been found on the island. The existing deposits of iron, manganese, nickel, and lead have not as yet been proved commercially exploitable.

Puerto Rico's forest reserves are too limited to support even a domestic furniture industry. Because of the island's small size, restricted even more by its dense population, it is impossible to enlarge the forest reserves to any marked degree.

By the same token, it is impossible to enlarge agricultural production to a great extent, especially of certain products like pineapples for which at least 8,000 acres are needed while only 4,700 are available. Agricultural production is moreover limited by the relatively restricted local

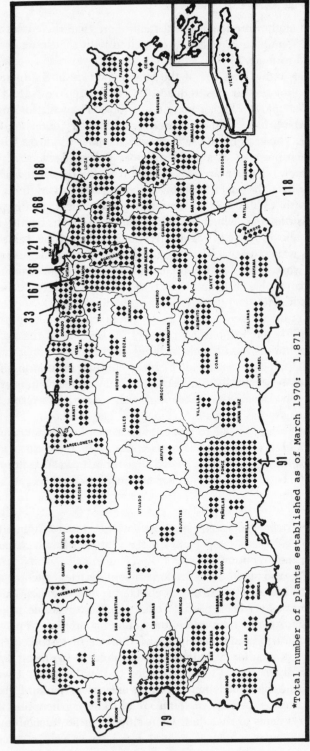

Figure 14.3. Established and Operating Factories Sponsored by the Economic Development Administration's Program, March 1970. (Source: Puerto Rico Industrial Development Company.)

market whose purchasing power is small when compared with that of the continental United States. Moreover, Puerto Rico's market is not protected by import duties which could compel greater consumption of domestic products. However, the levying of these duties can not, by itself, be the answer.

Puerto Rico's natural resources do not include enough fuels to sustain large industries. The coal and oil which are basic for industrial development are not found in commercial quantities; the demand for fuels is met by importation. The generation of hydroelectricity is limited by the smallness of the island's rivers. In 1945, hydraulic sources produced 55 per cent of the consumed 298 million kilowatt hours, the remainder came from thermal plants. The growing demand for electric energy has required the construction of new thermal generating plants and even a nuclear power plant. In 1970 the total production of electric energy in the island was 8,027 million kilowatt-hours, of which hydroelectric plants generated about 3 per cent and the rest came from plants burning petroleum derivatives. It is expected that future increases in the demand will be met by nuclear plants, like the one now being built in Aguirre.

FACTORS FAVORABLE FOR INDUSTRIALIZATION

The climate, which helps to reduce production costs by eliminating the need for heating factories at any time of the year, is one of the factors favoring industrialization, even though high, tropical temperatures demand air conditioning in offices and shops for improved output per worker.

The population, 14 or more years of age, is about 1.7 million and grows by some 30,000 annually. They constitute a labor force close to 850,000 who generally lack adequate education and industrial training despite the fact that both have been greatly advanced through vocational training in the industrial schools. Wages lower than those paid in the United States are regarded as favoring industrialization, though they have been affected by Federal minimum wage laws which prevent competition with Japan, the Philippines, and those European countries which pay wages lower than those of Puerto Rico.

Puerto Rico's capital has not been sufficient for the development of the various programs of economic growth. Of the $8,945 million invested in the island from 1947–58 to 1968–69 about 60 per cent came from private capital in the continental United States. The importation of private capital is necessary for the maintenance of the rate of growth in industrial production required for creating employment for the growing population. In order to attract capital for the creation of new factories, it was necessary to establish public relations centers in various parts of the United States and Europe. In 1967, of the 2,367 factories on the island, 865 were owned by residents of mainland United States or 58 foreign countries.

Puerto Rico's location between North and South America is another factor which favors industrialization, though the fact that it is an island involves costs for the maritime transportation of raw materials and finished products. The principal markets are in the United States, some 1,600 miles away. Shipping costs are relatively high because the U.S. Coastwise Shipping Act forbids the use of foreign ships with lower freight rates between Puerto Rico and mainland United States. On the whole, however, maritime transport is cheaper than the overland which is commonly used in the United States. For instance, it costs more to transport raw materials or finished products from California to New York by land than to embark them by ship from Puerto Rico to the eastern United States. Though the external transportation is complemented by a network of some 3,000 miles of roads in good condition, modern highways for a more direct and rapid communication between Ponce, San Juan, and other centers, are currently under construction.

The external commerce in Puerto Rican wares is based on a common market with the United States. Its total value (exports and imports) was $4,275 million in 1970, of which over 85 per cent originated in the United States. The duty-free common market in the U.S. permits Puerto Rico to trade with more than 200 million U.S. inhabitants who have the world's highest purchasing power. The common market is therefore the most important of the factors which favor the island's industrialization.

The government's attitudes and actions have furthered the utilization of the various industrial factors. The government offers incentives to private industry and contributes capital and technology for the promotion of industries. While several measures have contributed to the success of the industrial development program, that providing for tax exemption is outstanding. Several laws dealing with incentives for private enterprise have been in effect since the start of the program, but the one in effect at present, known as the Industrial Incentives Act of 1954, is the broadest.[17] Under that act various forms of tax exemption are offered to manufacturing ventures, hotels, and other specific industries. On corporate incomes, the exemption was overall for ten years; on personal incomes, seven years; on properties, varying with the amounts invested, they range from five to ten years; exemptions from municipal taxes run for ten years. On June 13, 1963, in an effort to decentralize the distribution of industries, the Legislature passed Act No. 57, known as the Industrial Incentives Act, which offers greater incentives to industries established outside of the San Juan Metropolitan Area (Fig. 14.4). That act provides for a tax exemption period of more than ten years, according to the location of the

17. Acts of Puerto Rico. Acts of the first special session and the second regular session of the Second Legislative Assembly of the Commonwealth of Puerto Rico (San Juan: Department of the Treasury, Purchase and Supply Service, Transportation Division, 1954), pp. 13–57.

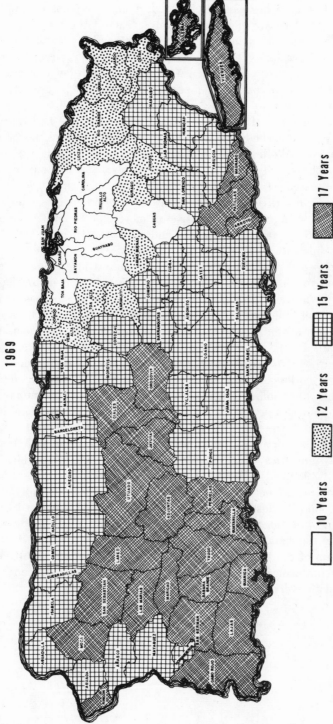

Figure 14.4. Industrial Tax Exemption by Municipalities in Accordance with Executive Order of the Governor of Puerto Rico, December 10, 1969. (Source: Puerto Rico Industrial Development Company.)

industry. Three zones were established, namely: regions outside of the metropolitan area are eligible for twelve years of tax exemption, except for those classified as underdeveloped, where the exemption from all taxes is in force for seventeen years; the metropolitan area continues to enjoy ten years of tax exemption. Other laws which favor industrial development provide for tax exemption for hotels, machinery, and industrial raw materials.

The effectiveness of those measures is attested by the fact that 83 per cent of the established new industries were attracted by the provisions for exemption. While it has been estimated that as a result of those laws the Commonwealth Treasury failed to receive $92 million in taxes in 1969, it *did* receive more than $60 million in taxes produced indirectly by the factories. In 1970, 313 industries whose periods of exemption had terminated, were paying annual taxes of more than $3 million. The figure does not include taxes on property and on dividends and shares owned by nonresidents.

Other special incentives for certain basic industries, beside tax exemption, tend to diminish the trend toward concentration in the San Juan Metropolitan Area. The Industrial Development Company has built typical industrial buildings outside the metropolitan zone, which are rented with certain advantages to industries willing to establish themselves in those parts of the island. Moreover, special buildings are erected for rental purposes to certain industries inclined toward permanence. Other incentives, no less important, are a direct subsidy for transporting equipment and other initial expenses, special training for operators of machinery, and sales promotion in external markets for goods manufactured in Puerto Rico. The Government Development Bank and the Puerto Rico Industrial Development Company (PRIDCO) offer long and short term credit to industries which require more capital for establishing themselves. By 1969 PRIDCO had in its books more than $30 million in loans and stock investments in new enterprises and over $160 million in the construction of industrial and commercial buildings. Between its organization and June 30, 1970, the Government Development Bank lent $107.4 million to the manufacturing industry.

The aim of the Bank is to extend credit to all feasible industrial projects, in consonance with its own objectives and the government's policy to stimulate every effort that tends toward economic growth.

15

Tourism

Tourism began to develop as an important economic factor near the end of the 1940's. Today, largely as a result of the government's "Operation Bootstrap" program, it is one of the island's most promising industries, stemming from the utilization of such advantages in Puerto Rico's geographic environment as location, topography, climate, and natural vegetation.

Tourism is extremely important in international commerce. Total expenditures by travelers in 1966 were estimated at some $10 billion. North American tourists spent about $3.6 billion and the United States is the country which contributes most to the tourist trade. In the Caribbean area, North American tourists spent some $210 million, or about 6 per cent of their expenditures throughout the world. In view of the proximity of the United States to the Caribbean centers, that sum is relatively small.

Puerto Rico is rich in the resources required for a thriving tourist industry. Its tropical climate, with no extreme temperatures throughout the year, is one of its major attractions. The average annual temperature is 76.5° F, and monthly averages vary between 73° and 79°. The cool trade winds and the sea and land breezes help to create a climate which is ideal for visitors. Those winds cool the island throughout the year, and even the summer season is excellent for rest and recreation.

Puerto Rico's average summer temperature (78.3° F) is lower than that of virtually all parts of the continental United States. In winter the average temperature is 73° F, offering visitors an extremely agreeable climate as an escape from the winter discomforts of many parts of the United States.

The visitor to Puerto Rico sees great contrast in natural vegetation, not far apart, such as desert vegetation and that of the subtropical rain forest. The year-long abundance of flowers also attracts the attention of visitors from other countries. Outstanding natural beaches exist on the island's coasts, and a number of them are well equipped for the bathers' comfort and safety (Fig. 15.1). Temperatures at those beaches are ideal throughout the year.

Puerto Rico, moreover, has several springs of sulfurous waters, like "Coamo Springs," whose curative properties were proclaimed by the early Spanish chroniclers. They are also found near Arroyo and Ponce and have attracted both local and foreign visitors. If they were well developed and had adequate facilities, they could serve as hotel centers as popular as Europe's famous "spas."

Figure 15.1. Luquillo Beach.

Sport fishing has become a tourist attraction in recent years. The Office of Tourism sponsors annual tournaments, attended by fans of the sport from a number of countries (Fig. 15.2).

Puerto Rico has preserved zones and monuments of extraordinary historic interest, dating from Spanish colonial days: buildings, streets, forts, ancient walls, military installations, as well as several ceremonial courts of the early Boriquén Indians, unique in the Antilles (Fig. 15.3). Several towns are noted for their Spanish colonial architecture, among them Ponce, San Germán, and Old San Juan, which show Spanish atmosphere and architectural traditions, adapted to the New World.

Visitors are also interested in some of Puerto Rico's cultural manifestations, such as knowledge of English and the island's close association with the United States which goes beyond political and economic relations. Spanish is the island's native tongue, English its second language; together, they help Puerto Ricans to understand visitors from North and South America and from Europe and to exchange ideas with them. This language tool plus Puerto Ricans' generous and innate hospitality give added pleasure to the visitor's stay on the island.

U.S. tourists find in Puerto Rico their own monetary system and good banks in practically every town and city. Besides, as the U.S. citizens do not need passports or visas for entering or leaving the island, there is a free interchange between Puerto Rico and the United States.

Figure 15.2. Sport-fishing Boats, Ready to Start an International Tournament. (Courtesy San Juan Yacht Club.)

Virtually all goods and services found in the continental United States are encountered in Puerto Rico's commerce. The island has good, modern hospitals, ready to serve the visitors' needs if so required. Foods, including water and milk, compare in quality with those of the United States. There are, moreover, good restaurants which specialize in various exotic foods such as Italian, Spanish, Mexican, French, German, Swiss, Chinese, and Japanese. (Fig. 15.4).

At the end of the 1940's, virtually all tourists came to San Juan, whose hotels provided altogether about 600 rooms. The island's small tourist movement meant that the hotel business was largely in the hands of local citizens. In recent years, however, many modern hotels have been built.

Figure 15.3. "Caleta de San Juan" Street. The street is at the foot of the Archbishop's Cathedral of San Juan, built by the Spaniards.

Figure 15.4. The "Swiss Chalet" Restaurant. International cuisine is offered here. In the background is the Hotel Pierre, under the same management.

In 1970, Puerto Rico had 63 tourist and commercial hotels with a total of 8,500 rooms. Today, San Juan alone has 6,700 rooms; the remaining 1,800 are in other parts of the island, either along the coasts or in the interior.

Puerto Rico's hotels compare favorably with the best in other countries. Their architecture ranges from the Spanish colonial style to the modern type, characterized by vertical construction. In San Juan, the city of Spanish architecture with typical narrow streets, an old convent has been restored and remodeled into a modern luxury hotel which, internally as well as externally, shows the subdued characteristics of colonial architecture (Fig. 15.5). In Santurce, outside the walled city, the new hotels are built in attractive modern style (Fig. 15.6).

The various hotels outside of the San Juan Metropolitan Zone offer wide varieties of scenic attractions and recreational facilities not found in the capital. In Dorado, west of San Juan and about thirty minutes away, are two hotels with excellent beaches, modern golf courses, and a landing field for small aircraft (Fig. 15.7). In the southwest, several small hotels in or near the picturesque fishing village of La Parguera offer facilities for sport fishing and night excursions to the luminous waters of "Phosphorescent Bay," a dramatic natural phenomenon. In the east, on a small island ten minutes from the beach of Fajardo, a "marina" offers facilities for yachtsmen, including a dry dock and anchorages, as well as docking facilities, for about a hundred vessels.

Recent years have seen the appearance of a new type of accommodation for visitors, characteristic of such tourist centers as Miami. That is

Figure 15.5. Hotel "El Convento" in San Juan.

the "guest house" which offers room service and cooking facilities at much lower prices than those charged in the standard hotels. Life in such guest houses, which resemble the European pensions is much less formal than that in the hotels and permits closer acquaintance with native Puerto Ricans and their customs. By the end of June 1970 a total of 482 rooms were available in guest houses. In San Juan's Metropolitan zone alone there were 35 guest houses. That type of hospitality is spreading to other parts of the island where seven guest houses have already been approved by the Tourist Development Company.

The above discussion of hotel establishments points to the importance of San Juan as a tourist center. The historic character of the city, founded early in the sixteenth century, and its location near the magnificent beaches of Santurce and Carolina and in the eastern part of the north coast, which gives easy access to other points of tourist interest on the coast and in the interior, make the Metropolitan Zone ideal for tourism. For such reasons, the decentralization of the tourist industry and its dispersal through the island is difficult. Nevertheless, to avoid undue concentration in the Metropolitan Zone, as in Miami, the government has recently begun to promote tourism in the rural areas. As this type of tourism does not require great luxury hotels, such dispersal would be less costly to visitors. It would moreover help to boost the considerable beauty of the island's interior with great benefits to the economy of the rural areas.

Figure 15.6. San Juan Hotel in Isla Verde, East of San Juan.

Cultural events, offered throughout the year, are of great interest to visitors. May and June, for instance, offer the annual Casals Festival, one of the world's great musical events in which famous artists participate under the direction of Maestro Pablo Casals (Fig. 15.8). Lovers of fine music from Puerto Rico and abroad attend the festival. Carnival is celebrated in February as a popular festivity, and June sees the "fiestas" of John the Baptist, the capital's patron saint, and many of the island's historic and folkloric customs may be observed.

The Institute of Puerto Rican Culture, created for the purpose of preserving, promoting, and enriching the island's cultural assets, contributes by developing attractions for tourists as well as for native Puerto Ricans. Within the walled city of San Juan, the Institute gives technical aid toward the restoration of old buildings and historic sites. In cooperation with the Institute, the Government Development Bank grants loans for such purposes. Through these efforts, a number of old run-down houses and commercial structures, historically and esthetically valuable, have been saved and restored. The Institute also organizes conferences and expositions of painting, architecture, sculpture, and typical Puerto Rican musical instruments.

The great upsurge of tourism began in the 1950's. In 1940, some 40,000 visitors came to the island, in 1950 nearly 65,000, and in 1970 over one million, plus those who came on cruise ships and naval and military personnel. Those visitors are divided into three classes according to their

Figure 15.7. Dorado Beach Hotel and Golf Course, West of San Juan.

lodgings: those who stay in hotels and guest houses; those who use the private quarters of friends and relatives; and those who do not patronize commercial establishments, like the military on leave and the cruise passengers who stay on their ships. The visitors who live in hotels and guest houses are the true tourists. Those who stay in private quarters are largely Puerto Ricans, visiting their island. The cruise passengers who remain on their ships generally stay only a very short time. Expenditures were as follows in 1970; $134 million by the visitors who stayed in hotels

Figure 15.8. Casals Festival Orchestra, Directed by Maestro Pablo Casals.

and guest houses; $81.2 million by visitors to private homes; and about $5.9 million by the military and cruise passengers. Of the 1,082,444 visitors in 1970, 491,618 stayed in hotels and guest houses and spent an average of $270 each. That figure represents an increase of $189 over the average per capita expenditure in 1950, caused partly by the growth in the number of tourists with high incomes and partly by increases in prices. In 1950 the major part of the tourists were summer vacationists, largely middle-income people from the United States. In 1966 about 66 per cent of the tourists were in the income bracket above $10,000, and comprised largely people who visit the island in the winter months of December to February.

The tourist expenditures go mainly to hotels and restaurants. In recent years, 61 per cent of the expenditures went for food and lodging, 19 per cent for recreation, 11 per cent for purchases (largely gifts), and the remaining 9 per cent for miscellaneous items.

In 1967 the average daily expenditure of hotel visitors was $46.59, approximately the same as in Hawaii. However, in Puerto Rico the average duration of the visitors' stay was about 5.74 days, compared to some 17 days in Hawaii. In 1961, Hawaii received 319,000 tourists, as compared to the 240,000 in Puerto Rico in 1963. But in Hawaii they spent four times as much as in Puerto Rico, showing that the latter's income from tourists would be larger if they stayed longer. New and better provisions for tourists will aid in prolonging their visits and increasing their numbers.

Puerto Rico receives about 404 tourists per 1,000 inhabitants; in Switzerland in 1967 the number was about 450. It is expected that in Puerto Rico the number will rise. Today, about 89.5 per cent of those who stay in hotels in the Metropolitan Zone come from the United States and the remaining 10.5 per cent from foreign countries. According to a study made by the Economic Development Administration, the majority of North American visitors, about 893 per 100,000 inhabitants, come from the New York State. Many come from other states in the eastern United States although to a lesser degree than from New York. The Middle West provides the fewest visitors, partly because of the greater travel distances involved.

Tourists come to Puerto Rico by plane primarily, and by ship. Those two forms of transportation should be efficient and low in cost to assure increase in the number of visitors. The growth of air transport, caused by the multiplication of passengers and the use of modern jet planes, required the construction of the modern International Airport in the San Juan Metropolitan Area, fifteen minutes from the heart of the city and three hours from New York. Its main building provides space for office facilities for the airlines and for passengers' accommodations and comfort, including a good hotel. The International Airport is one of the most modern in the western hemisphere and also one of the most active in the handling of freight and passengers. Nevertheless, the ever increasing service demands require its continuous expansion.

Elsewhere in Puerto Rico there are several small airports which facilitate the internal movement of passengers to sites of tourist interest. There are also daily flights from Puerto Rico to the other Caribbean islands. About half of the tourists who come to Puerto Rico also visit the Virgin Islands.

The movement of visitors to Puerto Rico is closely associated with the cost of transportation. On jet planes, the cost of a round trip from New York to San Juan is about $114–$152 for "tourist" fare, and $168–195 for first class accommodations. The cost of a ticket from Puerto Rico to New York and other cities is not high, considering the types of planes used and the service received by the passengers.

In 1970, 301 ships arrived in Puerto Rico with 136,604 tourists. Such ships follow fixed routes or itineraries, designed to bring large numbers of visitors to various countries. Freight vessels continue to bring a few passengers. However, because travel by ship is relatively expensive and slow, Puerto Rico's tourist industry relies largely on air transport.

Internal surface transportation is good in Puerto Rico and will improve with the projection and construction of new highways. The visitor can travel to all points of interest on paved roads, properly identified and provided with traffic safety signs such as maximum speeds. Most traffic is by common carriers called "públicos," regular automobiles licensed to provide public transportation. Most of their drivers speak English as well as Spanish and have been trained to provide courteous service for their passengers and to acquaint them with the island's points of interest. A number of companies offer car rental services to those who want private transportation. There are tourist centers in San Juan that give, free of charge, information on points of interest, help to plan trips, and hand out brochures and printed material on the island in general.

16

Commerce, Transportation and Finance

Commerce, transportation, and finance are essential for the success of our basic industries. The first two are factors of great economic importance to Puerto Rico because of their large contributions to the Commonwealth's income, the employment they generate, and their services to the other industries.

Commerce

Formerly, commerce occupied third place in the net income. Of the $225 million net income in 1940, commerce contributed 12 per cent; in 1969 it contributed 17.9 per cent of a net income of $3,403 million. The net income generated by commerce in the latter year, $608 million, was more than twenty-three times as large as the $26 million in 1940. In 1970 commerce generated about $675 million, more than any other activity except manufacturing.

In 1970, commerce employed 18.7 per cent of the 738,000 persons employed in Puerto Rico, which was an increase of 200 per cent over the 54,000 working in commerce in 1940.

According to a study made by the Department of Commerce, there were 45,000 business establishments in Puerto Rico in 1967, with sales and incomes totalling about $3,580 million. Within four years, the number of business firms increased by 4,000 while their income grew by $1,180 million. But the geographic distribution of that large increase was uneven. In 1967, 35 per cent of the business houses and 64 per cent of their income were found in the San Juan area. In the metropolitan area 55 per cent of the business establishments made 70 per cent of the sales.

As a result of industrialization and the growth of population income, the amount and nature of the island's external commerce has changed during the past two decades. Puerto Rico's total external trade, imports

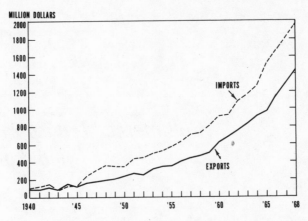

Figure 16.1. Value of Imports and Exports, 1940–1968.
(Source: Puerto Rico Planning Board.)

and exports, came to $199 million in 1940 (Fig. 16.1; Appendix F). The trade began to grow, though slowly, during World War II. Later, both imports and exports grew to the point of reaching $4,232 million in 1970. The per capita external trade rose to $1,575, one of the world's highest because the specialization of the island's commercial activities demands buying and selling elsewhere. The natural basis of Puerto Rico's commerce is its common market with the United States whose 200 million inhabitants have high purchasing power. In 1969–70, 90 per cent of merchandise exports went to the United States (excluding the Virgin Islands); the rest were sent elsewhere, especially to such Caribbean countries as Venezuela and to some European countries like Germany, France, and Spain. In that year 80 per cent of the imports came from the United States and the remainder from foreign countries. In 1970, the export of goods reached $1,719 million ($1,155 in 1966); this amounted to an increase of $1,727 million over the $92 million of exports in 1940 and of $1,484 million over the 1950 exports. In 1969, exports accounted for 37 per cent of the gross product; they originated primarily from manufacturing by the new industries, and not, as had been the case before 1940, from the sugar industry. In that year cane products (sugar, molasses, and rum) amounted to 68 per cent of the total exports (Appendix H).

While sugar was still important among the island's 1950 exports, it comprised only 5.8 per cent of the total in 1969. Less sugar was exported; in 1969 its export value was $83.7 million. The proportion occupied by sugar also decreased within the great increase of total exports. The change in the nature of exported goods resulted from the success of "Operation Bootstrap" with its emphasis on the promotion of manufacturing for export. In 1970, among $1,719 million worth of exported goods, about $1,289 million were new products manufactured in the factories promoted by the Economic Development Administration. From 1950 to 1968 the value of new products made in Puerto Rico had risen by $979 million. Clothing and textiles, which had long been important to Puerto Rico, increased $315 million. The export of gasoline, chemical products, and other derivatives of nonmetallic minerals, rose $225 million. Gasoline was refined from imported crude oils.

After 1940, imports as well as exports rose steadily in value and changed in composition. Imports of 1940 came to $107 million; in 1950, $350 million; and in 1970 to $2,513 million. The increase of imported durable goods, among which automobiles enjoyed the greatest rise, has been $245 million since 1950 (Appendix I). Imports of nondurable goods rose $419 million since 1950, of which more than $218 million were foodstuffs. Imports of raw materials and intermediate products increased from $144 million in 1950 to $1,200 million in 1970; the increase resulted largely from the new factories established after 1950. In the latter category the greatest increase was in crude oil, whose import value was about $98.6 million in 1969, a large part of which was subsequently exported in refined form, largely to the United States.

Comparison between the values of exports and imports show Puerto Rico's balance of trade to be "unfavorable" in that the imports exceed the exports in value. The unfavorable commercial balance is compensated for by the balance of payments, including investments from outside the island, expenditures by the Armed Forces of the United States as well as by various U.S. Government offices, payments to veterans, monies spent by tourists, allotments by the Federal Government for public works, and money sent by Puerto Ricans in the continental United States to their relatives on the island.

Transportation

MARITIME TRANSPORT

In today's economic system, transportation is indispensable to commerce. The importance of maritime transport is shown by the fact that about 99 per cent of Puerto Rico's external trade is carried by sea. As stated above, most of the island's external trade is with the United States because of the highly advantageous tariff union with that country. That situation, however, also has its disadvantages. The coastwise shipping laws dictate the use of American boats for cargos destined for ports regarded as domestic, like New York and San Juan. Although American-registered ships give regular and efficient service, their rates are higher than are those of other registries. The restrictions imposed by the coastwise shipping laws encourage monopolies and improper increases in rates. To protect consumers and industries, the Puerto Rican government is therefore constantly alert against unreasonable rate increases.

Despite such disadvantages, transportation by sea is cheaper than overland. For instance, it costs less to ship goods from any point in Puerto Rico to the eastern United States than to ship them from the Eastern U.S. to the Middlewest. Sending a pair of shoes from New York to Puerto Rico costs 4.3 cents; sending them from New York to Chicago, a shorter distance, costs 8.5 cents or almost twice as much. Some ten shipping companies operate between Puerto Rico and the mainland United States, providing more than 63 voyages monthly.

Of Puerto Rico's several ports, that of San Juan, which handles three quarters of the island's 5.7 million tons of maritime dry cargo, is by far the most important. About 82 per cent of the dry cargo arriving there comes in trailers or containers. Between 1950 and 1969 the movement of cargo in San Juan increased 129 per cent, and it is expected to grow another 45 per cent by 1975. In 1969, 3,075 ships put into San Juan harbor, several times more than five years earlier.

Next in importance after San Juan are the ports of Ponce and Mayagüez; they are being improved constantly to accommodate the cargoes which have recently increased about 5 per cent annually in both.

The San Juan harbor is being dredged at a cost of $10 million to accommodate heavy-tonnage ships. Works is also progressing on the new port zone of Puerto Nuevo, an area of 100 acres southeast of San Juan Bay. Puerto Nuevo should be able to handle virtually all the freight which now moves through San Juan. The new port zone contains thirteen berthing spaces for ships, refrigerated warehouses, and storage spaces for cargo. The new port also helps to reduce traffic congestion in San Juan, since most of the trucks now plying between the port and the capital's warehouses remain south of the bay. In the area of the Isla Grande airport, another port zone serves a number of lines handling trailer containers. The zone is being improved to offer space for much larger ships.

Ponce port has been greatly improved for the benefit of industry and general commerce. There are plans for building an industrial park near the port, to house new shops and factories with direct access to the piers.

Substantial improvements have been made in the Mayagüez port, the third in importance. In addition to a nearby industrial park, these include the establishment of the so-called "free trade zone," an international project of major importance to Puerto Rico, located near the port. The aim is to bring to it from abroad, duty free, raw materials and parts, to be processed and assembled in the zone for export, also duty free, to foreign countries. The arrangement should help to establish such industries as assembling automobiles and cutting and polishing gemstones. If the undertaking is successful some 25 or 30 factories, employing more than 3,000 workers, can be established in the zone. Today, it contains only seven factories.

The island's various ports are improved with government aid. The Ports Authority, a subsidiary of the Economic Development Administration, is in charge of new port facilities as well as of many now in existence. In 1966 the Authority handled, through its facilities in San Juan, 2.8 million tons of freight, of which only 102,124 were sugar in bulk.

AIR TRANSPORT

This type of transport is as basic for the movement of passengers as maritime transport is for freight. Virtually all the passengers coming to the island come by air. They use the modern international airport located in the San Juan Metropolitan Area. There are seven hundred commercial airports in the United States, of which 24 are rated as first class. An airport is considered first class if it handles more than one per cent of the total passenger movement. The fact that Puerto Rico's International Airport is ranked as number 16 means that it is among the highest in handling passengers. About a dozen airlines with fixed schedules, and others with no fixed schedules, operate there. In 1969 they made more than 80,200 flights. *Caribbean Atlantic Airways* (Caribair), a Puerto Rican company, is important for its 21,157 flights in 1969, principally between San Juan, Mayagüez, and the Virgin Islands. It was followed by *Pan American World Airways,* with 15,840, and *Eastern Airlines,* with 13,986. The total includes the arrival and departure of 32 daily flights by jet-propelled planes. Eastern proposed the acquisition of Caribair in 1971 and is now managing it.

In 1969 more than 4,217,000 passengers passed through the International Airport, as compared with 292,000 in 1950, coming from all parts of the world with which air traffic is maintained. The International Airport was opened in 1955 when it was thought that the movement of passengers would not exceed a million until 1970; that number had already been passed in 1958. It was therefore necessary to enlarge the airport and add a second runway in addition to new building facilities. Fortunately the original design permitted such expansion, since all the land was acquired before starting the project. The present runway is about 10,000 feet long, permitting landings and takeoffs by all classes of planes now in service. The second runway will have over 8,500 feet in length and will be used for landings only. The internal facilities have been doubled since inauguration of the airport. It is expected that the movement of passengers through the airport will exceed five million in 1975.

The island's other commercial airports, like those of Ponce, Mayagüez, and Arecibo, are small and used for internal service in which the move-

ment of passengers comes to about 350,000 and that of freight to some
8,300 tons. The runways vary between 2,300 and 3,900 feet in length,
which is sufficient for small, propeller-driven planes. An expansion is now
under way in the airports of Ponce and Mayagüez.

Air freight beyond Puerto Rico is efficient and rapid. The island's manufacturing industry is aided by the fact that the principal lines connect
almost daily with the great industrial zones of the United States, Canada,
France, Spain, and Germany. Air freight has increased considerably,
from 15,700 tons in 1955 to 60,866 in 1966, meaning that the tonnage increased fourfold in eleven years (Fig. 16.2). The service is rendered by
planes carrying only freight as well as by lines which also serve passengers.

LAND TRANSPORT

Internal transportation complements the external and aids Puerto
Rico's commerce and development. The growth of the island's economy
and the evolution of trucks demand constant improvements in overland
transportation. The increasing density of traffic creates problems of congestion which swell the number of accidents as well as the operating
costs of the industry. Puerto Rico's land transportation flows over a network of 6,500 kms. (3,300 miles) of roads, as of June 1970. There is a
small railroad for hauling sugar cane in various parts of the coastal plain,

Figure 16.2. Airplane Being Unloaded. (Courtesy of Pan American World
Airways.)

which helps to ease congestion on the roads, especially that of heavy trucks.

All Puerto Rican towns are interconnected by surfaced and asphalt roads, and a number of them are concreted. The old highways have been greatly improved and those being built today follow modern standards for speed and safety. The growth of traffic is indicated by the number of registered vehicles. In 1940 there were 26,800, and by 1970 the number had grown almost 25 times, to 656,000. About 78 per cent of the registered vehicles are private automobiles; the rest are trucks and trailers. That growth has congested the roads, especially in San Juan where some avenues are traveled by more than 45,000 vehicles daily (Fig. 16.3). In the Metropolitan Zone the Bus Authority operates a fleet of 367 units which transported 65 million passengers in fiscal year 1969. The tremendous growth of urban population has swelled public and private urbanizations outside the center of the city, which makes it difficult to provide satisfactory transportation services. Studies are under way to determine the types of rapid transit best suited to the metropolitan areas of San Juan, Ponce, and Mayagüez, tying up with the rest of the island. Meanwhile the work of building new highways and improving those now in use goes rapidly forward.

Finances

FUNCTIONS OF THE FINANCIAL SYSTEM

Finance is the art of administering funds. It comprises the processes by which institutions as well as individuals acquire, manage, and distribute monetary resources. The operations of the financial system are governed by a basic function: channeling the movement of funds according to the needs of the economy. In other words, the financial system is the mechanism by which the savings of individuals become invested in productive enterprises.

Puerto Rico's financial system is relatively simple. Its basic structure comprises the commercial banks, finance companies, savings and loan associations, personal loan companies, the fiscal agencies of the Puerto Rican and Federal governments, insurance companies, and other sources of credit such as credit cooperatives, pension funds, employees' associations, a mutual savings and a worker's bank. The functions of the system proper are complemented by those of other financial institutions such as security brokers, commission houses, discount houses, real estate and mortgage brokers. However, the island's system lacks certain special financial institutions, or at least their activities are extremely limited, such as stock exchanges, well-regulated pawnshops, dealers in real estate stocks and foreign currencies, or trust companies. Many of the basic func-

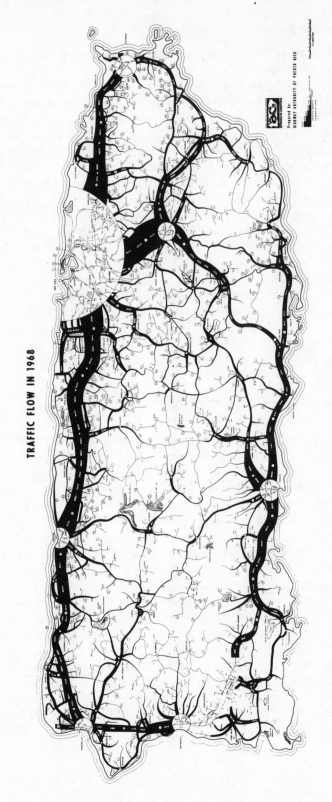

TRAFFIC FLOW IN 1968

Figure 16.3. Density of Traffic in Puerto Rico's Main Roads. Traffic flow in the San Juan Metropolitan Zone is indicated by figures.

326

tions of such institutions are performed by the commercial banks and other organizations which comprise the financial system.

The system as a whole has advanced extraordinarily during the past decades, both functionally as well as in the quantity of financial resources whose growth has paralleled the island's notable economic development. In general, the financial system has ably met the demands of Puerto Rico's economic development. The following discussions indicate progress achieved in the field of finance. Since the commercial bank is the core of the financial system, its history and an account of its current activities will precede discussions of the island's other financial institutions.

History of Commercial Banking in Puerto Rico

UNDER SPANISH RULE

The origin of Puerto Rico's commercial banks can be traced to the beginnings of the nineteenth century when in 1812, the colony's top financial officer, Intendente Alejandro Ramírez, proposed that a bank be established on the island. However, the first bank, the London Colonial Bank, was not established until 1850.[1] It was not accepted by the money lenders of the time who raised fierce competition which resulted in the disappearance of the bank three years after its founding. Savings banks were subsequently established, in San Juan in 1865 and in Mayagüez in 1874. Like the Colonial Bank, they failed to hold out long against competition from money lenders.

In 1881 the *Caja de Economías y Préstamos* (Loans) was established in San Germán; it managed to survive and remains today as Puerto Rico's oldest bank. The *Sociedad Americana de Crédito Mercantil* was founded in 1887 and liquidated the following year. In its place arose the *Banco Español de Puerto Rico* among whose functions was one of the most important of a central bank, that of issuing money.[2] After the change of sovereignty, in 1900, the *Banco Español* became the *Banco de Puerto Rico* and lost the power to issue money. It was reorganized in 1913 and changed into the *Banco Comercial de Puerto Rico*. It survived until the early 1930's when the world depression weakened its financial strength and it was acquired by the *Banco Popular de Puerto Rico*. Another bank established under Spanish rule which disappeared as a result of the economic chaos of 1929–33 was the *Territorial y Agrícola*, which operated from 1894 until the early 1930's.

During the last years of Spanish rule, two other commercial banks were created which are today solid pillars of the island's banking system,

1. Biagio Di Venuti, *Money and Banking in Puerto Rico* (Río Piedras: University of Puerto Rico, 1950), pp. 13–14.
2. Victor S. Clark, *Porto Rico and its Problems* (Washington, D.C.: The Brookings Institution, May 1930), pp. 374–75.

the *Banco Popular de Puerto Rico*, founded in 1893, and the *Banco Crédito y Ahorro Ponceño*, founded in 1895. The former is the largest domestic commercial bank, followed by the latter in resources and volume of transactions. In short, when Spanish rule ended, only four principal banks existed in Puerto Rico: the *Banco Español*, the *Territorial y Agrícola*, the *Popular*, and the *Crédito y Ahorro Ponceño*, of which only the last two survived. In those days, the combined resources of the four banks amounted barely to $6.3 million.

UNDER U.S. RULE

The island's banking system grew substantially during the twentieth century. The first bank established under the new regime, in 1899, was the *American Colonial Bank*. It was later acquired by the National City Bank,[3] established in 1918 and known today as the *First National City Bank*. Another important United States bank, the *Chase Manhattan* was established in Puerto Rico in 1933. Those two are today the only banks of the continental United States which have offices in Puerto Rico. Two Canadian banks were established during the first decade of the twentieth century as parts of the island's system: the *Royal Bank of Canada* and the *Bank of Nova Scotia*.

The domestic bank has also made notable progress during the present century. *Banco de Ponce* was founded in 1917 in Ponce; today it ranks among the highest in the matter of financial stability. The expansion of the domestic bank during the first half of the century is indicated by the founding of a number of native banking institutions. By 1948, their number had reached thirteen, ten of which had limited resources. Since then the expansion of the industry has been accompanied by a trend toward concentration, as a result of which some of the small banks were absorbed by the larger. Today only three of these remain: one in San Germán (*Banco de Economías y Préstamos*), one in Humacao (*Roig Commercial Bank*), and the third in San Juan (*Banco de San Juan*). All of them now have branches in San Juan and in other cities and towns.

COMPOSITION OF TODAY'S BANKING SYSTEM

Puerto Rico's banking system consists of thirteen commercial and two government banks. There is no central bank such as is generally known in other countries. The Government Development Bank for Puerto Rico carries out certain functions of a central bank, serving as a clearing house for the system and as a depository, though not the only one, for government funds. It makes loans to commercial banks, administers the current account of the Secretary of the Treasury, and acts as paying agent for government institutions. However, it lacks the power to issue money, is

3. Victor S. Clark, op. cit., p. 376.

not the depository for the legal reserves of the commercial banks, and cannot control the banking system's credit by establishing monetary policies.

Nine of the thirteen commercial banks are domestic, two are New York banks, and two are Canadian. The native banks, in the order of their importance, according to their resources and total deposits in 1969, are the following: Banco Popular de Puerto Rico; Banco Crédito y Ahorro Ponceño; Banco de Ponce; Banco de San Juan; Banco de Economías y Préstamos; Banco Obrero; Roig Commercial Bank; Banco Mercantil, and Banco Comercial de Mayagüez. The Banco Comercial de Mayagüez is the latest to be founded in Puerto Rico. The New York banks are: the First National City Bank and the Chase Manhattan Bank. The Canadian establishments are: the Royal Bank of Canada, and the Bank of Nova Scotia. Altogether, the thirteen commercial banks have a total of 185 banking units, 180 fixed and 5 mobile, amounting to one banking office for every 18 square miles (Fig. 16.4).

The two government banks, the Government Development Bank for Puerto Rico and the Housing Bank, complement the services of the commercial banks. The Cooperatives Bank, created by Act No. 209, May 3, 1951, was abolished by Act No. 90, June 21, 1966. Its resources and obligations became a part of the Cooperative Development Company which is empowered to establish a bank for cooperatives with powers similar to those of commercial banks.

Figure 16.4. Headquarters of Banco Popular in Hato Rey, San Juan's New Financial Center.

The *Banco Obrero de Ahorro y Préstamos* (Worker's Savings and Loan Bank) began operations in June 1960. To help defray the costs of organization, the Puerto Rican Treasury lent it $50,000, to be repaid within ten years after the bank was created by Act 86, June 14, 1960. The purpose of the institution is to promote the welfare of Puerto Rico's workers through the encouragement of regular, systematic savings, to provide credit for the workers, and to facilitate the creation, expansion, and improvement of sources of employment. While it is regarded as a commercial bank, there can be no doubt that it is a public enterprise, operated for the benefit of Puerto Rico's workers. By June 30, 1969, its assets totalled $28.4 million, its loans and net discounts were $15.3 million, and its deposits $21.7 million.

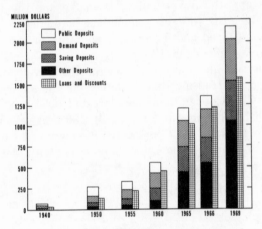

Figure 16.5. Deposits and Loans in Commercial Banks, 1940–1969.

The extraordinary growth of Puerto Rico's commercial banking is indicated by the following statistics. Between 1925 and 1969 the total deposits in commercial banks increased from $41.1 million to $2,185 million. The value of loans and net discounts was $1,572 million on June 30, 1969, compared to $36.6 million in 1925. Their capital grew from less than $6.5 million to $118 million during the same period (Fig. 16.5).

That great growth was accompanied by a significant transformation in the structure of the banking system. During the 1930's the system was dominated by the New York and Canadian banks; today these are superseded in importance by the native institutions. Table 16.1 shows that on June 30, 1969, 62.8 per cent of the total deposits and 62.6 per cent of the loans and discounts were in the hand's of native banks. The New York banks with offices in Puerto Rico held 31.2 per cent of the deposits and 29.4 per cent of the loans and discounts while the figures for the Canadian banks were 6 per cent and 8.0 per cent respectively.

Table 16.1. Deposits and loans by groups of banks in Puerto Rico, June 30, 1969
(figures in thousands of dollars)

Type	Deposits Total	Deposits Private	Deposits Government	Loans and Discounts (Net)
Local	1,468,431	1,168,348	129,273	947,371
N.Y. Branches	745,358	718,502	26,856	490,863
Canadian Branches	141,679	140,087	1,592	133,431
Government Development	29,370	730	28,640	88,672
Housing	2,302	332	1,970	9,952

The domestic banks stand above those from outside Puerto Rico, not only in the matter of deposits but also in loans, the most important aspect of the banking business. The expansion of domestic commercial banking is not confined to Puerto Rico; three of the island's institutions—Banco Popular de Puerto Rico, Banco de Ponce, and Banco Crédito y Ahorro Ponceño—have established branches in New York which receive deposits and render services on a similar basis with those incorporated in New York.

The progress and expansion of the domestic banks is also notable in other aspects of management. For instance, check clearings at par between the local system and banks operating in the continental United States began in 1958 with the inclusion of Puerto Rico in the Second District of the Federal Reserve System, which also brought about the insurance of deposits and the clearance of checks. Since 1952 the Government Development Bank has acted as an exchange for the banking system; today the deposits in the commercial banks are insured up to $20,000 by the Federal Deposit Insurance Corporation (FDIC), so increasing their reliability. Moreover, as mentioned above, most of the island's towns have banking services, either as permanent offices or mobile units which visit them regularly. The ideal, soon to be attained, is for every town to have its own permanent banking offices which are needed for the economic and social progress of every community.

Despite the above, certain phases of bank management could and should still be improved. Commercial banks, for instance, should extend more credit for long-term investments; to give greater protection to the depositing public and strengthen the financial solidity of the system, they should increase their somewhat limited capital. It would also be well to strengthen still more the relations with the Federal Reserve System which is legally the central bank for Puerto Rico's banking system, as well as with the Government Development Bank for Puerto Rico.

The island's commercial banks have been considerably complemented by the government's financial institutions. Today there are two public banks, namely, the Government Development Bank and the Housing Bank, in addition to such other sources of credit as the Industrial Development Company and the Agricultural Credit Corporation. Since these are specialized institutions, their credit operations are devoted to financing specific sectors of the economy. Of the above-mentioned four institutions, the ones which have given the most credit are the Government Development Bank and the Industrial Development Company. The basic functions of those institutions within the Puerto Rican financial system are outlined below.

Government Banking

The Government Development Bank originally created in 1942 received a new charter in 1948 (Act No. 17). It has two principal functions: (*a*) to grant long- and medium-term loans to private enterprises and (*b*) to act as fiscal agent for the Puerto Rican government. It was created to aid the government in the discharge of its fiscal duties and in meeting its "responsibility to develop Puerto Rico's economy, and especially its industrialization."[4] Its credit activities are designed to complement those of commercial banks and other institutions, working in close collaboration with them, but not in competition.

The categories listed below are typical of the types of loans in which the bank deals: (*a*) construction, expansion, and improvement of industrial and commercial structures; (*b*) acquisition of commercial and industrial structures, as well as machinery and equipment; (*c*) hotels and other essential tourist facilities; (*d*) operating capital in exceptional cases when the loan cannot be financed through private sources. Since the middle of the 1950–60 decade, loans were increased in participation with the commercial banks and other credit institutions, including the Small Business Administration and the Industrial Development Company.

At the end of 1969, the bank's total assets were $305.9 million and it had 1,650 loans outstanding (excluding those to students, veteran, and FHA mortgages) to private enterprises, with a total value of $102.6 million; at the same time it held 234 loans which were about to be disbursed, valued at $31.2 million, and was studying 65 applications for loans, with a value of $5.2 million. The total private loans made by the bank between its founding and June 30, 1969, exceeded $212 million.

The other basic function of the Government Development Bank is to serve as fiscal agent, or official borrowing agent, for the Commonwealth of Puerto Rico, the municipalities, and public corporations. In that capacity the Bank advises, plans, coordinates and executes all pertinent technical services. The Bank seeks to meet the financial needs of public entities in Puerto Rico on an orderly basis, using forms of borrowing that best suit the conditions of the U.S. capital market and the character of

4. Act No. 17, September 23, 1948, Section 1.

the borrower. To maintain close day-to-day contact with the mainland financial community, the Bank has an office on Wall Street, New York. Use of a single authorized fiscal agent offers certain valuable advantages. The services of the Government Development Bank offer flexibility in operations, eliminating duplication of organization and effort that would follow if each borrower acted independently. This system avoids disorderly competition for limited funds, and it provides an institutional means of accumulating experience for the benefit of all public borrowers.

Between its designation as a fiscal agent (May 15, 1945) and June 30, 1969, the bank negotiated more than $3,220 million worth of financing for the Commonwealth, municipalities, and public corporations. Of that sum $1,495 million were long-term bonds for permanent improvements.

The Housing Bank was created by Act No. 146, June 30, 1961, to provide credit for the acquisition of homes by people with small resources. Starting with $4 million assigned to it from government funds, the institution now has assets of more than $17.3 million. The need for the bank has been confirmed by its operation. By June 30, 1969, it had made 3,377 loans, totaling $15.1 million. The long-term (up to 40 years) mortgages average $5,200. In July 1966, the Housing Bank began to insure mortgages, so helping to make private savings available for the construction of low-cost housing. In order to expand its liquid resources, the Bank sells its mortgages to government pension funds and others.

As may be seen, the government's financial institutions are working to fill certain inevitable gaps in the credit policies of commercial banks.

Other Financial Institutions

There are other sources of specialized credit, whose activities have increased greatly, that form integral parts of Puerto Rico's financial system and are important to the development of the island's economy. The following are among them.

THE PUERTO RICO INDUSTRIAL DEVELOPMENT COMPANY (PRIDCO)

This is a specialized government agency whose principal function is the construction of industrial buildings to be leased or sold on favorable terms to new industrial enterprises which come to Puerto Rico. Its financial activities also include loans, investments, and the granting of special incentives to such concerns. The annual volume of its financial operations has been about $30 million, a notable aid to the island's economic growth.

THE FEDERAL FINANCING AGENCIES

The activities of these agencies consist largely of providing or guaranteeing long- or medium-term financing for agriculture, housing, public works, and, to a lesser extent, to the commercial and industrial sectors of the economy. The credit extended to agriculture, largely long-term, has varied between 50 and 70 million dollars during the past years. Most of the loans made to agriculture came through the Production Credit Association, the Baltimore Bank for Cooperatives, and the Federal Intermediate Credit Bank.

For financing homes and public works, the federal agencies, among which the Federal Housing Administration (FHA) is outstanding, have insured loans of $540.5 million during the past five-year period. Within the field of financing for commercial and industrial development, the Small Business Administration (SBA) has made over 38 million dollars' worth of loans during the recent four-year period. Altogether, these institutions have contributed direct resources of some $114.6 million annually to the agricultural, housing, and commercial sectors of the island's economy.

SAVINGS AND LOAN ASSOCIATIONS

This form of nonprofit, mutual association, whose principal aim is to stimulate savings and provide homes for the community, has grown spectacularly in Puerto Rico. The First Federal Savings and Loan Association of Puerto Rico, founded in 1948, was the first, organized with an initial capital of $250,000. On December 31, 1969, it held savings accounts totalling $147.6 million and loans outstanding of $159.7 million. Other such associations exist in San Juan, Caguas, Ponce, Mayagüez, Arecibo, Bayamón, and Humacao. This type of organization is one of the most important sources of housing credit. It devotes the greatest part of its funds to financing individual homes and other residential buildings as well as condominiums and a minimum part to commercial structures. As of December 31, 1970, the nine Puerto Rican associations held savings accounts totalling $316 million and mortgages outstanding for $341 million.

INSURANCE COMPANIES

Insurance, constituting another very important source of credit and savings, has grown considerably in recent years. Table 16.2 shows that the number of insurance companies in Puerto Rico grew from 73 to 247 between 1951 and 1968. There has also been a considerable growth in the types of insurance offered: life, accident, illness, automobile, property, marine disaster, fidelity, and title guarantee and insurance. The value of collected premiums rose 886 per cent between the calendar years 1951–68. During the same period the value of life insurance in effect increased 1,560 per cent, from $143 million to $2,244.5 million. The investments of these companies in Puerto Rico rose from $17.4 million to $333.5 million. The majority of those investments are in public and private securities, approximately 45 per cent in conventional mortgages and 42 per

Table 16.2. Insurance companies

Calendar Years	Number of Companies	Premium Collected (Millions of $)	Life Insurance in Force (Millions of $)	Investments in P.R. (Millions of $)
1951	73	16.7	143.0	17.4
1954	96	21.7	235.0	32.4
1960	154	45.0	696.5	89.4
1965	215	103.1	1540.5	231.5
1966	227	119.6	1880.8	205.0
1968	247	148.1	2244.5	333.5

Source: Annual Reports, Office of the Insurance Commissioner, 1951–52, 1954–55, 1960–61, 1962–66, 1968–69.

Note: The figures giving the numbers of companies are for the fiscal years; the others are for calendar years.

cent in all types of bonds. The growth of the insurance companies represents a large expansion of the island's sources of long-term credit.

CREDIT COOPERATIVES

Spurred by the programs of the Cooperative Development Administration, the number of credit cooperatives in Puerto Rico has risen from 172 to 431 between fiscal years 1958 and 1968 (Table 16.3). The table shows that the number of members roughly increased from 59,000 to 136,000 while the value of loans increased four times during the same period, from $16.4 million to $89.1 million, and the value of their assets was multiplied more than six times. The figures throw into bold relief the expansion achieved in that part of the island's financial system. Such progress is extremely important for the economy, since the cooperatives lend money almost exclusively to members of the middle class. It is precisely among people with limited means that the problem of usury arises in Puerto Rico. In a study of the problem it was found that in 1957 some

Table 16.3. Credit cooperatives

Fiscal Years	No. of Cooperatives	No. of Members	Total Loans (Millions $)	Total Assets (Millions $)
1957–58	172	58,839	16.4	12.1
1959–60	199	68,801	22.9	18.3
1961–62	255	85,500	30.2	25.9
1962–63	277	94,206	34.2	30.7
1963–64	316	97,282	44.0	37.7
1964–65	329	101,104	50.4	44.7
1965–66	351	110,000	60.6	54.7
1966–67	364	115,500	69.7	63.4
1967–68	431	135,867	89.1	74.6

Source: Plans and Budget Office, Cooperative Development Administration.

20 per cent of the workers turned to usurers for financial help. The average interest charged by the latter was estimated as 240 per cent annually.[5] This practice is insulting and humiliating. With the growth of credit cooperatives and the Worker's Bank, the usurers' chance to exploit the small borrower had been greatly reduced.

Another organization of the cooperative type, though controlled by a special law, is the Association of Government Employees which, during fiscal year 1969, made loans to its members totaling over $63 million. The pension funds for public employees are also highly important financial organizations. Those institutions, which deal with five retirement systems, those of government employees, judges, teachers, employees of the University of Puerto Rico, and employees of the Water Resources Authority, had by June 30, 1966, made investments totaling over $200 million. Almost 60 per cent of that amount, was in permanent investments, of which about ¾ was in mortgage loans, largely to members.

SMALL LOAN COMPANIES

Since the small loan companies were authorized by Act 106 of 1965 this type of credit institution has grown rapidly. In 1970 there were 51 companies with 162 offices operating in two-thirds of the municipalities. As of December 31, 1969, their active loans, limited to less than $600 each, totaled 226,700 with outstanding principal of over $93 million.

FINANCE COMPANIES

These organizations complement the services of the commercial banks and help to solve the financial problems of commerce and industry. In general, they provide credit for commerce, especially when the commercial banks do not do so, or provide it in limited measure. Some finance companies limit their financial activities to conditional sales, accounts receivables, inventories, equipment, and machinery. Such services provide flexibility and facilitate the development of the commercial activities of the economy. Sales on credit are important in Puerto Rico where about 80 per cent of the commercial deals are on installment buying. In fact, they have in large measure eased the problem of consumer credit. Today, many of those institutions provide financial facilities for consumers; in volumes of business, the General Motors Acceptance Corporation, the Universal C.I.T., and Talcott are outstanding among them.

According to the Economic Stabilization Administration, forty-two companies today finance purchases of automobiles, insurance, utensils, and equipment, as well as agricultural and industrial machinery. Nine of

5. Rafael Rodríguez Cantero, *Préstamos personales a familias de recursos moderados* [Personal loans to families with moderate income.] (San Juan: Division of Printing, Department of the Treasury, 1957).

these devote themselves to financing insurance; the rest engage in diverse kinds of financing.

SECURITIES BROKERS

In the field of securities, the well-known brokerage firm of Merrill, Lynch, Pierce, Fenner, & Smith has a branch in San Juan, established in 1952, whose volume of business has expanded considerably. In recent years it began to function as an investment bank when it redistributed the stock issues of the Puerto Rico Brewing Company and the Puerto Rico Cement Corporation. Other securities brokers are Eastman Dillon, Union Securities, Inc., Thompson and McKinnon, and Richard J. Buck & Co., which deal in stocks registered in the United States as well as those issued in Puerto Rico.

In the business of financing real estate and mortgages, the following are prominent: James T. Barnes & Co., the Housing Investment Corporation, and Berens Mortgage Bankers, Inc. In general, the principal activity of these institutions with island-wide coverage is financing the construction of urban developments and homes on a large scale, for the middle and upper classes.

INVESTMENT COMPANIES

There are also several investment companies on the island. The first to be established, in 1956, was the Compañía Financiera de Inversiones, Inc. (the Financial Investment Company, Inc.). Today, the Puerto Rico Capital Corporation, the International Investment Co. of Puerto Rico, and the First Investment Company of Puerto Rico are outstanding for their volume of business. The last-named is a holding company whose subsidiaries are the Talcott Inter-American Corporation and the Compañía Financiera de Inversiones, Inc. The former devotes itself largely to financing accounts due and grants loans guaranteed by inventories and machinery. Recently it has undertaken the financing of mortgages on real estate. The second, the Compañía Financiera de Inversiones, Inc., has operated as an investment bank, and at present deals in stocks of established Puerto Rican concerns. These institutions adequately complement the functions of the financial system, to meet the needs of Puerto Rico's economic and social development.

17

Projections of Economic and Social Development

A society's economic and social development depends basically on the quantity and quality of its productive factors and on the will and ability of its people to use them advantageously.

In Puerto Rico, two factors of production, land and capital, stand out for their scarcity and limitations, vis-á-vis labor.[1] Obviously, the island's economic progress will depend principally on the accumulation of capital and the training of labor.

Hitherto, the high rate of capital-formation in Puerto Rico resulted largely from the importation of capital, especially from the United States. Between 1947 and 1969, the fixed investment in Puerto Rico was about $9,682 million, of which $4,600 million, or about 49 per cent, came from beyond the island. As a result of the growth of local incomes, foreseen for the next few years, it is expected that the ratio of local investments to the total will increase substantially in the near future.

The magnitude and importance of economic projections are best understood on the basis of Puerto Rico's situation in those respects before 1940, followed by the evolution of its economy between 1940 and the present. After dealing briefly with those matters, the present discussion will proceed to the economic and social future as they have been projected as far as 1975.

The Economy Prior to 1940

Puerto Rico's agricultural potentials began to be developed during the eighteenth and nineteenth centuries with the cultivation for export of tobacco, coffee, and sugar cane. Agricultural development was slow until the island came under United States' rule in 1898. Stimulated by North

---

1. See Chapter 11, the section "Basic Factors of Production".

American capital, the sugar industry then grew rapidly, bringing about increases in domestic production and incomes. Nevertheless, it soon became obvious that economic and social well-being could not depend exclusively on agriculture. The century's first 40 years were marked by seasonal unemployment, low wages, large landed estates, and absentee ownership. The evil effects of those conditions were intensified as the population almost doubled in number in the course of 40 years. Unemployment reached extraordinary levels and working conditions were depressing even for those who did find work.

Puerto Rico's economy went through a critical period during the 1930's. The world depression had disastrous effects on the agricultural economy, based on the cultivation of sugar cane. The value of sugar production was reduced by the general lowering of prices. The flow of private North American capital to Puerto Rico fell off drastically, causing stagnation and deterioration in the sugar industry. The decline of the people's economic well-being was indicated by the fact that the per capita average annual income, which had been $122 in 1929–30, fell to $86 three years later. While the population continued its rapid growth, paralysis could be seen in all branches of the economy. But, with substantial financial help from the "New Deal" Administration, the economy entered a stage of slow recovery during the second half of the 1930–40 decade, and by 1940 the per capita average annual income reached $121.

From 1940 to 1970

The decade of 1940–50 was a period of decisive transformation in Puerto Rico's economic life. A new governor, Dr. Rexford G. Tugwell, the last nonPuerto Rican to be appointed to the governorship, came to power in 1940 and gave special attention and effort to the improvement of the island's economic and social conditions.

Despite World War II, the foundations for economic development were laid during the early years of the decade. Industrialization was regarded as the best course for providing work for the many unemployed; as the first step toward organizing and stimulating a program of industrialization, the government created three principal agencies: the Planning Board, the Industrial Development Company, and the Development Bank.[2]

The government also created, or reorganized, various public corporations to render basic services. Among them are the Water Resources Authority, the Aqueduct and Sewer Authority, the Transportation (today the Ports) Authority, and others. Those public entities and development companies were paid for through a surplus accumulated during the war,

2. See Chapters 14 and 16.

principally through the return to the Puerto Rican treasury of taxes on the sale of Puerto Rican rums on the continent.

During the first years after 1940, the government acquired and operated factories for making cement, glass, cardboard cartons, ceramics, and leather articles which, as stated in previous chapters, were soon sold to private enterprise.

A program for granting incentives for the promotion and stimulation of industrial development was launched in 1949. Among those which were adopted and are still in force are the following: tax exemption, the construction of factories for sale or rental to private companies, training skilled labor, technical assistance, and concessions of loans under favorable conditions. The program of tax exemption, going hand in hand with other incentives, has without a doubt been the foundation of the growth of Puerto Rico's private industry in recent years.

POLITICAL ASPECTS

In 1952, the island's political relations with the United States were newly and more clearly defined through a pact agreed to by the Congress of the United States and the people of Puerto Rico. The official status was thereby changed from that of an "unincorporated territory" into one which is officially called in English "Commonwealth" and in Spanish "Estado Libre Asociado" ("Free Associated State"), meaning a state which is free to govern itself in its internal matters while remaining voluntarily associated with the United States.

Recognizing that the present status can still be improved and that it does not rule out the eventual granting of either sovereign independence or federated statehood to Puerto Rico, the Commonwealth of Puerto Rico, asked the Congress of the United States on December 3, 1962, to define the various kinds of government to which it would agree, toward the end of establishing a clear record on Puerto Rico's final political status. The Congress then invited the Commonwealth's Legislature to participate in the creation of a commission to study "all the factors . . . which enter into the present and future relations between the United States and Puerto Rico." After completing its study in a democratic manner and hearing all interested witnesses, the commission with James Rowe presiding submitted its report which recommended, among other things, that: "It would be extremely useful for all interested parties if arrangements could be made for the expression of the will of Puerto Rican citizens through a plebiscite on the question of whether they wish to continue Commonwealth status with capacities for growth and development, or if they wish to choose statehood or independence."

On July 23, 1967, the Puerto Rican people were consulted on the three alternatives through a democratic plebiscite. Through an affirmative vote, amounting to more than 60 per cent of the total vote cast, the people confirmed their desire to continue their permanent relationship with the United States by means of Commonwealth status.

In addition to the incentives mentioned above, the present relationship itself helps the island's economy by offering the investor a series of advantages among which the following are the most important: free movement of people, merchandise (manufactured goods), and capital, between Puerto Rico and the continental United States and stability of currency and its freedom from exchange fluctuations since the dollar is Puerto Rico's currency. In addition, the North American investor rests assured that his legitimate rights of ownership will not be threatened on the island.

Puerto Rico's progress has been notable under that reaffirmed economic and political structure. Its economy has maintained a rate of growth which compares favorably with that of the world's most dynamic economies; its progress has awakened interest abroad. Today the island is visited by officials, students of government, industrialists, and managers, from all parts of the world, including Africa, Europe, the Far East, and Latin America, to observe the practices and policies which have contributed to the island's extraordinary economic transformation.

Progress is easily seen in Figures 17.1 and 17.2 and Appendixes F, O and P, which deal with four of the most important economic indicators, namely: gross product, fixed internal investments, per capita income, and external trade. The upward trend shown by the lines in the chart agrees perfectly with historic facts. During the 31 years between 1940 and 1971, the gross product increased 1,771 per cent, from $287 to $5,083 million. According to that indicator, the growth in the past decade has been about 10 per cent annually, one of the world's highest. In the course of the same period the net per capita income grew 1,285 per cent, from $121 to $1,556.

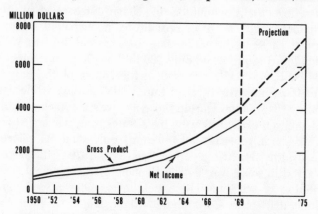

Figure 17.1. Gross Product and Net Income, 1950–1975.
(Source: Bureau of Economic and Social Analysis, Puerto
Rico Planning Board.)

Today's per capita income is more than five times as large as that of 1950, which was $279. In the case of Puerto Rico, where distribution is fairly equitable, per capita income is probably the best indication of the people's economic well-being. During the past nine years, that economic indicator grew at a rate of 9.4 per cent per year, and reached 9 per cent in 1970, as compared with the 2.5 per cent once fixed by the Alliance for Progress as a goal for the Latin American nations.

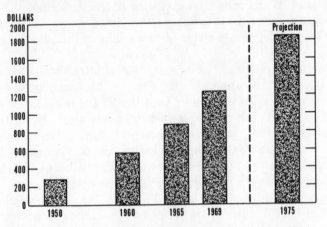

Figure 17.2. Net Income Per Capita 1950–1975. (Source: Bureau of Economic and Social Analysis, Puerto Rico Planning Board.)

Puerto Rico's economy, especially during the past decade, had transformed itself from one preponderantly agricultural into an economy which is more industrial and diversified. The economic sectors which pay good wages, principally manufacturing, have outstripped in importance those with low wages, such as agriculture, home needlework, and domestic service. In 1950, the net income from agriculture was $149 million while manufacturing produced only $89 million. The importance of those sectors has been drastically reversed in the course of the past two decades. In 1970, manufacturing contributed $953 million while agriculture brought only $184 million. During those 20 years, net income from manufacturing increased extraordinarily, by 970 per cent, while that from agriculture grew (largely because of inflation) only some 23 per cent (Fig. 17.3 and Appendix B). At the end of fiscal year 1970, 1,733 factories promoted or aided in some way by the Economic Development Administration operated in Puerto Rico. These include branches of well-known firms such as General Electric, Consolidated Cigar, Union Carbide, Parke and Davis, American Can, Phelps Dodge, W. R. Grace, Sperry Rand, and Phillips Petroleum. Those factories gave direct employment to about 102,400 workers and indirect employment to many others.

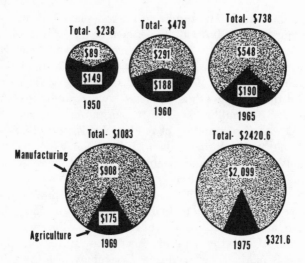

Figure 17.3. Net Income from Manufacturing and Agriculture, 1950–1975. (Source: Bureau of Economic and Social Analysis, Puerto Rico Planning Board.)

The high rate of investment in capital goods constitutes the fundamental basis for the structural transformation and growth of the island's economy (Fig. 17.4 and Appendix O). Those capital goods include industrial buildings, equipment, machinery, and highways. The 1970 total of capital goods reached $1,404 million, or more than 30 per cent of the gross product, compared with only $111 million in 1950 and $29 million in 1940.

As stated above, the formation of capital in Puerto Rico between 1947 and 1969 exceeded $11,000 million, of which about 49 per cent, came

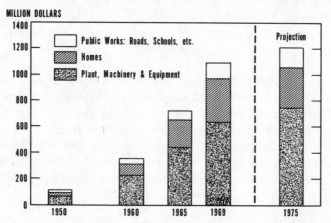

Figure 17.4. Gross Internal Investment of Fixed Capital, 1950–1975. (Source: Bureau of Economic and Social Analysis, Puerto Rico Planning Board.)

from outside the island. The public sector has played an important role in the formation of capital. About 38 per cent of the total fixed investment was public, as seen in better public services—highways, electric energy, aqueduct and sewer systems, and education—which form integral parts of the program of economic development. More than $323 million, almost 30 per cent of the fixed investments in 1969, were public investments. Of these, more than $46 million went for urban public housing; about $107 million went for the construction of roads, schools, and other capital improvement projects; while more than $170 million were invested in the physical plants, equipment, and machinery for the Commonwealth's public corporations and municipalities.

A large part of the public investment is financed through bond issues by the Commonwealth, the municipal governments, and the public corporations; these are generally sold in New York, the world's greatest financial center. Until the end of fiscal year 1970, the Government Development Bank had financed the Commonwealth government, its municipalities, and public corporations, to a total of $4.2 billion, of which $1.8 billion, or 43 per cent, were for capital improvement projects. Nevertheless, in 1969 the public debt of the Commonwealth and the municipalities was only $505 million. The payment of principal or interest has never defaulted or been delinquent. To investors another important characteristic of Puerto Rico's bond issues is that the income derived from them is exempt from federal, state, and local taxes.

The external trade is a dramatic reflection of industrialization. In 1970 exports reached the record figure of $1,719 million, or close to 40 per cent of the gross product. New products exported to the United States, largely made in factories promoted or aided by the Economic Development Administration, comprised 75 per cent of the exports. However, economic expansion is also indicated by imports which exceeded $2,513 million in 1970 as against $350 million in 1950. It should be noted, however, that in 1970 about 17 per cent of the total imports, or $465 million, were capital goods.

Most of Puerto Rico's exports go to the United States while its per capita purchases there exceed those of all other countries. Only four countries—Canada, Japan, Germany, and the United Kingdom—buy more in total from the United States than does Puerto Rico. In the western hemisphere only Canada surpasses Puerto Rico in that matter. While Puerto Rico's production is oriented largely toward the United States market, the island's domestic market for many products has expanded greatly, as a result of higher incomes and industrial integration.

SOCIAL PROGRESS

Jointly with its economic progress during the past quarter century, Puerto Rico has also experienced a great improvement in social matters.

Average life expectancy has risen from 46 years to 70, the same average as that in the United States. The birth rate dropped from an average of 39 per thousand to 24.8 in 1969. The death rate decreased from 18.2 to fewer than 6.1 per thousand, even lower than that of the United States as a whole. Great advances have been made in education; pupils in elementary schools today exceed 814,000. Students in universities and colleges of university level now number more than 65,000, as compared with barely 5,000 in 1940. It is estimated that the University of Puerto Rico will easily reach an enrollment of over 50,000 students within the next few years, or some 8,000 above the present numbers. Such figures speak for more and better employment opportunities, better housing, better sanitary and health facilities, and higher educational standards; in short, for a higher standard of living and greater welfare for Puerto Ricans in general.

Though the above is a source of pride and satisfaction, the forces which have made it possible must be kept viable. The per capita average annual income is expected to exceed $1,800 in 1975, and the per family income of 1970 should equal or exceed the 1950 average of several states of the continental United States.

As Puerto Rico continues to establish a sounder economy of greater abundance, the island is also expected to give greater attention to another goal which former Governor Luis Muñoz Marín called "Operation Serenity" and which he defined as follows:

Operation Serenity . . . aims to give some kind of effective command to the human spirit over the economic process. It attempts to make the human spirit an effective ruler, albeit a constitutional one limited by the strong parliament of economic forces. It aims at making high objectives for man's earthly life real, familiar and simple in the daily life of the community. Serenity may perhaps be defined as the habit of seeing your world whole, as the living society of men and forces and facts in which you as an individual conduct your life. To see it whole you must see it simply. And to see it with intelligent simplicity you must see it deeply. A society in which Operation Serenity had been successful would use its economic power increasingly for the extension of freedom, of knowledge, and of the understanding imagination rather than for a rapid multiplication of goods, in hot pursuit of a still more vertiginous multiplication of wants.[3]

"Operation Serenity" manifests itself in the restoration of historic areas like Old San Juan, in literary contests, in exhibitions of paintings and sculpture, in theatre and ballet performances, in the development of a San Juan Symphony Orchestra, and in such cultural activities as the

3. The Hon. Luis Muñoz Marín, Governor of the Commonwealth of Puerto Rico, Commencement Speech at Harvard University, mimeographed (June 16, 1955), p. 2.

Casals Music Festivals which every year attract innumerable lovers of good music.

Economic Projections

The preceding sections deal with the evolution of Puerto Rico's economy between 1940 and 1970, tracing the historic growth of the economic system, showing whence the island came and where it is today. The rest of the chapter will deal with the projection toward achievements expected by 1975, based on analysis of the growth potentials of the economy's main sectors. More than depicting an ideal goal for development, those projections arrive at possibilities in view of what has been accomplished to date, the economy's potentials for expansion, and the experiences accumulated in each program of planned development. A solid foundation on such factors lends to the projections a degree of realism which is indispensable for improved planning and coordination.

Prospects for 1975

GROSS PRODUCT AND NET INCOME

The probable growth of various sectors of the economy leads to the estimate that the gross product, in current prices, will increase from $1,645 million to $7,730 million between 1960 and 1975 (Appendix P).[4] In the course of that period, the net income is expected to increase five fold, from $1,362 to $6,484 million. That increase involves an annual growth rate of 8.8 per cent in current prices, or 6.3 per cent in 1965 prices. Considering the projected growth of population—3,280,000 by 1975—the net per capita income in current prices should reach $2,218 in that year, compared with only $582 in 1960.

In terms of average income per family, those projections lead to an expected increase from $2,649 to $5,800 in the course of those 15 years. The number of families with incomes about $3,000 will reach 456,800, compared to 128,000 in 1960 (Fig. 17.5 and Appendix R). The number of families with incomes below $3,000 will be reduced from 320,000 to about 200,000. Such changes will of course increase considerably the families' purchasing power and, as a result, the demand for goods and services provided by local commerce, various economic sectors, and the government. For example, there will be a need for more and better roads since the number of vehicles is expected to increase from 179,657 at the close of the past decade to close to 1 million in 1975. The growing demand for private

4. The statistics were prepared by the Bureau of Economic and Social Analysis of the Planning Board. Following that analysis, a report, "The Purpose of Puerto Rico" was published and partly legislated on. This report defines further the projections presented here.

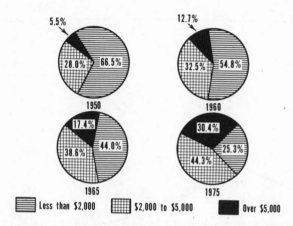

Figure 17.5. Distribution of Families by Income Level, 1950–1975. (Source: Bureau of Economic and Social Analysis, Puerto Rico Planning Board.)

homes is expected to bring the number of such occupied homes to 733,000 in 1975, compared to about 484,000 in 1960. The rate of increase in the number of those homes is greater than the rate of population growth.

INDUSTRIAL DEVELOPMENT

Industrialization continues to be the basis for future economic progress. The island's small internal market demands that industrialization must necessarily continue to orient itself toward the production of goods for export. Since Puerto Rico's exports today constitute a very small part of the total United States' market, the potentialities for industrial growth continue to be large. A study by the Economic Development Administration shows that in 1960 there were more than 160 products whose local manufacture could be economically successful in Puerto Rico but which were not made in 1960. Other factors favorable and promising for the island's economic future are: the improvement of the general level of education, industrial experience acquired in recent years, and the growing availability of skilled labor. Moreover, the improvement of basic services accelerates the process of capital formation which, in turn, will improve the island's economic infrastructure. That conjunction of factors augurs well for future industrial growth.

On the strength of the above—the progress achieved during the past decade, the present potential of the industrialization program, and its capacity for growth—it is expected that the following objectives will be reached: an increase in the net industrial income from $291 million in 1960 to $1,430 million in 1975, indicating an annual growth rate of 11.2 per cent compared to 14.4 per cent attained between 1958 and 1960; a gain

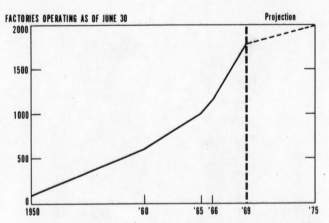

Figure 17.6. Number of Factories Promoted by the Economic Development Administration: Actual 1950–1969 and Projected 1975. (Source: Bureau of Economic and Social Analysis, Puerto Rico Planning Board.)

in employment in all factories, from 91,400 to 199,000, and in the productivity per worker from $3,185 to $6,899. The Industrial Development program of the Economic Development Administration (EDA) has undertaken to reach the following objectives during that time: (*a*) have two thousand factories in operation in 1975 (Fig. 17.6); (*b*) increase the net income (in current prices) originating from the new factories from $153 million in 1960 to $1,200 million in 1975; (*c*) increase by 160,000 the employment in factories promoted by EDA between 1960 and 1975 (Fig. 17.7); (*d*) increase the annual rate of production of the EDA-promoted factories by 5.3 per cent, so raising productivity in those factories from $3,400 to $7,500 by 1975.[5]

The increase of industrial employment by 160,000 should take place in factories promoted by the Economic Development Administration. These are expected to provide new jobs at an average annual rate of 7,100 between 1965 and 1975, compared with the annual growth of 2,950 jobs attained between 1955 and 1965. Such growth is postulated on the assumption that, during the period in question, productivity will increase at a rate not exceeding 5.3 per cent annually. Equilibrium between growth of employment and growth of income demands a growth of productivity sufficiently reasonable to prevent the high rate of wage increases experienced since 1956.

The aim of raising the net income generated by manufacturing, from $289 million to $1,430 million postulates an average annual rate of

5. Those gains will affect favorably other sectors of the economy, which will permit maintenance of the high rate of growth attained to date.

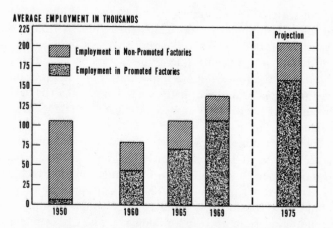

Figure 17.7. Employment in the Economic Development Administration Promoted Factories and in the Traditional Establishments: Actual 1950–1969 and projected 1975. (Source: Bureau of Economic and Social Analysis, Puerto Rico Planning Board.)

growth, between 1960 and 1975, of 11.2 per cent, compared with the 14.4 per cent attained during the last years of the past decade (Fig. 17.3 and Appendix B). For the factories promoted by the Economic Development Administration, the annual growth rate between 1958 and 1960 was 22.8 per cent. Realization of the program's objectives in the matter of new factories implies that in 1975 the income per promoted factory will be $600,000, representing an increase of 114 per cent over 1960. For factories not promoted by the government, the increase is expected to be 88 per cent. The prospects for those industries are good in general terms; however, a rate of growth as high as that experienced by new promoted factories is not to be expected.

AGRICULTURAL DEVELOPMENT

As stated in Chapters 11 and 18, Puerto Rico's geographic environment suffers from scarcities and limitations. Despite that fact, the value in the form of its agricultural production was $238 million in 1960; in the non-mountainous regions it was more than $200 per productive acre. The figures indicate a high rate of utilization of the island's scarce cultivable lands and natural resources. However, increased production on certain cultivated lands and on lands now idle which could be cultivated by means of more efficient, coordinated efforts is considered possible. The following paragraphs deal with prospects for the agricultural sector.

Poultry and Livestock. As a result of expected increases in the net per capita income, it is estimated that the per capita consumption of beef will rise from 22 pounds in 1960 to 47 in 1975. The demand will reach 154 million pounds of which 55.4 million are expected to be produced locally, in contrast to some 28 million in 1960. That will require virtually doubling the local production in 15 years, indicating that possibilities for expanding the industry are magnificent. Among the factors on which such expansion will be based, the following are important: (1) the program for improving pastures which, in 1960, had covered more than 200,000 acres; (2) improvement of beef cattle; and (3) the establishment of a modern, industrial slaughter house.

The production of pork is expected to rise to 45.6 millions pounds by 1975, from 22 million in 1960. The per capita consumption, considering the importance of pork and the growth of population, will increase from 34 pounds in 1959 to 45 pounds in 1975. The consumption of poultry is also expected to rise considerably, from 15 to 27 pounds, calling for an increase in production from 18 to 52 million pounds. Those increases will raise the value of domestic production from about $28.8 million in 1960 to $66.9 million in 1975, while the per capita consumption will increase from 79.5 to 130.1 pounds during the same years.

The prospect for the production of milk is that it will maintain the same high rate of growth that it showed during the past decade. The per capita consumption is expected to rise to 190 quarts in 1975, in contrast to 126 in 1960. The 1975 value of production will be about $100 million as against $43 million in 1959.

The projections also indicate a substantial increase in the per capita consumption of eggs, from 9 dozen to 20, between the two dates. The value of production will rise from 8 to 31 million dollars.

The value of production of the livestock and poultry industries together is expected to rise to $189 million in 1975, compared to $79.8 million in 1960.

Other Agricultural Industries. Among the rest of the island's agricultural industries, sugar is outstanding. However, since the beginning of the past decade, it has been affected by a series of adverse factors which caused a considerable lowering in production. No substantial increase is expected for the industry; on the contrary, an even greater reduction is probable in the areas planted to cane. There is, however, hope for increased production if efforts to increase the yield per acre are successful. That is important since nearly 200,000 acres cultivated in 1960, in farms of 250 acres or fewer, yielded only a low three tons of sugar per acre. Since yields of more than 4 tons are frequent, an improvement in that respect is probable and will result in substantial production increases in the island's first agricultural industry.

Prospects for the rest of the agricultural industry—coffee, tobacco, and other crops—indicate only a continuation of present production, though there is a possibility that commercial exploitation will be introduced on farms producing fruits and vegetables. The value of those products is expected to rise from $66.1 million in 1960 to $119 million in 1975.

It is estimated that total agricultural production will have a value of $450 million in 1975, or roughly $200 million more than that of 1960. Of that total value, $229 million, or over 50 per cent, will be in the poultry and livestock industry; the remainder, $221 million, will come from the other agricultural industries. Comparison of those figures with those of 1960—$82 million, or thirty per cent, from poultry and livestock and $156 million, or 70 per cent, from the remainder—shows that a substantial transformation of the agricultural sector is indicated. It will be noted that the poultry and livestock industry, taken together, is expected to surpass all other agricultural industries at the end of fiscal year 1975. That prospect is in line with a basic condition for economic development, viz: the channeling of activities toward the branches of highest per-worker productivity. In Puerto Rico's agriculture the channeling, or displacement, is toward poultry and livestock, whose productivity per employed worker is higher than that in the other agricultural industries. (Fig. 17.8 and Appendix K).

In the course of the fifteen projected years, the total net income of the agricultural sector is expected to increase 44 per cent, from $180 million in 1960 to $270 in 1975. That implies an annual growth rate of 2.5 per cent, which may be regarded as moderate. It is believed that the increase expected in the income generated by agriculture will constitute a diminishing proportion of the total, and that its proportion of the total will diminish from 14 to 6 per cent between 1960 and 1975.

Opportunities for employment in agriculture are expected to be reduced from 124,000 in 1960 to 60,000 in 1975, or by 64,000. The average

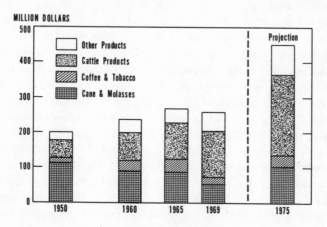

Figure 17.8. Value of Agricultural Production by Sectors,
1950–1975.

annual reduction will be about 3,000 workers, compared with an average annual reduction of 9,100 during the past decade. The decline anticipated in agricultural employment results from structural changes in the economy and from the growth of labor productivity in agriculture resulting from mechanization. The annual growth of productivity in that sector, during the past decade, was much greater than that in the general economy. The situation is expected to remain the same during the next years.

INVESTMENT AND THE CONSTRUCTION INDUSTRY

Puerto Rico's high rate of economic growth is based solidly on internal gross investment in fixed capital consisting of new constructions and the acquisition of machinery and equipment. That type of investment came to $5,144 million during 1965–70. According to the projections the annual figure should rise to $2,519 million in 1975. That anticipates an accumulated total of well over $15,000 million by 1975. On an annual basis, the investment is expected to mount from $348 million in 1960 to $2,519 million in 1975 (Fig. 17.4 and Appendix O). That increase indicates an average rate of growth higher than that of the gross product and affects the percentage relation between the two. The proportion was 21 per cent in 1960 and is expected to be well over 30 per cent in 1975.

The construction industry has played a very important role in the process of capital formation. Its enormous growth during the past decade (1960–1970) is seen everywhere. The value of new construction came to $1,448 million, distributed as follows: $542 million were invested in homes; $635 million in factories, hotels, commercial structures, electric power plants, and the like; the remaining $271 million were spent on essential public works such as roads and bridges. There can be no doubt that those investments constituted the basis for Puerto Rico's economic development. Venture investments[6] were determinant, reaching $2,921 million during the decade, of which $1,543 million were invested in machinery and equipment. It is expected that those venture investments, indispensable for the economy's continued growth, will rise from $210 million in 1960 to $849 million in 1975. The figures imply an annual rate of growth of 8.0 per cent, which is lower than that of recent years.

The value of construction is expected to rise from $227 million in 1960 to $1,177 million in 1975. It is expected that about 85 per cent of that sum will be invested in various enterprises,[7] and the remainder in public works. The annual value of private enterprise construction is expected to rise from $167 million in 1960 to $2,221 million in 1975, while the investment of government funds is expected to increase from $60 million to

6. Includes private as well as public investments.
7. Including government enterprises.

more than $190 million. In corporate investments the proportion going for machinery and equipment is expected to continue rising, since growth of production must be achieved mainly through the enlargement of established plants and the increasing use of modern, expensive machinery.

According to the projections, the number of occupied homes will increase from 484,200 in 1960 to 733,000 in 1975, or 248,800 units in 15 years as compared to 54,000 during the past decade. The rate of increase in the number of homes is expected to be higher than that of population growth, due to the tendency of young married couples to establish independent homes and that of young men between the ages of 20 and 30 years to start families. The large increase in the number of homes is expected to occur largely in the urban areas, since the population distribution of 44 per cent urban to 56 per cent rural, in 1960, will change to 61 and 39 per cent respectively by 1975. The value of home construction is expected to rise from $88 million (82 per cent private) in 1960 to $481.8 million (about 90 per cent private) in 1975. The last figure is about 25 per cent of the total investment of fixed capital in that year, a little higher than in 1960.

Total public investment by the Commonwealth and its municipalities in permanent improvements, such as roads, hospitals, and schools rose to $156 million in 1970 and is expected to rise to $291 in 1975, compared to $44 million in 1960.

In short, it is expected that all construction taken together, such as business and industrial, private homes, government housing, roads, and schools, will reach an annual value of more than eight times that of 1960, namely $1,800 million, compared to $227 million in 1960. That peak will be reflected in an increase in the net income of the construction industry, from $87 million to more than $700 million between the two dates.

OTHER ACTIVITIES

Governmental Sector. In the present decade the economic activity of the public sector is expected, as in the past decade, to continue as a vital factor in economic development. The policy of giving high priority to education, improvements planned in health and security services, and the rendering of indispensable services to permit economic development to continue its accelerating pace indicate substantial increases in incomes derived from the government. In view of those factors it is anticipated that the net income originated in the Commonwealth and municipal governments will multiply from $175 million in 1960 to more than $899 million in 1975.

Service Industries. A rosy future is expected for those industries during the projected period. The net income originating from them is calculated to grow from $132 million to $840 million and will in 1975 constitute some 13 per cent of the total net income, compared to less than 10 per cent in 1960.

Commerce. The prospects for commerce in general are splendid. In 1960 it produced $237 million or a little more than 17 per cent of Puerto Rico's total net income. It is expected to continue progressing, along the same lines as the general economy, and increase threefold ($719 million) within the fifteen year period between 1960 and 1975.

Other Services. The contributions to the total net income made by transportation and other public services, like those of finance, insurance, and real estate, will grow substantially, from $259 million in 1960 to $867 million in 1975. It is to be expected that all those industries will continue their high rate of development of the past decade, in terms of the demands of the general economic growth.

The Tourist Industry. Official figures testify eloquently to the extraordinary growth of Puerto Rico's tourist industry. In the course of only seven years, from 1953 to 1960, the number of guests in the island's hotels was tripled, from 45,000 to 146,000. In view of the potentials for expansion in Caribbean tourism, it is expected that 1.5 million will arrive in 1975. The number of hotel rooms needed at that time will be 13,700; at the end of 1960 there were only 2,922 rooms in the tourist and commercial hotels. The need for adding 7,000 more rooms during the period under review indicates a spectacular expansion in the hotel industry. Total expenditures on the island by visitors are expected to rise from $58 million ($29 million in hotels) in 1960 to $346.8 million ($236 million in hotels) in 1975, meaning that the net income from tourism will increase from $25.6 million to $135.7 million between the two dates. Other industries related to tourism, such as restaurants, travel agencies, and gift shops, will undoubtedly also benefit from the expansion of tourism.

Summary

According to the statistics and data given above, industrialization is expected to continue its rapid growth. At the end of the projected period, 1960–75, income from manufacturing is expected to constitute 44 per cent of the island's total net income, compared to 21 per cent in 1959–60 and only 14 per cent in 1949–50. However, despite a growth of more than $200 million in the value of its production, agriculture is expected to contribute only 4 per cent of the total income, in contrast to 14 per cent in 1960 and 24 per cent in 1950.

The transformation of the economic structure, from agricultural to industrial, is in line with modern economic developmental processes. Prospects regarding the contributions to the net income made by the economy's other sectors, taken together, are that they will be reduced somewhat during the present decade, though they will continue to contribute more than 60 per cent of the total net internal income.

In the matter of employment, the projections indicate that the number of persons gainfully employed will increase from 543,000 in 1960 to

Figure 17.9. Typical Middle Class Family Home.

355

960,000 in 1975, representing a growth of 417,000. The larger share of the growth will occur in the manufacturing sector, the main source of employment, with a total of 199,000. It is expected that 160,000 of those jobs will be in the 2,000 factories estimated to be in operation in 1975 under the program for economic development. Men and women are expected to hold those jobs in approximately equal numbers. As a result of the new work opportunities, a substantial reduction is expected, in the near future, in the migration to the continental United States by males fourteen years of age or older in search of work.

In the phase of employment by sectors, the structural transformation of employment observed during the past decade is expected to continue. The high rate of growth expected in agricultural productivity will permit increases in that sector's total production with fewer workers. As a result, the projection for 1975 is that agriculture will employ less than 10 per cent of the total in 1975, in contrast to 23 per cent in 1960. On the other hand, the prospects are that manufacturing will provide 21 per cent of the total employment in 1975, in contrast to only 17.7 per cent in 1960. In the other sectors, taken together, the proportion is expected to rise from 60 to 69 per cent of the total. It will be seen that the projections indicate a substantial increase in industrial employment. In turn, that increase will raise the demand for professional people, technicians and specialized operators, for a corps, in other words, of more highly trained and specialized workers. The special occupations which require more academic preparation will continue to supplant those requiring few or no skills.

The complete achievement of those objectives will of course contribute to the general, economic and social, well-being of Puerto Rico's people. As stated above, the per capita income is expected to rise above $2,000 in 1975. The average income per family will surpass $8,000 in that year, and 70 per cent of the families will receive incomes of more than $3,000. Those figures are far above those of 1960, when the average per-family income was $2,649 and only 29 per cent of the families had incomes above $3,000 (Fig. 17.9).

There is of course no mathematical assurance that those projections will be attained. Perhaps they merely express Puerto Rico's great opportunity in economic, social, and cultural matters to reach levels comparable to those of the earth's more prosperous societies. Naturally, such progress requires political stability and the continuation of the relations with the United States which have made much of the growth possible. A future of greater well-being is being worked out by the Puerto Ricans, with their continued effort and dedication to the ideals of democratic development which have already transformed Puerto Rico substantially in the short span of 30 years.

18

The Geographic Regions
of Puerto Rico

The preceding chapters are ·devoted to the description and analysis of various elements of the physical environment and its impact, together with historic, economic, and social factors, on the life of the Puerto Ricans. In the manner of a résumé, the present chapter presents the geography from the regional point of view as opposed to the systematic viewpoint used earlier. The repetition of certain data and concepts is therefore inevitable. After a brief recapitulation on the geographic environment and land utilization, this final chapter will proceed to describe Puerto Rico's regions as the author has outlined them in an earlier work.[1]

The island of Puerto Rico, located in the so-called American Mediterranean, is the smallest of the Greater Antilles. It occupies a central position in the arc of submerged mountains which extends between the two Americas and forms the Antillean Archipelago. The rest of the Greater Antilles—Hispaniola (the Dominican Republic and Haiti), Jamaica, and Cuba—lie west of Puerto Rico; the Lesser Antilles extend toward the southeast to the vicinity of the Venezuelan coast.

The geographic setting of Puerto Rico is characterized by diversity and by the intensive manner in which the population has utilized its scant natural resources. Puerto Rico is 111 miles long by 36 miles wide and has a total area of 3,435 square miles,[2] including its small adjoining islands: Vieques, Culebra, la Mona, El Monito, and Desecheo. The area is principal among the factors which limit exploitation of local resources.

San Juan is itself a small island, located a few yards from Puerto Rico, which once contained the most important commercial center. Its small size and narrow streets limit commercial growth which has spread to other areas, notably Santurce. (Located on the main island of Puerto

1. Rafael Picó, *The Geographic Regions of Puerto Rico* (Río Piedras: University of Puerto Rico Press, 1950).
2. See Appendix T for the equivalent in square kilometers.

Rico, Santurce is a section of the City of San Juan.) Nevertheless, the main offices of Puerto Rico's most important commercial and industrial establishments are still located in San Juan. The capital's urban population in 1970 was 444,952 and that of the metropolitan zone, 814,340.

The cities and towns near the metropolitan zone, as well as the rural areas, house many of those who work in the zone. The metropolitan zone includes the University of Puerto Rico and the International Airport. Economic activities of the rest of Puerto Rico are oriented toward the capital.

The resources are all the more restricted in view of the fact that Puerto Rico is one of the most densely populated areas in the world with 2,689,932 inhabitants in 1970, resulting in a density close to 800 per square mile, comparable to that of industrial countries like Holland and Belgium with intense commercial activity.[3] Nevertheless, despite territorial limitations and the density of population, the levels of living are higher in Puerto Rico than are those of many larger countries with more resources.

Topography and climate form the basis of the people's social-economic structure. The island is rugged from any point of view. It is estimated that 40 per cent of the total area is mountainous, 35 per cent hilly, and 25 per cent level. Fifty-eight per cent of the lands above altitudes of 1,000 feet slope more than 45 degrees; between 500 and 1,000 feet, the ratio is 49 per cent.[4]

The narrow coastal plains are flanked by hills and the interior mountains, with the Cordillera Central as the main part of the central axis. It begins near the west coast in the outskirts of the city of Mayagüez, bordered by the Cerro Las Mesas and the mountains of Uroyán, runs as far as the east coast in the Sierra de Cayey, and then turns northeast toward the Sierra de Luquillo. Altitudes above 2,800 feet predominate in the Cordillera Central; the highest is 4,398 feet at Cerro de Punta, south of Jayuya. In the mountains, erosion has created several interior valleys like those of the Loíza and La Plata rivers, and there remain highly eroded remnants of the St. John and Caguana peneplanes.[5]

The mountainous interior slopes abruptly southward to the south coastal plain. The northward slope is more gradual since the mountainous spine is located at about two-thirds of the island's width south of the north coast. The coastal valleys of the west, carved by the Culebrinas, Añasco, Yagüez, and Guanajibo rivers, are triangles, broadening from the mountains to the sea. In the east, the valleys and plains of Fajardo,

3. Data on the number of inhabitants are largely taken from the 1970 Census of Population (April 1970).

4. See Appendix T for the equivalent in meters.

5. H. A. Meyerhoff, *Geology of Puerto Rico* (Monographs of the University of Puerto Rico, Series B, No. 1) (Río Piedras: University of Puerto Rico, 1933).

Naguabo, Humacao, Yabucoa, and Maunabo cut similarly into the mountains.

The temperatures of Puerto Rico are high, as is the occurrence of rainfall. The relative humidity averages 70 per cent during the day and reaches as high as 85 per cent at night. Nevertheless, the air is tempered by the fresh trade winds and those of the valleys and mountains.

Puerto Rico is located in the tropical zone where there are no extremes of temperature at any time of the year. The average temperature is 76.5° F, with monthly fluctuations between 73° F and 79° F.[6] Between the coast and the interior, the changes between night and day temperatures vary from 10° to 20° F. Temperature zones are also differentiated through altitude: the "tierra caliente" (tropical) on the plains and low hills and the "tierra templada" (subtropical) in the higher mountains.

Precipitation varies much more than does the temperature, fluctuating between some 180 inches annually in the Sierra de Luquillo where it rains almost daily and fewer than 30 inches in the southwest which approaches tropical desert conditions. Precipitation is not well distributed in the course of the year. It is highest almost everywhere in the warmer months, from May to October, while the winter is generally drier. In the north and east, winter rainfall is relatively abundant because of the influence of the trade winds and rains of the orogenic type; the south and west, on the other hand, experience droughts.

The greatest diversity found in Puerto Rico is probably that of the soils. One hundred and fifteen soil series, encompassing 352 soil types and phases, have been classified within the island's small area.[7] Among them are the 251 soils of the humid and subhumid north while the other 101 are in the island's arid and semiarid south.[8] The large number of series and types of soils results primarily from the physical heterogeneity of Puerto Rico. Since it is virtually impossible to describe the 352 types in detail, reference is here made to the grouping of the 24 most important series into 11 groups as classified by J. A. Bonnet, which gives a sufficiently clear idea of the island's principal soils (Fig. 9.3).

Before the onset of colonization, the island was largely covered by forests, but in the course of four and a half centuries man has changed the natural landscape almost completely. Nevertheless, the manner in which the dense vegetation of the humid regions in the center of the island gradually changes until meeting the xerophytic plants typical of the south coastal plain can still be observed.

6. For conversion to degrees Centigrade, see Appendix T.

7. R. C. Roberts, *Soil Survey of Puerto Rico,* U.S. Department of Agriculture, Bureau of Plant Industry; University of Puerto Rico Agricultural Experiment Station (Washington, D.C., 1942).

8. Nathan Koenig, *A Comprehensive Agricultural Program for Puerto Rico* (U.S. Department of Agriculture; the Commonwealth of Puerto Rico) (Washington, D.C., 1953).

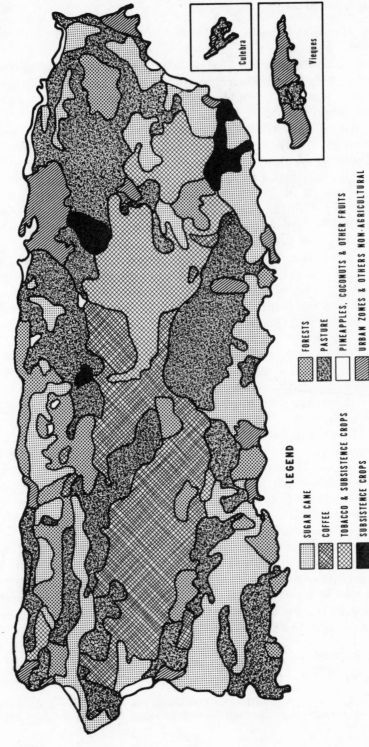

LEGEND

SUGAR CANE
COFFEE
TOBACCO & SUBSISTENCE CROPS
SUBSISTENCE CROPS

FORESTS
PASTURE
PINEAPPLES, COCONUTS & OTHER FRUITS
URBAN ZONES & OTHERS NON-AGRICULTURAL

Culebra

Vieques

Figure 18.1. Land Use in Puerto Rico. (Prepared by Héctor Berríos, Puerto Rico Planning Board.)

360

The 2,254,078 acres which comprise the territory of Puerto Rico are divided into 620,000 which are cultivated, 820,000 in pastures, 323,000 in woodlands (including 89,400 in forest reserves), and the remaining 474,078 acres in buildings, military reservations, and other uses which are agriculturally unproductive (Table 18.1 and Fig. 18.1).[9]

Despite the great physical and social-economic contrasts encountered in Puerto Rico, 11 geographic regions are recognized as relatively homogenous groupings in matters of soil, topography, climate, natural vegetation, and economic activities (Fig. 18.2).

Table 18.1. Land use, 1968
(acres)

Agricultural areas		1,763,000
Sugar cane	260,000	
Tobacco	8,000	
Coffee	180,000	
Minor food crops, fruits, etc.	172,000	
Total harvested	620,000	
Improved pastures	480,000	
Unimproved pastures	340,000	
Forests and woodlands	323,000	
Military reservations, reservoirs Highways, urban areas, rural villages, Homesites, etc.		474,000
Total, Puerto Rico		2,237,000

Source: Puerto Rico Department of Agriculture.

The Northern Coastal Lowlands

Though fourth in size, the northern coastal lowlands surpass all other regions in social-economic activity. The importance of the region stems largely from certain physical conditions which differ from those of the rest of the island, as well as from the train of historic development. The northern coastal lowlands extend from Aguadilla in the west to beyond the town of Luquillo in the east. As a region they comprise 301,389 acres, or 13.37 per cent of the island's total. Although it is about 100 miles long, its width does not exceed five.

The subregions are recognized in the northern coastal lowlands: the western subhumid limestone section and the humid alluvial section. The former extends from Aguadilla to Arecibo, the latter from Arecibo to Luquillo. The division is justified by certain physical and economic differences.

9. The Puerto Rican unit for land area is the "cuerda," or 0.9712 acre. Since the two units are so nearly alike, cuerdas are here called acres. See Appendix T for other equivalents of the "cuerda."

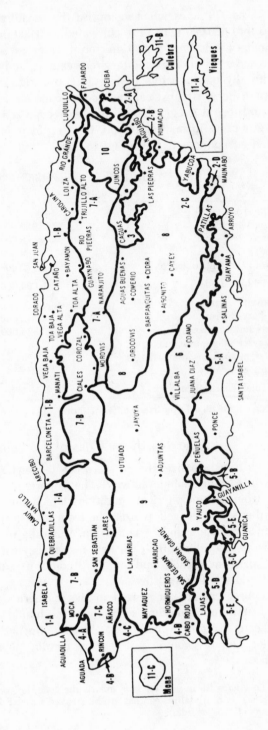

Figure 18.2. The Geographic Regions of Puerto Rico.

Table 18.2. The geographic regions

Geographic Regions	Acres	Per Cent of Total
Total	2,054,078	100.00
1. Northern coastal lowlands		301,389	13.37
a. Western subhumid limestone section	84,255	
b. Humid alluvial section	217,134	
2. Humid eastern coastal valleys		70,179	3.11
a. Fajardo section	24,900	
b. Naguabo-Humacao valleys	28,691	
c. Yabucoa Valley	12,468	
d. Maunabo Valley	4,120	
3. Caguas Valley		32,483	1.44
4. Wet–dry western coastal valleys		58,586	2.60
a. Culebrinas-Culebra valleys	10,645	
b. Corcega section	1,167	
c. Añasco Valley	11,776	
d. Guanajibo Valley	34,998	
5. Dry southern coastal lowlands		221,582	9.83
a. Ponce-Patillas alluvial plain	118,811	
b. Tallaboa Valley	5,578	
c. Guayanilla-Guánica section	15,348	
d. Lajas Valley	34,743	
e. Southwestern coastal hilly belt	47,102	
6. Semiarid southern foothills		222,822	9.89
7. Humid northern foothills		469,412	20.82
a. Northeastern Cretaceous section	167,991	
b. Inland limestone belt	241,961	
c. Atalaya Hills	59,460	
8. Humid east central mountains		337,149	14.96
9. Rainy west central mountains		432,081	19.17
10. Rainy Sierra de Luquillo		53,846	2.39
11. Outlying Puerto Rico		54,549	2.42
a. Vieques Island	34,016	
b. Culebra Island	6,714	
c. La Mona Island	13,792	

The western subhumid limestone section is characterized by a narrow beach, dotted with small sand dunes and bordered by the steep sea cliff which ascends to a more or less level plateau of Tertiary limestone.

The eastern section is a level alluvium plain which extends from Arecibo to the vicinity of Cape San Juan. Both sections contain limestone haystacks, from the west to near the town of Loíza; these, however, are more numerous in the east.

The western section is more arid than the eastern. The average annual rainfall is less than 60 inches; the Camuy zone is the driest, with 49.4 inches, though the precipitation increases somewhat from the coast toward the interior. In the eastern section the average annual precipitation is 58.8 inches at Barceloneta, and it increases toward the east, reaching 76.6 at Río Piedras.

The soils are largely products of topography and climate. Those of the northern coastal lowlands are limestone soils belonging, among others, to the Coto-Bayamón, Soller Aguilita, and Sabana Seca-Lares groups, in addition to areas of alluvium and peat. The Coto series is typical in the region northwest of the Quebradillas plain. The Bayamón series, similar to the Coto but more acid, is found from Arecibo to Río Piedras, where conditions are more humid. Both series are derived from Tertiary limestone, average in fertility, rich in iron and aluminium, but poor in nitrogen and phosphorus.

The alluvial soils of the humid and subhumid regions abound, east and west, along the north coast. Slightly acid and fertile, they are planted mostly to sugar cane.

The peat soils are found at or near the coast, in the swampy mangrove areas. Those of the north coast are found largely near the towns of Arecibo, Manatí and Loíza. They are very young soils, formed of recently decomposed organic matter, rich in humus but very poor in minerals, and often salty. Some areas, like those of Tiburones Swamp of Arecibo and the Loíza drainage project, have been drained to be used for pasture and for the production of sugar cane.

The northern coastal lowlands comprise the most densely populated region of Puerto Rico. With an urban population of 916,691, or almost 60 per cent of the island's urban total, it contains twenty towns and cities.[10]

San Juan, included in the region, is the oldest city on the island, founded in 1509. It is the seat of the central government of the Commonwealth.

Agriculture is still important in the economy of the region. In 1950 the cultivation of sugar cane embraced a little more than 100,000 acres, but by 1966 the area had been reduced by 55,000 acres. Many farmers of the humid alluvial section have converted to dairy farming or leave the land fallow, expecting it soon to be urbanized for residential or industrial uses.

The cultivation of fruits, especially pineapples and coconuts, is very important. The region includes more than 80 per cent of the 4,300 acres planted to pineapples in Puerto Rico in 1968. The area planted to coconuts is estimated to exceed 8,000 acres. Other important food crops are yams, beans, sweet potatoes, and yucca, which take up about 16,000 acres. Some tobacco and "Sea Island" cotton are produced in the western subhumid section, especially on the small farms. The small Isabela irrigation

10. The following urban centers are located in the northern coastal lowlands region: Arecibo, Barceloneta, Bayamón, Camuy, Carolina, Cataño, Dorado, Guaynabo, Hatillo, Isabela, Loíza Aldea and Canóvanas, Luquillo, Manatí, Quebradillas, Río Grande, San Juan, Toa Alta, Toa Baja and Levittown, Vega Alta, and Vega Baja.

system is used to a certain extent for the production of sugar cane and mixed vegetables in the western part of the section.

Dairy farming, today second in importance among Puerto Rico's agricultural industries, has by now become the first on the northern coastal plain, especially in the eastern section. The metropolitan market of San Juan favors dairy farming; the pasteurizing plants of that region sell 80 per cent of the milk produced in Puerto Rico. More than 30,000 acres are in improved or rotated pastures (pangola grass and malojillo); in addition, there are more than 90,000 acres in natural pastures, swampy or brush-covered and mixed with forests. About 70,000 acres in the region are covered by forests, mangrove swamps, or underbrush, or support urban developments and United States military establishments or reservations.

No other region equals that of the north coastal plain, especially the San Juan area, in matters of commerce and manufacturing. In part because of the capital's well-protected harbor, the metropolitan zone handles the largest part of the island's external trade. The zone contains more than 40 per cent of all the commercial establishments in Puerto Rico, together with 35 per cent of the direct employment in commerce. More than 40 per cent of all the factories in Puerto Rico, and 33 per cent of the people engaged in manufacturing, are found in the metropolitan zone, while it is estimated that that area generates 47 per cent of the island's net income.

The north coastal plain holds many tourist attractions. It possesses the majority of Puerto Rico's large hotels, especially in the San Juan metropolitan area. There are many beautiful natural beaches, and it is near other attractions such as the subtropical rain forest of Luquillo.

The Humid Eastern Coastal Valleys

The humid valleys of the east coast, separated by mountain spurs, extend from the city of Fajardo to Cape Mala Pascua at the southeastern corner of Puerto Rico. The region has been divided into four sections, containing a total of 70,179 acres: the Fajardo section, Naguabo-Humacao valleys, Yabucoa Valley, and Maunabo Valley. The Naguabo-Humacao Valleys are the largest, with 28,691 acres; the Maunabo Valley, with only 4,120 acres, is the smallest. The Fajardo section includes the Fajardo River and a series of narrow, short valleys; the other areas consist of the short but relatively wide valleys of several streams whose sources are in the mountain borders to the west.

Precipitation is generally abundant, with an annual minimum average of 75 inches, except for a strip southeast of Fajardo where the average is 67.2 inches. Parts of the region, where rainfall is heavier, may be regarded as being humid throughout the year. In Naguabo are stations whose annual precipitation is more than 85 inches. Humacao and Yabucoa receive similar quantities, which diminish somewhat in the Maunabo Valley. Precipitation increases east to west, from the coast toward the interior.

Temperatures in this section are typically tropical; Maunabo, with 79.6° F, has the highest annual average in Puerto Rico.

The soils of this region are largely alluvial, composed of materials brought down from the mountains by the streams. Clay and peat soils abound in the valleys. The drainage problem is serious and the provision of adequate drainage is expensive. The subsoils are heavy, generally medium, dark ochre or gray in color, fertile, and suited for mechanized farming.

Sugar cane, covering more than 30,000 acres, predominates in the humid eastern coastal valleys. More than 3,000 acres are planted to mixed vegetables which, together with 2,000 acres in coconuts, round out the greater part of the cultivated areas. Livestock farming is quite important; some 18,000 acres are in improved and natural pastures.

The region contains six urban centers[11] with a total population (1970) of 43,631. Fajardo, with 18,127 inhabitants, is the largest. The tourist industry is growing in the environs of Fajardo and its magnificent beaches; there are new hotels, improved beaches, and yacht basins. Humacao, seat of the senatorial district of the same name as well as of a regional college established by the University of Puerto Rico, is also an important industrial center. The rural population is typical of the sugar zones. Homes are scarce in the valleys planted to cane because the people live in the nearby towns and in the hills which border the valleys. Although it is a coastal region, there is a shortage of seaports. However, a number of suburbs on the coast, called "playas," serve as ports for the inland towns. The "Playa de Fajardo," in addition to being used by the city, is a fishing and commercial anchorage, as well as a base for the transportation of passengers between Puerto Rico, the islands of Vieques and Culebra, and the Virgin Islands.

The east coast is irregular, especially in the northeast, and has some good ports, like Ensenada Honda. It is promising region for the development of the fishing industry, despite its short shore line. The submarine platform is less than 250 feet deep and fish abound near the many islands and sand banks. The region is second in importance for commercial fishing and attracts a growing number of sport fishermen and yachtsmen. The "Isleta Marina," near Fajardo, shelters a large number of yachts and sport boats (Fig. 18.3).

11. Ceiba, Fajardo, Humacao, Maunabo, Naguabo, and Yabucoa.

The Caguas Valley

West of the humid east coast valleys, the Caguas Valley separates the Luquillo Range from the Sierra de Cayey. While only low hills divide the Caguas Valley from that of Naguabo, the area of the former, its economic importance, and its physical character, justify its classification as an independent geographic region. It receives its name from the city of Caguas, located in the center of the valley.

Figure 18.3. The Isleta Marina Yacht Basin, near Fajardo.

With an area of 32,483 acres, it is the largest of the interior valleys and the smallest of Puerto Rico's geographic regions. The Caguas Valley is the result of the erosional activities of the Loíza River, the widest in Puerto Rico, and its main tributary, the Gurabo.

The climate of the region is humid tropical, though the precipitation is less than that of the eastern valleys. In the city of Caguas, the typical station of the region, the average annual rainfall is 64.6 inches; farther east, in the town of San Lorenzo, it is 73.4 inches. In general, the precipitation is not well distributed; the months of February and March, when the rains amount to less than three inches monthly, are somewhat arid.

The soils of the Caguas Valley are largely derived from alluvium. They are deep, fertile, and little affected by erosion. Among the most extensive are the clays and loams of the Caguas and Toa series belonging, according to Bonnet, to the Sabana Seca-Lares group.

Sugar cane is the principal crop in the region and covers more than 10,000 acres, largely on alluvial lands. Tobacco used to be produced on about 10,000 acres; but has declined greatly. Caguas is still an important tobacco center, with one of the largest cigar factories in Puerto Rico. Mixed food crops occupy the rest of the tillable lands. Dairy farming is today more important in agriculture than is the production of sugar cane or tobacco. Together with raising beef cattle, the industry benefits from the markets for fresh milk in the city of Caguas and the San Juan metropolitan area, and from the establishment, in Caguas, of a modern slaughter house which processes many products derived from cattle, poultry, and pork. Improved pastures exceed 4,000 acres; natural pastures, worked in rotation or in other ways, occupy some 10,000.

The valley contains four urban centers[12] with a total population of 84,672 in 1970. Caguas, with 62,807 inhabitants, is the principal city, not only of the region but also of the entire interior of the island, being the fifth city of Puerto Rico in terms of population. This progressive city is supported by the agriculture and commerce of the region and is connected with San Juan by a modern four-land highway, 22 miles long.

Modern transportation facilities and direct communication to San Juan have contributed to the development of an important manufacturing center in Caguas, whose growth will eventually result in making it a part of the metropolitan zone. The physical and economic conditions of the valley continue to justify its classification as a geographic region apart from the northern coastal plains.

The Wet–Dry Western Coastal Valleys

The valleys of the west coast border on the western littoral extend from the Bay of Aguadilla in the north to a mile south of Puerto Real in Cabo Rojo (Red Cape). Three large river systems and a few consequent streams have developed four lowlands areas. From north to south they are: the Culebrinas-Culebra Valley, the Córcega section, the Añasco Valley, and the Guanajibo Valley. The valleys, like those on the east coast, are separated by mountains or low hills; their total area is 58,586 acres and they resemble the eastern coastal valleys in certain physical and economic ways.

The climate of these valleys is interesting because of the distribution of its rainfall. Precipitation is abundant from May to November but the months from December to March are dry. Despite the fact that the average annual rainfall is 75.9 inches at Mayagüez (the typical station of the region), the monthly average ranges from 2 inches in January to 11.1 inches in August, causing floods in the rainy season and droughts in win-

12. Caguas, Gurabo, Juncos, and San Lorenzo.

ter. That marked fluctuation between summer and winter is typical of Puerto Rico's entire western area.

The soils of those valleys, like those along the east coast, are derived largely from alluvium. They are very fertile but less acid than those in the east. Drainage, however, is a serious problem, and deep drainage ditches are needed in the Guanajibo and Culebrinas river valleys. In the adjoining hills there are true laterite soils of the Rosario-Nipe group, formed by the decomposition of the serpentine rocks in the hills near Mayagüez. They are relatively deep, reddish in color, rich in aluminium and iron, but poor in potassium, phosphorous, and calcium. Their fertility is slight and they may well be more valuable from the mineral than from the agricultural point of view. Most of the hills are covered by shrubs and trees, like the nonurban sections of Cerro Las Mesas in Mayagüez and the Monte de Maricao.

As in the humid eastern coastal valleys and the Caguas Valley, sugar cane, grown on 25,000 acres, is the principal crop. Mixed vegetables and fruits are other important crops of the region. Pastures occupy about 8,000 acres; the fact that they include large areas of natural and brush-covered pastures indicates that livestock culture is not very important in the western valleys.

The region contains ten urban centers[13] with a total population of 133,804, of which the port city of Mayagüez, with 69,485 inhabitants in 1970, is the largest. Mayagüez is the fourth largest city in Puerto Rico, an important industrial city and the traditional seat of the needlework industry. The College of Agriculture and Engineering of the University of Puerto Rico is located there, as an autonomous campus ("recinto"), as is the recently created "Free Trade Zone," the only one in Puerto Rico. The private Inter-American University is located in the nearby city of San Germán. Two seaports in the west, Mayagüez and Aguadilla, have contributed to the development of the economy of the region. Rincón, a center for nuclear experimentation, produced electric energy until recently.

Mayagüez contains three large plants in which imported tuna fish are canned. Local fishing is important in the west; more than 25 per cent of all the fresh fish consumed in Puerto Rico is caught in that region.

The Dry Southern Coastal Lowlands

The dry southern coastal lowlands region, with 22,582 acres, is clearly distinguished from its northern border, the semiarid southern foothills, by its level topography, greater aridity, and greater economic wealth.

13. Aguada, Aguadilla, Añasco, Cabo Rojo, Hormigueros, Mayagüez, Moca, Rincón, Sabana Grande, and San Germán.

Physiographically the region is divided into two subregions, the Ponce-Patillas alluvial plain and southwestern Puerto Rico which includes the Tallaboa Valley, the Guayanilla-Guánica section, the Lajas Valley, and the coastal hilly belt of the southwest corner of the island.

The Ponce-Patillas alluvial plain extends from near the city of Ponce to the town of Patillas. With the area of 118,811 acres, it is considered the richest agricultural region of Puerto Rico, despite the fact that it receives less rain than any of the other regions so far discussed. The general average annual precipitation is less than 50 inches; it decreases from east to west and from the interior toward the coast. Near the town of Arroyo, the average annual rainfall is 63.8 inches; in Guayama it is 59.9, and in Ponce 37.6. The monthly distribution is uneven, with extreme drought from December to April.

Nearly all the soils of this plain are of alluvial origin. The combination of a semiarid climate with the origin of the soils have contributed toward making those lands the most fertile of the island. Two groups of mature soils predominate: the Ponceña-Coamo and the Santa Isabel-Paso Seco. About 75,000 acres are irrigated, making them ideal for the production of sugar cane, and tomatoes and peppers. Cultivation of these two truck crops was started recently near Santa Isabel. The Ponceña-Coamo group is typical of the south coastal interior plains. It is formed of materials washed from the nearby hills, composed of clayey, calcareous shales, tuffs, and other rocks. The Santa Isabel-Paso Seco soils are found in the alluvial fans south of the Ponceña-Coamo. They are somewhat younger than the others and are very fertile.

The economy of the alluvial subregion is intimately related to the sugar industry. Of the 16 active sugar mills in 1969 in Puerto Rico, five are located in the region, and in 1970 they ground about 28 per cent of the island's total production. The area planted to sugar cane exceeds 58,000 acres and comprises about 40 per cent of the subregion.

In the region are seven urban centers[14] with a total 1970 population of 171,800. Ponce, with 125,926 inhabitants, (Fig. 18.4) is the third-largest city in Puerto Rico (Bayamón in the San Juan metropolitan area is now second). Its development stemmed largely from seaport activities, commerce, manufacturing, and education. The Catholic University of Puerto Rico (Regina Cleri) is located in Ponce, as well as the newly established regional college of the University of Puerto Rico.

There are more than 30,000 acres of pasture, about 35 per cent of which are improved, largely with guinea grass. Cattle culture, for fattening and milk, has always been the second agricultural industry of the region. About 2,000 acres are cultivated for mixed food crops, including plantains, bananas, corn, and beans. Only about 4,000 acres, consisting largely of mangrove swamps, are forested.

14. Arroyo, Guayama, Juana Díaz, Patillas, Ponce, Salinas, and Santa Isabel.

Figure 18.4. The City of Ponce from Mount El Vigía.

One of the most important petro-chemical complexes in Puerto Rico (Phillips Petroleum) is located near Guayama, using Jobos Bay for its port facilities.

Both physically and economically, the southwestern subregion is more diversified than the southeastern. With a total area of 102,771 acres, it contains three interior plains in addition to the coastal hilly belt of the island's southwest corner. The plains are (from east to west): the valley of Tallaboa, the Guayanilla-Guánica section, and the Lajas Valley.

The climate of the southwest is the most arid in Puerto Rico, with an average annual rainfall of less than 35 inches. The village of Ensenada receives an average of 30.3 inches annually and the town of Lajas about 41 inches. Like the Ponce area, the subregion requires irrigation for intensive dairying and crop farming. The arid climate has facilitated the production of salt along the coast from Ponce to Boquerón. Salt is evaporated from seawater in specially constructed ponds.

The soils of the southwestern valleys are less diversified than are those in other parts of the island. In the Tallaboa and Lajas valleys and in the Guánica and Guayanilla section, the soils, like those farther east, are largely alluvial and very fertile. In some irrigated zones, like the Lajas Valley, the soils tend to be quite heavy, difficult to drain, and affected by salt in a number of places. In the coastal hilly belt of the Southwest there are large areas of shallow and stony soils, extremely dry, and usable only for forests and extensive grazing.

As in the valleys described above, the cultivation of sugar cane is the main agricultural industry, utilizing some 22,500 acres, most of which are irrigated. Two sugar mills are located in the region; one of them Guánica "Central" is the largest in Puerto Rico.

The Tallaboa Valley has become an important petro-chemical center. In addition to refining petroleum, it now produces a large number of petroleum derivatives. The port of the sector has favored such industrial development. A pipeline from Guayanilla to San Juan transports gasoline and other derivatives for consumption in the northern coastal plain.

Some of the finest beaches in Puerto Rico are in the southwest: Guánica, Guayanilla, and Boquerón which, together with La Parguera, are fishing ports. The arid climates and the large sizes of the farms contribute to the fact that the rural population is almost as small and scattered as in some of the mountainous regions. Five small urban centers are located in or near the southwest region: Guánica, Guayanilla, Lajas, Peñuelas, and Yauco; their total combined population is 33,077.

The Semiarid Southern Foot Hills

This region of hills lies between the Central Mountains in the north and the southern coastal lowlands in the south. More than 80 miles long, with an average width of five miles, it has an area of more than 222,822 acres.

The climate of the region, though in general semiarid, may be regarded as intermediate. In Coamo, the driest part, the average annual rainfall is about 40 inches, increasing to more than 60 inches toward the northern, eastern and western borders. Precipitation, moreover, varies in the course of the year, with two marked rainy periods: May to June and August to November. Winters are dry, especially in February and March when the monthly precipitation is less than two inches.

The soils of this region are closely related to the forms of relief. Toward the east, soils of the Descalabrado-Guayama group predominate; in the west there are belts of Descalabrado-Guayama among the Soller-Aguilita, Múcara-Naranjito, and Ponce-Coamo groups. The Soller-Aguilita group is found toward the coast, and the Múcara-Naranjito toward the interior. The Ponceña-Coamo soils abound in the lowlands of the middle section. When the alluvial soils are irrigated they tend to be as productive as the soils of the southern coastal lowlands.

Because of aridity and impediments to irrigation posed by the topography and the lack of large rivers, the agriculture of this region is not as important as that of the south coastal plain. In spite of adverse conditions, however, the cultivated area totals about 50,000 acres, of which 24,000 produce sugar cane, the most important crop. About 5,000 acres are in coffee, largely in the north, near the Cordillera Central. The cultivation of mixed food crops is limited to those which grow rapidly and are resistant to drought, like corn, beans, and pigeon peas.

There are 138,000 acres in pastures, of which 29,000 are improved while 6,000 are worked in rotation. Guinea grass, excellent in the dry regions, has been planted extensively and today provides most of the feed, either grazed in the open or cut for barn-feeding. The dairy industry is very important and several good herds supply fresh milk for the markets in Ponce and even for the San Juan Metropolitan Area. Beef production is also important. The forested areas are large, totalling about 18,000 acres, beside more than 12,000 acres in second growth, especially in the more arid regions.

In general, the region is more densely populated than is the southern coastal plain, and the west central part has the highest demographic density. There are only two true urban centers, Coamo and Villalba, with a combined population of 16,032 (Fig. 18.5). The selection of the present sites of those two was greatly influenced in each case by the presence of a river and a valley in the vicinity, where water and relatively level lands were available to the settlers.

The Humid Northern Foothills

The humid northern foothills extend from east to west, north of the central mountains. With 469,412 acres, they are the largest of the geographic regions, comprising about 20.8 per cent of Puerto Rico's total

Figure 18.5. The City of Coamo from Mount Picó.

area. Their geology and soils, the amount and distribution of precipitation, and the economy, differentiate this agricultural region from the corresponding region in the south.

The humid northern foothills region contains five urban centers[15] with a total population of 36,531. Its rural areas are among the most densely populated of the island, with about 100,000 inhabitants.

The region is divided into three sections: the northeastern Cretaceous section, the inland limestone belt, and the Atalaya Hills.

The northeastern Cretaceous section extends from Ciales to Cape San Juan and has an area of 167,991 acres. Its topography is mountainous, with altitudes up to 2,000 feet. The climate is considered humid, with minimum annual rainfall of 80 inches. Near Corozal the precipitation averages 76.8 inches which increases eastward, surpassing 100 inches at Río Grande. The rainfall, moreover, is uniformly distributed throughout the year. Since the monthly precipitation is never less than five inches, there are no marked dry periods. Several important rivers, like the La Plata, the Bayamón, and the Loíza, cross the section, forming terraces and flood plains which are agriculturally very important. The rivers are used for generating limited electric energy and especially for supplying water to the population and industries in the region.

In so large a section, it is difficult to generalize as to soil characteristics. However, the soils are generally deep and the Múcara-Naranjito group is dominant. The texture of these deep and mediumly fertile soils is clayey and they are quite susceptible to erosion, especially at steep points. But they have the advantage of rapidly renewing their fertility, since the exposed fresh rock is rich in bases.

Agricultural diversification is notable in this section. Food crops receive special attention because the farms are small, the region is densely populated, and has access to the San Juan metropolitan area. Climatic conditions, moreover, permit harvesting two quick crops per year. Among the more important crops are yautía, yams, plantains, bananas, beans, truck, and others, occupying more than 24,000 acres.

Tobacco is an important crop for small farmers who devote more than 2,000 acres to its harvest, after which they use the land for growing corn or beans. The average yield in tobacco is not among the highest, but it varies with the agricultural methods used. The region has more than 6,000 acres in coffee. Sugar cane is also grown, though its importance has diminished because of high costs of production and small yields. Today cane is planted mostly on the alluvial terrains and the more productive plains.

15. Corozal, Morovis, Naranjito, San Sebastián, and Trujillo Alto. (The town of Trujillo Alto is part of the San Juan metropolitan area.)

Pastures occupy about 87,000 acres, which is a larger area than is that of the cultivated lands. In the eastern part of the section, dairy farming has attained some importance. The section contains about 12,000 acres of woodlands.

The inland limestone belt borders on the north coastal plain with its strings of conical limestone haystacks, or mogotes, sloping markedly toward the east (Fig. 18.6). It contains sinkholes, funnel-shaped depressions which are locally known as "sumideros." The soil of the haystacks is stony and shallow, belonging to the Los Guineos-Catalina-Alonso group. The sinkholes have fairly deep, stony soils, and there are a few clayey loams. An inland plain, known as the Cibao lowlands, borders the chain of haystacks and sinkholes on the south. The soils of this part are generally of medium depth. South of the Cibao lowlands begins another chain of haystacks and sinkholes whose shallow soils have little agricultural value.

The lands in pasture in this section are estimated at 72,600 acres, of which some 3,000 are worked in rotation, indicating that cattle raising is not very important.

Forests occupy 60,000 acres, and there are some 32,000 acres in the brush which covers many of the limestone haystacks.

The Atalaya Hills. The western part of the Atalaya Hills was one of the least accessible regions of Puerto Rico until the recent construction of several main and secondary highways which cross it. With an area of 59,460 acres, the section consists of a series of Cretaceous, sedimentary hills which begin south of San Sebastián.

The climate is generally humid, as indicated by the vegetation. At San Sebastián the average annual precipitation is about 91.8 inches, and at Aguada it is about 83.9". The winter months are dry, as on the west coast.

The soils of the Atalaya Hills are poor, stony, shallow, and very clayey. Often the ridges are so steep that the soil is washed away quite rapidly. Soils belonging to the Múcara-Naranjito series are found in the western part; in the northeast the Sabana Seca-Lares group is the most important and in the southeast the Guineos-Catalina-Alonso group.

The principal crop of the section is sugar cane, covering about 14,000 acres in the middle Culebrinas Valley and on the low hillsides bordering the region in the west.

Tobacco is the second crop in the section. Mixed food crops, especially plantains and bananas, are produced on some 6,000 acres. The rest of the area consists of shrub covered hills and haystacks.

The region is fairly densely populated, despite its inaccessibility; the people tend to be employed in nearby towns and adjacent agricultural regions.

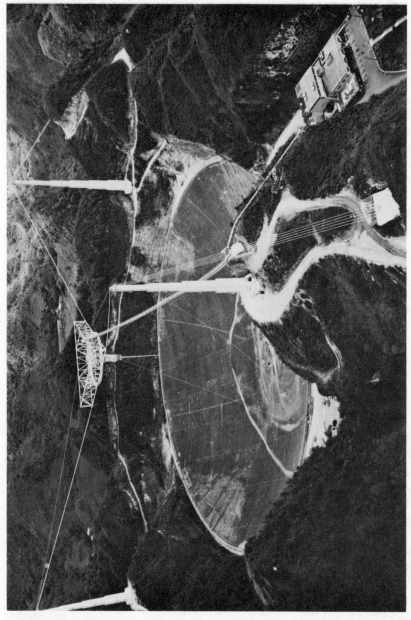

Figure 18.6. The Ionospheric Laboratory in the Inland Limestone Belt Subregion, Part of the Municipality of Arecibo.

The Humid East Central Mountains

The region of humid east central mountains has an area of 337,149 acres. Its southern border is marked by the Sierra de Cayey with its series of peaks which reach altitudes between 1,500 and 3,000 feet. North of the Sierra the topography is generally more gentle. The region contains various valleys like that carved out by the La Plata River, Puerto Rico's largest river, containing the town of Cayey where the river widens to create the valley.

The temperature of the region is ideal, with an annual average of 74° F above the altitude of 1,300 feet, where the "tierra templada" begins. The town of Aibonito, which is located on the remains of the St. John peneplane at some 2,000 feet, has an annual average of 71.4° F, and during the months from December to April it is less than 70° F. Because of the mild temperatures, towns like Aibonito and Barranquitas are popular summer resorts. Barranquitas has one of the best hotels outside of San Juan, a great attraction for Puerto Rican and foreign tourists.

The precipitation is less abundant than is that of the rainy west central mountains. The town of Cidra, whose rainfall is typical of almost the entire region, receives an annual average of 78.1 inches. Since there is no month during which precipitation averages less than three inches, the rainfall is fine for agriculture.

The principal soils of the region belong to the Múcara-Naranjito group, clayey or sandy in texture, derived largely from volcanic and sedimentary rocks. While those soils are excellent for tobacco farming, they are generally poor in minerals and subject to erosion.

The agriculture of the region is characterized by intensification and diversification. The principal tobacco region of Puerto Rico is found there, the crop once using more than 12,000 acres (Fig. 18.7). The industry has been integrated by the manufacture of cigars in Caguas, Cayey, and Comerío, where large factories produce machine-made cigars. Mixed food crops are raised on 48,000 acres, Important among them are plantains, bananas, yams, yautía, corn, sweet potatoes, and beans. Coffee, which is economically important in the region, is grown on about 11,000 acres, largely on the mountainous border of the Sierra Cayey. Sugar cane was formerly important, but its cultivation has ceased on the steep slopes. Today it is grown largely in valleys like that of Cayey, where mechanization is feasible.

The area in pastures exceeds that under cultivation by 168,000 acres. The fact that 63,000 of them are worked in rotation or improved gives an idea of the agricultural improvement of the region. The rest are largely natural pastures, often covered by brush.

Forests play an important role in the land use of the region. There are 38,000 acres in woodland, especially in the regions of steep slopes, plus some 10,000 acres in brush.

Figure 18.7. The Humid Eastern Mountains where Tobacco is Cultivated.

The Aibonito region has become the most important center for poultry farming in Puerto Rico. There is a modern slaughter house which processes chickens for distribution throughout the island.

In contrast to the western rainy mountains, the eastern humid mountains form one of the most densely populated regions in Puerto Rico. That fact is due in large measure to the more level topography, the many roads, access to the metropolitan area, and the importance of the tobacco industry. The region includes seven small urban centers[16] and the city of Cayey (21,372 inhabitants) with a total population of 57,790. The establishment of a University College in Cayey (as part of the University of Puerto Rico) with a four-year program is the most recent important development in the region, which will notably influence its future growth.

The Rainy West Central Mountains

The Rainy West Central Mountains with an area of 432,081 acres, are the second-largest region of Puerto Rico. Rectangular in shape, it extends

16. Aguas Buenas, Aibonito, Barranquitas, Cidra, Comerío, Las Piedras, and Orocovis.

from the center of the island to the vicinity of the west coast. Its mountains are generally higher than those in the east, and attain their maximum altitude in the Cerro de Punta (4,398 feet), south of the town of Jayuya. The terrain is generally rugged, with narrow valleys.

As explained in Chapter 5, copper mining operations are expected to start in the highland barrios of Utuado, Adjuntas and Lares. This $60 million a year industry should bring direct employment to 800 besides other economic and social advantages to a region that so far has benefited very little from "Operation Bootstrap."

The temperatures of the region, also classified as subtropical, are slightly lower than those in the east. At the El Guineo dam, for instance, at 3,000 feet altitude, the average annual temperature is 68.2° F, the lowest recorded in Puerto Rico.

Rainfall is abundant, with a general annual average of 95 inches, which diminishes in the deeper valleys. In the town of Adjuntas, for instance, it is 86 inches, while in the somewhat lower valley of Jayuya it is 58.7 inches. West of the region, the precipitation tends to diminish in winter, but it is more evenly distributed to the east. The rugged topography and abundant rainfall have been utilized for the construction of dams which, in addition to producing electric energy for the entire island, provide water when funnelled through the Cordillera Central, for irrigation and domestic as well as industrial use in the south coastal zone.

Figure 18.8. The Rainy Western Mountains and Their Coffee Plantations under Shade. In the background, the Haystacks, "Mogotes," bordering the Inland Limestone Belt.

Toro Negro, Garzas, and the Lajas Valley irrigation system are examples of intensive utilization of the geographic environment.

The soils of the region are deeper and more acid than those of the humid east central mountains. The Catalina-Los Guineos-Alonso group is present nearly everywhere. Near the towns of Utuado and Jayuya is a region with soils of the Múcara-Naranjito group, largely of the Utuado series derived from granitic materials where erosion is severe because the land is used primarily for farming, without the tree cover which is maintained for the cultivation of coffee.

The primitive, humid, subtropical vegetation is much more exuberant and better preserved than in the east, due partly to the higher rainfall and the form of land utilization.

The rainy west central mountains are Puerto Rico's greatest producers of coffee, with around 140,000 acres devoted to the crop (Fig. 18.8). The climate is generally favorable for coffee, except for the hurricanes which have caused large losses. However, with help from the government, the coffee region has largely rehabilitated itself. The coffee is produced under shade, and orange as well as banana trees provide provisional shade as well as producing good harvests of secondary fruits. Current government programs are aimed at retaining the coffee plantings on soils best suited for the crop.

Sugar cane is cultivated largely on the more level lands on the terraces and flood plains of the rivers. There were once several sugar mills in the region, but they disappeared because the planting of cane was curtailed due to low yields and high costs of production. Normally about 3,000 acres are planted to tobacco in the granitic soils of the Jayuya and Utuado regions. The cultivation of mixed food crops is very important, occupying more than 24,000 acres. Citron and bay oils are produced in the region in small quantities.

The area in pastures is estimated at 116,000 acres, of which 11,000 are planted in rotation with other crops and about 10,000 are improved. The remaining 95,000 acres are natural, shrub-covered pastures. Because of the topography of steep slopes, cattle culture is not important in the region. The forested areas are estimated as 88,000 acres, of which some 18,000 are in forest reserves such as those of Maricao, Prieto, and Toro Negro.

In comparison with the eastern region, the rural area is sparsely populated and the urban centers are small; the total population of the seven towns[17] is only 31,037 inhabitants. Part of the population of this region has migrated to the main cities of Puerto Rico in search of better living conditions. As a result all municipalities in the region lost population during 1960–70, according to the United States Census.

17. Adjuntas, Ciales, Jayuya, Las Marías, Maricao, Lares, and Utuado.

The Sierra de Luquillo

The most sparsely populated region of Puerto Rico is the Sierra de Luquillo, an area of monadnocks covered by exuberant vegetation. Climatically it is a part of the "tierra templada," with an average annual temperature 70.3° F, and below 70° F during five months.

It is the region of Puerto Rico with the most rain, with averages which range from 135.55 inches at La Perla, at an altitude of 1,200 feet, to about 180 inches at the meteorological station at La Mina at 2,000 feet. The Sierra de Luquillo is the most heavily forested region on the island, as well as a recreation center with great tourist activity (Fig. 18.9) The subtropical rain forest above 2,000 feet is the largest in Puerto Rico.

The soils of the region are typical of the rainy highlands and belong to the Guineos-Catalina-Alonso group. Steep slopes and many rocks inhibit agriculture. There are zones where the soil is classified as "rugged and stony," utilizable only for the forests which predominate in the region.

Timber resources constitute the major wealth. There are more than 31,000 acres in forests where timber-yielding trees like "tabonuco," "laurel," and other construction and cabinet woods are still standing, largely below altitudes of 3,000 feet. Above 3,000 feet the vegetation is natural, consisting largely of the sierra palm and tree ferns.[18] The importance of the region is not economic. It lies, rather, in its botanic and scientific interest, soil conservation, and recreational facilities for the population.

There are about 16,000 acres of pasture, of which more than 66 per cent are natural. The cultivated area is about 4,000 acres, of which some 800 produce coffee while the rest are planted largely to food crops. The rest of the land is covered by underbrush.

Vieques, Culebra and La Mona

The islands of Vieques and Culebra in the east (where, physiographically, the Lesser Antilles begin), and La Mona in the west, are parts of Puerto Rico in terms of cultural and political traditions, though differing widely from the main island in their physical and economic features. Nevertheless, the three have many geographic traits in common. All three are small, with similar topographies, relatively arid, and sparsely populated. Their predominant topographic forms are relatively low hills. Low elevations and reduced areas in a trade wind climate naturally result in very light rainfall, from 40 to 50 inches in all three cases.

18. The botanic name of the sierra palm is *Euterpe Globosa;* the giant fern belongs to the genera *Cyathea,* of the *Cya Theaceae* family, of which several species exist in the Sierra de Luquillo.

Figure 18.9. Natural Vegetation in the Sierra de Luquillo.

The largest and most important of the three islands is Vieques, with an area of 34,016 acres. Although its physical environment resembles that of the semiarid southern foothills, it is an agricultural community of 7,817 inhabitants who try to live off the land. Its population has gradually diminished and in recent decades it has lost more than 3,000 inhabitants.

The average annual rainfall of Vieques is 46.74 inches, diminishing slightly toward the east. The soils belong to the Descalabrado-Guayama series; they are rich in plant food and are clayey or loamey in texture. Physical conditions, especially the scant precipitation, restrict the island's agricultural importance. Moreover, about 71 per cent of the area of Vieques is occupied by the United States Navy and therefore can not be farmed. The land that can be farmed without restrictions has been reduced to 10,000 acres. The west central part of Vieques produces sugar cane which is carried to Puerto Rico in barges to be processed in the mills of Fajardo and Juncos.

The magnificent beaches of white sand in the southern part of Vieques offer possibilities for the development of the tourist industry. The construction of a modern hotel in the south has been comtemplated, to convert Vieques into one of the major tourist attractions of Puerto Rico.

The island of Culebra, with 6,741 acres, 20 miles east of Fajardo, is the most arid of the three which constitute the geographic region known as "Outlying Puerto Rico." It had 726 inhabitants in 1970. Precipitation is characterized by a rainy spring and fall and a dry winter. The vegetation is similar to that of Vieques and there are some clean natural pastures for cattle. The fact that the United States Navy uses parts of the island for maneuvers and target practice limits possibilities for agricultural or tourist development.

The island of La Mona is a limestone plateau of 13,792 acres, located some 50 miles southwest of Mayagüez, between Puerto Rico and the Dominican Republic. At present, the island is uninhabited. Because of its aridity and the extreme porosity of its soils, La Mona's vegetation is even poorer and scarcer than is that of southwestern Puerto Rico. Cacti and other thorny shrubs common to dry climates abound. There are relatively fine opportunities for fishing as well as hunting, such as for birds, goats and wild pigs. Because of its beauty and proximity to Puerto Rico, La Mona could be developed as a fine recreational and tourist center.

Appendices

Appendix A

Population by municipalities, actual and projected, 1940, 1950, 1960, 1970, 1975

Municipality	1940	1950	1960	1970	1975
Adjuntas	22,556	22,424	19,658	18,584	21,700
Aguada	17,923	20,743	23,234	25,166	29,100
Aguadilla	34,956	44,357	47,864	51,332	54,300
Aguas Buenas	14,671	15,565	17,034	18,702	19,600
Aibonito	16,819	18,191	18,360	19,834	20,900
Añasco	15,701	17,235	17,200	19,296	21,500
Arecibo	69,192	75,361	69,879	73,283	95,500
Arroyo	10,746	12,936	13,315	13,093	16,300
Barceloneta	18,545	19,897	19,334	20,628	22,300
Barranquitas	17,096	17,605	18,978	19,853	20,500
Bayamón	37,190	48,000	72,221	154,440	175,500
Cabo Rojo	28,586	29,546	24,868	25,569	30,500
Caguas	53,356	60,132	65,098	94,959	130,000
Camuy	18,922	20,886	19,739	19,796	21,600
Carolina	24,046	29,224	40,923	107,988	163,500
Cataño	9,719	19,865	25,208	26,056	30,700
Cayey	31,391	36,656	38,061	38,161	49,600
Ceiba	7,021	9,199	9,075	10,080	9,900
Ciales	22,906	19,464	18,106	15,422	19,600
Cidra	20,392	20,491	21,891	24,039	24,200
Coamo	22,772	26,485	26,082	26,179	31,500
Comerío	18,539	17,966	18,583	18,738	22,600
Corozal	20,458	23,087	23,570	24,194	26,300
Culebra	860	887	573	726	800
Dorado	9,481	11,749	13,460	17,264	24,900
Fajardo	20,405	22,116	18,321	22,856	26,400

Appendix A (continued)

Municipality	1940	1950	1960	1970	1975
Guánica	12,685	15,630	13,767	14,884	16,600
Guayama	30,511	32,807	33,678	36,159	50,900
Guayanilla	15,577	17,402	17,396	18,054	19,200
Guaynabo	18,319	29,120	39,718	65,557	80,000
Gurabo	15,870	16,395	16,603	18,219	20,700
Hatillo	18,322	20,877	20,238	21,549	22,000
Hormigueros	6,098	6,916	7,153	10,803	9,800
Humacao	29,833	34,853	33,381	35,655	41,900
Isabela	25,842	29,113	28,754	30,201	31,400
Jayuya	14,589	15,113	14,633	13,603	16,300
Juana Díaz	23,396	27,697	30,043	36,041	38,700
Juncos	19,464	21,654	21,496	21,762	24,500
Lajas	14,736	16,326	15,375	16,437	18,300
Lares	29,914	29,951	26,922	24,896	30,400
Las Marías	9,626	10,807	9,237	7,904	10,500
Las Piedras	15,389	16,208	17,047	18,048	19,100
Loíza	22,145	24,755	28,131	38,351	40,100
Luquillo	8,851	9,967	8,582	10,270	12,900
Manatí	29,366	30,449	29,354	30,274	38,900
Maricao	7,724	7,403	6,990	5,936	8,800
Maunabo	10,792	11,758	10,785	10,817	11,500
Mayagüez	76,487	87,307	83,850	86,267	127,300
Moca	19,716	21,614	21,990	22,266	24,700
Morovis	19,167	19,291	18,094	19,219	19,400
Naguabo	19,180	21,019	17,195	17,862	18,700
Naranjito	13,954	15,927	17,319	19,784	22,300
Orocovis	19,770	21,181	20,362	20,321	21,700
Patillas	17,319	18,851	17,106	17,819	18,600
Peñuelas	14,789	14,931	14,887	15,915	19,800
Ponce	105,116	126,810	145,586	156,498	241,000
Quebradillas	11,494	13,712	13,075	15,470	17,500
Rincón	9,256	9,888	8,706	9,350	10,600
Río Grande	16,116	16,651	17,233	21,978	28,400
Río Piedras	68,290	143,989	—	—	—
Sabana Grande	14,146	16,097	15,910	16,301	18,700
Salinas	19,400	23,435	23,133	21,816	28,900
San Germán	26,473	29,553	27,667	27,769	34,900
San Juan	169,247	224,767	—	—	—
San Lorenzo	26,627	29,248	27,950	27,598	30,600
San Sebastián	30,266	35,376	33,451	29,892	38,900
Santa Isabel	11,468	13,478	14,542	16,023	18,300
Toa Alta	13,371	14,155	15,711	18,537	19,800
Toa Baja	11,410	15,761	19,698	46,938	47,900
Trujillo Alto	11,726	13,605	18,251	30,351	32,500
Utuado	42,531	46,625	40,449	35,304	43,700

Appendix A (*continued*)

Municipality	1940	1950	1960	1970	1975
Vega Alta	14,329	16,521	17,603	22,857	18,900
Vega Baja	23,105	28,925	30,189	35,237	37,300
Vieques	10,362	9,228	7,210	7,817	7,800
Villalba	12,871	14,972	16,239	18,627	17,400
Yabucoa	27,438	28,810	29,782	29,947	34,400
Yauco	30,533	33,708	34,780	35,090	37,000
San Juan-Río Piedras[1]	–	–	451,658	455,421	578,300
Total	1,869,255	2,210,703	2,349,544	2,689,932	3,279,638
San Juan-Metropolitan Zone[2]	338,537	508,570	648,688	870,091	1,060,500

Source: Population Census, 1940, 1950, 1960, and 1970 (preliminary). Estimates for 1975, Bureau of Economic and Social Analysis, Puerto Rico Planning Board.
1. The Municipality and City of Río Piedras became part of San Juan in 1951.
2. For the years 1960 and 1975, the San Juan Metropolitan Zone includes Bayamón, Carolina, Cataño, Guaynabo, San Juan, and Trujillo Alto. For 1970 Levittown Village in Toa Baja with 30,278 has been added.

Appendix B

Net income by industrial origin, actual and projected, as of June 30, 1940, 1950, 1960, 1965, 1970, and 1975
(*millions of dollars*)

Industry	1940	1950	1960	1965	1970	1975
Agriculture	$ 71	$149	$ 180	$ 190	$ 184	$ 270
Manufacturing	27	89	289	557	953	2,886
Construction by contract	3	27	87	195	321	700
Trade	27	102	237	415	674	829
Government, state and Municipal	19	70	175	307	618	899
Mining	–	°	2	7	11	°
Others[1]	78	176	385	643	1,060	–
Total	$225	$614	$1,355	$2,314	$3,821	$6,484

Source: Bureau of Economic and Social Analysis, Puerto Rico Planning Board.
°Included in others.
1. Includes transportation and other public utilities, finances, securities, and real estate, etc.

Appendix C

Employment by industries, 1940, 1950, 1960, 1965, 1970

Industry	1940 thousands	%	1950 thousands	%	1960 thousands	%	1965 thousands	%	1970 thousands	%
All industries	536.0	100.0	595.8	100.0	543.0	100.0	680.0	100.0	738.0	100.0
Agriculture	230.0	42.9	216.3	36.3	124.0	22.9	119.0	17.5	74.0	10.0
Manufacturing	101.0	18.8	105.9	17.8	91.0	16.8	126.0	18.5	142.0	19.2
Home needlework	45.0	8.4	50.8	8.5	10.0	1.8	7.0	1.0	1.0	0.1
Others	56.0	10.4	55.1	9.3	81.0	15.0	119.0	17.5	141.0	19.1
Construction	16.0	3.0	27.4	4.6	45.0	8.3	63.0	9.3	83.0	11.2
Trade	54.0	10.1	89.7	15.0	97.0	17.9	123.0	18.1	138.0	18.7
Government[1]	12.6	2.4	44.6	7.5	62.0	11.4	87.0	12.8	113.0	15.3
Others[2]	122.4	22.8	111.9	18.8	123.0	22.7	162.0	23.8	188.0	25.6

Source: Bureau of Economic and Social Analysis, Puerto Rico Planning Board and Bureau of Labor Statistics, Department of Labor, San Juan.
  1. Includes the Commonwealth and Federal Governments.
  2. Includes mining, finances, insurance and real estate, transportation, communications and public utilities, and services.

Appendix D

Number of establishments, workers, and wages paid in manufacturing, 1909, 1919, 1939, 1949, 1958, 1963, 1967

Year	Establishments	Workers	Wages (*in thousands*)
1909	939	15,582	$ 3,639
1919	619	15,985	6,766
1939	798	23,484	9,220
1949	1,998	47,735	35,736
1958	2,042	60,047	93,320
1963	2,243	83,940	178,897
1967	2,367	103,952	279,522

Source: U.S. Department of Commerce, *Puerto Rico: Census of Manufacturers, 1939, 1958, 1963, and 1967* (Washington, D.C.: U.S. Government Printing Office).
Note: Coffee roasting and tobacco stemming and redrying included since 1949.

Appendix E

Number of workers and wages paid in the sugar and tobacco industries, 1909, 1919, 1939, 1949, 1958, 1963, 1967

Year	Sugar		Tobacco[1]	
	workers	*wages*	*workers*	*wages*
1909	5,062	$ 1,227,585	7,025	$ 1,479,567
1919	7,490	2,832,022	5,098	2,267,204
1939	9,658	4,741,126	445	123,615
1949	12,900	13,253,674	1,098	442,578
1958	6,136	11,833,000	1,571	2,117,000
1963	5,752	14,067,118	1,957	3,804,988
1967	4,516	11,737,000	6,702	15,869,000

Source: U.S. Department of Commerce, *Puerto Rico: Census of Manufacturers 1939, 1958, 1963, 1967* (Washington, D.C.: U.S. Government Printing Office).
1. Includes only the manufacture of cigars and chewing tobacco.

Appendix F

Value of exports and imports, as of June 30, 1940–1970
(millions of dollars)

Year	Exports	Imports
1940	$ 92	$ 107
1941	88	128
1942	106	152
1943	92	84
1944	148	129
1945	118	141
1946	161	244
1947	179	311
1948	192	362
1949	204	351
1950	235	350
1951	271	438
1952	257	448
1953	319	496
1954	348	525
1955	353	575
1956	406	633
1957	446	711
1958	467	728
1959	503	807
1960	622	915
1961	687	927
1962	757	1,092
1963	829	1,168
1964	919	1,363
1965	974	1,514.6
1966	1,155	1,659.4
1967	1,321	1,798.9
1968	1,449	1,969
1969	1,606	2,263
1970	1,719	2,513

Source: Puerto Rico Planning Board.

Note: The exports and imports of 1960–70 include the Virgin Islands. They do not include shipments made by the Food Administration of the United States Government.

Appendix G

Unadjusted value of external trade, as of June 30, 1950, 1960, 1966, 1970
(millions of dollars)

Item	1950	1960	1966	1970
Imports, Total	$345	$915	$1,659	$2,556
From the United States	318	761	1,357	1,964
From foreign countries	27	154	302	592
Exports, Total	235	622	1,155	1,719
To the United States	210	594	1,055	1,534
To foreign countries	25	28	100	196
Imbalance	110	293	540	837
United States	108	167	302	430
Foreign countries	2	126	202	396

Source: Bureau of Economic and Social Analysis, Puerto Rico Planning Board.
Note: Figures for 1950 exclude the Virgin Islands.

Appendix H

Composition and value of exports, as of June 30, 1950 and 1970
(millions of dollars)

Nature	1950	1970	Increase
Traditional products (sugar, rum, etc.)	$202	$ 430	$ 228
New manufactured products	33	1,289	1,256
Clothing and textiles	21	396	375
Machinery, electric appliances, and Metallurgic products	1	142	141
Footwear and similar goods	1	82	81
Cigars and tobacco	3	95	92
Gasoline, chemical products and other derivatives of nonmetallic minerals, petroleum and petroleum derivatives	3	361	358
Other manufactured products and income	4	213	209
Total Exports	$235	$1,719	$1,484

Source: Bureau of Economic and Social Analysis, Puerto Rico Planning Board.
Note: Data for 1950 exclude the Virgin Islands.

Appendix I

Composition and value of imported goods, as of June 30, 1950 and 1970
(millions of dollars)

Nature	1950	1970	Increase
Consumer goods	$184	$ 848	$ 664
Durable	23	268	245
Automobiles	6	103	97
Electric appliances	6	59	53
Other durable goods	11	106	95
Nondurable	162	581	419
Foodstuffs	89	307	218
Alcoholic beverages and tobacco	21	38	17
Other nondurable goods	51	236	185
Capital goods	23	465	442
Raw materials and intermediate products	144	1,200	1,056
Grand Total	$350	$2,513	$2,163

Source: Bureau of Economic and Social Analysis, Puerto Rico Planning Board.
Note: Figures for 1950 exclude purchases from the Virgin Islands.

Appendix J

Balance of payments, fiscal 1970
(millions of dollars)

Nature		
Commerce in goods		
Imports	$−2,513	
Exports	1,747	
Balance of commerce in goods		−766
Trade in services		
Expenditures	−1,110	
Income	640	
Balance of trade in services		−470
Balance of trade in goods and services		−1,236
Net unilateral payments		
Private remittances	66	
U.S. government to Commonwealth government	230	
U.S. and state governments to individuals and private corporations	29	
Receipts in unilateral payments		325
Current balance (largely investments from the outside)		−911

Source: Bureau of Economic and Social Analysis, Puerto Rico Planning Board.

Appendix K

Farm value of agricultural products by sectors actual and projected,
1960, 1965, 1967, 1970
(millions of dollars)

Products	1960	1965	1967	1970
Cane and molasses	$ 90	$ 86	$ 85	$ 52
Coffee and tobacco	29	36	23	17
Cattle products	82	105	115	132
Other products plus subsidies	37	46	45	70
Total	$238	$273	$268	$271

Source: Bureau of Economic and Social Analysis, Puerto Rico Planning Board.

Appendix L

Production of sugar (96°), 1900–1970
(tons)

Year	Quantity	Year	Quantity
1900	81,526	1934	1,113,697
1901	103,152	1935	780,741
1902	100,576	1936	926,392
1903	139,096	1937	996,345
1904	151,088	1938	1,077,128
1905	214,480	1939	851,969
1906	206,864	1940	1,018,802
1907	230,095	1941	932,821
1908	277,093	1942	1,147,677
1909	346,786	1943	1,037,935
1910	349,840	1944	723,360
1911	371,070	1945	963,747
1912	398,004	1946	909,087
1913	351,666	1947	1,087,879
1914	346,490	1948	1,108,261
1915	345,490	1949	1,277,482
1916	483,589	1950	1,286,435
1917	503,081	1951	1,227,622
1918	453,794	1952	1,359,841
1919	406,002	1953	1,170,440
1920	485,071	1954	1,190,382
1921	489,818	1955	1,152,641
1922	408,325	1956	1,137,799
1923	379,172	1957	978,522

Appendix L (continued)

Year	Quantity	Year	Quantity
1924	447,587	1958	922,938
1925	660,512	1959	1,072,673
1926	606,464	1960	1,006,385
1927	630,203	1961	1,095,751
1928	748,691	1962	996,626
1929	586,580	1963	978,307
1930	872,327	1964	978,128
1931	783,796	1965	886,676
1932	992,433	1966	873,408
1933	834,310	1967	808,119
		1968	637,288
		1969	477,858
		1970	455,000

Source: Department of Agriculture of Puerto Rico.

Appendix M

Production of coffee, 1897–1971
(in hundredweights)

Year	Quantity	Year	Quantity
1897	117,837	1942	307,059
1898–1909	°	1943	169,590
1910	527,177	1944	222,317
1911–1919	°	1945	300,947
1920	532,093	1946	150,815
1921	441,942	1947	295,800
1922	383,679	1948	237,619
1923	253,710	1949	243,800
1924	289,083	1950	224,500
1925	341,772	1951	172,000
1926	363,346	1952	300,097
1927	391,247	1953	174,178
1928	323,933	1954	315,000
1929	184,466	1955	193,000
1930	53,000	1956	309,000
1931	60,000	1957	155,000
1932	100,902	1958	350,000
1933	113,811	1959	247,151
1934	90,000	1960	345,000
1935	80,000	1961	260,000
1936	258,555	1962	340,000

Appendix M (continued)

Year	Quantity	Year	Quantity
1937	205,370	1963	375,000
1938	166,392	1964	305,000
1939	189,491	1965	375,000
1940	326,520	1966	300,000
1941	162,314	1967	284,000
		1968	325,000
		1969	260,000
		1970	225,000
		1971	325,000

Source: Department of Agriculture of Puerto Rico.
*No data available.

Appendix N

Production of tobacco, 1910–1971
(in hundredweights)

Year	Quantity	Year	Quantity
1910	108,280	1939	138,250
1911	*	1940	281,000
1912	128,000	1941	302,000
1913	150,000	1942	318,000
1914	130,000	1943	94,000
1915	120,000	1944	285,000
1916	*	1945	372,650
1917	254,090	1946	320,000
1918	257,720	1947	230,000
1919	193,630	1948	254,000
1920	253,390	1949	270,000
1921	250,000	1950	260,000
1922	225,000	1951	255,000
1923	260,000	1952	281,000
1924	250,000	1953	343,000
1925	230,000	1954	341,000
1926	360,000	1955	340,000
1927	500,000	1956	300,000
1928	270,000	1957	240,000
1929	280,000	1958	267,000
1930	325,000	1959	256,000
1931	273,000	1960	281,000
1932	60,000	1961	255,000

Appendix N (continued)

Year	Quantity	Year	Quantity
1933	167,830	1962	307,000
1934	250,000	1963	343,000
1935	225,000	1964	319,125
1936	260,000	1965	379,000
1937	349,830	1966	165,400
1938	440,690	1967	123,000
		1968	112,000
		1969	80,000
		1970	63,000
		1971	55,000

Source: Department of Agriculture of Puerto Rico.
*No data available.

Appendix O

*Gross internal investment of fixed capital, actual and projected, as of June 30,
1950, 1960, 1965, 1967, 1970, 1975
(millions of dollars)*

Nature	Years					Projection
	1950	1960	1965	1967	1970	1975
Plant, machinery and equipment	$ 67	$216	$440	$541	$ 912	$1,564
Homes	25	88	212	269	336	664
Public Works: road, schools, etc.	19	44	70	74	156	291
Total	$111	$348	$722	$884	$1,404	$2,519

Source: Bureau of Economic and Social Analysis, Puerto Rico Planning Board.

Appendix P

Gross product, total net income, per capita income, actual and projected,
as of June 30, 1940–1975
(millions of dollars)

Item	Years						Projection
	1940	1950	1960	1965	1970	1971	1975
Gross product	$287	$755	$1,645	$2,721	$4,607	$5,083	$7,730
Net income	225	614	1,362	2,289	3,821	4,228	6,484
Net per capita income (in current dollars)	121	279	582	884	1,427	1,556	2,218

Source: Bureau of Economic and Social Analysis, Puerto Rico Planning Board.

Appendix Q

Number of factories promoted, average employment in factories promoted and
not promoted by the economic development administration, actual and projected,
fiscal 1950, 1960, 1965, 1970, 1975

Items	Actual				Projection
	1950	1960	1965	1970	1975
Promoted factories in operation June 30	83	604	1,005	1,733	2,000
Average employment (thousands)					
in promoted factories	4.9	44.2	74.4	102.4	160.0
in non-promoted factories	.0	47.0	51.6	31.9	47.0

Sources: Bureau of Economic and Social Analysis, Puerto Rico Planning Board and Puerto Rico Industrial Development Company.

Appendix R

Distribution of families by levels of income, actual and projected, 1947, 1950,
1960, 1965, 1975

Level of Incomes	Actual				Projection
	1947	1950	1960	1965	1975
	%	%	%	%	%
$2,000 or less	89.0	66.5	54.8	44	25
$2,000–$5,000	8.8	28.0	32.5	39	44
$5,000 or more	2.2	5.5	12.7	17	31
Total	100.0	100.0	100.0	100.0	100.0

Source: Bureau of Economic and Social Analysis, Puerto Rico Planning Board.

Appendix S

The geographic regions and the population of their cities and towns, 1970

Geographic Regions	Urban Population	Per Cent of Total
Total	1,536,399	100.00
I Northern coastal lowlands	916,691	59.67
A. Subhumid limestone section	19,370	
1. Camuy	3,882	
2. Hatillo	2,791	
3. Isabela	9,884	
4. Quebradillas	2,813	
B. Humid alluvial section	897,321	
1. Arecibo	35,420	
2. Barceloneta	4,486	
3. Bayamón	146,363	
4. Carolina	94,635	
5. Cataño	26,056	
6. Dorado	4,361	
7. Guaynabo	53,785	
8. Canóvanas and Loíza Aldea	6,069	
9. Luquillo	2,412	
10. Manatí	13,433	
11. Río Grande	4,125	
12. San Juan	444,952	
13. Toa Alta	3,154	
14. Toa Baja and Levittown	32,310	
15. Vega Alta	8,752	
16. Vega Baja	17,014	
II Humid eastern coastal valleys	43,631	2.84
1. Ceiba	2,146	
2. Fajardo	18,127	
3. Humacao	12,332	
4. Maunabo	1,819	
5. Naguabo	4,136	
6. Yabucoa	5,071	
III The Caguas Valley	84,672	5.51
1. Caguas	62,807	
2. Gurabo	6,255	
3. Juncos	7,911	
4. San Lorenzo	7,699	

Appendix S (*continued*)

Geographic Regions	Urban Population	Per Cent of Total
IV Wet-dry western coastal valleys		133,804	8.71
1. Aguada	4,512	
2. Aguadilla	21,087	
3. Añasco	4,402	
4. Cabo Rojo	7,158	
5. Hormigueros	6,428	
6. Mayagüez	69,485	
7. Moca	2,323	
8. Rincón	1,534	
9. Sabana Grande	5,556	
10. San Germán	11,319	
V Dry southern coastal lowlands		213,090	13.87
A. Ponce-Patillas alluvial plain	180,013	
1. Arroyo	5,410	
2. Guayama (includes the villages of Jobos and Puerto Jobos)	23,785	
3. Juana Díaz	8,729	
4. Patillas	2,518	
5. Ponce	125,926	
6. Salinas (includes the villages of Coquí, Central Aguirre and San Felipe)	9,102	
7. Santa Isabel	4,543	
B. The southwest of Puerto Rico	33,077	
1. Guánica	8,538	
2. Guayanilla	5,156	
3. Lajas	3,364	
4. Peñuelas	3,139	
5. Yauco	12,880	
VI Semiarid southern foothills		16,042	1.04
1. Coamo	11,957	
2. Villalba	4,085	
VII Humid northern foothills		36,531	2.38
1. Corozal	5,085	
2. Morovis	2,905	
3. Naranjito	3,285	
4. San Sebastián	7,039	
5. Trujillo Alto	18,217	

Appendix S (continued)

Geographic Regions	Urban Population	Per Cent of Total
VIII Humid east central mountains		57,790	3.76
1. Aguas Buenas	3,432		
2. Aibonito	7,564		
3. Barranquitas	4,399		
4. Cayey	21,372		
5. Cidra	6,348		
6. Comerío	6,267		
7. Las Piedras	4,625		
8. Orocovis	3,783		
IX Rainy west central mountains		31,037	2.02
1. Adjuntas	5,309		
2. Ciales	3,994		
3. Jayuya	3,800		
4. Lares	4,505		
5. Las Marías	475		
6. Maricao	1,479		
7. Utuado	11,475		
X Outlying Puerto Rico		3,111	0.20
1. Vieques (Isabel Segunda)	2,385		
2. Culebra Municipality	726		

Source: 1970 Census of Population (Preliminary Report), August 1970.

Note: The cities and towns that lie near borders are included in the region to whose economy they are most closely related. The Sierra de Luquillo (Region X) has no towns or cities.

Appendix T

Measures and their equivalents

1 cuerda	42,300 square feet
	3,929.798 square meters
	0.9712 acre
	0.3930 hectare
658.944 cuerdas	1 square mile
1 acre	43,560 square feet
	4,840 square yards
	0.404685 hectare
	1.0297 cuerdas
	4,046.8564 square meters
640 acres	1 square mile

Appendix T (*continued*)

1 hectare	107,639.1 square feet
	2.4710 acres
	10,000 square meters
258.999 hectares	1 square mile
1 mile	5,280 feet
	1,609.344 meters
	1,760 yards
	1.6093 kilometers
1 square mile	2.59 square kilometers
	258.999 hectares
	640 acres
1 kilometer	3,280.8 feet
	0.6214 mile
1 square kilometer	0.3861 square miles
1 foot	0.3048 meters
1 square foot	0.0929 square meter
1 meter	3.2808 feet
	1.0936 yards
1,000 meters	1 kilometer
1 square meter	10.76391 square feet
	1.19599 square yards
1 yard	0.9144 meter
	3 feet
1 square yard	0.8361 square meter
8 fluid ounces	½ pint
16 fluid ounces	½ quart
32 fluid ounces	¼ gallon
1 gallon	3.7853 liters
	0.833 English gallons
16 ounces	1 pound
100 pounds	1 quintal

Appendix T (continued)

2,000 pounds	1 short or net ton
2,240 pounds	1 long or gross ton
1 fathom (braza)	1.733 meters
Conversion of temperatures	
Degrees Centigrade	$\dfrac{(\text{Degrees Fahrenheit} - 32)\,5}{9}$
Degrees Fahrenheit	$\dfrac{\text{Degrees Centigrade} \times 9 - 32}{5}$

Bibliography

Puerto Rico and the Antilles

Abbad Lasierra, Fray I. *Historia geográfica, civil y natural de San Juan Bautista de Puerto Rico*. Annotated by José Julián Acosta. San Juan: Imprenta Acosta, 1866.

Asenjo, C. *Geografía de la Isla de Puerto Rico*. San Juan: Cantero Fernández & Co., Inc., 1927.

Augelli, J. P. *Caribbean Lands*. Grand Rapids, Mich.: The Fideler Co., 1965.

Brameld, T., and H. Burghard. *The Remaking of a Culture; Life and Education in Puerto Rico*. New York: Harper, 1959.

Capó, C. *The Island of Puerto Rico: A Compilation of Facts and Some Comments on the Geography of the Country*. San Juan: The Globe Publishing Co., 1925.

Clark, S. A. *All the Best in Bermuda, the Bahamas, Puerto Rico and the Virgin Islands*. New York: Dodd, Mead & Co., 1965.

————. *All the Best in the Caribbean*. (Including Puerto Rico and the Virgin Islands.) New York: Dodd, Mead & Co., 1965.

Fernández García, E. *El Libro de Puerto Rico*. San Juan: El Libro Azul Publishing Co., 1923.

Gandía Córdoba, R. "Datos históricos del estudio de la geografía en Puerto Rico." *Revista de obras publicas de Puerto Rico* 5 (January 1928); pp. 1485–87.

Gaztambide Vega, F. *La Isla de Puerto Rico*. New York: Rand McNally, 1941.

González Ruíz, R. *Geografía elemental de Puerto Rico con nociones de geografía astronómica, física, social y política*. San Juan: Editorial Imprenta Venezuela, 1941. Translated to English in 1943.

Gruber, R. *Puerto Rico: Island of Promise*. New York: Hill and Wang, 1960.

Hanson, E. P. *Puerto Rico, Land of Wonders*. New York: Knopf, 1960.

————. *Transformation: The Story of Modern Puerto Rico*. New York: Simon and Schuster, 1955.

————. "Tropical Adaptation: a Revaluation." Paper presented at the annual meeting of the Association of American Geographers, March 1951.

Meyerhoff, H. A., and R. Picó. "Comparisons and Contrasts in Puerto Rico and the Dominican Republic." Pp. 207–8. Reproduced from Proceedings of the Eighth American Scientific Congress, Washington, D.C., May, 1940.

Miller, P. G. *Dodge's Geography of Puerto Rico*. Chicago: Rand McNally, 1921.

Nones, A. "La Isla de Puerto Rico." *Historical and Geographical Description Presented to the Society of Geography of Lisbon in 1899*. 3rd ed. San Juan: Imprenta Venezuela, 1927.

Page, H. *Puerto Rico: The Quiet Revolution*. New York: Viking Press, 1963.

Picó, R. "Comparisons and Contrasts in the Greater Antilles." In *Hispanic American Studies*. No. 2, pp. 132–42. Coral Gables, Fla.: University of Miami, January 1941.

————. *Puerto Rico* (Mapa físico-político). Escala 1:125,000. New York: Rand McNally, 1962.

————. *Puerto Rico*. Reprint of *Las Antillas de la Geografía Universal*. Vol. 19, pp. 352–420. Barcelona: Editores Montaner y Simón, S. A., 1958.

Picó, R., and W. Haas. "Puerto Rico." In *The American Empire: A Study of the Outlying Territories of the United States*. Edited by W. Haas, pp. 29–91. Chicago: The University of Chicago Press, 1940.

Puerto Rico, Departamento de Estado, Oficina de Asuntos Externos. *Puerto Rico, desarrollo político, social y económico*, 2nd ed. San Juan, 1965.

Puerto Rico, Departamento de Instrucción. *Puerto Rico y su historia, lecturas escogidas*. San Juan: Department of Education, Curriculum Division, 1964.

Ramos de Santiago, C. *El Gobierno de Puerto Rico*. Río Piedras: University of Puerto Rico Press, 1965.

Whitbeck, F. *Porto Rico*. Frye-Atwood Geographical Series, Supplement to the New Geography, book two. Boston: Ginn & Co., 1925.

————. *The Pupil's workbook in the geography of Porto Rico*. Boston: Ginn & Co., 1923.

Geographic Environment

Buitrago de Santiago, Z. *Caguas*. San Juan: Department of Education Press, 1965.

————. *Las Marías*. San Juan: Department of Education Press, 1965.

Esteves, V. R., and V. Guzmán Soto. *El Problema del desempleo en Puerto Rico*. San Juan: Government Development Bank for Puerto Rico, January 1963.

Hernández, M. "Economic Classification of the Lands in Southwestern Puerto Rico." Mimeographed. Río Piedras: University of Puerto Rico Agricultural Experiment Station, January 1948.

Jones, Clarence F., and Rafael Picó, eds. *Symposium on the Geography of Puerto Rico*. Río Piedras: University of Puerto Press, 1955.

Picó, R. "El Ambiente geográfico y los problemas del riego de Isabela." In *Revista de Agricultura, industria y comercio de Puerto Rico* 27, no. 1 (May 1936).

————. "The Commonwealth of Puerto Rico." In *Focus* 14, no. 2 (October 1963). The American Geographical Society, New York.

————. "Evaluación de nuestros recursos naturales." Lecture delivered at the Seventh Social Work Convention in Puerto Rico, May 3, 1952. Mimeographed.

————. "The Geographic Foundation of Life in Puerto Rico." In *Hispanic American Studies*. No. 2, pp. 143–51. Coral Gables, Fla.: University of Miami Press, January 1941.

————. *Geografía de Puerto Rico.* Parte I, Geografía Física. Río Piedras: University of Puerto Rico Press, 1954.

————. *Geografía de Puerto Rico.* Parte II, Geografía Económica. Río Piedras: University of Puerto Rico Press, 1964.

————. "Studies in the Economic Geography of Puerto Rico." *The University of Puerto Rico Bulletin,* ser. 8, no. 1. Río Piedras: University of Puerto Rico, 1937.

Puerto Rico, Departament de Instrucción. *Puerto Rico. Su ambiente Geografico.* Ser. 4. San Juan: Department of Education Press, 1955.

Torres Zayas, J. A. "Social Change in a Puerto Rican Rural Community: a Study on Sociological Ambivalence." Mimeographed. Río Piedras: University of Puerto Rico Social Science Research Center, 1965.

Whitbeck, F. "Geographical Influences in the Development of Puerto Rico." In Albert L. Sieman, *Geography of Middle America.* Pp. 186–91. Seattle: The Washington Book Store. Also in *The Journal of Geography,* 1926.

Relief

Bonnet, J. A. "Geología del valle de Lajas." *Revista de Agricultura de Puerto Rico* 38, no. 1 (January–April 1947), pp. 35–38.

Fettke, C. R. "The Geology of the Humacao District, Puerto Rico." In New York Academy of Sciences, *Scientific Survey of Porto Rico and the Virgin Islands.* Vol. 2, pt. 2. New York, 1931.

Galloway, J. J. and C. E. Hemingway. "The Tertiary Foraminifera of Porto Rico." In New York Academy of Sciences, *Scientific Survey of Porto Rico and the Virgin Islands.* Vol. 3, pt. 4, pp. 275–1491. New York, 1941.

Gandía Córdova, R. "Los temblores de tierra del 11 de octubre de 1918." *Revista del Colegio de Ingenieros de Puerto Rico* 7, no. 4 (October–December 1946), pp. 80–83.

Hodge, E. T. "Geology of the Coamo-Guayama District." In New York Academy of Sciences, *Scientific Survey of Porto Rico and the Virgin Islands.* Vol 1, pt. 2. New York, 1920.

Holmes, A. "A Revised Geological Time Scale." Pt. 3, p. 204. Edinburgh Geological Society Transactions 17 (1960).

Hubbard, B. "The Geology of the Lares District, Porto Rico." In New York Academy of Sciences, *Scientific Survey of Porto Rico and the Virgin Islands.* Vol. 2, pt. 1. New York, 1923.

Lobeck, A. K. "The Physiography of Porto Rico." In New York Academy of Sciences, *Scientific Survey of Porto Rico and the Virgin Islands.* Vol. 1, pt. 4. New York, 1922.

Martínez Alvarez, A. "Datos históricos y científicos relacionados con la geofísica de Las Antillas." *Revista de obras publicas de Puerto Rico* 12, no. 6 (June 1935).

Meyerhoff, H. A. *Geology of Puerto Rico.* Puerto Rico, ser. B, no. 1. Río Piedras: University of Puerto Rico, 1933. Monographs of the University of Puerto Rico.

————. "The Geology of the Fajardo District, Porto Rico." In New York Academy of Sciences, *Scientific Survey of Porto Rico and the Virgin Islands.* Vol. 2, pt. 3. New York, 1931.

————. "Geology of the Virgin Islands, Culebra, and Vieques." In New York Academy of Sciences, *Scientific Survey of Porto Rico and the Virgin Islands.* Vol. 4, pts. 1 and 2. New York, 1926–27.

————. "Tertiary Physiographic Developments of Porto Rico and the Virgin Islands." *Geological Society of America Bulletin* 38 (December 1927).

————. "The Texture of Karst Topography in Cuba and Puerto Rico." *Journal of Geomorphology* 1, no. 4 (December 1938).

Mitchell, G. J. "Geology of the Ponce District." In New York Academy of Sciences, *Scientific Survey of Porto Rico and the Virgin Islands.* Vol. 1, pt. 3. New York, 1922.

Mitchell, Raoul C. "A Survey of the Geology of Puerto Rico." University of Puerto Rico Agricultural Experiment Station. Technical Paper No. 13. Río Piedras, June 1954.

Monroe, W. "Dominio litológico en la formación de algunas formas de relieve en Puerto Rico." In *Geografía Internacional, Conferencia Regional Latino-americana.* Proceedings, Mexico, 1967.

Nevares, R., Jr., and J. C. Dunlap. "Datos de ingeniería y geología alrededor de la sedimentación de embalses en Puerto Rico." *Revista de Agricultura de Puerto Rico* 42, nos. 1–2 (January–December 1951), pp. 169–89.

Picó, R. *Cartography in Puerto Rico.* With the collaboration of Leticia Lopez and Hector Berríos. San Juan: Government Development Bank for Puerto Rico, 1964.

Puerto Rico University, Institute of Caribbean Studies. "Status of Geological Research in the Caribbean." Compiled by J. D. Weaver. Mayaguez, Puerto Rico, 1965.

Reed, H. F., and S. Taber. *The Porto Rico Earthquake of 1918.* U.S. Congress, House, 66th Cong., doc. no. 269. Washington, D.C., 1919.

Report of the Governor of Porto Rico to the Secretary of War, 1919, Data on the 1918 earthquakes. Washington, D.C.: Government Printing Office, 1919.

Semmes, D. R. "The Geology of the San Juan District, Porto Rico." In New York Academy of Sciences, *Scientific Survey of Porto Rico and the Virgin Islands.* Vol. 1, pt. 1. New York, 1919.

Serra, G. "El Area Montañosa de Puerto Rico y su rehabilitación." Lecture delivered on March 21, 1940 at the University of Puerto Rico, at a public forum on various aspects of the economy of the island, under the auspices of the Social Sciences Faculty. San Juan: Department of Education, 1950.

Thorp, J. "The Asymmetry of the Pepino Hills of Puerto Rico in Relation to the Trade Winds." *The Journal of Geology* 42, no. 5 (July–August 1934).

U.S. Department of the Interior, Geological Survey. Professional papers. U.S. Geological Survey Publication 317-A, B, C. Washington, D.C.: U.S. Geological Survey, 1959–65.

U.S. Department of the Interior, Geological Survey. Bulletins. U.S. Geological Survey Publication 817, 1042-I, 1082-C, 1105, 1184. Washington, D.C.: U.S. Geological Survey, 1930–65.

————. Circulars. U.S. Geological Survey Publications 451, 456. Washington, D.C.: U.S. Geological Survey, 1961.

————. *Geologic Quadrangle Maps.* U.S. Geological Survey Publication CO-191, 197; I-318, 319, 326, 334, 335, 336, 337, 347, 392, 421. Washington, D.C.: U.S. Geological Survey, 1960–65.

————. *Geological Survey Research.* U.S. Geological Survey Publication 400-A, B; 424-A, B, C; 450-A, D; 475-A, B; 501-A, B. Washington, D.C.: U.S. Geological Survey, 1960–64.

————. *Hydrologic Investigations Atlases.* U.S. Geological Survey Publication HA-77; 128; 197. Washington, D.C.: U.S. Geological Survey, 1962–66.

————. *Oil and Gas Map.* U.S. Geological Survey Publication 85. Washington D.C.: U.S. Geological Survey, 1948.

————. *Topographic Map of Puerto Rico.* 65 quadrangles. Washington, D.C.: U.S. Geological Survey, 1946.

Zapp, A. D., H. R. Berquist, and C. R. Thomas. "Tertiary Geology of the Coasta¹ Plains of Puerto Rico, 1948." Prepared for the Puerto Rico Development Company. Geology by A. D. Zapp. Base from topographic maps of the U.S. Geological survey, prepared in cooperation with the Government of Puerto Rico. Geologic map of the north coastal plain of Puerto Rico. Geologic map of the south coastal plain of Puerto Rico.

Hydrography

Arnow, T., and J. W. Crooks. *Public Water Supplies in Puerto Rico.* Washington, D.C.: U.S. Geological Survey, 1960.

Bogart, D. B., and others. *Water Problems of Puerto Rico and a Program of Water Resources Investigations.* Washington, D.C.: U.S. Geological Survey, 1960.

————. *Water Resources of Puerto Rico, A Progress Report.* Washington, D.C.: U.S. Geological Survey, 1964.

Cataldo, V. M., and R. R. Ramírez. "Reforma del sistema de distribución de energía eléctrica del Area Metropolitana de San Juan de Puerto Rico." *Revista del Colegio de Ingenieros de Puerto Rico* 10, no. 4 (October–December 1949), pp. 30–36; 12, no. 2 (March–April 1951), pp. 22–25.

Cuevas, S. "La hulla blanca, fuente de energía y progreso." *Revista del Colegio de Ingenieros de Puerto Rico* 1, no. 3 (July–September 1940), pp. 50–52.

Ferré, L. A. "Fuerza eléctrica derivada de la industria azucarera para complementar el desarrollo hidroeléctrico de Puerto Rico." *Revista del Colegio de Ingenieros de Puerto Rico* 5, no. 2 (April–June 1944), pp. 36–40.

Fidalgo, M. H. "El proyecto hidroeléctrico de Caonillas." *Revista del Colegio de Ingenieros de Puerto Rico* 10, no. 2 (April–June 1949) pp. 2, 4–9; 10, no. 3 (July–September 1949), pp. 31–39.

González, R. A. "Conferencia sobre el sistema de riego de Isabela para la Asociación de Tecnólogos Azucareros de Puerto Rico." *Revista de Agricultura, Industria y Comercio de Puerto Rico,* June 1930.

Labadie Eurite, J. "Suministro de agua potable en la zona rural de Puerto Rico." *Revista de Agricultura de Puerto Rico* 51, no. 1 (January–June 1964), pp. 192–99.

Lucchetti, A. *Concerning the Construction and Operation of the Hydroelectric and Irrigation Systems of the South Coast and of the Hydroelectric System of Utilization of the Water Resources of the Government of Puerto Rico.* Bulletin of the Insular Department of the Interior, January 1936.

————. "La electrificación rural y la agricultura." *Almanaque Agricola de Puerto Rico,* pp. 67–82. San Juan: Departamento de Agricultura y Comercio, 1944.

————. "El proyecto del suroeste de Puerto Rico y su aportación a la salud pública." *Revista del Colegio de Ingenieros de Puerto Rico* 10, no. 1 (January–March 1949), pp. 14, 21–23.

————. "Puerto Rico Water Resources Authority: A Vital Force in the Island's Social and Economic Progress." Report to the American Society of Civil Engineering, November 1962.

————. *Rural Electrification in Puerto Rico, an Insular Government Undertaking.* Third World Power Conference, sec. 6, no. 17. Washington, D.C.: Government Printing Office, 1936.

Mújica Dueño, M. A. "Construcción de represas pequeñas." *Revista de Agricultura de Puerto Rico* 42, nos. 1–2 (January–December 1951), pp. 190–99.

Passalacqua, C. M., and R. Sánchez. "Proyecto de suministro de aguas a San Juan y once municipalidades limítrofes, consideraciones en torno a la selección de la fuente del Río Grande de Loíza." *Revista del Colegio de Ingenieros de Puerto Rico* 9, no. 2 (April–June 1948), pp. 58–69; no. 3 (July–September 1948), pp. 78–83.

Puerto Rico, Aqueduct and Sewer Authority. "Ground Water Resources of Puerto Rico." By Charles L. McGuinness, geologist, U.S. Geological Survey. Prepared in cooperation with the Geological Survey, U.S. Department of the Interior, 1948. Mimeographed.

Puerto Rico, Autoridad de las Fuentes Fluviales. *Energía eléctrica y riego en Puerto Rico, 1945–1955.* Tercera memoria general sobre la utilización de las fuentes fluviales de Puerto Rico. San Juan: Autoridad de las Fuentes Fluviales, December 1958.

————. "Historia breve de la Autoridad de las Fuentes Fluviales de Puerto Rico." Mimeographed. San Juan, n.d.

Puerto Rico, Servicio de Riego de Isabela. *Informes anuales del Ingeniero Jefe al Honorable Comisionado del Interior, años fiscales 1934–35 a 1949–50.* San Juan: General Supplies Administration, Printing Division, 1936–1952.

Puerto Rico, Water Resources Authority. *Annual Reports.* San Juan, 1964–69.

————. *Bonus: Nuclear Electric Generating Station in Puerto Rico.* San Juan: Puerto Rico Water Resources Authority, 1965.

————. Caonillas hydroelectric project, descriptive data. San Juan: Puerto Rico Water Resources Authority, 1951.

————. *Second General Report on the Utilization of the Water Resources of Puerto Rico, 1935–45.* By Antonio Lucchetti, executive director. San Juan: Service Office of the Government of Puerto Rico. Printing Division, 1945.

————. "Statistical Summary of Power Projects." Mimeographed. San Juan: Puerto Rico Water Resources Authority, August 1951.

Puerto Rico Water Resources Authority, Engineering and Construction Division. "Preliminary Engineering Report on the Proposed Coamo-Bauta Irrigation and Power Project." Prepared by the Planning Department of the Engineering and Construction Division. Mimeographed. San Juan, February 1948.

————. "Report on Caonillas Spillway Capacity." By Miguel Quinones, principal engineer. Mimeographed, June 1945.

————. "Report on the Southwestern Puerto Rico project." San Juan, March 1948.

Ramírez, R. "Desarrollos hidroeléctricos en Puerto Rico—estudio novel sobre justificación económica." Trabajo presentado ante la 22a. asamblea anual del Colegio de Ingenieros de Puerto Rico. Mimeographed. San Juan, November 1959.

Ramírez, R. R., and V. M. Cataldo. "Desarrollo de la red de líneas de transmisión en Puerto Rico. *Revista del Colegio de Ingenieros de Puerto Rico* 11, no. 6 (November–December 1950), pp. 34–41.

Rullan, E. "El Proyecto hidroeléctrico Garzas." *Revista del Colegio de Ingenieros de Puerto Rico* 2, no. 4 (October–December 1941), pp. 73–74.

U.S. Department of the Interior, Geological Survey. Water supply papers. U.S. Geological Survey Publications 1460-A, 1547. Washington, D.C.: U.S. Geological Survey, 1957–62.

Urrutia, R. V. "La electrificación rural en Puerto Rico." *Revista de Agricultura de Puerto Rico* 51, no. 1 (January–June 1964), pp. 182–91.

Ward, P. E., and L. S. Truxes. "Water Wells in Puerto Rico." Washington, D.C.: U.S. Geological Survey, 1964.

Minerals

Ackerman, D. H. "Mining and the Environment." *Industrial Puerto Rico*, February–March, 1970.

Briggs, R. P. *Mineral Resources of Puerto Rico, an Outline with Remarks on Conservation.* Report presented at the Conference of Natural Resources organized by the School of Law, University of Puerto Rico, Río Piedras campus, November 1967. Reprinted from *Revista del Colegio de Ingenieros, Arquitectos y Agrimensores de Puerto Rico* 19, no. 2 (April–June 1969), pp. 27–40.

Caribbean Commission. *The Cement Trade of the Caribbean.* External Trade Bulletin no. 2. Washington, D.C.: Kaufman Press, 1949.

Colony, R. J., and H. A. Meyerhoff. *The Magnetite Deposit near Humacao, P.R.* The American Institute of Mining and Metallurgical Engineers, Technical Bulletin no. 587, February 1935.

Committee on Mineral Resources of Puerto Rico, Report. San Juan, 1933 and 1934.

Diamond, W. G., and M. D. Turner. *"The Mineral Industry of the Commonwealth of Puerto Rico, the Panama Canal Zone and the Virgin Islands.* Reprint from *Bureau of Mines Yearbook,* 1957.

Font, M. "El agua de mar en el mezclado de hormigón." *Revista del Colegio de Ingenieros de Puerto Rico* 1, no. 3 (October–December 1940), pp. 75–77.

López Sanabria, M. "Aportaciones del campo de la geología y la mineralogía y la minería a la integración de nuestra cultura." *Revista del Colegio de Ingenieros de Puerto Rico* 1, no. 3 (July–September 1940).

Miranda Siragusa, F. *Minerales, rocas y suelos.* Río Piedras: University of Puerto Rico, Agricultural Extension Service, December 1964.

Nieves Rivera, C. "Hierro en Juncos. Extraen 800 toneladas al día de yacimientos de 'La Mina'." *El Mundo,* San Juan, June 29, 1951.

Puerto Rico Bureau of Mines. "Report of the Bureau of Mines on the Mineral Resources of Puerto Rico." An appendix to the *Annual Report of the Bureau of Mines for the Fiscal Years 1939–1941 to the Honorable Commissioner of the Interior of Puerto Rico.* San Juan: Bureau of Supplies, 1941.

Puerto Rico. Comisión de Minería. *Reglamento para la explotación, arrendamiento y producción de minerales comerciales en Puerto Rico.* Effective November 21, 1967. Commonwealth of Puerto Rico, Office of the Governor, Mining Commission.

Puerto Rico Mining Commission. *Oil and Gas Possibilities of Northern Puerto Rico.* Washington, D.C.: U.S. Geological Survey, 1961.

Throp, J., and L. R. Smith. "Concerning the Origin of the White Quartz Sands of Northern Puerto Rico." *The Journal of the Department of Agriculture of Puerto Rico* 17, no. 2 (April 1933).

Willoughby, W. F. "Mineral Industries of Porto Rico." In *U.S. Bureau of the Census Bulletin* no. 6, 1904.

Marine Resources

Barnés, Jr., V. "Aspecto biológico de la pesca en Puerto Rico, 1943." Unpublished typewritten report found in the library of the Fishing Laboratory at Mayaguez, Puerto Rico.

Bird, E. A. *Fishing off Puerto Rico*. New York: A. S. Barnes & Co., Inc. London: Thomas Yoseloff, 1960.

Bonnet Benítez, L. C. "Desarrollo y planes para la pesca de agua dulce en Puerto Rico." *Revista de agricultura, industria y comercio de Puerto Rico* 33 (July–September 1941), pp. 339–46.

Caribbean Commission, Central Secretariat. *The Fish Trade of the Caribbean*. External Trade Bulletin no. 3. Washington, D.C.: Kaufman Press, 1948.

de Jesús Martinez, A. "El fomento de la industria pesquera en Puerto Rico y sus perspectivas." Typewritten thesis. Río Piedras: University of Puerto Rico, Social Sciences College, December 21, 1970.

Díaz Pacheco, S. "Practices and Operating Costs of Puerto Rican Fishermen." Report no. 21. Mimeographed. Río Piedras: University of Puerto Rico Agricultural Experiment Station, 1943.

Evermann, W., and M. C. Marsh *Investigations of the Aquatic Resources and Fisheries of Puerto Rico by the U.S. Fish Commission Steamer, Fish Hawk in 1899*. U.S. Commission of Fish and Fisheries Bulletin, 1900, pp. 1–350.

Iñigo, F., R. Juhl and J. A. Suárez Caabro. "El fomento de la industria pesquera en Puerto Rico y sus perspectivas." *Contribuciones Agropecuarias y Pesqueras* 2, no. 3 (May 1970). Department of Agriculture of Puerto Rico.

Jarvis, N. D. *The Fisheries of Puerto Rico*. Investigational report no. 13, Bureau of Fisheries, U.S. Department of Commerce. Washington, D.C.: Government Printing Office, 1932.

Lucas, C. R. "The War and Puerto Rico's Edible Fishery Imports." *Revista de agricultura, industria y comercio de Puerto Rico* 34, no. 2 (1942), p. 213.

Marrero, M. A. "Refrigeración en la industria pesquera." *Revista del Colegio de Ingenieros de Puerto Rico* 3, no. 4 (October– December 1942) pp. 83–84.

Martin, H. R. "Development of Fresh-Water Fisheries in Puerto Rico." *Revista de agricultura, industria y comercio de Puerto Rico* 39, no. 2 (July–December 1948), pp. 218–20.

Picó, R. "La industria pesquera en Puerto Rico: estudio de las condiciones económicas." Typewritten report. August, 1932.

"Problema de la Industria Pesquera." *Revista de Agricultura, industria y comercio de Puerto Rico*, 32 (January–March 1940), pp. 109–10.

Puerto Rico, Departamento de Agricultura, División de Pesca y Vida Silvestre. "Anotaciones sobre programas de fomento pesquero." Por Félix Inigo. n.d.

Puerto Rico, Department of Agriculture. "La Pesca en Puerto Rico." *Revista de Agricultura de Puerto Rico* 50, no. 1 (January–June 1963).

Puerto Rico, Department of Agriculture and Commerce, Division of Ornithology and Pisciculture. *Fishery Bulletin of Puerto Rico* 1, nos. 1, 2, 3 (1943–1944). San Juan: Bureau of Supplies, Printing Division.

Puerto Rico, Departamento de Comercio. "Informe sobre proyecto piloto para el mejoramiento de la industria pesquera y de las condiciones de vida de los pescadores." Preparado por el Secretario de Comercio, Sr. Jenaro Baquero y sometido al Hon. Gobernador de Puerto Rico, December 1965.

Puncochar, J. F. "Aims of the Fishery Research Laboratory of Puerto Rico." *Revista de Agricultura, industria y comercio de Puerto Rico* 34, no. 2 (1942), p. 200.

Sacarello, R. "El Departamento de Agricultura está poblando de peces las aguas dulces de Puerto Rico." *Revista de Agricultura, industria y comercio de Puerto Rico* 31 (January–March 1939), pp. 28–38.

————. "La pesca comercial en Puerto Rico." *Revista de Agricultura, industria y comercio de Puerto Rico* 31 (July–September 1939), pp. 451–61.

Soler, P. J. "A Bibliography on the Fishes and Fisheries of Puerto Rico." *Proceedings of the Gulf and Caribbean Fisheries Institute*, 3rd annual session. Appendix 1 pp. 143–49. Miami Beach, November 1950.

Suárez Caabro, J. A. "Puerto Rico's Fishery Statistics 1968–1969." *Contribuciones Agropecuarias y Pesqueras* 2, no. 1 (March 1970). Department of Agriculture of Puerto Rico.

Vélez, M., S. Díaz Pacheco, and P. B. Vázquez Calcerrada, "La Pesca y distribución de pescado en Puerto Rico." Bulletin no. 66. Río Peidras: University of Puerto Rico Agricultural Experiment Station, June 1945.

Vergne Roig, P. Economics of the Fisheries and Fishery Resources of Puerto Rico. Mimeographed. Mayagüez, Puerto Rico: Fisheries Research Laboratory of the U.S. Fish and Wildlife Service, n.d.

Climate

Alcalá, J. L. *Desastres naturales: huracanes, marejadas, inundaciones.* Río Piedras: University of Puerto Rico Agricultural Extension Service, 1965.

Barnes, Robert W. *Weather and Climate in Puerto Rico.* Río Piedras, 1967.

Berry, F. A. *Handbook of Meteorology.* Edited by F. A. Berry, Jr., F. Bollay, and N. R. Beers. 1st ed. New York: McGraw–Hill, 1945.

Briscoe, C. B. "Weather in the Luquillo Mountains of Puerto Rico." Forest Service Research Paper ITF no. 3. Río Piedras: Institute of Tropical Forestry, 1966.

Byers, H. R., and D. C. McDowell. "Weather on the Southeast (Atlantic) route." *Bulletin of the American Meteorological Society* 26, no. 6 (June 1945), pp. 220–34.

Colón, J. A. "On the Wind Structure above the Tropopause over Puerto Rico." *Bulletin of the American Meteorological Society* 32, no. 2 (February 1951), p. 52.

Fassig, O. L. "The Trade Winds of the Eastern Caribbean." *American Geophysical Union Transactions*, Fourteenth Annual Meeting, 1933.

————. "The Climate of Porto Rico." *Puerto Rico Review of Public Health* 4 (1928), p. 199.

Gray, R. W. "Annual Meteorological Summary with Comparative Data, 1935–37." San Juan: U. S. Department of Agriculture, Weather Bureau, 1936.

————. "La distribución anual y geográfica de lluvia en Puerto Rico." *Almanaque agrícola de Puerto Rico para el año 1944.* Pp. 47–57.

Hanson, E. P. "Are the Tropics Unhealthy?" *Harper's*, October 1933.

Harris, M. F. "La temperatura de Puerto Rico." *Almanaque agrícola de Puerto Rico para el año 1947.* Pp. 75–82. San Juan: Administración general de suministros, 1947.

Hartwell, F. E. "San Ciprián, Hurricane of September 26–27, 1932." *Monthly Weather Review*, September 1932. Includes data on other hurricanes.

Howarth, M. "Climatic Studies in Puerto Rico." M.A. thesis. Worcester, Mass.: Clark University, 1934.

McDowell, D. C. "Results of a High-Altitude Rawinsonde Flight over Puerto Rico." *Bulletin of the American Meteorological Society* 30, no. 2 (February 1949), pp. 65–66.

———. "Weather Variations in the Caribbean." Report 30. Río Piedras: University of Puerto Rico, Institute of Tropical Meteorology, January 1950.

Netzer, D. L. "Climate and Agricultural Cropland Use in Puerto Rico." Thesis. Ann Arbor: University of Michigan, University Microfilms, 1954.

Picó, R. "Huracanes en el Caribe." *Ambito*, revista universitaria, October 1935.

Puerto Rico, Experiment Station, Mayagüez. "Climatic Features in Relation to Agriculture." *Report of the Puerto Rico Experiment Station*, 1935. Washington, D.C.: Government Printing Office, 1936.

Ramírez de Arellano, R. W. "Los Huracanes de Puerto Rico. Mapas y tablas de estadisticas." *Boletín de la Universidad de Puerto Rico*, ser. 3, no. 2 (December 1932).

Riehl, H. "Note on Tropical Storm North of Puerto Rico on September 13, 1945." *Bulletin of the American Meteorological Society* 26, no. 9 (November 1945), pp. 357–60.

Salivia, L. A. *Historia de los temporales de Puerto Rico*. San Juan: Imprenta La Milagrosa, 1950.

Smedley, D. "Climate of Puerto Rico and U.S. Virgin Islands." In *Climate of the States*. Washington, D.C.: U.S. Weather Bureau, 1961.

Tannehill, I. R. *The Hurricane*. Miscellaneous publication no. 197. Washington, D.C.: U.S. Department of Agriculture, July 1934.

———. *Hurricanes, their Nature and History, Particularly Those of the West Indies and the Southern Coasts of the United States*. Princeton, N.J.: Princeton University Press, 1938.

Thorp, J. "Climate and Settlement in Puerto Rico and the Hawaiian Islands." *Yearbook of Agriculture, 1941–Climate and Man*. Pp. 217–26. Washington, D.C.: Government Printing Office, 1941.

U.S. Department of Agriculture. *Studies of Rainfall Distribution in Puerto Rico*. Averages for 20 or more years compiled and graphed in 14–day periods. Published in blueprints by the Puerto Rico Emergency Reconstruction Administration, 1935.

U.S. Weather Bureau. *Puerto Rico and United States Virgin Islands; Climatic Summary of the United States*. Supplement for 1951 through 1960. 1965.

Natural Vegetation

Alberts, H. W., and O. García Molinari. *Pastures of Puerto Rico and their Relation to Soil Conservation*. Miscellaneous publication no. 513. Washington, D.C.: U.S. Department of Agriculture, May 1943.

Bevan, A. "The Forest Problem in Puerto Rico." *Revista de Agricultura, industria y comercio de Puerto Rico* 32 (July–September 1940), pp. 447–48.

"Bosques de Puerto Rico." July–September issue of the *Revista de Agricultura de Puerto Rico* (devoted to forests) 49, no. 1 (January–June 1962).

"Classificación general de las especies madereras más importantes en los bosques naturales de Puerto Rico." *Revista de Agricultura de Puerto Rico* 38, no. 2 (May–December 1947), pp. 135–36.

Cook, M. T., and H. A. Gleason. "Ecological Survey of the Flora of Puerto Rico." *Journal of the Department of Agriculture of Puerto Rico* 12, nos. 1 and 2 (January and April 1928).

Durland, W. "Forest Regeneration of Puerto Rico." *Economic Geography* 5, no. 4 (October 1929).

Garcia Molinari, O. "Succession of Grasses in Puerto Rico." *Revista de Agricultura, industria y comercio de Puerto Rico* 39, no. 2 (July–December 1948), pp. 199–217.

Gilormini, J. A. *Manual para la propagación de árboles y el establecimiento de plantaciones forestales en Puerto Rico.* 2nd ed. Río Piedras, 1949.

Gleason, H. A., and M. T. Cook. "Plant Ecology of Porto Rico." *Scientific Survey of Porto Rico and the Virgin Islands.* Vol. 7, pt. 1. New York: New York Academy of Sciences, 1927.

Gregory, L. E. "Notes of the Yarey Palm of Puerto Rico and the Straw Industry Derived from It." *The Caribbean Forester* 1, no. 4 (July 1940).

Hadley, E. W. "Subsistence Homesteads on Public Forest Lands of Puerto Rico." *Revista de Agricultura, industria y comercio de Puerto Rico* 33 (April–June 1941), pp. 317–22.

Holdridge, L. R. "Forestry in Puerto Rico." *The Caribbean Forester* 1, no. 1 (October 1939).

––––––. "Some Notes on the Mangrove Swamps of Porto Rico." *The Caribbean Forester* 1, no. 4 (July 1940).

Murphy, L. S. *Forests of Porto Rico, Past, Present, and Future, and their Physical and Economic Environment.* Washington, D.C.: Government Printing Office, 1916.

Otero, J. I., R. A. Toro, and L. Pagán de Otero. *Catálogo de los nombres vulgares y científicos de algunas plantas puertorriqueñas.* 2nd ed. Reprint of bulletin no. 37. Second edition revised and amplified by courtesy of the Agricultural Experiment Station of the University of Puerto Rico. San Juan: General Supplies Administration, 1946.

Puerto Rico, Departamento de Agricultura. "Los recursos forestales de Puerto Rico." Por Benjamín R. Seda, Chief, Forest Reservation Program. October 1965.

Puerto Rico, Departamento de Agricultura y Comercio. *Informes anuales del Comisionado de agricultura y comercio, ejercicio 1935–36 a 1949–50.* San Juan: General Supplies Administration, 1936–51.

Puerto Rico, Department of Agriculture and Commerce, Forest Service. *Insular Forest Atlas.* 2 vols. Río Piedras: Forest Service, 1948.

Puerto Rico, University, Agricultural Experiment Station. *The Interior Management of Tropical Forages in Puerto Rico.* By José V. Chandler and others. Bulletin no. 187. Río Piedras, December 1964.

Teesdale, L. V., and J. W. Girard. *Wood Utilization in Puerto Rico.* Washington, D.C.: U.S. Department of Agriculture, Forest Service, 1945.

Upson, A. T. "Forests and Land Tenure in Puerto Rico." Caribbean Commission, Caribbean Land Tenure Symposium, pp. 233–37. Washington, D.C.: 1946.

U.S. Department of Agriculture, Forest Service. *National Forest of Puerto Rico.* Washington, D.C.: Government Printing Office, 1940.

––––––. *The Caribbean Forester.* Río Piedras: Tropical Forest Experiment Station, 1938 to date.

––––––. *Common Trees of Puerto Rico and the Virgin Islands.* By Elbert L. Little, Jr., and Frank H. Wadsworth. Agriculture Handbook no. 249, 1964.

––––––. "Recreational Notes and Discussions." Luquillo Unit, Caribbean National Forests. Mimeographed. Washington, D.C.

––––––. "Suggestions for a Forestry Program for the Commonwealth of Puerto Rico." By Frank H. Wadsworth. Mimeographed.

_____. *Trees of Puerto Rico.* By L. R. Holdridge, Vol. 50. Occasional Paper No. 1, March 1942.

Wadsworth, F. H. "Los bosques de Puerto Rico." *Revista del Café* 20, no. 12 (October 1965).

_____. "El cultivo forestal como una práctica de conservación de suelos en Puerto Rico." *Revista de Agricultura de Puerto Rico* 42, nos. 1–2 (January–December 1951), pp. 127–32.

_____. "Notas sobre los bosques climáticos de Puerto Rico y su destrucción y conservación con anterioridad al 1900." *The Caribbean Forester* 2, no. 1 (1950), pp. 47–56.

_____. "Ordenación forestal en las montañas de Luquillo." *The Caribbean Forester* 12 no. 3 (July 1951), pp. 115–32.

White D. G. *Bamboo Culture and Utilization in Puerto Rico.* Circular 29. Washington, D.C.: U.S. Department of Agriculture, Puerto Rico Experiment Station in Mayagüez, April 1948.

Soils

Asón, E. R. "Algunas consideraciones teóricas acerca del valor y el uso de los terrenos en Puerto Rico." Mimeographed. Río Piedras: University of Puerto Rico, College of Business Administration, Business Research Center, August 1967.

Berríos, A. T. "Apreciación de suelos." Río Piedras: University of Puerto Rico Agricultural Extension Service, June 1966.

Bonnet, J. A. *Chemical Data of Puerto Rico Soils. Correlation of Data for Humid and Arid Areas. Field Response of Crops to Available Phosphorous and Potash in Soil.* Research bulletin no. 1. Río Piedras: University of Puerto Rico Agricultural Experiment Station, 1941.

_____. "Laboratory and Field Studies in an Alkaline Earth Solonchak Area of Puerto Rico to be Irrigated." *Soil Science Society of America Proceedings,* 11 (1946), pp. 480–93.

_____. "The Nature of Laterization as Revealed by Chemical, Physical, and Mineralogical Studies of Lateritic Soil Profile from Puerto Rico." A Doctor's Thesis. *Soil Science* 48 no. 1 (July 1939), pp. 25–40.

_____. "Pérdidas por erosión en Puerto Rico y factores que las afectan." *Revista de Agricultura de Puerto Rico* 42 nos. 1–2 (January–December 1951), pp. 86–91.

_____. "Series importantes de suelos de Puerto Rico." *Almanaque agrícola de Puerto Rico,* 1944, pp. 83–90.

_____. "Los suelos de la zona cafetalera de Puerto Rico." *Revista del Cafe* 2, fourth year (July 1948), pp. 5–11.

_____. "Tracing the Calcium, Phosphorous and Iron from a Limed and Unlimed Lateritic Soil to the Grass and to the Animal Blood." *Soil Science Society of America Proceedings* 11, (1946), pp. 295–97.

Bonnet, J. A., and M. A. Lugo López. *Soil Studies in the Projected Coamo Irrigation Area.* Río Piedras: University of Puerto Rico Agricultural Experiment Station, 1950.

Bonnet, J. A., and P. Tirado Sulsona. *Soil Studies in Lajas Valley.* Río Piedras: University of Puerto Rico Agricultural Experiment Station, 1950.

Canals, C. S. "Características generales de los suelos en las áreas pantanosas que circundan la Bahía de San Juan, Puerto Rico." *Revista del Colegio de Ingenieros de Puerto Rico* 12 no. 2 (March–April, 1951), pp. 18–20.

Colon Torres, R. "La Conservación de los recursos agrícolas de Puerto Rico: Función de buen liderato y buena técnica." *Revista de Agricultura de Puerto Rico* 42, nos. 1–2 (January–December 1951), pp. 4–10.

————. *Proyección para el uso intensivo y balanceado de los recursos agrícolas en Puerto Rico.* San Juan: Department of Education, 1950.

————. "Soils of Puerto Rico, Classified by Geological Formation, Series, Types and Phases, with Productivity Rating of Each Based on Inherent Qualities of the Land, Area and Per Cent of Total Area." Report no. 19. Mimeographed. Río Piedras: University of Puerto Rico, Agricultural Experiment Station, 1941.

Córdova, J. P. "Classificación de terrenos basada en su capacidad productora." *Revista de Agricultura de Puerto Rico* 42, nos. 1–2 (January–December 1951), pp. 69–81.

Helfenbein, H. F. "Principios y funciones fundamentales de un programa de conservación de suelos para un distrito." *Revista de Agricultura de Puerto Rico* 42, nos. 1–2 (January–December 1951), pp. 47–52.

Hernández, M. "La Conservación del suelo y su vinculación al bienestar de Puerto Rico." *Revista de Agricultura de Puerto Rico* 42, nos. 1–2 (January–December 1951), pp. 11–22.

————. "Soil Conservation and Its Relation to Puerto Rico's Welfare." Mimeographed. Río Piedras: University of Puerto Rico Agricultural Experiment Station, September 1948.

Hernández Agosto, M. A. "La Importancia del vivero forestal en el programa de conservación de suelos y aguas." *Revista de Agricultura de Puerto Rico* 42, nos. 1–2 (January–December 1951), pp. 122–26.

Hopkins, E. F., and others. "Iron and Manganese in Relation to Plant Growth and Its Importance in Puerto Rico." *Journal of Agriculture of the University of Puerto Rico* 28 (April 1944), pp. 43–101.

Lugo López, M. A. "Características del suelo que determinan su resistencia o susceptibilidad a la erosión." *Revista de Agricultura de Puerto Rico* 42, nos. 1–2 (January–December 1951), pp. 92–97.

Marrero, J. F. "El Servicio de conservación de suelos en Puerto Rico." *Revista de Agricultura de Puerto Rico* 42, nos. 1–2 (January–December 1951), pp. 23–24.

Miranda Siragusa, F. "Apuntos sobre suelos de Puerto Rico." Mimeographed. Río Piedras: Agricultural Extension Service, February 1965.

————. "Roturación del subsuelo y abonamiento profundo." Río Piedras: University of Puerto Rico Agricultural Extension Service, May 1965.

Nazario, L. A. "La Economía insular y la conservación de nuestros recursos naturales." *Revista de Agricultura de Puerto Rico* 42, nos. 1–2 (January–December 1951), pp. 17–22.

Nolla, J. A. B., and G. L. Crawford. *La conservación del suelo en Puerto Rico.* Puerto Rico Soil Conservation Service, U.S. Department of Agriculture, 1941.

"Our Work in Puerto Rico." *Soil Conservation* 6, no. 1 (1940).

Puerto Rico, Administración de Terrenos. *Informe Anual 1962–63.* San Juan: Talleres Gráficos Interamericanos, 1963.

Puerto Rico, Autoridad de Tierras. *Informe general sobre programa de mejoramiento de suelos pantanosos y áridos.* San Juan: Autoridad de Tierras, División de Promoción y relaciones públicas, March 1956.

Puerto Rico, Servicio de Conservación de Suelos. "Investigaciones sobre conservación en Puerto Rico." *Revista de Agricultura de Puerto Rico* 42, nos. 1–2 (January–December 1951), pp. 140–50.

Puerto Rico, University, Agricultural Experiment Station. *Detailed Salinity Survey of Lajas Valley*. By J. A. Bonnet and E. J. Brenes. Bulletin no. 141. Río Piedras: July 1958.

_____. *A Survey of the PH Status of the Soils of Puerto Rico*. By George Samuels. Technical paper no. 42. Río Piedras: June 1966.

Thorp, J. "Some Important Soil Profiles of Southern Puerto Rico." *Soil Science* 34, no. 4 (October 1932).

Thorp, J., and L. R. Smith. "Concerning the Origin of the White Quartz Sands of Northern Puerto Rico." *Journal of the Department of Agriculture of Puerto Rico* 17, no. 2 (April 1933).

U.S. Department of Agriculture. *Soil Survey of Puerto Rico*. By R. C. Roberts and others. Washington, D.C.: Government Printing Office, 1942.

_____. "Soils of Puerto Rico and the Virgin Islands." *Yearbook of Agriculture, 1938: Soils and Man*. Pp. 1137–47. Washington, D.C.: Government Printing Office, 1938.

U.S. Department of Agriculture, Soil Conservation Service. *Generalized Soil Map of Puerto Rico*. August 1937.

_____. *Reconnaissance Erosion Survey of Puerto Rico, 1937*.

Vicente J., and R. R. Caro. "Los pastos mejorados conservan y mejoran la tierra y producen más leche y carne." *Revista de Agricultura de Puerto Rico* 42, nos. 1–2 (January–December 1951), pp. 133–39.

Wadsworth, F. H. "El cultivo forestal como una práctica de conservación de suelos en Puerto Rico." *Revista de Agricultura de Puerto Rico* 42, nos. 1–2 (January–December 1951), pp. 127–32.

Population and Land

Brau, S. *Historia de Puerto Rico*. New York: D. Appleton & Co., 1914.

Carrero, T. "El Arrabal urbano, su eliminación y la renovación urbana." Mimeographed. April 23, 1952.

Committee on Human Resources. *Puerto Rico's Manpower Needs and Supply*. San Juan: Department of Labor, Puerto Rico Planning Board, November 1957.

Cruz Monclova, L. *Historia of Puerto Rico: Siglo 19*. Vol. 1, *1808–1868;* vol. 2, pt. 1 *1868–1874;* vol. 2, pt. 2, *1875–1885;* vol. 3, pt. 3, *1885–1898*. Río Piedras: University of Puerto Rico Press, 1957–64.

Durand Manzanal, R. *El Grupo trabajador civil en Puerto Rico*. Special bulletin. San Juan: Department of Labor, Bureau of Labor Statistics, September 1948.

Hernandez Colon, R. *La Zona histórica de Ponce, lo que es y lo que no es*. Ponce: Advisory Commission in the Ponce Historical Zone, 1965.

Hill, R. *The Family and Population Control. A Puerto Rican Experiment in Social Change*. Chapel Hill: University of North Carolina Press, 1959.

Janer, J. L. "Population Growth in Puerto Rico and its Relation to Time Changes in Vital Statistics." Reprinted from *Human Biology, a Record of Research* 17 (December 1945), p. 4.

Miller, P. G. *Historia de Puerto Rico*. Chicago: Rand McNally & Co., 1939.

Niddrie, D. L. "The Problems of Population Growth in Puerto Rico." Reprint from the *Journal of Tropical Geography* 20 (June 1965). Singapore: Department of Geography, University of Singapore and the University of Malaya.

Puerto Rico, Junta de Planificación. *A City is People—Una ciudad, un pueblo.* New York: Aldus Printers, 1954.

————. *Mapa de municipios y barrios.* Memorias para los 76 municipios de Puerto Rico. San Juan: Service Office of the Government of Puerto Rico, Printing Division, 1945–1948.

————. *Delimitación regional en Puerto Rico—informe preliminar, April 1957.* San Juan: Bureau of Comprehensive Planning.

————. *Proyección y empleo residencial.* Puerto Rico, January 1964.

————. Puerto Rico. "Características físicas, uso de terrenos y transportación." San Juan: Bureau of Master Plans, n.d.

————. *Puerto Rico and its Population Problem.* By Frederick P. Bartlett and Brandon Howell. Translated to Spanish by René Jiménez Malaret. San Juan: General Supplies Administration, Services Office, Printing Division, 1946.

————. "Refomento municipal." Por el Dr. Rafael Picó. Address before the Fifth Meeting of the Inter-American Congress of Municipalities. San Juan: December 6, 1954. Mimeographed.

Puerto Rico, Universidad, Estación Experimental Agrícola. *Estudio socio-económico de dos comunidades establecidas por la 'Administración de Programas Sociales de Puerto Rico.* Por José M. Ríos y P. B. Vázquez Calcerrada. Bulletin no. 135. Río Piedras, October 1956.

Steward, J. H. *Social Class and Social Change in Puerto Rico.* Urbana: University of Illinois Press, 1956.

Tunim, M. M. *Social Class and Social Change in Puerto Rico.* Princeton, N.J.: Princeton University Press, 1961.

U.S. Bureau of the Census. *Population of Puerto Rico.* Washington, D.C.: Government Printing Office, 1900–1970.

University of Chicago. "The Population of Puerto Rico, 1950–1975." Part of the workshop studies of the Program of Education and Research in Planning, June 1956.

Economic Structure

Andic, F. M. *El desarrollo económico y la distribución del ingreso en Puerto Rico.* Technical report no. 2. San Juan: Government Development Bank for Puerto Rico, 1964.

Baer, W. *The Puerto Rican Economy and the United States Economic Fluctuations.* Río Piedras: University of Puerto Rico, Social Science Research Center, 1962.

Baggs, W. C. *Puerto Rico: Showcase of Development.* Reprinted from the *1962 Britannica Book of the Year.*

Bourne, D. D. and R. James. *Thirty Years of Change in Puerto Rico.* New York: Praeger, 1966.

Castañeda Hernández, R. *Interpretaciones en torno al problema de balance o desbalance en el desarrollo económico.* Río Piedras, 1964.

Clark, V. S. et al. *Porto Rico and Its Problems.* Washington, D. C.: The Brookings Institution, 1930.

Descartes, S. L. *Basic Statistics on Puerto Rico, 1946.* Washington, D.C.: the Office of Puerto Rico in Washington.

————. *Capacidad económica de Puerto Rico para la seguridad social, 1949.*

————. "The Economic and Social Situation of Puerto Rico, 1963." Mimeographed report.

————. *The Outlook of the Puerto Rican Economy for the Next Decade, 1961.*

_____. *Política contributiva insular, 1949.*

_____. *The Public Debt of Puerto Rico, 1954.*

Esteves, V. R. "Economic Policy for Puerto Rico." Thesis. Cambridge: Harvard University Library, Photographic Department, 1948.

Freyre, J. *El Servicio de la inversión externa en países importadores de capital: El Caso de Puerto Rico.* San Juan: Government Development Bank for Puerto Rico, 1963.

Indicadores económicos de Puerto Rico, 27 de junio, 1967. San Juan: Puerto Rico Planning Board, Bureau of Economic and Social Analysis.

Labadie Eurite, J. "Sound investment climate accelerates growth in Puerto Rico." *Quarterly Report to Investors in Puerto Rican Securities.* San Juan: Government Development Bank for Puerto Rico 14, no. 2 (June 1967), pp. 5–6.

Montalvo, R. "External Investment in Puerto Rico, the Role of the Government Development Bank for Puerto Rico." Paper presented at the Seminar of Economic Planning, October 27 to November 28, 1958. Mimeographed.

Movimiento económico del mes en Puerto Rico, 1952–63. San Juan: Puerto Rico Planning Board, Bureau of Economic and Social Analysis.

Munoz Marín, L. "The Will to Develop." Address before the Sixth World Conference of the Society for International Development, March 16, 1964. San Juan: Government Development Bank for Puerto Rico, 1964.

Perloff, H. S. *Puerto Rico's Economic Future.* Chicago: University of Chicago Press, 1950.

_____. *Puerto Rico's Economic Future.* Condensed by Daisy D. Reck, translated to Spanish by Antonio J. Colorado. San Juan, 1957.

Picó, R. *El Banco Gubernamental de Fomento y la economía puertorriquena.* San Juan: Government Development Bank for Puerto Rico, May 1964.

_____. *The Government Development Bank and Puerto Rico's Economic Program.* Briefing session, American Management Association, Hotel Astor, April 2, 1959. San Juan: Treasury Department, Purchase and Supplies Service, Printing Division, 1959.

_____. *Diez Anos de Planificación en Puerto Rico.* San Juan: Treasury Department, Purchase and Supplies Service, Printing Division, 1954.

_____. *Economic Development in Puerto Rico.* Paper presented in October 1962 to United Nations at Geneva. Reprint from *Science, Technology and Development.* Vol. 10 pp. 35–41. Washington, D.C.: Government Printing Office, 1963.

_____. *El Progreso de Puerto Rico.* Lecture delivered at the Casa de la Cultura Ecuatoriana, Quito, Ecuador, February 25, 1955. Mimeographed.

_____. *Puerto Rico: Planificación y acción.* San Juan: Government Development Bank for Puerto Rico, 1962.

_____. *Puerto Rico's Successful Development Program.* Lecture delivered October 24, 1963, before the Municipal Bond Women's Club of New York. San Juan: Government Development Bank for Puerto Rico.

_____. *Los recursos económicos de Puerto Rico.* Lecture delivered, February 14, 1949 at the University of Puerto Rico, at a public forum on various aspects of Puerto Rico's economy, held under the auspices of the Social Sciences Department. Río Piedras: Tipografia Porvenir, 1949.

Puerto Rico, Departamento de Estado. *Puerto Rico: desarrollo político, social y económico.* 2nd ed. San Juan: Department of State, August 1965.

Puerto Rico, Government Development Bank. *Proceedings of the Seminar on the Contribution of Physical Planning to Social and Economic Development in a Regional Framework, May 23–27, 1960.* Edited by Alvin Mayne. Govbank Technical Papers, no. 3. San Juan: Government Development Bank for Puerto Rico, 1965.

————. *The Puerto Rico Chart Book, 1967, 1968, 1970.* San Juan: Talleres Gráficos Interamericanos.

————. *Puerto Rico in Figures, 1970.* Prepared by the Economic Research Department of the Government Development Bank for Puerto Rico.

Puerto Rico, Junta de Planificación. *Statistical Yearbook, 1964.* San Juan: 1965.

————. *Annual Reports,* Fiscal Years 1965–66 to 1968–69.

————. *Economic Report to the Governor, 1969.* San Juan, 1969.

————. *Four-Year Financial Program 1966–69.*

Rodríguez, G. *Los problemas y el progreso de Puerto Rico.* New York: Municipal Forum, 1956.

Agriculture

Arrillaga, F. A. "The Agricultural Development Program of the Land Authority of Puerto Rico." Mimeographed. San Juan: Land Authority of Puerto Rico, Division of Promotion and Public Relations, May 26, 1955.

Colón, E. *Datos sobre la agricultura de Puerto Rico antes de 1898.* San Juan: Tipografía Cantero, Fernández & Co., 1930.

————. *La Gestión agrícola después de 1898.* Edited by Jaime Bagué. San Juan: Imprenta Venezuela, 1948.

Descartes, S. L. *A Credit Study of 167 Tobacco Farms, Puerto Rico, 1939–40.* In cooperation with Julio O. Morales. Bulletin no. 69. Río Piedras: University of Puerto Rico Agricultural Experiment Station, March 1946.

————. *Food Consumption Studies in Puerto Rico.* In cooperation with S. Díaz Pacheco and J. R. Noguera. Bulletin no. 59. Río Piedras: University of Puerto Rico Agricultural Experiment Station, June 1941.

————. "Land Reform in Puerto Rico's Problem of Economic Advancement." In *Family Farm Policy.* Chicago: University of Chicago Press, 1947.

————. *Organization and Earnings on 130 Sugar Cane Farms in Puerto Rico.* In English and Spanish. Bulletin no. 47. Río Piedras: University of Puerto Rico Agricultural Experiment Station, May 1938.

————. "Perspectivas de la agricultura puertorriqueña para el 1975." Mimeographed. 1964.

————. *La Situación hipotecaria rural en Puerto Rico.* Bulletin no. 42. Río Piedras: University of Puerto Rico Agricultural Experiment Station, January 1936.

García Molinari, O., *Grasslands and Grasses of Puerto Rico.* Río Piedras: University of Puerto Rico Press, 1952.

Gayer, A. D. *The Sugar Economy of Puerto Rico.* New York: Columbia University Press, 1938.

González Chapel, A. *Planificación e implementación de un programa de desarrollo agrícola en el Valle de Lajas.* Bulletin no. 192. Río Piedras: University of Puerto Rico Agricultural Experiment Station, 1965.

Hernández Agosto, M. A. *Conversión de nuestra agricultura de caña de azúcar al maquinismo.* San Juan: Land Authority of Puerto Rico, 1963.

Irizarry, G. "Problemas encontrados y técnicas empleadas en relación a la planificación económica en el desarrollo de programas y proyectos de agricultura de Puerto Rico." In *Seminario de planificación de Puerto Rico*. Pp. 175–95. Mexico, 1960.

————. *La Política agraria de Puerto Rico: parte de una fructífera política económica*. San Juan: Treasury Department, 1965.

Koenig, N. *A Comprehensive Agricultural Program for Puerto Rico*. Washington, D.C.: U.S. Department of Agriculture, The Commonwealth of Puerto Rico, 1953.

McCord, J. E., J. J. Serralles, Jr., and R. Picó. *Tipos de explotación agrícola en Puerto Rico*. Bulletin no. 41. Río Piedras: University of Puerto Rico Agricultural Experiment Station, 1935.

MacPhail, D. D. *Puerto Rico Dairying: A Revolution in Tropical Agriculture*. Reprinted from *The Geographical Review* 53, no. 2 (1963).

Negrón Ramos, P. "Reestructuración de la agricultura puertorriqueña. La Experiencia de los últimos diez años." Paper read at a meeting of the Puerto Rican Economic and Statistical Association and the College of Agronomists of Puerto Rico. Mimeographed. San Juan: Department of Agriculture of Puerto Rico, July 1963.

Picó, R. *Funciones del Banco Gubernamental de Fomento y su relación con el desarrollo de nuestra economía agrícola*. Reprinted from *Revista de Agricultura de Puerto Rico* 45, no. 1 (January–June 1958), pp. 53–57.

————. "Inventario del uso de la tierra en Puerto Rico." Paper presented before the Third Pan American Consultation on Geography held in Washington, D.C., July 25–August 4, 1952. Mimeographed.

————. *Planificación en la zona rural*. Reprinted from *Almanaque Agrícola de Puerto Rico, Year 1944*. Pp. 59–65.

————. "Value of the Rural Land Classification Program of Puerto Rico for Purposes of Economic Development." Paper presented at the Presidential Program of the Annual Meeting of the Association of American Geographers, Cincinnati, Ohio, April 2, 1957.

Puerto Rico, Autoridad de Tierras. *Programa de fomento de ganadería de carne*. San Juan, n.d.

Puerto Rico, Banco Gubernamental de Fomento. *Estudio de crédito de la fase agrícola para la mecanización de la industria cañera*. Prepared by the Economic Research Department. May 1960.

Puerto Rico, Consejo Angrícola. "Análisis de aspectos económicos y agrícolas de la industria azucarera." By Guillermo Irizarry. Mimeographed. San Juan: Department of Agriculture of Puerto Rico, February 5, 1960.

————. "Análisis de la industria ganadera en Puerto Rico." By Guillermo Irizarry. Mimeographed. San Juan: Department of Agriculture of Puerto Rico, January 17, 1959.

————. "Informe sobre el examen de la industria azucarera realizado por el Consejo Agrícola y sobre las recomendaciones adoptadas para atender los problemas de dicha industria." By Bartolomé M. Morell. Mimeographed. San Juan: Department of Agriculture of Puerto Rico, August 10, 1962.

Puerto Rico, Departamento de Agricultura. *Industria cafetalera de Puerto Rico*. San Juan, 1965.

Rivera Santos, L. "La Agricultura en una economía en desarrollo." In *Seminario de planificación de Puerto Rico*. Pp. 161–74. Mexico, 1960.

United States Bureau of the Census. *Census of the United States: Agriculture of Puerto Rico*. Washington, D.C.: Government Printing Office, 1940, 1950, 1960, 1970.

Manufacturing

Amadeo, F. *La Administración de Fomento Económico y la Compañia de Fomento Industrial.* Reprint of Supplement to *Quarterly Bulletin of Center of Latin America Monetary Studies (CEMLA)*, September 1961.

Barton, H. C., Jr., "Economic Characteristics of the New Industries." Statement at the Briefing Conference on Doing Business in Puerto Rico. Mimeographed. New York, February 6, 1958.

————. "Planificación del desarrollo industrial en Puerto Rico." *Seminario de planificación económica de Puerto Rico.* Pp. 217–40. Mexico, 1960.

————. "Puerto Rico's Industrial Development Program, 1942–1960." Pre-publication copy of paper presented at a Seminar of the Center held in Cambridge, Mass., October 29, 1959. Cambridge, Mass.: Harvard University Center for International Affairs.

Barton, H. C., Jr., and R. A. Solo. *The Effect of Minimum Wage Laws on the Economic Growth of Puerto Rico.* Cambridge, Mass.: Harvard University Center of International Affairs, 1959.

Bordon, B. L. "El programa de fomento industrial de Puerto Rico y su posible aplicabilidad en el desarrollo económico del Paraguay." Thesis. Río Piedras: University of Puerto Rico, College of Social Sciences, 1965.

Economic Associates. *Industrial Supply and Distribution in Puerto Rico.* Prepared for the Economic Development Administration of the Commonwealth of Puerto Rico under the Small Business Administration management research grant program. Project director, Amadeo Francis. Washington, D.C., 1963.

Hibben, T., and R. Picó. *Industrial Development of Puerto Rico and the Virgin Islands of the United States.* Report of the United States Section, Caribbean Commission, July 1948. Port of Spain: Guardian Commercial Printery, 1948.

Industry in Puerto Rico. Prepared by the Economic Research Division of the Chase Manhattan Bank, July 1967.

Lastra, C. J. *The Impact of Minimum Wages on a Labor-Oriented Industry.* Govbank Technical Papers, no. 1. San Juan: Government Development Bank for Puerto Rico, 1965.

Little, A. D., Inc. "New Industries for Puerto Rico." Report to Puerto Rico Industrial Development Company. San Juan, 1943.

Mayne, A., and E. Ramos. *Planning for Social and Economic Development in Puerto Rico.* May 1959.

Moscoso, T. "El fomento industrial en Puerto Rico." Lecture given at the Seminar of Economic Planning. San Juan, October 27–November 28, 1958. Mimeographed.

Perloff, H. S. *Puerto Rico's Economy.* 1. "Characteristics, Trends and Recent Developments"; 2–6, "A Study of the Potentialities of the Puerto Rican Economy." Preliminary report for review and suggestions only. Río Piedras: University of Puerto Rico, Social Sciences Research Center, 1946–1948.

Puerto Rico, Economic Development Administration. *Stimulating Greater Local Investment in Manufacturing Enterprises in Puerto Rico.* Prepared by the Local Industries Research Section, Office of Economic Research, Economic Development Administration. Washington, D.C.: 1960.

Puerto Rico, Government Development Bank. *A Special Report on PRIDCO,* February 1967.

Puerto Rico, Industrial Development Company. *Annual Reports,* 1965 to 1969.

Puerto Rico, Junta de Planificación. "Evaluaciones del programa de pequeñas industrias comunales." Prepared by the Division of Finance and Master Plans. Mimeographed. San Juan, July 2, 1957.

Reynolds, L., and P. Gregory. *Wages, Productivity and Industrialization in Puerto Rico*. With the assistance of Luz M. Torruellas. Homewood, Ill.: R. D. Irwin, 1965.

Ross, D. F. *The Long Uphill Path: A Historical Study of Puerto Rico's Program of Economic Development*. San Juan: Talleres Graficos Interamericanos, 1966.

Taylor, M. C. *Industrial Tax-Exemption in Puerto Rico*. Madison: University of Wisconsin Press, 1957.

United States Bureau of the Census. *Census of the United States. Puerto Rico: Census of Manufactures 1939, 1958, 1963, 1967*. Washington, D.C.: Government Printing Office.

Tourism

"Annual Analysis of the Puerto Rico Hotel Industry." Prepared by Accountant, Howarth Hotel, San Juan. Each year since 1959.

Barasorda, M. A. "Tourism in Development Planning." *Seminar on Planning Techniques and Methods*. Caribbean Organization, February 1963.

Barton, H. C. *Towards the Development of a Policy for Tourism*. San Juan: Economic Development Administration, February 16, 1955.

Benítez Carle, R. "The Puerto Rico Tourist Industry." Statement to the Civil Aeronautics Board on Docket No. 7375. San Juan: Economic Development Administration, 1956.

Bouret, R. "Puerto Rico's Tourism: Island-Wide and Tax-Free Opportunities." *Investment Dealers' Digest*, Sec. 2 (June 17, 1963), pp. 18–21.

Cadilla, C. G. *Expansión turística y las nuevas facilidades hoteleras en Puerto Rico*. San Juan: Government Development Bank for Puerto Rico, 1959.

Cosandey, P. "The Hotel School of Puerto Rico." Report on the First Hotel Seminar, Caribbean Tourist Association, October 1959.

Fine, S. M. *Analysis of Demand for Tourist Facilities in Puerto Rico*. San Juan: Economic Development Administration, 1956.

Francis, A. I. D. *Developments in the Hotel Sector of the Business Economy between 1949 and 1954*. San Juan: Economic Development Administration, January 12, 1956.

————. "Tourism in Puerto Rico." Address to the St. Thomas Chamber of Commerce, August 22, 1958.

Informe Proyecto La Ruta. San Juan: Department of Public Works, October 1963.

Izcoa, E. "The Impact of the Tourist Industry on the Economy of Puerto Rico." Master's Thesis in economics. Washington, D.C.: Catholic University of America, August 22, 1958.

Martínez, C. J. *La Contribución económica y social del turismo a Puerto Rico*. Río Piedras: 1964.

Martocci, F. T. 1949 Master Plan for the Development of Tourism. San Juan: Economic Development Administration.

————. 1957 Master Plan for the Development of Tourist Facilities. San Juan: Economic Development Administration.

Meek, H. B. *Code of Minimum Standards for the Tax-Exempt Hotels of Puerto Rico*. San Juan: Economic Development Administration, May 7, 1953.

Puerto Rico, Economic Development Administration. *Qué Pasa en Puerto Rico.* Monthly information bulletin. San Juan: Department of Tourism, 1949 to date.

————. *Selected Statistics on the Visitors and Hotel Industry in Puerto Rico.* October 1963–64. Published annually.

————. *Tourist Information from the Post Card Surveys of Hotel Guests.* Beginning 1957.

Rivera Boucher, M. *Selected Statistics—Hawaii and Puerto Rico.* San Juan: Economic Development Administration, December 4, 1962.

Robbins, S. J. *Report to PRIDCO on the Tourist Industry of Puerto Rico, with Particular Reference to the Development Companies, Relation to and Continuing Interest in It.* San Juan: Economic Development Administration, December 4, 1962.

Rosa, S. *Aspectos económicos del turismo externo en Puerto Rico y sus perspectivas.* San Juan: Puerto Rico Planning Board, Bureau of Economic and Social Planning, April 1963.

Sánchez, R. "Ports Authority Reflects Growth of Tourism and the Entire Economy." *Quarterly Report to Investors in Puerto Rican Securities* 11, no. 3 (September 1964), pp. 3–4. San Juan: Government Development Bank for Puerto Rico.

"Tourism Advisory Board's Programs." Mimeographed. San Juan: Tourism Advisory Board, April 21, 1950.

"Tourism—A Winner in Puerto Rico's Growth." *Quarterly Report To Investors in Puerto Rican Securities* 13, no. 2 (June 1966) pp. 1–2. San Juan: Government Development Bank for Puerto Rico.

"Tourism Contributing Greatly to Puerto Rico's Economy." *Quarterly Report to Investors in Puerto Rican Securities* 12, no. 2 (June 1965), pp. 1–3. San Juan: Government Development Bank for Puerto Rico.

Whitcomb, E. J. *Development of Tourism in Puerto Rico.* A research study for the Puerto Rico Development Company. San Juan: March 15, 1945.

Wolff, R., and R. J. Voyles. *Tourist Trends in the Caribbean, 1951–1955.* Coral Gables, Fla.: University of Miami, Bureau of Economic Research, 1956.

Commerce, Transportation and Finance

Cadilla, C. G. *El Banco Gubernamental de Fomento para Puerto Rico.* Reprint of the Supplement to the *Quarterly Bulletin of the Center of Latin American Monetary Studies (CEMLA),* May 1961.

Cadwalder, Wickersham & Taft. *Economic and Financial Analysis. The Commonwealth of Puerto Rico.* New York: Cadwalder, Wickersham & Taft, January 1954.

De Beers, J. S. *Instruments of the Capital Market in Puerto Rico.* Revised by Carlos G. Cadilla and submitted to the Fifth Meeting of Central Bank Technicians of the American Continent, Bogotá, Colombia, 1962.

————. *A Study of Puerto Rico's Banking System.* San Juan: Finance Council of Puerto Rico, 1960.

De Jesus Toro, R. "Efectos de la continuada importación de capital sobre el futuro ritmo de crecimiento de la economía de Puerto Rico." Report submitted to the Economic and Statistical Division of the Puerto Rico Planning Board, May 31, 1960. Mimeographed.

Descartes, S. L. *The Banking System of Puerto Rico, 1950.*

_____. *Financing Economic Development in Puerto Rico 1941–1949*. Conference prepared for Meeting of Experts on Financing Economic Development, Lake Success, N.Y., October 24–November 2, 1949. San Juan: Government of Puerto Rico, Department of Treasury, June 1950.

_____. *Fortalecimiento fiscal de los gobiernos municipales de Puerto Rico.* San Juan: Senate of Puerto Rico, 1968.

_____. *The Public Debt of Puerto Rico.* San Juan, 1954.

_____. *Savings and Investments in Puerto Rico, 1956.*

Di Venuti, B. *Banking Growth in Puerto Rico.* San Juan: Treasury Department, 1955.

_____. *Money and Banking in Puerto Rico.* Río Piedras: University of Puerto Rico Press, 1950.

Eastman, S. E. *Ships and Sugar: An Evaluation of Puerto Rican Offshore Shipping.* Río Piedras: University of Puerto Rico Press, 1953.

Financing Economic Development in Puerto Rico. Reprinted from *Monthly Review.* Federal Reserve Bank of New York, May 1961.

Galbraith, J. K. *Marketing Efficiency in Puerto Rico.* Cambridge, Mass.: Harvard University Press, 1955.

Kirk, J. *Puerto Rico: Survival in the Sun.* Reprinted from *Banking,* Journal of the American Bankers Association, January 1966.

Morales Arroyo, D. *El colmado del área metropolitana de San Juan, Puerto Rico, 1950 y 1963.* Un estudio sobre ajuste de la firma comercial pequeña al cambio comercial metropolitano de una economia en desarrollo. Río Piedras, 1965.

Picó, R. *Cómo estimular el flujo de capital del exterior: la experiencia de Puerto Rico.* Paper presented before the Sixth Meeting of Central Bank Technicians of the American Continent, Guatemala, November 1960. San Juan: Department of Education, Printing Office, 1961.

_____. "The Dynamic Role of Puerto Rico's Banking System in a Growing Economy." Address at the Annual Convention of National Association of Supervisors of State Banks, San Juan, October 21, 1964. Mimeographed.

_____. *Financial Progress in Puerto Rico.* English and Spanish. New York: The Municipal Forum, January 26, 1962.

_____. *The Financial Structure of Puerto Rico.* Reprinted from the *Export Trade and Shipper* 78, no. 6 (September 8, 1958).

_____. "Financing for Economic Development." Lecture delivered at the Seminar on Planning Techniques and Methods, sponsored by the Caribbean Commission, San Juan, January 30–February 7, 1963. Mimeographed.

_____. "Función del Banco de Fomento en la política de desarrollo económico y social de Puerto Rico." Primera Reunión Latinoamericana de Instituciones Financieras de Desarrollo bajo los auspicios del Banco Interamericano de Desarrollo, Washington, D.C., November 29–December 2, 1964. Mimeographed.

_____. "A New Look at Debt Limits." Paper presented at the 56th Annual Conference of Municipal Finance Officers Association of the United States and Canada, Boston, Mass., May 29, 1962. Mimeographed.

Puerto Rico, Autoridad de Carreteras. *Informe Anual, 1965–66, 1966–67, 1968–69.* San Juan: Talleres gráficos Interamericanos.

Puerto Rico, Autoridad Metropolitana de Autobuses. "Apreciaciones de la AMA en torno a las recomendaciones del informe de transportación de la firma de consultores W. C. Wilman and Co., December 1963." Mimeographed.

_____. *Special Study of the Metropolitan Bus Authority: San Juan Metropolitan Area.* Vol. 1. Prepared for the Department of Public Works of Puerto

Rico and the Puerto Rico Planning Board by W. C. Gilman and Co., December 1963.

Puerto Rico, Autoridad de los Puertos. *Financial Master Plan Study for the Puerto Rico Ports Authority.* Interim report by James C. Buckley, Inc., Industrial and Transportation Consultants, New York. August 1, 1960.

————. *Informe Anual, 1955 a 1969.* Autoridad de los Puertos, San Juan, Puerto Rico.

Puerto Rico, Government Development Bank. *Annual Reports,* 1944 to 1969.

————. *Instituciones financieras que operan en Puerto Rico.* San Juan: Talleres Gráficos Interamericanos, 1964.

————. *Financial Facts, 1969.*

————. *Puerto Rico: A Thriving Field for Investment.* San Juan, 1960.

————. *A Special Report on the Commonwealth of Puerto Rico. November 1969.*

Puerto Rico, Treasury Department. Office of Economic and Financial Studies "Boletín estadístico trimestral, enero 1958–marzo 1968." Mimeographed.

————. *Economía y Finanzas, años 1955–1966.* Published annually. San Juan: Treasury Department, Purchase and Supplies Services, Printing Division.

Puerto Rico, Treasury Department, Bureau of Bank Examinations. "Consolidated Report on Conditions of Banks in Puerto Rico." Published monthly. June 1957 to date. Mimeographed.

Quintero Ramos, A. M. *Promedios e índices del mercado de valores.* Río Piedras: College of Business Administration, Business Research Center, 1959.

Rivera, H. J. *Introducción a la moneda y la banca.* Río Piedras: University of Puerto Rico Press, 1965.

Rodríguez Massa, G. S. "Interrelación entre balanza de pagos y desarrollo económico: Puerto Rico 1947–1965." M.A. thesis. Río Piedras, 1967.

Rodríguez, S. *Investment Yardstick for Municipal Bonds Applied to Puerto Rican Obligations.* San Juan: Government Development Bank for Puerto Rico, 1960.

Study of Lending Activities of the Government Development Bank for Puerto Rico and PRIDCO. Prepared by Bloch, Descartes, and Kalmonoff of Zinder International L.T.D., November 15, 1964, and June, 1965.

U.S. Department of Commerce, Bureau of the Census. *U.S. Trade with Puerto Rico and U.S. Possessions: FT 800 Report.* Published monthly. Washington, D.C.: Government Printing Office, June 1948–June 1965.

————. *Puerto Rico: 1967 Census of Business.* Washington, D.C., December 1970.

Economic Projections

Baquero, J. "Outlook for Puerto Rico Business Community Viewed by Secretary of Commerce." *Quarterly Report to Investors in Puerto Rican Securities* 14, no. 4 (December 1967), pp. 7–8. San Juan: Government Development Bank for Puerto Rico.

Chase, S. *"Operation Bootstrap" in Puerto Rico. Report on Progress, 1951.* Prepared for the NPA Business Committee on National Policy, Washington, D.C., 1951.

García Santiago, R. "The Puerto Rico Economy—Status and Projections." *Quarterly Report to Investors in Puerto Rican Securities* 14, no. 4 (December 1967), pp. 1–3. San Juan: Government Development Bank for Puerto Rico.

Perloff, H. S. *Puerto Rico's Economic Future, a Study in Planned Development.* Chicago: University of Chicago Press, 1950.

Puerto Rico, Asamblea Legislativa, Comisión para el Estudio del Próposito de Puerto Rico. *Informe a la Asamblea Legislativa.* En cumplimiento del mandato expresado en la Resolución II del 26 de mayo de 1965. San Juan: Treasury Department, Purchase and Supplies Service, Printing Division, 1968.

Puerto Rico, Industrial Development Company. *The Dynamics of Economic Development in Puerto Rico.* By Robert Hannah, William Leech, Donald O'Sell, and James Hartring, under the direction of Lloyd O. Wadleigh, Chairman, Department of Economics and Business Administration. Waukesha, Wis.: Carroll College, 1967.

————. *Over-all Economic Development Plan for the Commonwealth of Puerto Rico.* First revision, February 1967. San Juan.

————. *Physical Facilities for Commercial Development in the San Juan Metropolitan Area, a Master Plan Study.* By Samuel Weiss Research Associates. Washington, D.C., October 1957.

Puerto Rico, Junta de Planificación. "El desarrollo Económico de P. R. y su reafirmación para el futuro." Documento presentado por el Sr. Ramón García Santiago al Comité Económico de la Asamblea de Programa y Reglamento del PPD, 22 de julio de 1964. Mimeographed.

Puerto Rico, Junta de Planificación Negociado de Analisis Económico y Social. "Plan general de desarrollo, 1965–75." Elementos sociales, económicos. 2da. parte del Informe Económico al Gobernador, 1965–66. December 1966.

————. "Planning for Social and Economic Development in Puerto Rico." By Alvin Mayne and Evelyn Ramos. Mimeographed. May 1959.

————. *Programa de mejoras a la comunidad para la erradicación y prevención de zonas de desarrollo.*

————. "Un Programa propuesto para viviendas a bajo costo." English and Spanish. Mimeographed. September 22, 1958.

————. "Ritmos de crecimiento anual." Mimeographed. June 1967.

Spotlights Puerto Rico. Published by the *Investment Dealers Digest,* June 13, 1966, June 19, 1967.

Geographic Regions

Hernández, P. H. *Bosquejo histórico de Utuado.* Utuado: Editorial Uber, 1965.

Mayne, A. *Designing and Administering a Regional Economic Development Plan, with Specific Reference to Puerto Rico.* Paris: Organization for Economic Cooperation and Development, 1961.

Picó, R. *The Geographic Regions of Puerto Rico.* Río Piedras: University of Puerto Rico Press, 1950.

Picó, R., and L. López. "Planning and Regional Development of Puerto Rico." Paper presented before the Fifth Inter-American Planning Congress, Mexico, September 28–October 3, 1964, under the auspices of the Inter-American Planning Society.

Puerto Rico, Planning Board. "Comprehensive Regional Planning in Puerto Rico." Mimeographed. June 1958.

————. "Towards a Comprehensive Regional Development Scheme for Puerto Rico." Mimeographed. September 1957.

Torres Grillo, H. *Historia de la ciudad de Caguas; la invicta del Turabo.* Barcelona: Ediciones Rumbos, 1965.

Index

427